# BHAGAVADGĪTĀ

The Dialogue between Śrī Kṛṣṇa and Arjuna

# BHAGAVADGĪTĀ

The Dialogue between Śrī Kṛṣṇa and Arjuna

Including
Sanskrit Text, Roman Transliteration, English
Translation and Commentaries

*Translation and Commentaries from Sanskrit to Portuguese*

GLORIA ARIEIRA

*Translation from Portuguese to English*

RICKY TOLEDANO

MOTILAL BANARSIDASS PUBLISHERS
PRIVATE LIMITED • DELHI

*First Edition: Delhi, **2016***



ISBN: 978-81-208-4011-9 (Cloth)
ISBN: 978-81-208-4012-6 (Paper)

*Also Available at*

MOTILAL BANARSIDASS
41 U.A. Bungalow Road, Jawahar Nagar, Delhi 110 007
8 Mahalaxmi Chamber, 22 Bhulabhai Desai Road, Mumbai 400 026
203 Royapettah High Road, Mylapore, Chennai 600 004
236, 9th Main III Block, Jayanagar, Bengaluru 560 011
8 Camac Street, Kolkata 700 017
Ashok Rajpath, Patna 800 004
Chowk, Varanasi 221 001

*MLBD Cataloging-in-Publication Data*
Bhagavadgītā
*The Dialogue between Śrī Kṛṣṇa and Arjuna*
*Translation and Commentaries from Sanskrit to Portuguese* : GLORIA ARIEIRA
*Translation from Portuguese to English* : RICKY TOLEDANO
Includes Epithets of Arjuna, Kṛṣṇa and References
ISBN: 978-81-208-4011-9 (Cloth)
ISBN: 978-81-208-4012-6 (Paper)
I. Hinduism II. Bhagavadgītā—Translation : Sanskrit,
Portuguese, English III. Kṛṣṇa IV. Arjuna V. Arieira, Gloria
VI. Toledano, Ricky VII. Mattos, Victor

*Printed in India*
by Aegean Offset Printing Press, Delhi and
published by JP Jain for Motilal Banarsidass Publishers (P) Ltd,
41 U.A. Bungalow Road, Jawahar Nagar, Delhi-110007

ओं श्री गुरुभ्यो नमः

*oṃ śrī gurubhyo namaḥ*

Salutations to the teachers

# Foreword

The *Bhagavadgītā* is the most renowned Hindu text in the West. *Bhagavat* means "he who possesses wealth", meaning the Lord; the word *Gītam*, which is neutral, means "song". The compound word *Bhagavadgītā*, where *t* converts to *d* for phonetic reasons, means "the Song of the Lord" and becomes feminine, since it is a text that feeds our soul, as a mother feeds her child. In the West, for the sake of clarity, the title is often separated into Bhagavad *Gītā*. It is also often referred to as the *Gītā*.

The very first translation to a Western language was the "Bhagavat-geeta, or Dialogues of Kreeshna and Arjoon", published in 1785 in London by Charles Wilkins, who had originally gone to India in 1770 as a writer and typographer of the East India Company. His facility for languages allowed him to learn Bengali and Persian quickly. In 1784, he moved to Varanasi, where he began studying Sanskrit with a pundit and dedicated himself to translating the *Mahābhārata* (the epic poem of which the *Gītā* is part), which he did not conclude. He later created the first printing font for *Devanāgarī* (the characters traditionally used to write in Sanskrit), just as he had also created for Bengali and Persian. In 1808, he published the "Grammar of the Sanskrita Language".

The Wilkins translation of the *Gītā* was then translated into French (1787) and German (1802), and had a great influence in European literature of the period, as well as increasing interest in Hindu philosophy.

The first translation directly from Sanskrit into German,

by Friedrish Schlegel in 1808, contained parts of the *Gītā*. His brother, August, published the journal Indishe Bibliothek (1823-1830), which included translations of the *Gītā* and the *Rāmāyaṇa* (another eminent Hindu epic). These texts marked the beginning of Sanskrit studies in Germany, which later developed enormously, and the texts of Hinduism influenced the German writers and philosophers.[1]

What had fascinated Wilkins, the brothers Schlegel, and countless other Westerners before and afterwards was the facility with which the *Gītā* speaks to the hearts of men. *Arjuna*'s questions and self-doubt, as well as the best way to proceed with his life, are the very same questions of each and every one of us. The barriers of time and space are immediately overcome as we feel ourselves in the place of *Arjuna*, paying close attention to the explanations of *Kṛṣṇa*.

Some academics place the composition of the *Gītā* between the 5$^{th}$ and 2$^{nd}$ centuries BC. Others, based on differences in literary style, argue that the *Gītā* had been added to the *Mahābhārata* afterwards. The authorship of the *Mahābhārata*, and thus the *Gītā*, has been attributed to *Vyāsa*. This preoccupation with establishing dates and authors is typical of the Western culture, since we see the individual as separate from the Whole.

Hinduism has an oral tradition of transmitting knowledge from one generation to the next with incredible precision over thousands of years. The Brahmins taught their children from an early age to recite the *Vedas* by heart in the exact meter and precise intonation. The four *Vedas* (*Ṛg*, *Yajur*, *Sāma* and *Atharva*) are called *Śruti*, "that which has been heard". Only much later in history were these texts written with a stylus on banana leaves.

---

1 Wikipedia

The beginning part of each *Veda*, called *Karma Kaṇḍa*, deals with actions and their results. The final part, called *Jñāna Kaṇḍa*, covers the topics of knowledge of the individual, the Absolute, and the relationship between the two. This latter part of the *Vedas* is comprised of the *Upaniṣads*, which is collectively called *Vedānta*, which means the end of the *Vedas*.

The *Gītā* was composed after the *Vedas*, therefore it is part of the category called *Smṛti*, “that which is remembered”, but its importance in terms of revealing knowledge places it at the same level of the *Vedas*, thus it is called the 5th *Veda*. It is as much a philosophical treatise - as far as it covers the individual, the Absolute, and the relationship between the two - as it is a practical guide to everyday life, with instructions on how to act, how to deal with the mind, how to meditate, etc.

The *Gītā* is like a mother who welcomes us as we are with words of comfort regarding our limitations. It seems to come into our lives by chance - if you believe things actually happen by chance.

In my case this chance happened in 1966, when I was doing an interchange program in the United Sates, where I found a copy in the library of the school I was attending. It was a paperback edition with an introduction by Aldous Huxley, a famous writer at the time. I knew nothing of Hinduism, but I quite liked Huxley; I had read some of his books.

In his introduction, Huxley explained what he called Perennial Philosophy, which found expression, sometimes partial, sometimes complete, in different ways and in different cultures, be it in *Vedānta*, in the Hebrew prophecies, in the Tao, in the dialogues of Plato, in the Gospel of St. John, in the Buddhist Mahayana theology, in the Persian Sufis, in the

Christian Mystics of the Middle Ages and the Renaissance.[2]

According to Huxley, the *Gītā* is the most systematic expression of Perennial Philosophy. This introduction captivated me and I brought a copy of this edition back with me to Brazil.

For many years I read this book, little by little, at times with an irresistible attraction, at times hindered by cultural and religious baggage. I was often confused by the many passages that are apparently contradictory.

Only in 1979, when I began studying *Vedānta* with Gloria Arieira, was I able to finally recognize the true greatness of the *Gītā*.

Gloria had just returned from India, where she had been studying *Vedānta* for four and half years with Swami Dayananada, under the traditional method, in Sandipani Sadanalaya, Bombay, today Mumbai. She had also studied Sanskrit in depth, allowing her to translate the texts she would teach to her students directly from Sanskrit into Portuguese.

The *Gītā* may be interpreted in different way, according to the diverse traditions of Hinduism. The tradition that Gloria represents is called *Advaita Vedānta*, or Non-Dualism, which was systematized by *Śaṅkara* (7th Century, AD). He commented on all the verses of instruction in the *Gītā* (Chapters 2 to18, since the first is just a list of warriors preparing for battle), explaining word for word, clarifying all doubts and apparent contradictions.

There are other traditions, notably those of Ramanuja (11th Century, AD), of *Viṣiṣṭa Advaita Vedānta*, Qualified Non-Dualism and of Madhva (12th Century AD) of Dvaita *Vedānta*, or Dualism. This later tradition is represented by

---

2 The Song of God Bhagavad-Gita, translation by Swami Prabhavananda and Christopher Isherwood, introduction by Aldous Huxley, The New American Library of World Literature, 6th, 1959.

the Hare Krishna movement, which has translated the *Gītā* into more than 50 languages.

Among modern commentators, Mahatma Gandhi must be highlighted. He considered the *Gītā* his greatest inspiration, although he often cited the Bible, especially the Sermon on the Mount, and the Koran. In 1929, he wrote a translation of the *Gītā* in Gujarati, his native language, which was translated to English in 1935 by Mahadev Desai, his secretary, and then from there to many other languages. Curiously, Gandhi had started his study of the *Gītā* during his stay in England (1888-1891) to attend law school. Until that time, Gandhi has shown no special interest in religion, but two vegetarian brothers that he had met were members of the Theosophical Society. They told him about the *Gītā*, since they were reading a translation by Edwin Arnold, and invited him to study the *Gītā* in the original Sanskrit. Gandhi confessed that he had little knowledge of the *Gītā* and that his Sanskrit was weak, but decided to study with them. It was a revelation: he found the book immeasurably valuable. Gandhi saw in the *Gītā* an allegory, where the battlefield is the human soul and *Arjuna* is the higher impulse to fight against evil.

All these traditions deserve respect; the best one being that which speaks directly to your heart.

***João Mazza***

# Contents

# Preface

The Vedic tradition is unique and incomparable. It is part of the patrimony of humanity for its approach on the various facets of human life and society. It is only within this tradition that the specific themes of *dharma* and *mokṣa* have been encountered with such depth and profoundness. In the Vedic literature these words, as well as others, such as *sannyāsa*, and therefore *sannyāsin* (one who lives a life of *sannyāsa*), are unique and difficult to be translated.

"That which sustains something or someone" is called *dharma* in Sanskrit and it has three different meanings. *Dharma* is the role of each and every one of us, for as long as we have been included as individuals into various and different relationships. It is also the understanding and practice of ethics, of universal values. Lastly, *dharma* is the essential and immutable nature of everything. Revealing *dharma*, and inspiring the human being to follow it, is the object of the *Vedas*.

*Mokṣa* is the human being's liberation from the constant feeling of limitation and insufficiency. This liberation can be attained by the understanding that the Self is eternal and limitless. The *Vedas* demonstrate that the cause of suffering is due to the ignorance of the true nature of the Self. Revealing this knowledge of the Absolute – the essential nature of the human being, the Creator and the Universe all at once – is the main objective of the *Vedas*. Nothing can be found in any other sacred text that compares with the clarity, the logic and the profoundness of the *Vedas* with regard to the dilemma of the human being and its solution.

The Vedic society is divided into stages of life, or varna: brahmacarin (the student), *gṛhastha* (the married householder), vanaprastha (one retired from family duties) and *sannyāsin* (the renunciate). The *sannyāsin* is one who leaves aside all ordinary duties, dedicating oneself to studies, meditation and teaching. It involves total dedication to a life of self-knowledge and to the renunciation of everything else. Nevertheless, if one – after completing much study – is prepared for and desirous of a life of total dedication to self-knowledge, even if from young age, one may go through a ritual and become a *sannyāsin*.

Since the *Vedas* are very particular in enjoining human beings to contribute to society and to its orderly maintenance, these stages of life were ordained to be strictly followed by everyone. In order to enjoy a harmonious society, one must do one's duty, *dharma*. Naturally, one may satisfy one's own desires, but only when such desires are not in opposition to *dharma*.

Thus, according to the *Vedas*, being a "drop-out" from society was not an option. Only an individual who has gone through all the three stages of life is entitled to leave aside all duties and dedicate oneself entirely to self-knowledge and a life of meditation – and it is role of society to support this individual in doing so.

A *sannyāsin* lives a life of *sannyāsa*. Often this word is translated as and confused with a "mendicant" because this individual does not formally work, neither does this person receive a salary: all such an individual possesses has been given to him by society; whereas a mendicant in Western society is quite different: this person is often seen as rebellious or forfeiting. In Vedic society, all are happy to have a *sannyāsin* among its members, since such an individual is committed to truth, to a quiet contemplative life, and to help and to inspire other members of society. From this standpoint, this individual is far from being a "drop-out".

*Sannyāsa* is also called tyaga, which means renunciation. In the *Vedas*, renunciation is emphasized as a means for self-knowledge, but it is not just as simple as giving up or dropping out: it requires an emotional maturity, a preparation of the mind, and an analysis of one's utmost goal in life - besides the resolute certainty of how to reach this goal. This kind of renunciation is associated to the desire for *mokṣa*, which is freedom from the sense of limitation which can only be acquired through knowledge of oneself as being complete and not separate or different from *Īśvara*, the cause of the universe.

*Sannyāsa*, *mokṣa* and *dharma* are words particular to the *Vedas*, and we decided to maintain them in Sanskrit, in order not to present an opportunity for misunderstanding by fixing a single word as a translation.

There are four *Vedas*: *Ṛg*, *Sama*, *Yajur* and *Atharva* - each of which can be divided into two parts. The first part teaches rituals and *mantras*, revealing appropriate and inappropriate actions according to one's role in life - denominated *dharma* and *adharma*, respectively - as well as their corresponding positive consequences, *puṇyam*, or negative consequences, *pāpam*. The *Vedas* emphazise that the human being is free to choose his or her actions, but the individual is bound to the results of his or her choices.

The second part of the *Vedas* is called *Vedānta*, and it is here where the dialoguess between gurus and their disciples can be found in what is called the *Upaniṣads*. *Vedānta* states that the actions of human beings are done in pursuit of four objects, known as *puruṣārthas* in Sanskrit: *ārtha*, security; *kāma*, pleasure; *dharma*, a better future (in both this and the next life); and *mokṣa*, the liberation from the sense of limitation and need. This latter object is considered the *parama-puruṣārtha*, the final objective of human life.

*Vedānta* teaches us that the essential truth of all and everything is but one. Eternal and ever-present, it is the very nature of the subject. The sense of mortality and the feeling that something is missing, which is shared by all human beings, is due to the ignorance of one's true nature. Therefore, the solution to this fundamental problem is self-knowledge. And to acquire knowledge, a means of knowledge, a *pramāṇam*, is necessary.

*Vedānta* is a means of knowledge in the form of words. It reveals the indivisible identity among *jīva*, the individual; *Īśvara*, the cause of the Universe; and *jagat*, the world. The phrase that best summarizes this teaching is "*tat tvam asi*", or "you are that", meaning that *jīva* is equal to *Īśvara*. The pupil, after a process of studying, reflection and contemplation, realizes: aham *Brahma asmi* – I am the limitless *Brahman*. This realization is what is called *mokṣa*, and it is the highest goal of human life.

The *Bhagavadgītā* – although not part of the *Vedas* – has the same value as an *Upaniṣad* and is therefore often called "the 5th *Veda*", since it contains the same knowledge and is presented in the same format as the *Vedas*. The *Gītā* can be found in the epic *Mahābhārata*, which is incomparable work – not only for the sheer size of it – but for its understanding of the problems facing humanity and the individual mind, as well as how to solve them. It has been said that what cannot be found in the *Mahābhārata* simply cannot be found anywhere.

The oral tradition has a saying about *Gītā*:

गीता सुगीता कर्तव्या किम् अन्यैः शास्त्रविस्तरैः ।

*gītā sugītā kartavyā kim anyaiḥ śāstravistaraiḥ |*

Meaning, '*Gītā*, which is well sung and taught (by the master *Śrī Kṛṣṇa*), must be studied. What need is there to study other texts?'

Besides the study of *ātman*, the Self, and its identity with the Absolute, *Brahman* (which is not separate from the Universe), the *Bhagavadgītā* discusses in detail the lifestyle that prepares an individual for a clear understanding of this self-knowledge. This way of life is called *yoga*.

The teacher of the *Gītā* is *Śrī Kṛṣṇa* and the disciple is *Arjuna*. The *Gītā* is divided into three parts, just as the previously mentioned *mahāvākya*: "*tat tvam asi*" ("You are That"). The first part of the *Gītā* refers to *tvam* - you; the second part deals with *tat*, which is *Īśvara* - That which is Everything; the third part is *asi* - the identity between the two. The three parts of the *Gītā* are divided into six chapters each, for a total of 18 chapters. The *Gītā*'s 700 verses are part of the *Mahābhārata*, the longest epic ever written.

The *Gītā* is the most famous text of the Vedic tradition. The words of *Śrī Kṛṣṇa* can reach each and every one, regardless of culture, since its subject matter is universal and the teaching easily understood.

***Gloria Arieira***

# Translator's note

In 1500, Pedro Álvares Cabral set out to overcome a great obstacle: the Arab, Turkish and Italian monopoly of the Indian spice trade. The Portuguese had little choice but to take a detour – as often one must do to get round an obstacle – and in doing so, the great mariner inadvertently encountered the very large land mass that would come to be known as Brazil. As one of the infinite results of that encounter, almost 500 years later, Gloria Arieira also took a detour: she left her native Brazil in search of India – but not for spices. At that time, she probably had no idea why a girl from Rio de Janeiro in the 1970s would cast aside all that her family and society had prepared her for in order to go to India to study Sanskrit and *Vedānta*, just as I had no real idea why I left my native Chicago for Rio de Janeiro in the 1990s to become a teacher and translator. Then, I unintentionally took yet another detour and discovered India via an unusual route: there I was sitting on the floor in front of Gloria Arieira in a studio in Copacabana to study the *Bhagavadgītā*. I still cannot believe it. Even today it seems odd to me. India had been the furthest thing on my mind when I came to Brazil so many years ago.

It is not necessary, however, to take a major detour in life and go to another country in order for you discover that you are not exactly the author of your own story. As you are about to learn in the pages ahead, while you may employ your free will to choose your actions, under no circumstances do you decide upon the results of your actions. The results are delivered to you according to an infallible order that you do not control. This concept is very difficult to explain - not to mention accept - therefore, here in one of the greatest stories ever told, our hero *Arjuna* asks, and our guide *Kṛṣṇa* explains, again and again, in an attempt to overcome a great obstacle on this voyage: words.

Words are limitations that can facilitate us as much as they can represent great obstacles. You set sail - just like Cabral did, because at some point one must stop deliberating and must make a choice - and maybe everything runs smoothly until you encounter a barrier like the word 'consciousness'. What does one do? Before you lies one of the most elusive words consigned to language, and it may very well be described as the purpose of life just to discover its meaning. Do you really know what it means? I am not sure I do yet, but I began contemplating it years ago under the careful guidance of Gloria Arieira, in Portuguese - which I found a bit easier because the language offered fewer options for this word; in English, I saw some confusing detours signs pointing me in the direction of synonyms such as 'awareness' and 'mindfulness'. There was no choice but to stop and begin a process of contemplation, which is exactly part of the process of *Vedānta*: the discovery of the true Self, which is pure 'Consciousness', the illumination that allows one to see even one's own intellect at work. This 'awareness' can come in what is apparently some of the most inopportune moments, such as in the middle of a battlefield, which is exactly where a warrior by the name of *Arjuna* finally encountered the words to ask the right questions to overcome the anguish of indecision. It was a defining moment. Not surprisingly, it is in these moments that the teacher always appears: for *Arjuna*, it was *Kṛṣṇa*; and as for me, I am fortunate enough to have had Gloria Arieira by my side patiently monitoring my understanding of such concepts as

I translated the voice of her knowledge into English. This knowledge of *Vedānta* is transformational; I am forever indebted to Gloria Arieira. Thus, when the opportunity arose to translate her Portuguese version of the *Bhagavadgītā* into English, I saw a chance not only to show my gratitude, but also an opportunity to invite people along on a voyage, navigating around such elusive words and contemplating their meanings, as well as to be 'mindful' of the words we did not translate, because the Sanskrit words simply do not have any equivalent and must be elaborated in order to deliver their meaning. Among such choices, we have included *dharma, sannyāsa, sannyāsin, brahman, ātman, brāhmaṇa, yoga, yogin,* and *saṁsāra*. These terms will be explained by Gloria throughout the course of this text.

*Rāgas* and *dveṣas* are Sanskrit antonyms that are paramount to understanding the human dilemma of bondage to the material world filled with things that one likes and dislikes - as these two words have often been translated. However, as I learned from Gloria, this concept is much more than one liking chocolate and disliking eggplant. I despised eggplant, and then later acquired a taste for it. Dealing with one's own tastes, however, is not often so easy - not to mention dealing with other people's tastes. Therefore, here in this *Gītā*, I have decided to remain with the Portuguese-equivalent words with which I learned this concept: tastes and aversions, because likes and dislikes simply did not seem to cover the constant duality of objects in this world that leads one astray from self-knowledge by distracting one with the endless search for pleasure and avoidance of pain, as well as the acceptance of the tastes and aversions one has and does not control - despite all efforts.

Struck by what was about to unfold in the middle of the battlefield, *Arjuna* asks which way of life is best: one of action or one of renunciation. Much of the *Gītā* is dedicated to describing this bifurcation of life, both of which lead to the self-knowledge that is the final liberation from human suffering. In Sanskrit, these two paths have two specific names: *karmayoga* and *sannyāsa*. The Sanskrit grammar allows for corresponding parts of speech to describe individuals on these paths – *karmayogin* and *sannyāsin*. Portuguese's Latin grammar could often mirror the geometry of its ancient Sanskrit ancestor. English, however, can be quite unruly: its huge lexicon can break off into a plethora of apparent synonyms that are actually quite different in meaning and often carry strong connotations. It left me with heavily charged words like actor/agent and renouncer/renunciant that I found either too vague or disagreeable for the contemporary English ear.

As previously mentioned, there is a final objective of human life, which is called *mokṣa* in Sanskrit. At the end of the *Gītā, Arjuna* declares that he has understood the meaning of this word. There are those that have dedicated their lives to comprehending its meaning. Gloria chose the Portuguese-equivalent word of 'liberation' for her public in Brazil. My choice in English was a little more complicated with words like 'freedom'. As far as I can see, both terms are equally appropriate; even so, I imagined *Arjuna* pounding his fist, demanding freedom (from bondage); then I imagined him imploring for liberation (to be what he had always been). The latter term somehow seemed wider and arrived in my ear more generously. I had to make the call; I hoisted my sail and moved on to continue my voyage between the two more distant places on the globe, India and Brazil.

I shall not dare assume to know why the author of my story sent me to Brazil, but I like to think that if there is one reason why I had come to Brazil, it was probably to discover

India, and lend what little help I can to Gloria.

It should be so simple...

Just as it was for *Arjuna*, for Gloria, and for Pedro Alvares Cabral, all paths are part of a journey to discover the Self – just as they are for each and every one of us – especially when chosen inadvertently.

***Ricky Toledano***

***January 2013***

# Acknowledgments

Within the *Mahābhārata*, we find a rare and precious jewel: the dialogue between the teacher *Kṛṣṇa* and the disciple *Arjuna*, which is called the *Bhagavadgītā*. It is through this very text that *Kṛṣṇa* and *Arjuna* have been with me since 1974, the year I met them in India. They were introduced to me by my dear teacher, Swami Dayananda Saraswati, to whom I owe everything.

When I returned to Brazil in 1979, it was the first text I translated in order to teach my students. In the beginning, I only translated enough verses to see me through for each class. After having translated the 700 verses, I made some revisions. I have only recently returned to this text to prepare it for publishing. There are those that have collaborated with me over the years, such as Laís Leite and César Monhoz.

For the Portuguese edition, I have counted on the excellent and constant work of Adélia Monteiro de Faria and Paula Haas Ornelas for the formatting and editing of the texts in *Devanāgarī* and its transliteration, as well as for their review of the translation of the verses and chapter summaries. They worked at my side with much ability, dedication and care.

Once the book in Portuguese was published, my nephew Vitor Arieira Harres, who also studied in India with *Śrī* Swami Dayanandaji for more than five years, desired to have the book published in English. Vitor contacted Ricky Toledano - an American who lives in Brazil for a very long time and who has a great admiration of the Vedic tradition - while they were both in Rishikesh, India. Ricky has studied with me for many years and goes often to India to visit "his Indian family". Since Ricky works with the English language, teaching and translating from Portuguese, and he is familiar with *Vedānta* and holds it dearly, he was the perfect person to do the job of rendering my Sanskrit-to-Portuguese translation of the *Bhagavadgītā* into English.

Ricky Toledano did the translation work quickly, from May 2012 to December 2012 and together we have gone through each word. It was a pleasure for me to sit with him for so many Friday afternoons. He is a dedicated person, careful and precise with words. He has taken the care to translate, maintaining the true essence of the *Bhagavadgītā* and using words and phrases so that the English speaking "native", as he often said, could easily enjoy the depth of this teaching, avoiding possible misunderstandings. I am grateful to Ricky Toledano for his dedicated work and to Vitor for having had the idea to trust this cherished translation of the *Gītā* in his hands.

I must mention that Sanskrit is the vehicle by which the singular knowledge of the *Vedas* has been transmitted, and its translation to another language may not always be exact. It is a great challenge to change even one word of a language to another, since it is the most profound understanding of the meaning of the words that must be translated. At times the best option is to maintain the original word and explain its meaning in an attempt to minimize any loss in translation. Therefore, we have chosen to maintain some of the original Sanskrit words, placed in italics, such as *dharma*, *sannyāsa*, *sannyāsin*, *brahman*, *ātman*, brahmana, *yoga*, *yogin*, and samsara. Furthermore, we have also chosen to leave them in their noun base wihout any case ending. The translation, however, is not exactly as may be found in dictionaries, since the meanings of some words have been entirely based on the commentary of *Śrī Śaṅkara*, the greatest teacher of *Advaita Vedānta* of all time.

I thank the great teacher of the *Bhagavadgītā*, *Śrī Kṛṣṇa*, who with patience and wisdom instructed *Arjuna* and all of us through his words.

I thank *Arjuna*, with whom we can identify through his excellent questions.

I also thank Vyasa, who first related the dialogue between *Śrī Kṛṣṇa* and *Arjuna* and the entire story of the *Mahābhārata* for our reflection.

I thank *Śrī Śaṅkara*, whose commentary enlightens the meaning of the words, phrases and all of the *Vedas*. I thank my teacher, Swami Dayananda Saraswati, who taught me the tradition of *Advaita Vedānta* and the value of the *Gītā*. I also thank Swami Chinmayananda who inspired me, and made it possible for me to study in his ashram in India. I would also like to thank and to acknowledge the support of some people who made my five-year stay in India possible: Walter Alvarenga, Kaushik Bhatt (today Swami Brahmatmananda), Harihara Subramaniam (today Swami Paramarthananda), and K. Chandra and her family. Without their support I wouldn't have been successful during those five years.

I must also thank each and every one of my students who, since 1979, have *sat* before me, listened, and have thus given me the opportunity to reflect on and contemplate the singular knowledge that is *Advaita Vedānta* over and over again.

There are so many other people I must thank who have not been mentioned and who have helped me along the entire process of this book. It is only through the support of all these people that this book has been made possible.

***Gloria Arieira***

# Introduction

*Gītādhyānam – Verses of meditation on the Bhagavadgītā*

ओं पार्थाय प्रतिबोधितां भगवता नारायणेन स्वयं
व्यासेन ग्रथितां पुराणमुनिना मध्ये महाभारतम् ।
अद्वैतामृतवर्षिणीं भगवतीमष्टादशाध्यायिनीमम्ब
त्वामनुसन्दधामि भगवद्गीते भवद्वेषिणीम् ॥१॥

*oṁ pārthāya pratibodhitāṁ bhagavatā nārāyaṇena svayaṁ*
*vyāsena grathitāṁ purāṇamuninā madhye mahābhāratam |*
*advaitāmṛtavarṣiṇīṁ bhagavatīmaṣṭādaśādhyāyinīmamba*
*tvāmanusandadhāmi bhagavadgīte bhavadveṣiṇīm ||1||*

**1.** *Oṁ*. O Mother *Bhagavadgītā*! You were taught to *Pārtha* [*Arjuna*] by the very Lord *Nārāyaṇa* [*Kṛṣṇa*], told by the ancient sage *Vyāsa*, in the middle of *Mahābhārata*; You who possess eighteen chapters emanating the nectar of non-duality; who are filled with qualities [and is] the enemy of *saṁsāra*, the life of constant transformation, I meditate upon you.

नमोऽस्तु ते व्यास विशालबुद्धे
फुल्लारविन्दायतपत्रनेत्र ।
येन त्वया भारततैलपूर्णः
प्रज्वालितो ज्ञानमयः प्रदीपः ॥२॥

*namo'stu te vyāsa viśālabuddhe*
*phullāravindāyatapatranetra |*
*yena tvayā bhāratatailapūrṇaḥ*
*prajvālito jñānamayaḥ pradīpaḥ ||2||*

**2.** Salutations to you, O *Vyāsa*, whose intellect knows no limits [and] whose eyes are like the long petals of the lotus in bloom. It was for you that the lamplight of knowledge was lit, overflowing with oil from the *Mahābhārata*.

प्रपन्नपारिजाताय तोत्रवेत्रैकपाणये ।
ज्ञानमुद्राय कृष्णाय गीतामृतदुहे नमः ॥३॥

*prapannapārijātāya totravetraikapāṇaye |*
*jñānamudrāya kṛṣṇāya gītāmṛtaduhe namaḥ ||3||*

**3.** Salutations to *Kṛṣṇa*, who is as the tree that satisfies the desires of those that surrender to Him, who in one hand holds the symbol of knowledge and in the other, the whip. It is He who milked the nectar of the *Gītā*.

सर्वोपनिषदो गावो दोग्धा गोपालनन्दनः ।
पार्थो वत्सः सुधीर्भोक्ता दुग्धं गीतामृतं महत् ॥४॥

*sarvopaniṣado gāvo dogdhā gopālanandanaḥ |*
*pārtho vatsaḥ sudhīrbhoktā dugdhaṁ gītāmṛtaṁ mahat ||4||*

**4.** All the *Upaniṣads* are the cows, *Gopālanandana* [*Kṛṣṇa*], the one who milks. *Pārtha* [*Arjuna*] is the calf and also all those whose intellect is mature enough to enjoy that milk which is the great nectar of the *Gītā*.

वसुदेवसुतं देवं कंसचाणूरमर्दनम् ।
देवकीपरमानन्दं कृष्णं वन्दे जगद्गुरुम् ॥५॥

*vasudevasutaṁ devaṁ kaṁsacāṇūramardanam |*
*devakīparamānandaṁ kṛṣṇaṁ vande jagadgurum ||5||*

**5.** I salute Lord *Kṛṣṇa*, son of *Vasudeva*, destroyer of *Kaṁsa* and *Cāṇūra*, the greatest joy of *Devakī*, the teacher of the Universe.

भीष्मद्रोणतटा जयद्रथजला गान्धारनीलोत्पला
शल्यग्राहवती कृपेण वहनी कर्णेन वेलाकुला ।
अश्वत्थामविकर्णघोरमकरा दुर्योधनावर्तिनी
सोत्तीर्णा खलु पाण्डवै रणनदी कैवर्तकः केशवः ॥६॥

*bhīṣmadroṇataṭā jayadrathajalā gāndhāranīlotpalā*
*śalyagrāhavatī kṛpeṇa vahanī karṇena velākulā |*
*aśvatthāmavikarṇaghoramakarā duryodhanāvartinī*
*sottīrṇā khalu pāṇḍavai raṇanadī kaivartakaḥ keśavaḥ ||6||*

**6.** With *Bhiṣma* and *Droṇa* at its banks, *Jayadratha* as its water, king *Gāndhāra* [*Śakuni*] as the blue lilly, *Śalya*, the shark, *Kṛpa*, its current, *Karṇa*, the breakers, *Aśvatthāmā* and *Vikarṇa*, the terrible crocodiles, [and] *Duryodhana*, the whirlpool, the river of battle was indeed crossed by the *Pāṇḍavas*, [because] the boatman was *Keśava* [*Kṛṣṇa*].

पाराशर्यवचःसरोजममलं गीतार्थगन्धोत्कटं
नानाख्यानककेसरं हरिकथासम्बोधनाबोधितम् ।
लोके सज्जनषट्पदैरहरहः पेपीयमानं मुदा
भूयाद्भारतपङ्कजं कलिमलप्रध्वंसि नः श्रेयसे ।।७।।

*pārāśaryavacaḥsarojamamalaṁ gītārthagandhotkaṭaṁ*
*nānākhyānakakesaraṁ harikathāsambodhanābodhitam |*
*loke sajjanaṣaṭpadairaharahaḥ pepīyamānaṁ mudā*
*bhūyādbhāratapaṅkajaṁ kalimalapradhvaṁsi naḥ śreyase ||7||*

**7.** May the spotless lotus *Mahābhārata* - blooming from the lake of words of the son of *Pārāśara* [*Vyāsa*] - be for us a source of plenitude and liberation; having the meaning of the *Bhagavadgītā* as its sweet fragrance; having its [many] stamen as the countless stories; fully opened with the stories of *Hari* [*Kṛṣṇa*], relished, day after day, by those qualified as honeybees of this world; as the destroyer of blemishes of this era called Kali Yuga.

मूकं करोति वाचालं पङ्गुं लङ्घयते गिरिम् ।
यत्कृपा तमहं वन्दे परमानन्दमाधवम् ।।८।।

*mūkaṁ karoti vācālaṁ paṅguṁ laṅghayate girim |*
*yatkṛpā tamahaṁ vande paramānandamādhavam ||8||*

**8.** I salute *Mādhava* [*Kṛṣṇa*], whose nature is plenitude, by whose grace the mute become eloquent [and] the crippled cross mountains.

यं ब्रह्मावरुणेन्द्ररुद्रमरुतः स्तुन्वन्ति दिव्यैः स्तवैः
वेदैः सङ्गपदक्रमोपनिषदैर्गायन्ति यं सामगाः ।
ध्यानावस्थिततद्गतेन मनसा पश्यन्ति यं योगिनः
यस्यान्तं न विदुः सुरासुरगणा देवाय तस्मै नमः ।।९।।

*yaṁ brahmāvaruṇendrarudramarutaḥ stunvanti divyaiḥ stavaiḥ*
*vedaiḥ saṅgapadakramopaniṣadairgāyanti yaṁ sāmagāḥ |*
*dhyānāvasthitatadgatena manasā paśyanti yaṁ yoginaḥ*
*yasyāntaṁ na viduḥ surāsuragaṇā devāya tasmai namaḥ ||9||*

**9.** Salutations to the Lord that *Brahmā* [the Creator], *Varuṇa* [the water god], *Indra* [the king of gods], *Rudra* [*Śiva*, the Transformer] [and] *Marut* [the wind god] glorify in the Vedic hymns. Those that know the *Sāmaveda* sing [in His praise], with the knowledge of diction, language and the *Upaniṣads*; the contemplative *yogins* see Him with the unwavering mind of meditation; neither celestial beings nor demons know Him; unto Him, the Lord, my salutations.

# Chapter 1

## *The sorrow of Arjuna*

The knowledge transmitted via the dialogue between *Kṛṣṇa* and *Arjuna* in the *Bhagavadgītā* happens on the battlefield known as *Kurukṣetra*, just before the beginning of the war between the *Pāṇḍavas* and the *Kauravas*. In order to get a better understanding of the historical context, some characters and the situation at hand should be explained.

Kings are always concerned about the continuity of their reign through their sons, the princes who inherit the throne. There were three brothers, *Dhṛtarāṣṭra*, *Pāṇḍu* and *Vidura*. *Dhṛtarāṣṭra*, the eldest son, was born blind and thus he could not inherit the throne. His younger brother *Pāṇḍu*, although weak of health, was therefore crowned king, and he successfully governed and expanded the kingdom. *Vidura* was not a legitimate heir, since he was in fact the son of a servant. He was a very wise man, good and just, and was a minister and counselor.

*Dhṛtarāṣṭra* was an envious and competitive man who never accepted the coronation of his younger brother as king. Despite never having demonstrated it openly, he despised his brother's sons, who he believed were in the way of his own son being crowned king. Somehow *Dhṛtarāṣṭra* felt that if his own son were to be crowned king, it would make up for all the hurt and suffering of having his name surpassed for that of his brother, *Pāṇḍu*.

*Dhṛtarāṣṭra*'s sons, especially the eldest, *Duryodhana*, inherited all the envy and competitiveness of their father, as well as his father's hatred of his cousins.

*Bhiṣma*, the uncle of these three brothers, had committed

himself to supporting the continuation of the kingdom; he was a man of great sacrifice and dedication.

*Droṇa* was the *ācārya*, the teacher of all the princes, both the sons of *Dhṛtarāṣṭra* and of *Pāṇḍu*.

*Pāṇḍu*, after having strengthened the kingdom and conquered lands, went with his two wives, *Kuntī* and *Mādrī*, to retire to the forest, where their five children (who were in fact also sons of deities) were born. *Yudhiṣṭhira*, the eldest, was the son of the god *Dharma*, Justice, and was thus committed to the truth and righteousness. *Bhīma*, son of *Vāyu*, the Wind (just as *Hanumat*), was extremely strong. *Arjuna*, the greatest hero of his time, was son of *Indra* and a great bowman; he was the favorite of his teacher *Droṇa*. *Nakula* and *Sahadeva* were twins, both calm and wise; they were the sons of the *Aśvins*. The five brothers were quite united. When their father Pandu died, the five brothers went with their mother, *Kuntī*, to live in the palace where they were raised by their uncle *Dhṛtarāṣṭra* and the other members of the family.

While Pandu and his two wives had been living in the forest, *Dhṛtarāṣṭra* heard that his brother would have his first son. He worried that his brother's son would be the new heir to the kingdom, and therefore *Dhṛtarāṣṭra* also wished to have sons – and thus he had many. Therefore, he was quite concerned when his nephews returned to the palace after the death of their father, but he pretended to be affectionate and dedicated to his orphaned nephews, who always honored him and paid him respects.

*Duryodhana* tried to kill his cousins in vain, several times.

After the marriage of the *Pāṇḍavas* with the beautiful princess *Draupadī*, *Dhṛtarāṣṭra* was advised to divide the kingdom with the sons of his late brother. He agreed, but chose an arid and abandoned land to offer them. *Yudhiṣṭhira* accepted the offer, since he could no longer stand the situation of living with the cousins. Yet, much to *Duryodhana*'s dismay, the *Pāṇḍavas* turned the wretched land into the richest, most prosperous and beautiful of all, and also conducted a great ritual by which *Yudhiṣṭhira* was able to conquer other kingdoms, thereby becoming an emperor. *Kṛṣṇa* was their cherished cousin, friend and advisor of the *Pāṇḍavas*.

Meanwhile, *Duryodhana* convinced his father to invite the five cousins to a game of dice, and such an invitation became an obligation for them to play. The maternal uncle of *Duryodhana* played in his place with rigged dice, whereby the *Pāṇḍavas* lost everything they possessed by gambling. The cheating cousins of the *Pāṇḍavas* were insulting and abusive under the silent consent of their father. *Duryodhana* even offended and paid great disrespect to Queen *Draupadī* by trying to strip her of her clothing.

At the request of *Duryodhana*, they would resolve such great adversity by throwing the dice one final time: the winner taking all and the loser retreating to the forest for twelve years. Upon the thirteenth year, the loser would stay in an obvious place, yet remain disguised - if recognized, the loser would return to the forest for more twelve years.

The *Pāṇḍavas* lost yet once again, went to the forest, and after thirteen years returned to claim what was rightfully theirs. *Duryodhana* refused to restore their kingdom to them; he wanted nothing less than war. Many kings, including *Kṛṣṇa*, tried to negotiate peace with *Duryodhana* in order to avoid war, but he would have none of it. He was more than confident of victory considering the great number of allies and armies at his disposal; moreover, he was completely unwilling to divide his kingdom with the cousins he despised so much.

A great council of kings was held and, since *Duryodhana*

refused to cede anything at all, war was inevitable, and both sides prepared for battle. *Kṛṣṇa* was approached by both *Arjuna* and *Duryodhana* to gain his favor. The impartial *Kṛṣṇa* told the two adversaries he had but two things to offer: either himself with no weapons, or all his armed forces. The *Pāṇḍavas* preferred *Kṛṣṇa* on their side even if he refused to fight; the *Kauravas* (sons of *Dhṛtarāṣṭra*) were quite content with the armies and weapons of *Kṛṣṇa*.

The day the war was to begin finally arrived. At dawn, everyone gathered as described in the first chapter of the *Bhagavadgītā*. *Arjuna* began a dialogue with *Kṛṣṇa*, his charioteer for the battle ahead. The *Bhagavadgītā* is precisely the dialogue between the teacher, or *guru*, *Kṛṣṇa*, and his disciple, *Arjuna*.

*Arjuna* knew that war was inevitable, and that he and his brothers would have to fight in order to reestablish *dharma*, order. Of this fact he was completely aware. However, when he saw his relatives and friends united behind enemy lines – including his grandfather and teacher – he was overcome by great emotion. It was in that very moment that *Arjuna* realized the real conflict that was within him: neither fighting (to do what must be done as prince and warrior) nor retreating (abandoning his role) could bring him happiness. Winning would give him and his brothers success on Earth; dying would give them Heaven, after having duly perished as warriors, which was their role in life. However, winning also meant slaughtering friends and relatives.

It was in this moment that *Arjuna* understood the meaning of *saṁsāra-cakra*, the wheel of *saṁsāra*, the continuous cycle of life, with the constant ups and downs of happiness and sadness that never provide complete fulfillment. Any win will inherently involve a loss; likewise, any loss will come together with a win. *Arjuna* realized that action that satisfies the desire for security and pleasure – even if governed by *dharma* – can never satisfy completely. There always remains a desire for further satisfaction and fulfillment.

Desire is a symptom of someone who is not complete. It may not necessarily be an object that one desires, but there is a desire to be rid of the sensation that there is something missing, something through which one can be different and content. The individual has concluded that he or she is unhappy and incomplete; therefore, there is a desire to change the way one is feeling at a given moment, the feeling of being limited and unfulfilled.

Desire, and its subsequent action to be different and fulfilled, is the very impulse that pushes the wheel of *saṁsāra*, which is the constant transformation of life and inevitable unfulfillment. An individual, who by definition is limited, together with an infinite number of limited gains and achievements, will always remain limited, and therefore, unsatisfied. Something acquired may make an individual feel more comfortable; however, if there is truly a way to be happy and fulfilled, it is not by means of a process of transformation, but rather by means of discovering the Self that is already complete, fulfilled and eternal. Is it possible to stop the endless search to be different, and therefore, to be happy?

It is necessary to discover the mind that says: "Enough! I want to understand my suffering, its cause, and the solution for this fundamental problem of the human being". It is only in this moment that a person becomes a seeker of the true Self, a seeker of liberation from the imprisonment of the wheel of *saṁsāra* – the unending wheel of desire.

There are two paths for human life: one is a search to produce something new via action; the other is a search to recognize what already exists via knowledge. One search is to acquire something that has not yet been attained; the other is to acquire what one already has (although not recognized).

Human desire is always changing: at times, it is a desire to acquire something, while at other times, it is a desire to release something. However, what lies behind both of these two instances is the desire for fulfillment. Whereas the desire for objects is situational and the objects themselves are constantly changing, the desire for happiness is fundamental and accompanies every single individual throughout life. Not knowing how to solve this fundamental problem, we try to flee from ourselves, by running from discomfort or pain by taking a trip, making some kind of change, or by creating a distraction. No problem, however, can be solved by either running from it or changing a way of being or living.

Solving this dissatisfaction is the main goal of life. It is important to understand the problem in order to look for a way of solving the problem where it resides. It is not merely enough to search for a solution; one must understand the nature of the problem in order to recognize the nature of the solution.

Situational problems will always occur: they are solved, and then new ones appear. *Arjuna* is not complaining about just any specific situational problem. He desires a solution to the problem of the human feeling of insufficiency and inadequacy. Despite all his training as a warrior, he feels helpless and does not know what to do. He turns to *Śrī Kṛṣṇa* for a solution.

The *Bhagavadgītā* begins with the word "*dharma*" and ends, in chapter 18 verse 78, with the word "mama" (my), since the subject of the *Gītā* is mama *dharma*. At the individual level, it is what must be done by each and every one of us in the various roles in life. *Dharma* at the general level means "that which is correct, appropriate". In its general meaning, they are the universal values, such as always speaking the truth and practicing non-violence.

*Dharma* is the cosmic law of cause and effect that governs action and its corresponding result. An appropriate action brings a positive result, called *puṇya*; an inappropriate action, *adharma*, brings a negative result, called *pāpa*.

*Dharma* has an even more fundamental meaning that refers to the greater good of the human being, its eternal nature - and it is knowledge of this eternal nature that is the highest goal of human life.

*Arjuna* and his brothers, together with *Śrī Kṛṣṇa* defend *dharma*; *Dhṛtarāṣṭra*, *Duryodhana* and his brothers defend *adharma*.

There is a conflict between them that must be resolved so that peace may reign again.

## Summary of the verses

In verses 1 to 20, there is a description of the two armies and the sounding of the conches, signaling the beginning of war.

In verses 3 to 11, *Duryodhana* speaks to his teacher, the great *Droṇa*, instigating him to fight with all his might, since he knows that his heart, as well as the heart of *Bhiṣma*, is with the enemy, the *Pāṇḍavas*.

In verses 21 to 25, *Arjuna* asks *Śrī Kṛṣṇa*, his charioteer, to place the chariot right in between the two armies so that he can see against whom he shall fight.

In verses 26 to 30, upon seeing his relatives and friends, *Arjuna* loses the clarity of his intellect and is overcome by emotion, no longer seeing that this very war was caused by his cousins' disregard for *dharma*, for order and justice, which caused *Śrī Kṛṣṇa*, *Arjuna* and his allies to take the decision to defend *dharma*, meaning that which is righteous and just.

In verses 31 to 35, *Arjuna* questions himself about what he really wants.

Verses 36 to 47 describe the state of disillusion in which *Arjuna* finds himself. He wants a way out of this state, but does not yet know what to do. He wishes to flee the war to escape the suffering he is feeling at the moment, and wants to convince *Śrī Kṛṣṇa* that this is indeed the best solution, since he is not sure about the problem or the solution anyway. Therefore, suffering and disheartened, he drops his bow and arrows. He sits without knowing what to do.

# अथ श्रीमद्भगवद्गीता

***atha śrīmadbhagavadgītā***

**The** *Bhagavadgītā*

## अथ प्रथमोऽध्यायः

***atha prathamo'dhyāyaḥ***

**Chapter one**

धृतराष्ट्र उवाच
धर्मक्षेत्रे कुरुक्षेत्रे समवेता युयुत्सवः ।
मामकाः पाण्डवाश्चैव किमकुर्वत सञ्जय ॥१॥

*dhṛtarāṣṭra uvāca*
*dharmakṣetre kurukṣetre samavetā yuyutsavaḥ |*
*māmakāḥ pāṇḍavāścaiva kimakurvata sañjaya ||1||*

**1.** *Dhṛtarāṣṭra* spoke:
— O *Sañjaya*! When assembled together, desiring to fight, what in fact did the sons of *Pāṇḍu* and my [sons] do on the field of *Kurukṣetra*, where *dharma* [that which is virtuous] rules?

सञ्जय उवाच
दृष्ट्वा तु पाण्डवानीकं व्यूढं दुर्योधनस्तदा ।
आचार्यमुपसङ्गम्य राजा वचनमब्रवीत् ॥२॥

*sañjaya uvāca*
*dṛṣṭva tu pāṇḍavānīkaṁ vyūḍhaṁ duryodhanastadā |*
*ācāryamupasaṅgamya rājā vacanamabravīt ||2||*

**2.** *Sañjaya* spoke:
— King *Duryodhana*, having seen the army of the *Pāṇḍavas* arranged for battle, then approached his teacher, and spoke these words:

पश्यैतां पाण्डुपुत्राणामाचार्य महतीं चमूम् ।
व्यूढां द्रुपदपुत्रेण तव शिष्येण धीमता ॥३॥

*paśyaitāṁ pāṇḍuputrāṇāmācārya mahatīṁ camūm |*
*vyūḍhāṁ drupadaputreṇa tava śiṣyeṇa dhīmatā ||3||*

**3.** "O teacher, behold the great army of the sons of *Pāṇḍu*, led by your talented apprentice, the son of *Drupada*.

अत्र शूरा महेष्वासा भीमार्जुनसमा युधि ।
युयुधानो विराटश्च द्रुपदश्च महारथः ॥४॥

*atra śūrā maheṣvāsā bhīmārjunasamā yudhi |*
*yuyudhāno virāṭaśca drupadaśca mahārathaḥ ||4||*

**4.** Here are heroes, mighty archers, equal to *Bhīma* and *Arjuna* in the field of battle, *Yuyudhāna*, the king of *Virāta* and *Drupada*, great warriors;

धृष्टकेतुश्चेकितानः काशिराजश्च वीर्यवान् ।
पुरुजित्कुन्तिभोजश्च शैब्यश्च नरपुङ्गवः ॥५॥

*dhṛṣṭaketuścekitānaḥ kāśirājaśca vīryavān |*
*purujitkuntibhojaśca śaibyaśca narapuṅgavaḥ ||5||*

**5.** the strong and valient *Dhṛṣṭaketu, Cekitāna,* the king of *Kāśī, Purujit, Kuntibhoja* and the famous *Śaibya;*

युधामन्युश्च विक्रान्त उत्तमौजाश्च वीर्यवान् ।
सौभद्रो द्रौपदेयाश्च सर्व एव महारथाः ॥६॥

*yudhāmanyuśca vikrānta uttamaujāśca vīryavān |*
*saubhadro draupadeyāśca sarva eva mahārathāḥ ||6||*

**6.** the mighty *Yudhāmanyu* and the valient *Uttamaujas;* the son of *Subhadrā* and the sons of *Draupadī,* all great warriors.

अस्माकं तु विशिष्टा ये तान्निबोध द्विजोत्तम ।
नायका मम सैन्यस्य सञ्ज्ञार्थं तान् ब्रवीमि ते ॥७॥

*asmākaṁ tu viśiṣṭā ye tānnibodha dvijottama |*
*nāyakā mama sainyasya sañjñārthaṁ tān bravīmi te ||7||*

**7.** But look, o great *brāhmaṇa,* amongst us are the most renowned leaders of my army. For your information, I shall name them for you.

भवान् भीष्मश्च कर्णश्च कृपश्च समितिञ्जयः ।
अश्वत्थामा विकर्णश्च सौमदत्तिर्जयद्रथः ॥८॥

*bhavān bhīṣmaśca karṇaśca kṛpaśca samitiñjayaḥ |*
*aśvatthāmā vikarṇaśca saumadattirjayadrathaḥ ||8||*

**8.** Your lordship, *Bhīṣma, Karṇa, Kṛpa*, victorious in war; *Aśvatthāmā, Vikarṇa*, the son of *Somadatta* and also *Jayadratha*,

अन्ये च बहवः शूरा मदर्थे त्यक्तजीविताः ।
नानाशस्त्रप्रहरणाः सर्वे युद्धविशारदाः ॥९॥

*anye ca bahavaḥ śūrā madarthe tyaktajīvitāḥ |*
*nānāśastrapraharaṇāḥ sarve yuddhaviśāradāḥ ||9||*

**9.** and many other heroes who are determined to give their lives for my sake; armed with various weapons, all are very skilled in war.

अपर्याप्तं तदस्माकं बलं भीष्माभिरक्षितम् ।
पर्याप्तं त्विदमेतेषां बलं भीमाभिरक्षितम् ॥१०॥

*aparyāptaṁ tadasmākaṁ balaṁ bhīṣmābhirakṣitam |*
*paryāptaṁ tvidameteṣāṁ balaṁ bhīmābhirakṣitam ||10||*

**10.** Our army is not complete, protected by *Bhīṣma*; whereas their army, [though] complete, is under the protection of *Bhīma*.[1]

---

1 *Duryodhana* uses the antonyms "*aparyāptaṁ*" and "*paryāptaṁ*" to describe the two armies. He begins the verse by saying: "*aparyāptaṁ tadasmākaṁ balaṁ*", or rather, "our army is *aparyāptaṁ*". The word "*aparyāptaṁ*" can mean "incomplete, insufficient" as well as "that which cannot be dominated". In the second phrase of the verse "*paryāptaṁ tvidameteṣāṁ balaṁ*" "whereas their army is *paryāptaṁ*". The word "*paryāptaṁ*" can also have more than one meaning: "complete, extensive, sufficient" or "conquerable, limited". Therefore, two translations are possible, according to the tradition of *Advaita Vedānta*. The version that has been chosen for this book: "Our army is not complete, protected by *Bhīṣma*; whereas their army, [though] complete, is under the protection of *Bhīma*". Another possible translation, which remains within the tradition, would be: "Our army cannot be dominat-

अयनेषु च सर्वेषु यथाभागमवस्थिताः ।
भीष्ममेवाभिरक्षन्तु भवन्तः सर्व एव हि ॥११॥

*ayaneṣu ca sarveṣu yathābhāgamavasthitāḥ |*
*bhīṣmamevābhirakṣantu bhavantaḥ sarva eva hi ||11||*

**11.** And, placed in their respective positions, in all the army lines, may all indeed protect *Bhīṣma*."

तस्य सञ्जनयन्हर्षं कुरुवृद्धः पितामहः ।
सिंहनादं विनद्योच्चैः शङ्खं दध्मौ प्रतापवान् ॥१२॥

*tasya sañjanayanharṣaṁ kuruvṛddhaḥ pitāmahaḥ |*
*siṁhanādaṁ vinadyoccaiḥ śaṅkhaṁ dadhmau pratāpavān ||12||*

**12.** Pleasing him [*Duryodhana*], the dignified grandfather, the eldest of the family of *Kurus*, blew [his] conch out loud like the roar of a lion.

ततः शङ्खाश्च भेर्यश्च पणवानकगोमुखाः ।
सहसैवाभ्यहन्यन्त स शब्दस्तुमुलोऽभवत् ॥१३॥

*tataḥ śaṅkhāśca bheryaśca paṇavānakagomukhāḥ |*
*sahasaivābhyahanyanta sa śabdastumulo'bhavat ||13||*

**13.** Then, suddenly, conches, drums, cymbals and trumpets were struck and the sound was tremendous.

---

ed, it is under the protection of *Bhīṣma*; whereas their army, which is conquerable, is under the protection of *Bhīma*." The object of *Duryodhana* was to win the heart of his teacher, so that he would fight with all his might, since he knew well that *Droṇa* had a soft spot for the *Pāṇḍavas*, whom he would face in battle shortly.

ततः श्वेतैर्हयैर्युक्ते महति स्यन्दने स्थितौ ।
माधवः पाण्डवश्चैव दिव्यौ शङ्खौ प्रदध्मतुः ॥१४॥

*tataḥ śvetairhayairyukte mahati syandane sthitau |*
*mādhavaḥ pāṇḍavaścaiva divyau śaṅkhau pradadhmatuḥ ||14||*

**14.** Then *Mādhava* [*Kṛṣṇa*] and the *Pāṇḍava* [*Arjuna*], who were in a great chariot pulled by white horses, also sounded out their divine conches.

पाञ्चजन्यं हृषीकेशो देवदत्तं धनञ्जयः ।
पौण्ड्रं दध्मौ महाशङ्खं भीमकर्मा वृकोदरः ॥१५॥

*pāñcajanyaṁ hṛṣīkeśo devadattaṁ dhanañjayaḥ |*
*pauṇḍraṁ dadhmau mahāśaṅkhaṁ bhīmakarmā vṛkodaraḥ ||15||*

**15.** *Hṛṣīkeśa* [*Kṛṣṇa*] blew [the conch called] *Pāñcajanya*, *Dhanañjaya* [*Arjuna*] blew [the conch called] *Devadatta*, *Vṛkodara* [*Bhīma*], he of great deeds, blew the great conch *Pauṇḍra*.

अनन्तविजयं राजा कुन्तीपुत्रो युधिष्ठिरः ।
नकुलः सहदेवश्च सुघोषमणिपुष्पकौ ॥१६॥

*anantavijayaṁ rājā kuntīputro yudhiṣṭhiraḥ |*
*nakulaḥ sahadevaśca sughoṣamaṇipuṣpakau ||16||*

**16.** King *Yudhiṣṭhira*, son of *Kuntī*, [blew the conch called] *Anantavijaya*. *Nakula* and *Sahadeva* [blew] *Sughoṣa* and *Maṇipuṣpaka*.

काश्यश्च परमेष्वासः शिखण्डी च महारथः ।
धृष्टद्युम्नो विराटश्च सात्यकिश्चापराजितः ॥१७॥
द्रुपदो द्रौपदेयाश्च सर्वशः पृथिवीपते ।
सौभद्रश्च महाबाहुः शङ्खान्दध्मुः पृथक् पृथक् ॥१८॥

*kāśyaśca parameṣvāsaḥ śikhaṇḍī ca mahārathaḥ |*
*dhṛṣṭadyumno virāṭaśca sātyakiścāparājitaḥ ||17||*
*drupado draupadeyāśca sarvaśaḥ pṛthivīpate |*
*saubhadraśca mahābāhuḥ śaṅkhāndadhmuḥ pṛthak pṛthak ||18||*

**17/18.** The king of *Kāśi*, excellent of bow and arrow; *Śikhaṇḍī*, great warrior; *Dhṛṣṭadyumna*; *Virāṭa*; the invincible *Sātyaki*; *Drupada*; the sons of *Draupadī* and the son of *Subhadrā*, of the strong arms, each blew their respective conch, o lord of the Earth [*Dhṛtarāṣṭra*].

स घोषो धार्तराष्ट्राणां हृदयानि व्यदारयत् ।
नभश्च पृथिवीं चैव तुमुलो व्यनुनादयन् ॥१९॥

*sa ghoṣo dhārtarāṣṭrāṇāṁ hṛdayāni vyadārayat |*
*nabhaśca pṛthivīṁ caiva tumulo vyanunādayan ||19||*

**19.** That tremendous noise, reverberating the sky and earth with echos, burst the hearts of the sons of *Dhṛtarāṣṭra*.

अथ व्यवस्थितान्दृष्ट्वा धार्तराष्ट्रान्कपिध्वजः ।
प्रवृत्ते शस्त्रसम्पाते धनुरुद्यम्य पाण्डवः ॥२०॥
हृषीकेशं तदा वाक्यमिदमाह महीपते ॥२१॥

*atha vyavasthitāndṛṣṭvā dhārtarāṣṭrānkapidhvajaḥ |*
*pravṛtte śastrasampāte dhanurudyamya pāṇḍavaḥ ||20||*
*hṛṣīkeśaṁ tadā vākyamidamāha mahīpate ||21||*

**20/21.** Then, O lord of the Earth [*Dhṛtarāṣṭra*], the son of *Pāṇḍu* [*Arjuna*], *Kapidhvaja* [*Arjuna*], seeing the sons of *Dhṛtarāṣṭra* prepared for the first clash of weapons, raised his bow, and said these words to *Hṛṣīkeśa* [*Kṛṣṇa*]:

अर्जुन उवाच
सेनयोरुभयोर्मध्ये रथं स्थापय मेऽच्युत ॥२१॥
यावदेतान्निरीक्षेऽहं योद्धुकामानवस्थितान् ।
कैर्मया सह योद्धव्यमस्मिन् रणसमुद्यमे ॥२२॥

*arjuna uvāca*
*senayorubhayormadhye rathaṁ sthāpaya me'cyuta ||21||*
*yāvadetānnirīkṣe'haṁ yoddhukāmānavasthitān |*
*kairmayā saha yoddhavyamasmin raṇasamudyame ||22||*

**21/22.** *Arjuna* spoke:
— O *Acyuta* [*Kṛṣṇa*], place my chariot between the two armies; so that I may see those arranged [here], hungry for battle. I must know, at the beginning of this war, with whom shall I have to fight.

योत्स्यमानानवेक्षेऽहं य एतेऽत्र समागताः ।
धार्तराष्ट्रस्य दुर्बुद्धेर्युद्धे प्रियचिकीर्षवः ॥२३॥

*yotsyamānānavekṣe'haṁ ya ete'tra samāgatāḥ |*
*dhārtarāṣṭrasya durbuddheryuddhe priyacikīrṣavaḥ ||23||*

**23.** I want to see those assembled here, prepared for battle, aiming to please *Duryodhana*, whose way of thinking is wrongful.

सञ्जय उवाच
एवमुक्तो हृषीकेशो गुडाकेशेन भारत ।
सेनयोरुभयोर्मध्ये स्थापयित्वा रथोत्तमम् ॥२४॥
भीष्मद्रोणप्रमुखतः सर्वेषां च महीक्षिताम् ।
उवाच पार्थ पश्यैतान्समवेतान्कुरूनिति ॥२५॥

*sañjaya uvāca*
*evamukto hṛṣīkeśo guḍākeśena bhārata |*
*senayorubhayormadhye sthāpayitvā rathottamam ||24||*
*bhīṣmadroṇapramukhataḥ sarveṣāṁ ca mahīkṣitām |*
*uvāca pārtha paśyaitānsamavetānkurūniti ||25||*

**24/25.** *Sañjaya* spoke:
— O *Bhārata* [king *Dhṛtarāṣṭra*], having been commanded by *Guḍākeśa* [*Arjuna*], *Hṛṣīkeśa* [*Kṛṣṇa*] placed the most important chariot between the two armies, in front of *Bhīṣma*, *Droṇa* and all the kings, [and] said: "O *Pārtha* [*Arjuna*], behold the *Kurus* assembled".

तत्रापश्यत्स्थितान्पार्थः पितॄनथ पितामहान् ।
आचार्यान्मातुलान्भ्रातॄन्पुत्रान्पौत्रान्सखींस्तथा ॥२६॥
श्वशुरान्सुहृदश्चैव सेनयोरुभयोरपि ।
तान्समीक्ष्य स कौन्तेयः सर्वान्बन्धूनवस्थितान् ॥२७॥
कृपया परयाविष्टो विषीदन्निदमब्रवीत् ॥२८॥

*tatrāpaśyatsthitānpārthaḥ pitṝnatha pitāmahān |*
*ācāryānmātulānbhrātṝnputrānpautrānsakhīṁstathā ||26||*
*śvaśurānsuhṛdaścaiva senayorubhayorapi |*
*tānsamīkṣya sa kaunteyaḥ sarvānbandhūnavasthitān ||27||*
*kṛpayā parayāviṣṭo viṣīdannidamabravīt ||28||*

**26/27/28.** *Pārtha* [*Arjuna*] saw all those who were part of both armies: fathers, grandfathers, teachers, maternal uncles, brothers, uncles, grandsons, colleagues, fathers-in-law, and also friends. *Kaunteya* [*Arjuna*], upon seeing all of the relatives present, was overtaken by profound compassion, and said despairingly:

अर्जुन उवाच
दृष्ट्वेमं स्वजनं कृष्ण युयुत्सुं समुपस्थितम् ॥२८॥
सीदन्ति मम गात्राणि मुखं च परिशुष्यति ।
वेपथुश्च शरीरे मे रोमहर्षश्च जायते ॥२९॥

*arjuna uvāca*
*dṛṣṭvemaṁ svajanaṁ kṛṣṇa yuyutsuṁ samupasthitam ||28||*
*sīdanti mama gātrāṇi mukhaṁ ca pariśuṣyati |*
*vepathuśca śarīre me romaharṣaśca jāyate ||29||*

**28/29.** *Arjuna* spoke:
— o *Kṛṣṇa*, seeing my people assembled and anxious for war, my limbs sink and my mouth is dry. My body shakes and born [in me] is the sensation of horror.

गाण्डीवं स्रंसते हस्तात्त्वक्चैव परिदह्यते ।
न च शक्नोम्यवस्थातुं भ्रमतीव च मे मनः ॥३०॥

*gāṇḍīvaṁ sraṁsate hastāttvakcaiva paridahyate |*
*na ca śaknomyavasthātuṁ bhramatīva ca me manaḥ ||30||*

**30.** The [bow] *Gāṇḍīva* falls from [my] hand and [my] skin is burning; I cannot remain standing, and my mind is whirling.

निमित्तानि च पश्यामि विपरीतानि केशव ।
न च श्रेयोऽनुपश्यामि हत्वा स्वजनमाहवे ॥३१॥

*nimittāni ca paśyāmi viparītāni keśava |*
*na ca śreyo'nupaśyāmi hatvā svajanamāhave ||31||*

**31.** I see bad omens, O *Keśava* [*Kṛṣṇa*]! And I do not see any good in killing my people in battle.

न काङ्क्षे विजयं कृष्ण न च राज्यं सुखानि च ।
किं नो राज्येन गोविन्द किं भोगैर्जीवितेन वा ॥३२॥

*na kāṅkṣe vijayaṁ kṛṣṇa na ca rājyaṁ sukhāni ca |*
*kiṁ no rājyena govinda kiṁ bhogairjīvitena vā ||32||*

**32.** I do not desire victory, O *Kṛṣṇa*, neither kingdom nor pleasures. What is a kingdom to us, O *Govinda* [*Kṛṣṇa*]? For what are pleasures, or even life?

येषामर्थे काङ्क्षितं नो राज्यं भोगाः सुखानि च ।
ते इमेऽवस्थिता युद्धे प्राणांस्त्यक्त्वा धनानि च ॥३३॥
आचार्याः पितरः पुत्रास्तथैव च पितामहाः ।
मातुलाः श्वशुराः पौत्राः श्यालाः सम्बन्धिनस्तथा ॥३४॥

*yeṣāmarthe kāṅkṣitaṁ no rājyaṁ bhogāḥ sukhāni ca |*
*te ime'vasthitā yuddhe prāṇāṁstyaktvā dhanāni ca ||33||*
*ācāryāḥ pitaraḥ putrāstathaiva ca pitāmahāḥ |*
*mātulāḥ śvaśurāḥ pautrāḥ śyālāḥ sambandhinastathā ||34||*

**33/34.** Those for which we desire kingdom, pleasures and comforts are invovled in war, sacrificing their lives and wealth; they are: teachers, paternal uncles, sons, grandparents, maternal uncles, fathers-in-law, grandsons, brothers-in-law, and also [other] relatives.

एतान्न हन्तुमिच्छामि घ्नतोऽपि मधुसूदन ।
अपि त्रैलोक्यराज्यस्य हेतोः किं नु महीकृते ॥३५॥

*etānna hantumicchāmi ghnato'pi madhusūdana |*
*api trailokyarājyasya hetoḥ kiṁ nu mahīkṛte ||35||*

**35.** These, O *Madhusūdana* [*Kṛṣṇa*], I do not wish to kill, even if I am killed [by them]. Not even for the three worlds do I wish to kill them, much less for earth.

निहत्य धार्तराष्ट्रान्नः का प्रीतिः स्याज्जनार्दन ।
पापमेवाश्रयेदस्मान्हत्वैतानाततायिनः ॥३६॥

*nihatya dhārtarāṣṭrānnaḥ kā prītiḥ syājjanārdana |*
*pāpamevāśrayedasmānhatvaitānātatāyinaḥ ||36||*

**36.** What will be our satisfaction, O *Janārdana* [*Kṛṣṇa*], to kill the sons of *Dhṛtarāṣṭra*? Slaying these murderers will only bring evil upon us.

तस्मान्नार्हा वयं हन्तुं धार्तराष्ट्रान्स्वबान्धवान् ।
स्वजनं हि कथं हत्वा सुखिनः स्याम माधव ॥३७॥

*tasmānnārhā vayaṁ hantuṁ dhārtarāṣṭrānsvabāndhavān |*
*svajanaṁ hi kathaṁ hatvā sukhinaḥ syāma mādhava ||37||*

**37.** Therefore we should not kill the sons of *Dhṛtarāṣṭra*, our kinsmen. How could we be happy, O *Mādhava* [*Kṛṣṇa*], killing our own people?

यद्यप्येते न पश्यन्ति लोभोपहतचेतसः ।
कुलक्षयकृतं दोषं मित्रद्रोहे च पातकम् ॥३८॥
कथं न ज्ञेयमस्माभिः पापादस्मान्निवर्तितुम् ।
कुलक्षयकृतं दोषं प्रपश्यद्भिर्जनार्दन ॥३९॥

*yadyapyete na paśyanti lobhopahatacetasaḥ |*
*kulakṣayakṛtaṁ doṣaṁ mitradrohe ca pātakam ||38||*
*kathaṁ na jñeyamasmābhiḥ pāpādasmānnivartitum |*
*kulakṣayakṛtaṁ doṣaṁ prapaśyadbhirjanārdana ||39||*

**38/39.** Although those who have the mind blinded by ambition see neither the evil in destroying family nor in betraying friends, we, those that see clearly the evil in destroying family, should we not learn to retreat from such error, O *janārdana* [*Kṛṣṇa*]?

कुलक्षये प्रणश्यन्ति कुलधर्माः सनातनाः ।
धर्मे नष्टे कुलं कृत्स्नमधर्मोऽभिभवत्युत ॥४०॥

*kulakṣaye praṇaśyanti kuladharmāḥ sanātanāḥ |*
*dharme naṣṭe kulaṁ kṛtsnamadharmo'bhibhavatyuta ||40||*

**40.** In the destruction of family, the ancient *dharma* of the family vanishes. When the *dharma* is lost, *adharma* takes control of the family.

अधर्माभिभवात्कृष्ण प्रदुष्यन्ति कुलस्त्रियः ।
स्त्रीषु दुष्टासु वार्ष्णेय जायते वर्णसङ्करः ॥४१॥

*adharmābhibhavātkṛṣṇa praduṣyanti kulastriyaḥ |*
*strīṣu duṣṭāsu vārṣṇeya jāyate varṇasaṅkaraḥ ||41||*

**41.** By the power of *adharma*, the women of the family decline morally, O *Kṛṣṇa*. When women are corrupted, O *Vārṣṇeya* [*Kṛṣṇa*], confusion among society is born.

सङ्करो नरकायैव कुलघ्नानां कुलस्य च ।
पतन्ति पितरो ह्येषां लुप्तपिण्डोदकक्रियाः ॥४२॥

*saṅkaro narakāyaiva kulaghnānāṁ kulasya ca |*
*patanti pitaro hyeṣāṁ luptapiṇḍodakakriyāḥ ||42||*

**42.** The confusion [leads] the destroyers of family and the family, indeed, to hell. The ancestors, deprived of the offerings of balls of rice and water, fall [upon bad destiny].

दोषैरेतैः कुलघ्नानां वर्णसङ्करकारकैः ।
उत्साद्यन्ते जातिधर्माः कुलधर्माश्च शाश्वताः ॥४३॥

*doṣairetaiḥ kulaghnānāṁ varṇasaṅkarakārakaiḥ |*
*utsādyante jātidharmāḥ kuladharmāśca śāśvatāḥ ||43||*

**43.** With these evil acts by the destroyers of family who bring confusion upon society, the eternal *dharma* of society and of the family is destroyed.

उत्सन्नकुलधर्माणां मनुष्यानां जनार्दन ।
नरके नियतं वासो भवतीत्यनुशुश्रुम ॥४४॥

*utsannakuladharmāṇāṁ manuṣyānāṁ janārdana |*
*narake niyataṁ vāso bhavatītyanuśuśruma ||44||*

**44.** O *janārdana* [*Kṛṣṇa*], we have heard that men whose family *dharma* is destroyed remain in Hell.

अहो बत महत्पापं कर्तुं व्यवसिता वयम् ।
यद्राज्यसुखलोभेन हन्तुं स्वजनमुद्यताः ॥४५॥

*aho bata mahatpāpaṁ kartuṁ vyavasitā vayam |*
*yadrājyasukhalobhena hantuṁ svajanamudyatāḥ ||45||*

**45.** Alas! We, who are prepared to kill our own people for the ambition of power and pleasure, have decided to commit a grave error.

यदि मामप्रतीकारमशस्त्रं शस्त्रपाणयः ।
धार्तराष्ट्रा रणे हन्युस्तन्मे क्षेमतरं भवेत् ॥४६॥

*yadi māmapratīkāramaśastraṁ śastrapāṇayaḥ |*
*dhārtarāṣṭrā raṇe hanyustanme kṣemataraṁ bhavet ||46||*

**46.** If the armed sons of *Dhṛtarāṣṭra* were to kill me, unarmed and submissive in war, this would be better for me.

सञ्जय उवाच
एवमुक्त्वार्जुनः सङ्ख्ये रथोपस्थ उपाविशत् ।
विसृज्य सशरं चापं शोकसंविग्नमानसः ॥४७॥

*sañjaya uvāca*
*evamuktvārjunaḥ saṅkhye rathopastha upāviśat |*
*visṛjya saśaraṁ cāpaṁ śokasaṁvignamānasaḥ ||47||*

**47.** *Sañjaya* spoke:
— Having spoken this way on the battle field and casting away his bow and arrows, *Arjuna sat* on the chariot, with the mind completely overcome by sorrow.

ओं तत्सदिति श्रीमद्भगवद्गीतासूपनिषत्सु ब्रह्मविद्यायां योगशास्त्रे श्रीकृष्णार्जुनसंवादेऽर्जुनविषादयोगो नाम प्रथमोऽध्यायः ॥

*oṁ tatsaditi śrīmadbhagavadgītāsūpaniṣatsu brahmavidyāyāṁ yogaśāstre śrīkṛṣṇārjunasaṁvāde'rjunaviṣādayogo nāma prathamo'dhyāyaḥ ||*

*Oṁ*, this is the Truth. Thus is the first chapter, the subject [of which] is called "*Arjuna-viṣāda*" [the sorrow of *Arjuna*], in the glorious *Bhagavadgītā*, [which is equivalent to] the *Upaniṣads*, [the subject of which is] the knowledge of *Brahman* [and] *yoga*, in the dialogue between *śrī Kṛṣṇa* and *Arjuna*.

# Chapter 2

## *The knowledge*

Chapter 2 is called *Sāṅkhya*, knowledge, because it covers the knowledge of the essential nature of the Self. The *Gītā* could very well finish right here with this chapter, because all that is needed to say about this topic is expressed herein. However, since *Arjuna* does not understand and expresses doubt, therefore, chapter 3 and all the subsequent chapters until the final chapter 18 become necessary.

*Sañjaya*, the minister and confidant of *Dhṛtarāṣṭra*, received a special power of clairvoyance from *Vyāsa* to see and to hear everything that occurs on the battlefield. He relates everything that is happening to the king, seated in the palace in *Hastināpurā*.

*Arjuna* is confused and disheartened: he can neither fight nor abandon the war. Lord *Kṛṣṇa* provokes him with strong words, trying to get *Arjuna* to think about his mental state and about the purpose of his actions.

*Kṛṣṇa*'s words hit their target. *Arjuna*, trying to explain what he thinks and feels, discovers that what he really desires is knowledge of the Absolute - that which is limitless. He discovers that no amount of wealth, fame or power will help him to solve the fundamental problem of human life: the feeling of unfulfillment despite any triumphs. He begins to feel he wants a life of complete dedication to acquiring *śreyas* - the greater good - the complete satisfaction that does not depend on the presence or absence of objects. To acquire *śreyas*, he recognizes the fact that he must acquire self-knowledge, and therefore, he surrenders himself as the disciple of *Kṛṣṇa*.

*Kṛṣṇa* accepts him as a disciple, teaching him to solve the timeless problem common to all humanity, and not just the situational problem of whether or not to fight.

His lesson begins with verse 11 with a negative word, "*aśocyān*", meaning "those whose suffering is illegitimate". With this word, *Śrī Kṛṣṇa* refers to liberation from suffering by refuting the limitation which is caused by the ignorance of one's self.

Although the suffering of *Arjuna*, or indeed any individual, is undoubtedly real, the reason for suffering is illegitimate. For such a problem, the only solution can be self-knowledge: the individual's awareness that his essential nature is free of limitation.

The human being feels limited by objects, by time and by knowledge. Constantly feeling unfulfilled, there is always something missing, and there are indeed so many objects to be possessed. Furthermore, the individual knows that one day he or she will cease to exist, and the very idea of one's death is intolerable. Moreover, having acquired much knowledge about many things does not dissipate one's ignorance of the self, and often one tries in vain to fill the emptiness caused by the apparent limitations of objects, time and knowledge. Legitimate problems can be solved by various degrees of effort; however, an illegitimate problem must be recognized for it to be dissipated. *Śrī Kṛṣṇa* explains that any experience involves the subject who experiences and the objects that are experienced. Whereas objects are under constant transformation, the subject remains the same.

The truth of the Self is that which is always present, that which cannot be denied. The body, the senses, the mind, the intellect, knowledge and ignorance, are objects of perception, although they are sometimes identified as the subject, in such phrases as: "I am fat", "I am nervous", "I am beautiful".

There is an "I" that is always present, which is always the same. It is the conscious self whose very nature is Consciousness, the existence of which depends upon nothing.

*Sāṅkhya*, the knowledge taught in the *Gītā*, is about the Self that is always present, which is pure Consciousness, the basis of any knowledge, and free from any limitation whatsoever.

Once this knowledge is clearly evident and undeniable, it frees the individual from the feeling of unfulfillment, which will always exists as long as the individual identifies himself exclusively with the mind and body - which are limited by nature. It is for this reason that suffering is illegitimate and must be recognized as such.

In order to get a better understanding of what happens to a person who possesses such knowledge, *Arjuna* asks what a wise man is and how the wise relate to the world around them. *Śrī Kṛṣṇa* explains that happiness comes from neither objects, which are limited and under constant transformation, nor from within the person. The fundamental nature of the Self is plenitude, which lacks absolutely nothing. This state of being is not completely unknown to the individual; it is experienced is some special moments, such as deep sleep, when the individual is free from desires and accommodates the entire universe. The heart of the wise is like the ocean: always full, despite waters entering and exiting all the time. This plentitude is the true self and must be discovered as such, so that is can be accessed, despite situations and experiences of limitation.

In this chapter, *Śrī Kṛṣṇa* also presents to *Arjuna* the qualifications necessary for the mind in order to acquire self-knowledge.

It is in the mind where all the conclusions about oneself are housed. It is in the mind where we store all our tastes and aversions that are the result of past experiences, and by which we become attached to objects - always running after some and fleeing from others - as a source of happiness.

In order to acquire knowledge, it is necessary to study in a process of listening to, reflection upon and contemplation of the words contained in the *Vedas*, under the orientation of a teacher who can employ logic with relevant illustrations.

However, in order for this study to be done successfully, the mind must be prepared with the capacity to focus, *antaḥkaraṇanaiścalyam*, and the mind must not react to situations that occur, whether they be pleasant or disagreeable - this capacity of the mind is called *antaḥkaraṇaśuddhiḥ*. In order to prepare the mind, *yoga* is prescribed, which includes various practices and disciplines, such as *karmayoga*.

In this chapter, we encounter the main verses on *karmayoga*, as well as two definitions of *yoga* in verses 48 and 50. Later, in chapter 6, *Śrī Kṛṣṇa* gives us yet another definition in verse 23. In chapter 18, verse 46, the great teacher of the *Gītā* completes his lesson by stating that the attitude of *karmayoga* depends on the comprehension of *Īśvara*. *Īśvara* is the cause of the manifestation of the universe; the universe itself with all its duality; the various laws that govern it; as well as the cosmic Order that maintains it cohesive.

*Īśvara* is *karmaphaladātā* - that which gives the result of action. It is for this reason that in chapter 2, verse 47, it is said that the individual's choice is in his action and not in the result of his action, which is delivered according to laws. The comprehension of *Īśvara* capacitates the individual to receive whatever may come, without reacting, thereby acquiring the emotional maturity necessary to assimilate the knowledge of the Self. This process of knowledge negates the reason for suffering, rendering it illegitimate. That is why the *Bhagavadgītā* begins with a negation in verse 11 of this chapter and ends with verse 66 of chapter 18 with yet another negation, *mā śucaḥ*, "do not be sad".

## Summary of the verses

Verse 1: *Sañjaya* tells king *Dhṛtarāṣṭra* that the mental state of *Arjuna* is one of sadness and disillusion, and that *Śrī Kṛṣṇa* turns to *Arjuna* after listening to him for some time.

Verses 2 and 3: *Śrī Kṛṣṇa* tries to shake *Arjuna* with words.

Verses 4 to 8: *Arjuna* analyzes his suffering and discovers the fundamental problem. He requests that *Śrī Kṛṣṇa* be his teacher and bless him with the necessary instruction.

Verses 9 and 10: *Sañjaya* comments on what happened.

Verses 11 to 38: *Śrī Kṛṣṇa* responds to *Arjuna* and presents his argument as to why he must fight. He says that the Self is eternal and immortal; and even if the Self was subject to transformation, *Arjuna* must not lament: since all that is born is subject to death, and is then born in another form. There is no point in lamenting that which is inevitable, whether death or separation from the beloved; and moreover, from the perspective of a *Kṣatriya*, as prince and warrior, *Arjuna* must consider what is best for society, and thus establish order without hesitation, waging war, if necessary. Also, doing contrary to what must be done will produce *pāpa*, the negative result; therefore, the least he can do to avoid *pāpa* is to go to war. And finally, in order to defend his good name, he should fight.

Verse 39: *Śrī Kṛṣṇa* introduces a new theme, *karmayoga*.

Verses 40 to 46: The importance of *karmayoga* is described.

Verse 47: The concept of *karmayoga* is that a person may choose an action, but not the result of action, which depends on cosmic laws that govern action and its results. At the same time, however, inaction is not a solution. Having exacted an action, one must be prepared for its result.

Verse 48: *Yoga* is defined as the mind's capacity to remain unwavering in any situation, whether in success or failure.

Verses 49 to 53: *Karmayoga* is newly presented as an attitude upon taking action. With the mind stable through *yoga*, knowledge becomes possible.

Verse 54: *Arjuna* wants to know what the characteristics of a person who is resolute in self-knowledge are.

Verses 55 to 72: *Śrī Kṛṣṇa* explains the characteristics of a person who possesses knowledge of one's true nature, free of limitation, and compares the mind to an ocean that is always full, regardless of the waters that enter and exit it. Finally he states that clear and unwavering knowledge is called *Brahmī Sthiti*, the state of *Brahman*. One who reaches this state becomes free from delusion, a *jīvanmukta* (liberated in life), and after death, becomes one with *Brahman*.

# अथ द्वितीयोऽध्यायः

## *atha dvitīyo'dhyāyaḥ*

## Chapter two

सञ्जय उवाच
तं तथा कृपयाविष्टमश्रुपूर्णाकुलेक्षणम् ।
विषीदन्तमिदं वाक्यमुवाच मधुसूदनः ॥१॥

*sañjaya uvāca*
*taṁ tathā kṛpayāviṣṭamaśrupūrṇākulekṣaṇam |*
*viṣīdantamidaṁ vākyamuvāca madhusūdanaḥ ||1||*

**1.** *Sañjaya* spoke:
— Then *Madhusūdana* [*Kṛṣṇa*] pronounced these words to him [*Arjuna*] who was sad, filled with compassion [and] whose eyes were filled with tears.

श्रीभगवानुवाच
कुतस्त्वा कश्मलमिदं विषमे समुपस्थितम् ।
अनार्यजुष्टमस्वर्ग्यमकीर्तिकरमर्जुन ॥२॥

*śrībhagavānuvāca*
*kutastvā kaśmalamidaṁ viṣame samupasthitam |*
*anāryajuṣṭamasvargyamakīrtikaramarjuna ||2||*

**2.** The Lord [*Kṛṣṇa*] spoke:
— How, in this inappropriate place, O *Arjuna*, has weakness - which does not lead to heaven, causes irreputation and is improper of a respectable person - overcome you?

क्लैब्यं मा स्म गमः पार्थ नैतत्त्वय्युपपद्यते ।
क्षुद्रं हृदयदौर्बल्यं त्यक्त्वोत्तिष्ठ परन्तप ॥३॥

*klaibyaṁ mā sma gamaḥ pārtha naitattvayyupapadyate |*
*kṣudraṁ hṛdayadaurbalyaṁ tyaktvottiṣṭha parantapa ||3||*

**3.** O *Pārtha* [*Arjuna*], effemination is unfitting [of you]; this is unbecoming of you. Abandon the negative weakness of heart. Get up, O *Parantapa* [*Arjuna*]!

अर्जुन उवाच
कथं भीष्ममहं सङ्ख्ये द्रोणं च मधुसूदन ।
इषुभिः प्रतियोत्स्यामि पूजार्हावरिसूदन ॥४॥

*arjuna uvāca*
*kathaṁ bhīṣmamahaṁ saṅkhye droṇaṁ ca madhusūdana |*
*iṣubhiḥ pratiyotsyāmi pūjārhāvarisūdana ||4||*

**4.** *Arjuna* spoke:
— O *Madhusūdana* [*Kṛṣṇa*], how can I fight on the battlefield with arrows against *Bhīṣma* and *Droṇa*, who deserve respect, O *Arisūdana* [*Kṛṣṇa*]?

गुरूनहत्वा हि महानुभावान्
श्रेयो भोक्तुं भैक्ष्यमपीह लोके ।
हत्वार्थकामांस्तु गुरूनिहैव
भुञ्जीय भोगान्रुधिरप्रदिग्धान् ॥५॥

*gurūnahatvā hi mahānubhāvān*
*śreyo bhoktuṁ bhaikṣyamapīha loke |*
*hatvārthakāmāṁstu gurūnihaiva*
*bhuñjīya bhogānrudhirapradigdhān ||5||*

**5.** Indeed it is better not to kill the venerable teachers and live the life of a beggar in this world. By slaying these teachers who wish [us] well, I will benefit here in this world from pleasures stained with blood!

न चैतद्विद्मः कतरन्नो गरीयो
यद्वा जयेम यदि वा नो जयेयुः ।
यानेव हत्वा न जिजीविषाम-
स्तेऽवस्थिताः प्रमुखे धार्तराष्ट्राः ॥६॥

*na caitadvidmaḥ kataranno garīyo*
*yadvā jayema yadi vā no jayeyuḥ |*
*yāneva hatvā na jijīviṣāma-*
*ste'vasthitāḥ pramukhe dhārtarāṣṭrāḥ ||6||*

**6.** And we do not know which is better for us: whether it is our conquest, or theirs. Having slain the sons of *Dhṛtarāṣṭra*, assembled before us, we shall not wish to live.

कार्पण्यदोषोपहतस्वभावः
पृच्छामि त्वां धर्मसंमूढचेताः ।
यच्छ्रेयः स्यान्निश्चितं ब्रूहि तन्मे
शिष्यस्तेऽहं शाधि मां त्वां प्रपन्नम् ॥७॥

*kārpaṇyadoṣopahatasvabhāvaḥ*
*pṛcchāmi tvāṁ dharmasaṁmūḍhacetāḥ |*
*yacchreyaḥ syānniścitaṁ brūhi tanme*
*śiṣyaste'haṁ śādhi māṁ tvāṁ prapannam ||7||*

**7.** I, overcome by cowardness, with the mind incapacitated to decide between right and wrong, ask you: teach me once and for all that which is best for me. I am your disciple, teach me. I surrender to you.

न हि प्रपश्यामि ममापनुद्याद्
यच्छोकमुच्छोषणमिन्द्रियाणाम् ।
अवाप्य भूमावसपत्नमृद्धं राज्यं
सुराणामपि चाधिपत्यम् ॥८॥

*na hi prapaśyāmi mamāpanudyād*
*yacchokamucchoṣaṇamindriyāṇām |*
*avāpya bhūmāvasapatnamṛddhaṁ*
*rājyaṁ surāṇāmapi cādhipatyam ||8||*

**8.** I do not see what would take away the sadness that dries my senses, even if I obtained a prosperous and unrivaled kingdom on Earth, or the dominion of celestial creatures.

सञ्जय उवाच
एवमुक्त्वा हृषीकेशं गुडाकेशः परन्तपः ।
न योत्स्य इति गोविन्दमुक्त्वा तूष्णीं बभूव ह ॥९॥

*sañjaya uvāca*
*evamuktvā hṛṣīkeśaṁ guḍākeśaḥ parantapaḥ |*
*na yotsya iti govindamuktvā tūṣṇīṁ babhūva ha ||9||*

**9.** *Sañjaya* spoke:
— Having spoken to *Hṛsīkeśa* [*Kṛṣṇa*] this way, *Guḍākeśa Parantapa* [*Arjuna*] said to *Govinda* [*Kṛṣṇa*]: "I shall not fight" [and] fell silent.

तमुवाच हृषीकेशः प्रहसन्निव भारत ।
सेनयोरुभयोर्मध्ये विषीदन्तमिदं वचः ॥१०॥

*tamuvāca hṛṣīkeśaḥ prahasanniva bhārata |*
*senayorubhayormadhye viṣīdantamidaṁ vacaḥ ||10||*

**10.** O *bhārata* [*Dhṛtarāṣṭra*], in the middle of the two armies, *Hṛsīkeśa* [*Kṛṣṇa*], as if he were smiling, said these words to him [*Arjuna*], who was anguished.

श्रीभगवानुवाच
अशोच्यानन्वशोचस्त्वं प्रज्ञावादांश्च भाषसे ।
गतासूनगतासूंश्च नानुशोचन्ति पण्डिताः ॥११॥

*śrībhagavānuvāca*
*aśocyānanvaśocastvaṁ prajñāvādāṁśca bhāṣase |*
*gatāsūnagatāsūṁśca nānuśocanti paṇḍitāḥ ||11||*

**11.** The Lord [*Kṛṣṇa*] spoke:
— You grieve for those who do not deserve grief, yet you speak wise words. The wise grieve for neither those whose breath has gone [the dead], nor those whose breath has not yet gone [the living].

न त्वेवाहं जातु नासं न त्वं नेमे जनाधिपाः ।
न चैव न भविष्यामः सर्वे वयमतः परम् ॥१२॥

*na tvevāhaṁ jātu nāsaṁ na tvaṁ neme janādhipāḥ |*
*na caiva na bhaviṣyāmaḥ sarve vayamataḥ param ||12||*

**12.** Never have I not existed, neither have you nor these kings. Nor will any of us cease to exist in the future.

देहिनोऽस्मिन्यथा देहे कौमारं यौवनं जरा ।
तथा देहान्तरप्राप्तिर्धीरस्तत्र न मुह्यति ॥१३॥

*dehino'sminyathā dehe kaumāraṁ yauvanaṁ jarā |*
*tathā dehāntaraprāptirdhīrastatra na muhyati ||13||*

**13.** Just as for the individual in the body, there is childhood, adulthood, and old age; there is also the acquisition of another body. Regarding this, the wise do not delude themselves.

मात्रास्पर्शास्तु कौन्तेय शीतोष्णसुखदुःखदाः ।
आगमापायिनोऽनित्यास्तांस्तितिक्षस्व भारत ॥१४॥

*mātrāsparśāstu kaunteya śītoṣṇasukhaduḥkhadāḥ |*
*āgamāpāyino'nityāstāṁstitikṣasva bhārata ||14||*

**14.** The contact of the senses with objects brings about cold, heat, happiness and sadness; they are short-lived and impermanent, O *Kaunteya* [*Arjuna*]. O *Bhārata* [*Arjuna*], may you bear them.

यं हि न व्यथयन्त्येते पुरुषं पुरुषर्षभ ।
समदुःखसुखं धीरं सोऽमृतत्वाय कल्पते ॥१५॥

*yaṁ hi na vyathayantyete puruṣaṁ puruṣarṣabha |*
*samaduḥkhasukhaṁ dhīraṁ so'mṛtatvāya kalpate ||15||*

**15.** These [sensations] do not afflict one who employs discernment, who remains the same before pleasure and pain, O *Puruṣarṣabha* [*Arjuna*]. This [person] is qualified for liberation.

नासतो विद्यते भावो नाभावो विद्यते सतः ।
उभयोरपि दृष्टोऽन्तस्त्वनयोस्तत्त्वदर्शिभिः ॥१६॥

*nāsato vidyate bhāvo nābhāvo vidyate sataḥ |*
*ubhayorapi dṛṣṭo'ntastvanayostattvadarśibhiḥ ||16||*

**16.** For the unreal, there is no existence; for the real, there is no non-existence. But the reality of both has been completely revealed to those that know the truth.

अविनाशि तु तद्विद्धि येन सर्वमिदं ततम् ।
विनाशमव्ययस्यास्य न कश्चित्कर्तुमर्हति ॥१७॥

*avināśi tu tadviddhi yena sarvamidaṁ tatam |*
*vināśamavyayasyāsya na kaścitkartumarhati ||17||*

**17.** Know that which is indestructible, which pervades everything. No one is capable of destroying that which is unchanging.

अन्तवन्त इमे देहा नित्यस्योक्ताः शरीरिणः ।
अनाशिनोऽप्रमेयस्य तस्माद्युध्यस्व भारत ॥१८॥

*antavanta ime dehā nityasyoktāḥ śarīriṇaḥ |*
*anāśino'prameyasya tasmādyudhyasva bhārata ||18||*

**18.** The bodies of the One who inhabits the body – that which is eternal, indestructible and unknownable – have been ordained perishable. Therfore, fight, O *Bhārata* [*Arjuna*]!

य एनं वेत्ति हन्तारं यश्चैनं मन्यते हतम् ।
उभौ तौ न विजानीतो नायं हन्ति न हन्यते ॥१९॥

*ya enaṁ vetti hantāraṁ yaścainaṁ manyate hatam |*
*ubhau tau na vijānīto nāyaṁ hanti na hanyate ||19||*

**19.** One who considers this [Self] the slayer, and one who considers this [Self] as the slain: both do not understand that [the Self] neither slays nor is slain.

न जायते म्रियते वा कदाचिन्-
नायं भूत्वाभविता वा न भूयः ।
अजो नित्यः शश्वतोऽयं पुराणो
न हन्यते हन्यमाने शरीरे ॥२०॥

*na jāyate mriyate vā kadācin-*
*nāyaṁ bhūtvābhavitā vā na bhūyaḥ |*
*ajo nityaḥ śaśvato'yaṁ purāṇo*
*na hanyate hanyamāne śarīre ||20||*

**20.** This [Self] is neither born nor dies; existing, it shall never not exist again. It is not born; it is eternal, unchanging, always the same. When the body is destroyed, it is not destroyed.

वेदाविनाशिनं नित्यं य एनमजमव्ययम् ।
कथं स पुरुषः पार्थ कं घातयति हन्ति कम् ॥२१॥

*vedāvināśinaṁ nityaṁ ya enamajamavyayam |*
*kathaṁ sa puruṣaḥ pārtha kaṁ ghātayati hanti kam ||21||*

**21.** O *Pārtha* [*Arjuna*], how can one who knows the Self as indestructible, eternal, not-born and unchanging, be capable of killing or instigate the killing of the same?

वासांसि जीर्णाणि यथा विहाय
नवानि गृह्णाति नरोऽपराणि ।
तथा शरीराणि विहाय जीर्णा-
न्यन्यानि सम्याति नवानि देही ॥२२॥

*vāsāṁsi jīrṇāṇi yathā vihāya*
*navāni gṛhṇāti naro'parāṇi |*
*tathā śarīrāṇi vihāya jīrṇā-*
*nyanyāni samyāti navāni dehī ||22||*

**22.** Just as a person abandons old clothes [and] puts on new ones, the One who inhabits the body abandons used bodies and goes for new ones.

नैनं छिन्दन्ति शस्त्राणि नैनं दहति पावकः ।
न चैनं क्लेदयन्त्यापो न शोषयति मारुतः ॥२३॥

*nainaṁ chindanti śastrāṇi nainaṁ dahati pāvakaḥ |*
*na cainaṁ kledayantyāpo na śoṣayati mārutaḥ ||23||*

23.Weapons do not cut it, nor does fire burn it. Water does not wet it, nor does the wind dry it.

अच्छेद्योऽयमदाह्योऽयमक्लेद्योऽशोष्य एव च ।
नित्यः सर्वगतः स्थाणुरचलोऽयं सनातनः ॥२४॥

*acchedyo'yamadāhyo'yamakledyo'śoṣya eva ca |*
*nityaḥ sarvagataḥ sthāṇuracalo'yaṁ sanātanaḥ ||24||*

**24.** It [the Self] cannot be cut, burned, wetted, nor dried. He is eternal, all-pervading, unwavering, immovable, ancient yet always the same.

अव्यक्तोऽयमचिन्त्योऽयमविकार्योऽयमुच्यते ।
तस्मादेवं विदित्वैनं नानुशोचितुमर्हसि ॥२५॥

*avyakto'yamacintyo'yamavikāryo'yamucyate |*
*tasmādevaṁ viditvainaṁ nānuśocitumarhasi ||25||*

**25.** It is said It [the Self] is unmanifest, neither an object of thought nor subject to transformation. Therefore, knowing it as such, you should not grieve.

अथ चैनं नित्यजातं नित्यं वा मन्यसे मृतम् ।
तथापि त्वं महाबाहो नैवं शोचितुमर्हसि ॥२६॥

*atha cainaṁ nityajātaṁ nityaṁ vā manyase mṛtam |*
*tathāpi tvaṁ mahābāho naivaṁ śocitumarhasi ||26||*

**26.** Furthermore, even if you consider it as continually being born and dying, you should not grieve this way, O *Mahābāhu* [*Arjuna*]!

जातस्य हि ध्रुवो मृत्युर्ध्रुवं जन्म मृतस्य च ।
तस्मादपरिहार्येऽर्थे न त्वं शोचितुमर्हसि ॥२७॥

*jātasya hi dhruvo mṛtyurdhruvaṁ janma mṛtasya ca |*
*tasmādaparihārye'rthe na tvaṁ śocitumarhasi ||27||*

**27.** Indeed, for one who is born, death is certain, and for the dead, birth is certain. Therefore, you should not grieve over an inevitable fact.

अव्यक्तादीनि भूतानि व्यक्तमध्यानि भारत ।
अव्यक्तनिधनान्येव तत्र का परिदेवना ॥२८॥

*avyaktādīni bhūtāni vyaktamadhyāni bhārata |*
*avyaktanidhanānyeva tatra kā paridevanā ||28||*

**28.** In the beginning, beings are unmanifest, in the middle, manifest, and [again] unmanifest in the end. Why grieve over this fact, O *Bhārata* [*Arjuna*]?

आश्चर्यवत्पश्यति कश्चिदेनम्-
आश्चर्यवद्वदति तथैव चान्यः ।
आश्चर्यवच्चैनमन्यः शृणोति
श्रुत्वाप्येनं वेद न चैव कश्चित् ॥२९॥

*āścaryavatpaśyati kaścidenam-*
*āścaryavadvadati tathaiva cānyaḥ |*
*āścaryavaccainamanyaḥ śṛṇoti*
*śrutvāpyenaṁ veda na caiva kaścit ||29||*

**29.** Some see this [the Self] as incredible, others call it incredible; yet others hear it is incredible, and others, even hearing about it, are unaware of it.

देही नित्यमवध्योऽयं देहे सर्वस्य भारत ।
तस्मात्सर्वाणि भूतानि न त्वं शोचितुमर्हसि ॥३०॥

*dehī nityamavadhyo'yaṁ dehe sarvasya bhārata |*
*tasmātsarvāṇi bhūtāni na tvaṁ śocitumarhasi ||30||*

**30.** This [Self], which inhabits the body of all [beings], is always indestructible, O *Bhārata* [*Arjuna*]. Therefore, you should not grieve for any creature.

स्वधर्ममपि चावेक्ष्य न विकम्पितुमर्हसि ।
धर्म्याद्धि युद्धाच्छ्रेयोऽन्यत्क्षत्रियस्य न विद्यते ॥३१॥

*svadharmamapi cāvekṣya na vikampitumarhasi |*
*dharmyāddhi yuddhācchreyo'nyatkṣatriyasya na vidyate ||31||*

**31.** Furthermore, taking into consideration your own *dharma* [your role], you must not vacillate. Indeed, for a *kṣatriya* [a warrior], there is nothing better than a just war.

यदृच्छया चोपपन्नं स्वर्गद्वारमपावृतम् ।
सुखिनः क्षत्रियाः पार्थ लभन्ते युद्धमीदृशम् ॥३२॥

*yadṛcchayā copapannaṁ svargadvāramapāvṛtam |*
*sukhinaḥ kṣatriyāḥ pārtha labhante yuddhamīdṛśam ||32||*

**32.** O *Partha* [*Arjuna*], happy are the *kṣatriyas* to have a battle such as this, which was attained without effort and is a gate open to heaven [a better future] .

अथ चेत्त्वमिमं धर्म्यं सङ्ग्रामं न करिष्यसि ।
ततः स्वधर्मं कीर्तिं च हित्वा पापमवाप्स्यसि ॥३३॥

*atha cettvamimaṁ dharmyaṁ saṅgrāmaṁ na kariṣyasi |*
*tataḥ svadharmaṁ kīrtiṁ ca hitvā pāpamavāpsyasi ||33||*

**33.** Now let us suppose you do not undertake this righteous fight: then, abandoning your own *dharma* [your role] and your reputation, you shall acquire *pāpa* [demerit].

अकीर्तिं चापि भूतानि कथयिष्यन्ति तेऽव्ययाम् ।
सम्भावितस्य चाकीर्तिर्मरणादतिरिच्यते ॥३४॥

*akīrtiṁ cāpi bhūtāni kathayiṣyanti te'vyayām |*
*sambhāvitasya cākīrtirmaraṇādatiricyate ||34||*

**34.** People will also speak of your undying dishonor; and for people of honor, dishonor is worse than death.

भयाद्रणादुपरतं मंस्यन्ते त्वां महारथाः ।
येषां च त्वं बहुमतो भूत्वा यास्यसि लाघवम् ॥३५॥

*bhayādraṇāduparataṁ maṁsyante tvāṁ mahārathāḥ |*
*yeṣāṁ ca tvaṁ bahumato bhūtvā yāsyasi lāghavam ||35||*

**35.** The great warriors will think that you, out of fear, retreated from battle. And you, who had been highly esteemed by them, will become the object of ridicule.

अवाच्यवादांश्च बहून्वदिष्यन्ति तवाहिताः ।
निन्दन्तस्तव सामर्थ्यं ततो दुःखतरं नु किम् ॥३६॥

*avācyavādāṁśca bahūnvadiṣyanti tavāhitāḥ |*
*nindantastava sāmarthyaṁ tato duḥkhataraṁ nu kim ||36||*

**36.** And your enemies, ridiculing your capacity, will say unspeakable words [about you]. What greater pain can there be than that?

हतो वा प्राप्स्यसि स्वर्गं जित्वा वा भोक्ष्यसे महीम् ।
तस्मादुत्तिष्ठ कौन्तेय युद्धाय कृतनिश्चयः ॥३७॥

*hato vā prāpsyasi svargaṁ jitvā vā bhokṣyase mahīm |*
*tasmāduttiṣṭha kaunteya yuddhāya kṛtaniścayaḥ ||37||*

**37.** Winning, you shall enjoy the Earth; or dying, you shall reach Heaven. Therefore, stand up resolute to fight, O *Kaunteya* [*Arjuna*]!

सुखदुःखे समे कृत्वा लाभालाभौ जयाजयौ ।
ततो युद्धाय युज्यस्व नैवं पापमवाप्स्यसि ॥३८॥

*sukhaduḥkhe same kṛtvā lābhālābhau jayājayau |*
*tato yuddhāya yujyasva naivaṁ pāpamavāpsyasi ||38||*

**38.** Confronting pain and pleasure, gain or loss, success or defeat, with the same attitude, prepare for battle! This way you shall not acquire *pāpa* [the negative result of action].

एषा तेऽभिहिता साङ्ख्ये बुद्धिर्योगे त्विमां शृणु ।
बुद्ध्या युक्तो यया पार्थ कर्मबन्धं प्रहास्यसि ॥३९॥

*eṣā te'bhihitā sāṅkhye buddhiryoge tvimāṁ śṛṇu |*
*buddhyā yukto yayā pārtha karmabandhaṁ prahāsyasi ||39||*

**39.** This knowledge of *Ātman* has been revealed to you, but now listen to [the knowledge of] *yoga*. In possession of this knowledge, O *Pārtha* [*Arjuna*], you shall leave behind the bondage inherent in action.

नेहाभिक्रमनाशोऽस्ति प्रत्यवायो न विद्यते ।
स्वल्पमप्यस्य धर्मस्य त्रायते महतो भयात् ॥४०॥

*nehābhikramanāśo'sti pratyavāyo na vidyate |*
*svalpamapyasya dharmasya trāyate mahato bhayāt ||40||*

**40.** Here there is no effort without success, no possibility of loss. Even a little knowledge of *karmayoga* protects one from great fear.

व्यवसायात्मिका बुद्धिरेकेह कुरुनन्दन ।
बहुशाखा ह्यनन्ताश्च बुद्धयोऽव्यवसायिनाम् ॥४१॥

*vyavasāyātmikā buddhirekeha kurunandana |*
*bahuśākhā hyanantāśca buddhayo'vyavasāyinām ||41||*

**41.** Here [in the search for liberation], O descendent of *Kuru*, there is but one clear and decisive understanding, but for the undiscriminating, there are many and varied concepts.

यामिमां पुष्पितां वाचं प्रवदन्त्यविपश्चितः ।
वेदवादरताः पार्थ नान्यदस्तीति वादिनः ॥४२॥
कामात्मानः स्वर्गपरा जन्मकर्मफलप्रदाम् ।
क्रियाविशेषबहुलां भोगैश्वर्यगतिं प्रति ॥४३॥
भोगैश्वर्यप्रसक्तानां तयाऽपहृतचेतसाम् ।
व्यवसायात्मिका बुद्धिः समाधौ न विधीयते ॥४४॥

*yāmimāṁ puṣpitāṁ vācaṁ pravadantyavipaścitaḥ |*
*vedavādaratāḥ pārtha nānyadastīti vādinaḥ ||42||*
*kāmātmānaḥ svargaparā janmakarmaphalapradām |*
*kriyāviśeṣabahulāṁ bhogaiśvaryagatiṁ prati ||43||*
*bhogaiśvaryaprasaktānāṁ tayā'pahṛtacetasām |*
*vyavasāyātmikā buddhiḥ samādhau na vidhīyate ||44||*

**42/43/44.** The ignorant, enchanted by the words of the *Vedas*, O *Pārtha* [*Arjuna*], desiring heaven, argue "there is nothing more [than this]", filled with desire, they speak flowery words of the particular actions for acquiring the pleasures and power that lead to rebirth and the fruits of action. There is no clear knowledge in the mind of those attached to pleasure and power, [since their mind] has been robbed by such [words].

त्रैगुण्यविषया वेदा निस्त्रैगुण्यो भवार्जुन ।
निर्द्वन्द्वो नित्यसत्त्वस्थो निर्योगक्षेम आत्मवान् ॥४५॥

*traiguṇyaviṣayā vedā nistraiguṇyo bhavārjuna |*
*nirdvandvo nityasattvastho niryogakṣema ātmavān ||45||*

**45.** The subject of the *Vedas* is associated to the three *guṇas* [qualities]. O *Arjuna*, be free of the three qualities, of the pairs of opposites, be eternally fixed in the quality of *sattva*, free from the acquisition and possession of objects, and be a person who dominates the mind and senses.

यावानर्थ उदपाने सर्वतः संप्लुतोदके ।
तावान्सर्वेषु वेदेषु ब्राह्मणस्य विजानतः ॥४६॥

*yāvānartha udapāne sarvataḥ saṁplutodake |*
*tāvānsarveṣu vedeṣu brāhmaṇasya vijānataḥ ||46||*

**46.** A small well is as useful in a flood as the *Vedas* are useful to a person who holds knowledge of the Absolute.

कर्मण्येवाधिकारस्ते मा फलेषु कदाचन ।
मा कर्मफलहेतुर्भूर्मा ते सङ्गोऽस्त्वकर्मणि ॥४७॥

*karmaṇyevādhikāraste mā phaleṣu kadācana |*
*mā karmaphalaheturbhūrmā te saṅgo'stvakarmaṇi ||47||*

**47.** Your choice is that of action alone, never its result. May you not [desire to] be the cause of the result of action, nor may you be attached to inaction.[2]

2 We often see the sentence – "*mā karmaphalaheturbhūḥ*" (translated here as "May you not [desire] to be the cause of the result of action.") translated as – May you not be one who holds the fruit of action as the cause. According to the compound word in Sanskrit, this translation is also correct. However, my teacher, *śrī* Swami Dayananda Saraswati, says that what *śrī Kṛṣṇa* is saying here is that the cause of the fruit of action is *Īśvara* and not *Arjuna*, or anyone else. Although *Arjuna* may consider himself the cause of action, by no means is he the cause of the result of his action; hence, our translation as given here.

योगस्थः कुरु कर्माणि सङ्गं त्यक्त्वा धनञ्जय ।
सिद्ध्यसिद्ध्योः समो भूत्वा समत्वं योग उच्यते ॥४८॥

*yogasthaḥ kuru karmāṇi saṅgaṁ tyaktvā dhanañjaya |*
*siddhyasiddhyoḥ samo bhūtvā samatvaṁ yoga ucyate ||48||*

**48.** Steadfast in *yoga*, perform actions without attachment, having the same attitude whether in success or in failure. O *Dhanañjaya* [*Arjuna*], [this] steadiness of mind is called *yoga*.

दूरेण ह्यवरं कर्म बुद्धियोगाद्धनञ्जय ।
बुद्धौ शरणमन्विच्छ कृपणाः फलहेतवः ॥४९॥

*dūreṇa hyavaraṁ karma buddhiyogāddhanañjaya |*
*buddhau śaraṇamanviccha kṛpaṇāḥ phalahetavaḥ ||49||*

**49.** Indeed, action is much inferior to *buddhiyoga* [action with correct attitude]. Seek refuge in this attitude, O *Dhanañjaya* [*Arjuna*]. Greedy are those that hold the fruit of action as their motive.

बुद्धियुक्तो जहातीह उभे सुकृतदुष्कृते ।
तस्माद्योगाय युज्यस्व योगः कर्मसु कौशलम् ॥५०॥

*buddhiyukto jahātīha ubhe sukṛtaduṣkṛte |*
*tasmādyogāya yujyasva yogaḥ karmasu kauśalam ||50||*

**50.** One who has a correct attitude abandons, here in this world, the action that will bring both positive and the negative results. Therefore, dedicate yourself to *karmayoga* [correct attitude]. *Yoga* is skill in action.

कर्मजं बुद्धियुक्ता हि फलं त्यक्त्वा मनीषिणः ।
जन्मबन्धविनिर्मुक्ताः पदं गच्छन्त्यनामयम् ॥५१॥

*karmajaṁ buddhiyuktā hi phalaṁ tyaktvā manīṣiṇaḥ |*
*janmabandhavinirmuktāḥ padaṁ gacchantyanāmayam ||51||*

**51.** Indeed those who are discriminating, endowed with this attitude – having abandoned the result born of action, [becoming] free from the bondage of birth, free from suffering – attain liberation.

यदा ते मोहकलिलं बुद्धिर्व्यतितरिष्यति ।
तदा गन्तासि निर्वेदं श्रोतव्यस्य श्रुतस्य च ॥५२॥

*yadā te mohakalilaṁ buddhirvyatitariṣyati |*
*tadā gantāsi nirvedaṁ śrotavyasya śrutasya ca ||52||*

**52.** When your mind crosses the impurity called delusion, then you shall attain an indifference to all that has been heard and shall be heard.

श्रुतिविप्रतिपन्ना ते यदा स्थास्यति निश्चला ।
समाधावचला बुद्धिस्तदा योगमवाप्स्यसि ॥५३॥

*śrutivipratipannā te yadā sthāsyati niścalā |*
*samādhāvacalā buddhistadā yogamavāpsyasi ||53||*

**53.** When your mind, tormented by the declarations of the *Vedas*, becomes free from restlessness [and] resolute in the *Ātman*, then you shall reach *yoga*.

अर्जुन उवाच
स्थितप्रज्ञस्य का भाषा समाधिस्थस्य केशव ।
स्थितधीः किं प्रभाषेत किमासीत व्रजेत किम् ॥५४॥

*arjuna uvāca*
*sthitaprajñasya kā bhāṣā samādhisthasya keśava |*
*sthitadhīḥ kiṁ prabhāṣeta kimāsīta vrajeta kim ||54||*

**54.** *Arjuna* spoke:
— O *Keśava* [*Kṛṣṇa*], what is the description of a person whose knowledge is unwavering [and] resolute in the *Ātman*? How does a person with such awareness speak, sit [and] walk?

श्रीभगवानुवाच
प्रजहाति यदा कामान्सर्वान्पार्थ मनोगतान् ।
आत्मन्येवात्मना तुष्टः स्थितप्रज्ञस्तदोच्यते ॥५५॥

*śrībhagavānuvāca*
*prajahāti yadā kāmānsarvānpārtha manogatān |*
*ātmanyevātmanā tuṣṭaḥ sthitaprajñastadocyate ||55||*

**55.** the Lord [*Kṛṣṇa*] spoke:
— O *Pārtha* [*Arjuna*], when [an individual] leaves behind all the desire that comes into mind, becoming satisfied with oneself, through the self, it is then said that one's knowledge is unwavering.

दुःखेष्वनुद्विग्नमनाः सुखेषु विगतस्पृहः ।
वीतरागभयक्रोधः स्थितधीर्मुनिरुच्यते ॥५६॥

*duḥkheṣvanudvignamanāḥ sukheṣu vigataspṛhaḥ |*
*vītarāgabhayakrodhaḥ sthitadhīrmunirucyate ||56||*

**56.** [One who is] exempt from desire, fear and anger, free from the thirst for pleasures, unaffected by adverse situations [and] whose knowledge is unwavering, is called wise.

यः सर्वत्रानभिस्नेहस्तत्तत्प्राप्य शुभाशुभम् ।
नाभिनन्दति न द्वेष्टि तस्य प्रज्ञा प्रतिष्ठिता ॥५७॥

*yaḥ sarvatrānabhisnehastattatprāpya śubhāśubham |*
*nābhinandati na dveṣṭi tasya prajñā pratiṣṭhitā ||57||*

**57.** One who is free from attachment in any situation, who neither rejoices upon achieving the pleasant, nor disdains the unpleasant, has unwavering knowledge.

यदा संहरते चायं कूर्मोऽङ्गानीव सर्वशः ।
इन्द्रियणीन्द्रियार्थेभ्यस्तस्य प्रज्ञा प्रतिष्ठिता ॥५८॥

*yadā saṁharate cāyaṁ kūrmo'ṅgānīva sarvaśaḥ |*
*indriyaṇīndriyārthebhyastasya prajñā pratiṣṭhitā ||58||*

**58.** And, just as a turtle completely withdraws its limbs, when one is able to withdraw the sense organs from the objects of the senses, one's knowledge is resolute.

विषया विनिवर्तन्ते निराहारस्य देहिनः ।
रसवर्जं रसोऽप्यस्य परं दृष्ट्वा निवर्तते ॥५९॥

*viṣayā vinivartante nirāhārasya dehinaḥ |*
*rasavarjaṁ raso'pyasya paraṁ dṛṣṭvā nivartate ||59||*

**59.** The objects retire from one who no longer feeds the senses, but the taste [for the objects] remains. By beholding the absolute, even the taste [for the objects] disappears.

यततो ह्यपि कौन्तेय पुरुषस्य विपश्चितः ।
इन्द्रियाणि प्रमाथीनि हरन्ति प्रसभं मनः ॥६०॥

*yatato hyapi kaunteya puruṣasya vipaścitaḥ |*
*indriyāṇi pramāthīni haranti prasabhaṁ manaḥ ||60||*

**60.** Indeed, even for one who makes an effort and who possesses discernment, O *Kaunteya* [*Arjuna*], the turbulent sense organs rob the mind by force!

तानि सर्वाणि सम्यम्य युक्त आसीत मत्परः ।
वशे हि यस्येन्द्रियाणि तस्य प्रज्ञा प्रतिष्ठिता ॥६१॥

*tāni sarvāṇi samyamya yukta āsīta matparaḥ |*
*vaśe hi yasyendriyāṇi tasya prajñā pratiṣṭhitā ||61||*

**61.** Keeping all those [sense organs] under one's command, may this discriminating person sit in contemplation, holding me as the highest goal. For this person, whose sense organs are under control, knowledge is unwavering.

ध्यायतो विषयान् पुंसः सङ्गस्तेषूपजायते ।
सङ्गात्सञ्जायते कामः कामात्क्रोधोऽभिजायते ॥६२॥

*dhyāyato viṣayān puṁsaḥ saṅgasteṣūpajāyate |*
*saṅgātsañjāyate kāmaḥ kāmātkrodho'bhijāyate ||62||*

**62.** Attachment to objects is born to one who meditates upon them. From attachement, comes desire. From desire, comes anger.

क्रोधाद्भवति सम्मोहः सम्मोहात्स्मृतिविभ्रमः ।
स्मृतिभ्रंशाद्बुद्धिनाशो बुद्धिनाशात्प्रणश्यति ॥६३॥

*krodhādbhavati sammohaḥ sammohātsmṛtivibhramaḥ |*
*smṛtibhraṁśādbuddhināśo buddhināśātpraṇaśyati ||63||*

**63.** From anger, mental delusion arises. From this mental delusion, there is a loss of memory. From this loss of memory comes the incapacitation of the intellect. From the incapacitation of the intellect, one is destroyed.

रागद्वेषवियुक्तैस्तु विषयानिन्द्रियैश्चरन् ।
आत्मवश्यैर्विधेयात्मा प्रसादमधिगच्छति ॥६४॥

*rāgadveṣaviyuktaistu viṣayānindriyaiścaran |*
*ātmavaśyairvidheyātmā prasādamadhigacchati ||64||*

**64.** As long as one whose mind has been disciplined moves among the objects of the senses with his sense organs under one's command, free from tastes and aversions, one reaches tranquility.

प्रसादे सर्वदुःखाणां हानिरस्योपजायते ।
प्रसन्नचेतसो ह्याशु बुद्धिः पर्यवतिष्ठते ॥६५॥

*prasāde sarvaduḥkhāṇāṁ hānirasyopajāyate |*
*prasannacetaso hyāśu buddhiḥ paryavatiṣṭhate ||65||*

**65.** When [the mind] is tranquil, the destruction of all suffering occurs, since indeed knowledge becomes unwavering for one whose mind is tranquil.

नास्ति बुद्धिरयुक्तस्य न चायुक्तस्य भावना ।
न चाभावयतः शान्तिरशान्तस्य कुतः सुखम् ॥६६॥

*nāsti buddhirayuktasya na cāyuktasya bhāvanā |*
*na cābhāvayataḥ śāntiraśāntasya kutaḥ sukham ||66||*

**66.** For one who is still not tranquil, there is no knowledge. For one who is not tranquil, there is no contemplation, and for one who is not contemplative, there is no peace. For one who has no peace, how can there be happiness?

इन्द्रियाणां हि चरतां यन्मनोऽनुविधीयते ।
तदस्य हरति प्रज्ञां वायुर्नावमिवाम्भसि ॥६७॥

*indriyāṇāṁ hi caratāṁ yanmano'nuvidhīyate |*
*tadasya harati prajñāṁ vāyurnāvamivāmbhasi ||67||*

**67.** Indeed, the mind that follows the wandering sense organs steals one's awareness, just as the wind carries off a boat on water.

तस्माद्यस्य महाबाहो निगृहीतानि सर्वशः ।
इन्द्रियाणीन्द्रियार्थेभ्यस्तस्य प्रज्ञा प्रतिष्ठिता ॥६८॥

*tasmādyasya mahābāho nigṛhītāni sarvaśaḥ |*
*indriyāṇīndriyārthebhyastasya prajñā pratiṣṭhitā ||68||*

**68.** Therefore, O *Mahābāhu* [*Arjuna*], knowledge is unwavering for one whose sense organs are completely withdrawn from [their respective] objects.

या निशा सर्वभूतानां तस्यां जागर्ति सम्यमी ।
यस्यां जाग्रति भूतानि सा निशा पश्यतो मुनेः ॥६९॥

*yā niśā sarvabhūtānāṁ tasyāṁ jāgarti samyamī |*
*yasyāṁ jāgrati bhūtāni sā niśā paśyato muneḥ ||69||*

**69.** One whose senses are under one's command is lucid to what might be darkness to all other beings. For what might be lucid to all other beings is darkness to the wise that sees.

आपूर्यमाणमचलप्रतिष्ठं
समुद्रमापः प्रविशन्ति यद्वत् ।
तद्वत्कामा यं प्रविशन्ति सर्वे
स शान्तिमाप्नोति न कामकामी ॥७०॥

*āpūryamāṇamacalapratiṣṭhaṁ*
*samudramāpaḥ praviśanti yadvat |*
*tadvatkāmā yaṁ praviśanti sarve*
*sa śāntimāpnoti na kāmakāmī ||70||*

**70.** Just as the waters enter the unchanging full ocean, objects enter [the wise] the same way. It is [the wise] who attain peace, not the one who desires objects.

विहाय कामान्यः सर्वान्पुमांश्चरति निस्पृहः ।
निर्ममो निरहङ्कारः स शान्तिमधिगच्छति ॥७१॥

*vihāya kāmānyaḥ sarvānpumāṁścarati nispṛhaḥ |*
*nirmamo nirahaṅkāraḥ sa śāntimadhigacchati ||71||*

**71.** Abandoning all desire, the person who moves free from attachment [and] from the sense of "mine" [and] "me" reaches peace.

एषा ब्राह्मी स्थितिः पार्थ नैनां प्राप्य विमुह्यति ।
स्थित्वास्यामन्तकालेऽपि ब्रह्मनिर्वाणमृच्छति ॥७२॥

*eṣā brāhmī sthitiḥ pārtha naināṁ prāpya vimuhyati |*
*sthitvāsyāmantakāle'pi brahmanirvāṇamṛcchati ||72||*

**72.** This is remaining in *Brahman*. [One who] obtains this does not delude himself, O *Pārtha* [*Arjuna*]. Remaining there, even at the hour of death, one attains liberation.

ओं तत्सदिति श्रीमद्भगवद्गीतासूपनिषत्सु ब्रह्मविद्यायां योगशास्त्रे श्रीकृष्णार्जुनसंवादे साङ्ख्ययोगो नाम द्वितीयोऽध्यायः ॥

*oṁ tatsaditi śrīmadbhagavadgītāsūpaniṣatsu brahmavidyāyāṁ yogaśāstre śrīkṛṣṇārjunasaṁvāde sāṅkhyayogo nāma dvitīyo'dhyāyaḥ ||*

*Oṁ*, this is the Truth. Thus is the second chapter, the subject [of which] is called "*Sāṅkhya*" [the knowledge], in the glorious *Bhagavadgītā*, [which is equivalent to] the *Upaniṣads*, [the subject of which is] the knowledge of *Brahman* [and] *yoga*, in the dialogue between *śrī Kṛṣṇa* and *Arjuna*.

# Chapter 3

## *Action*

*Arjuna* receives from his teacher the knowledge that the true nature of the Self is already plenitude. Therefore, it is this knowledge that frees the mind from the desire to be happy, since one is already complete.

*Arjuna* thinks that he must abandon desire in order to be happy; furthermore, he thinks that he will undoubtedly discover the plenitude of which *Śrī Kṛṣṇa* speaks of by living a life far from objects of desire. However, at the same time, he is not sure if that renunciation is the correct course of action, since *Kṛṣṇa* had instructed him earlier (chapter 2, verse 37) to get up and fight. *Arjuna* then asks him which path is the best for someone who wants liberation: the path of action or the path of knowledge. He sees the two ways as opposites. Knowledge reveals what already exists; action produces something new. Therefore, *Arjuna* requests that *Kṛṣṇa* tell him which one is better.

Meanwhile, *Arjuna* also reaches the conclusion that if it is action that agitates the mind, then it is better not to act. After *Kṛṣṇa*'s instruction, he decides it would be better to retire from the world and meditate to discover peace, since action will always include expectations, results, judgments, reactions and problems.

*Śrī Kṛṣṇa*, however, knows there are some obstacles to acquiring knowledge that can only be overcome by action. These obstacles are none other than the individual's tastes and aversions, which are present in every single mind, and they are responsible for one's reactions and self-judgment.

Each and every one of us believes that if the world were

the way we liked it, then we would be happy. This conclusion is simply not true - if not for the fact one's very own tastes and aversions are constantly changing.

The feeling of dissatisfaction is simply not caused by the world, but rather the fantasies about how the world should be. Therefore, tranquility of the mind can only be possible once a clear objectiveness regarding the world has been established, meaning the capacity to accept the world as it is, and only then take action, if necessary.

In order to reach this objective, one's tastes and aversions must be neutralized, since eliminating them entirely is impossible; they formulate the personality of each individual. When acting on the impulse of tastes and aversions, if the individual deliberately does not react to the result of such action when it arrives, the tastes and aversion can thereby be neutralized; there will be no judgment regarding success or failure. A mind under the power of tastes and aversions cannot cultivate an awareness of the Self; such a mind will only be under the power of the reactions and judgments born of those very tastes and aversions.

Fearing reactions and self-judgement - which obstruct knowledge of the Self as being plentitude itself - *Arjuna* insists on renouncing the world, thereby abandoning problems.

*Kṛṣṇa* wants him to comprehend that by taking action with a different attitude, he can neutralize the negative power of the tastes and aversions, acquire a mind of relative peace, and finally, attain self-knowledge.

However, whereas choosing which action to take is a human possibility, choosing the result of one's action is not. Furthermore, to do nothing - not act - is simply not an option available to the human condition.

The universe is governed by laws and sustained by a cosmic order, known as *Īśvara* in Sanskrit.

When the result of an action occurs, it happens according to these very laws: this result is not subject to anyone's choice, whatsoever; therefore, the result is always suitable to the action.

Accepting the result of action, even if yet another action is subsequently produced to correct a previous one, is to have an attitude that is called *prasāda-buddhi*.

By neutralizing this power of the tastes and aversions that cause the mind to react, one may act on one's impulses, but should be mindful not to react when the result of action comes. Another way to deal with the mind and neutralize the power of tastes and aversions is at the level of the action itself, not upon receiving the results. Holding *Īśvara* as the order that maintains the universe in harmony, an individual chooses a suitable course of action while avoiding acting under the power of tastes and aversions, choosing that which is correct, and renouncing any wrongdoing. This attitude is called *Īśvara-arpaṇa-buddhi*, an attitude that sacrifices action to *Īśvara*. One leaves aside tastes and aversions and does only what is to be done. Both attitudes are *karmayoga*: the consequence of this practice is the acquisition of an objective mind that does not react and is available to learn from experience.

At the end of the chapter, *Arjuna* wants to know what is it that makes a person act even when not wanting to do so. *Śrī Kṛṣṇa* explains to him how desire is transformed into anger when not satisfied. Anger is the great devourer of objects that can rob one of peace, just as an enemy can. Just before desire is manifested in the mind, there is a slight agitation that grows and takes over the body and mind of a person. It is desire that blinds the discriminating mind and its knowledge. In the end, *Śrī Kṛṣṇa* instigates *Arjuna* to destroy this enemy.

## Summary of the verses

Verses 1 and 2: *Arjuna* tells *Śrī Kṛṣṇa* that he is confused by what seems to be a contradiction in terms. He requests that his teacher decide which way will lead him to liberation: knowledge or action.

Verse 3: *Śrī Kṛṣṇa* responds that there are two ways of life that are called *jñānayoga-niṣṭhā* (a life of isolation, totally dedicated to knowledge) and *karmayoga-niṣṭhā* (a life within society that includes the search for self-knowledge).

Throughout the *Bhagavadgītā, Śrī Kṛṣṇa* says that *karmayoga-niṣṭhā* is best, since it gives the individual the opportunity of acquiring the skills necessary for self-knowledge.

Verses 4 to 8: *Śrī Kṛṣṇa* criticizes inaction, and praises a sincere life of discernment and action.

Verses 9 to 20: *Kṛṣṇa* explains the attitude of *karmayoga* as an offering to *Īśvara,* who, having created the universe and mankind, has given them the choice of discernment that will help mankind to mature, to grow internally and to give them the sensitivity necessary for self-knowledge. When an individual takes from the universe while contributing with his or her part, the individual acts maturely. By taking and not contributing, the person becomes indebted. *Karmayoga* is an attitude that maintains the harmony of the universe; it is to comply with the obligation of each and everyone so that everything works accordingly for the benefit of all.

Finally, *Kṛṣṇa* cites the example of King *Janaka,* who attained liberation via knowledge, without ever having abandoned action.

Verses 21 to 29: *Kṛṣṇa* speaks on the role of the wise within society. He considers himself and *Arjuna* as *śreṣṭha,* a leader, someone who stands apart because of his position in society and for his knowledge - a person whose example will be followed by others. Therefore, *Arjuna* should comply with the role of the *kṣatriya* that he is, and set an example for the others. That said, just as the ignorant should act to prepare the mind, the wise should act as an example for others: the difference between the two is that the former will act with attachment and expectation to the fruit of action, and the latter with detachment and satisfaction with the Self as is.

Verse 30: *Kṛṣṇa* summarizes the attitude of *karmayoga*.

Verses 31 and 32: *Śrī Kṛṣṇa* says that he who follows a life of *karmayoga* will attain liberation and those that do not follow this knowledge are doomed to delusion.

Verses 33 to 35: *Kṛṣṇa* states that tastes and aversion are a natural part of the mind and that it is not easy to control them. Therefore, it is always best to act according to *dharma* - that which must be done - and not according to tastes and aversions.

Verse 36: *Arjuna* asks what is it that makes a person act inappropriately, against one's will. What force is it that pushes a person to do so?

Verse 37 to 43: *Kṛṣṇa* responds by analyzing desire and anger - the enemies of knowledge that shroud the discriminating mind and steal peace. A mind free from the force of desire makes self-knowledge possible.

be followed by others. Therefore, Arjuna should comply with the role of the Kshatriya (warrior) and set an example for others. It is said, just as the ignorant should act to prepare their minds the wise should act as an example for others, the difference between the two is that the former will act with attachment and expectation to the fruit of action, and the latter with detachment and satisfaction with the self alone.

Verses 30 to 32 summarize the attitude of karma yoga (selfless action) and here Sri Krishna says that he who follows a life of karma yoga will attain liberation and those that do not follow this knowledge are doomed to delusion.

Verses 33 to 35 Krishna states that desires and aversions are a natural part of the mind and that it is not easy to control them. Therefore, it is always best to act according to dharma, that which must be done – and not according to tastes and aversions.

Verse 36: Arjuna asks what it is that makes a person act inappropriately, against one's will. What force is it that pushes a person to do so?

Verses 37 to 43 Krishna responds by saying the desire and anger – the enemies of knowledge that shroud the discriminating mind and steal peace. A mind free from the force of desire makes self-knowledge possible.

# अथ तृतीयोऽध्यायः

***atha tṛtīyo'dhyāyaḥ***

**Third chapter**

अर्जुन उवाच
ज्यायसी चेत्कर्मणस्ते मता बुद्धिर्जनार्दन ।
तत्किं कर्मणि घोरे मां नियोजयसि केशव ॥१॥

*arjuna uvāca*
*jyāyasī cetkarmaṇaste matā buddhirjanārdana |*
*tatkiṁ karmaṇi ghore māṁ niyojayasi keśava ||1||*

**1.** *Arjuna* spoke:
— If you consider knowledge superior to action, *Janārdana* [*Kṛṣṇa*], then why do you instigate such cruel action for me, O *Keśava* [*Kṛṣṇa*]?

व्यामिश्रेणेव वाक्येन बुद्धिं मोहयसीव मे ।
तदेकं वद निश्चित्य येन श्रेयोऽहमाप्नुयाम् ॥२॥

*vyāmiśreṇeva vākyena buddhiṁ mohayasīva me |*
*tadekaṁ vada niścitya yena śreyo'hamāpnuyām ||2||*

**2.** With apparently contradictory terms, you seem to wish to confuse my reasoning. Deciding once and for all, name one [thing] by which I can attain liberation.

श्रीभगवानुवाच
लोकेऽस्मिन्द्विविधा निष्ठा पुरा प्रोक्ता मयानघ ।
ज्ञानयोगेन साङ्ख्यानां कर्मयोगेन योगिनाम् ॥३॥

*śrībhagavānuvāca*
*loke'smindvividhā niṣṭhā purā proktā mayānagha |*
*jñānayogena sāṅkhyānāṁ karmayogena yoginām ||3||*

**3.** the Lord [*Kṛṣṇa*] spoke:
— O *Anagha* [*Arjuna*]! In this world, there are two styles of life that have been taught by me since the beginning [of creation] – for renouncers, a life dedicated to knowledge; for those involved in action, a life dedicated to action.

न कर्मणामनारम्भान्नैष्कर्म्यं पुरुषोऽश्नुते ।
न च सन्न्यासनादेव सिद्धिं समधिगच्छति ॥४॥

*na karmaṇāmanārambhānnaiṣkarmyaṁ puruṣo'śnute |*
*na ca sannyāsanādeva siddhiṁ samadhigacchati ||4||*

**4.** A person does not attain a state of inaction by not performing actions; neither does one attain liberation by mere renunciation.

न हि कश्चित्क्षणमपि जातु तिष्ठत्यकर्मकृत् ।
कार्यते ह्यवशः कर्म सर्वः प्रकृतिजैर्गुणैः ॥५॥

*na hi kaścitkṣaṇamapi jātu tiṣṭhatyakarmakṛt |*
*kāryate hyavaśaḥ karma sarvaḥ prakṛtijairguṇaiḥ ||5||*

**5.** In fact, no one - not even for an instant - exists without performing action. Everyone has no choice but to act according to the qualities born of nature.

कर्मेन्द्रियाणि संयम्य य आस्ते मनसा स्मरन् ।
इन्द्रियार्थान्विमूढात्मा मिथ्याचारः स उच्यते ॥६॥

*karmendriyāṇi saṁyamya ya āste manasā smaran |*
*indriyārthānvimūḍhātmā mithyācāraḥ sa ucyate ||6||*

**6.** One who sits, controlling [one's] organs of action, while thinking about the objects of the senses, is deluded [and] his conduct is said to be false.

यस्त्विन्द्रियाणि मनसा नियम्यारभतेऽर्जुन ।
कर्मेन्द्रियैः कर्मयोगमसक्तः स विशिष्यते ॥७॥

*yastvindriyāṇi manasā niyamyārabhate'rjuna |*
*karmendriyaiḥ karmayogamasaktaḥ sa viśiṣyate ||7||*

**7.** But one who does *karmayoga* with the organs of action - devoid of attachment and controlling the organs of the senses with the mind - is far superior, O *Arjuna*.

नियतं कुरु कर्म त्वं कर्म ज्यायो ह्यकर्मणः ।
शरीरयात्रापि च ते न प्रसिध्येदकर्मणः ॥८॥

*niyataṁ kuru karma tvaṁ karma jyāyo hyakarmaṇaḥ |*
*śarīrayātrāpi ca te na prasidhyedakarmaṇaḥ ||8||*

**8.** Perform the action that must be done, for action is superior to inaction. Even the maintenance of your body would not be possible for you without action.

यज्ञार्थात्कर्मणोऽन्यत्र लोकोऽयं कर्मबन्धनः ।
तदर्थं कर्म कौन्तेय मुक्तसङ्गः समाचर ॥९॥

*yajñārthātkarmaṇo'nyatra loko'yaṁ karmabandhanaḥ |*
*tadarthaṁ karma kaunteya muktasaṅgaḥ samācara ||9||*

**9.** This world [people] is bound by action, except that which is done as an offering. O *Kaunteya* [*Arjuna*], perform action with this proposal [as a sacrifice to *Īśvara*], free from attachment [to its result].

सहयज्ञाः प्रजाः सृष्ट्वा पुरोवाच प्रजापतिः ।
अनेन प्रसविष्यध्वमेष वोऽस्त्विष्टकामधुक् ॥१०॥

*sahayajñāḥ prajāḥ sr̥ṣṭvā purovāca prajāpatiḥ |*
*anena prasaviṣyadhvameṣa vo'stviṣṭakāmadhuk ||10||*

**10.** In the beginning, the Creator, having made mankind along with *yajña* [action as sacrifice], said: "May you grow by this [*yajña*]. May this [action as sacrifice] be for you as the wishfulfilling cow".

देवान्भावयतानेन ते देवा भावयन्तु वः ।
परस्परं भावयन्तः श्रेयः परमवाप्स्यथ ॥११॥

*devānbhāvayatānena te devā bhāvayantu vaḥ |*
*parasparaṁ bhāvayantaḥ śreyaḥ paramavāpsyatha ||11||*

**11.** By this [*yajña*], may you conquer the grace of the gods. May the gods bless you, [and] blessing one another, you shall reach the supreme good.

इष्टान्भोगान्हि वो देवा दास्यन्ते यज्ञभाविताः ।
तैर्दत्तानप्रदायैभ्यो यो भुङ्क्ते स्तेन एव सः ॥१२॥

*iṣṭānbhogānhi vo devā dāsyante yajñabhāvitāḥ |*
*tairdattānapradāyaibhyo yo bhuṅkte stena eva saḥ ||12||*

**12.** The gods, nourished by *yajña*, will undoubtedly give you the objects desired. One who enjoys that which is offered by them, while not offering them anything [in return], is in fact a thief.

यज्ञशिष्टाशिनः सन्तो मुच्यन्ते सर्वकिल्बिषैः ।
भुञ्जते ते त्वघं पापा ये पचन्त्यात्मकारणात् ॥१३॥

*yajñaśiṣṭāśinaḥ santo mucyante sarvakilbiṣaiḥ |*
*bhuñjate te tvaghaṁ pāpā ye pacantyātmakāraṇāt ||13||*

**13.** Those that eat [after] having first offered [to *Īśvara*] are free from all impurity, but those that perform inappropriate action cook for themselves, they nourish themselves with suffering.

अन्नाद्भवन्ति भूतानि पर्जन्यादन्नसम्भवः ।
यज्ञाद्भवति पर्जन्यो यज्ञः कर्मसमुद्भवः ॥१४॥

*annādbhavanti bhūtāni parjanyādannasambhavaḥ |*
*yajñādbhavati parjanyo yajñaḥ karmasamudbhavaḥ ||14||*

**14.** Living beings are born of food; food is born of rain; rain is born of *yajña*; *yajña* is born of action.

कर्म ब्रह्मोद्भवं विद्धि ब्रह्माक्षरसमुद्भवम् ।
तस्मात्सर्वगतं ब्रह्म नित्यं यज्ञे प्रतिष्ठितम् ॥१५॥

*karma brahmodbhavaṁ viddhi brahmākṣarasamudbhavam |*
*tasmātsarvagataṁ brahma nityaṁ yajñe pratiṣṭhitam ||15||*

**15.** Know that action comes from *Veda*, and *Veda* comes from the Imperishable. Therefore, the all-pervading *Brahman* always resides in *yajña*.

एवं प्रवर्तितं चक्रं नानुवर्तयतीह यः ।
अघायुरिन्द्रियारामो मोघं पार्थ स जीवति ॥१६॥

*evaṁ pravartitaṁ cakraṁ nānuvartayatīha yaḥ |*
*aghāyurindriyārāmo moghaṁ pārtha sa jīvati ||16||*

**16.** One who does not follow, here in this world, the wheel as placed in motion [by *Īśvara*], who lives by his inappropriate actions and is satisfied only by the sense, lives in vain, O *Pārtha* [*Arjuna*]!

यस्त्वात्मरतिरेव स्यादात्मतृप्तश्च मानवः ।
आत्मन्येव च सन्तुष्टस्तस्य कार्यं न विद्यते ॥१७॥

*yastvātmaratireva syādātmatṛptaśca mānavaḥ |*
*ātmanyeva ca santuṣṭastasya kāryaṁ na vidyate ||17||*

**17.** But [for] one who remains only in the Self, satisfied and happy with the Self, there is no further action to be taken.

नैव तस्य कृतेनार्थो नाकृतेनेह कश्चन ।
न चास्य सर्वभूतेषु कश्चिदर्थव्यपाश्रयः ॥१८॥

*naiva tasya kṛtenārtho nākṛteneha kaścana |*
*na cāsya sarvabhūteṣu kaścidarthavyapāśrayaḥ ||18||*

**18.** For this person there is certainly no need to act or not to act here in this world; neither is there any dependence on another living being in order to acquire anything at all.

तस्मादसक्तः सततं कार्यं कर्म समाचर ।
असक्तो ह्याचरन्कर्म परमाप्नोति पूरुषः ॥१९॥

*tasmādasaktaḥ satataṁ kāryaṁ karma samācara |*
*asakto hyācarankarma paramāpnoti pūruṣaḥ ||19||*

**19.** Therefore, free from attachment, always perform the action that must be done. Indeed, by performing action without attachment, man reaches the highest goal.

कर्मणैव हि संसिद्धिमास्थिता जनकादयः ।
लोकसङ्ग्रहमेवापि सम्पश्यन्कर्तुमर्हसि ॥२०॥

*karmaṇaiva hi saṁsiddhimāsthitā janakādayaḥ |*
*lokasaṅgrahamevāpi sampaśyankartumarhasi ||20||*

**20.** Surely, [king] *Janaka* and others attained liberation through action. At least considering the protection of others, you must act.

यद्यदाचरति श्रेष्ठस्तत्तदेवेतरो जनः ।
स यत्प्रमाणं कुरुते लोकस्तदनुवर्तते ॥२१॥

*yadyadācarati śreṣṭhastattadevetaro janaḥ |*
*sa yatpramāṇaṁ kurute lokastadanuvartate ||21||*

**21.** Everything a leader does, the others do; that which he sets as an example will be followed by others.

न मे पार्थास्ति कर्तव्यं त्रिषु लोकेषु किञ्चन ।
नानवाप्तमवाप्तव्यं वर्त एव च कर्मणि ॥२२॥

*na me pārthāsti kartavyaṁ triṣu lokeṣu kiñcana |*
*nānavāptamavāptavyaṁ varta eva ca karmaṇi ||22||*

**22.** O *Pārtha* [*Arjuna*], there is nothing left to be done by Me. In the three worlds, there is nothing to be attained that has not already been reached [by Me]. Nevertheless, I devote myself to action.

यदि ह्यहं न वर्तेयं जातु कर्मण्यतन्द्रितः ।
मम वर्त्मानुवर्तन्ते मनुष्याः पार्थ सर्वशः ॥२३॥

*yadi hyahaṁ na varteyaṁ jātu karmaṇyatandritaḥ |*
*mama vartmānuvartante manuṣyāḥ pārtha sarvaśaḥ ||23||*

**23.** [Though I have nothing to acquire,] but hardly lazy, were I not to remain permanently in action [as an example to all], mankind would follow my example in every way, O *Pārtha* [*Arjuna*].

उत्सीदेयुरिमे लोका न कुर्यां कर्म चेदहम् ।
सङ्करस्य च कर्ता स्यामुपहन्यामिमाः प्रजाः ॥२४॥

*utsīdeyurime lokā na kuryāṁ karma cedaham |*
*saṅkarasya ca kartā syāmupahanyāmimāḥ prajāḥ ||24||*

**24.** Were I not to perform action, people would be destroyed. I would be responsible for chaos [within society] and I would destroy mankind.

सक्ताः कर्मण्यविद्वांसो यथा कुर्वन्ति भारत ।
कुर्याद्विद्वांस्तथाऽसक्तश्चिकीर्षुर्लोकसङ्ग्रहम् ॥२५॥

*saktāḥ karmaṇyavidvāṁso yathā kurvanti bhārata |*
*kuryādvidvāṁstathā'saktaścikīrṣurlokasaṅgraham ||25||*

**25.** Just as the unwise act attached to [the results of] action, the wise should act without attachment for the protection of others, O *Bhārata* [*Arjuna*].[3]

3 What is meant here is the wise should act with the same enthusiasm as the unwise, albeit without attachment. While people always act with the objective of reaching a specific result from their action, it is the wise who calmly wait to see what will be the result of their action, knowing that the appropriate result will be infallibly delivered from the cosmic order that is *Īśvara*. Yet others not only desire a specific result from their actions but also become so attached to the desired result that they become dissatisfied and frustrated if they do not get it. Results from their actions are their only objective, whereas the wise act as an example for all. The *yogin* acts for what must be done; the ignorant act just to get a result.

न बुद्धिभेदं जनयेदज्ञानां कर्मसङ्गिनाम् ।
जोषयेत्सर्वकर्माणि विद्वान्युक्तः समाचरन् ॥२६॥

*na buddhibhedaṁ janayedajñānāṁ karmasaṅginām |*
*joṣayetsarvakarmāṇi vidvānyuktaḥ samācaran ||26||*

**26.** One should not confuse the minds of the ignorant, [who are] attached to action. The wise, unwavering [in knowledge], should encourage [others] to perform all actions.

प्रकृतेः क्रियमाणानि गुणैः कर्माणि सर्वशः ।
अहङ्कारविमूढात्मा कर्ताहमिति मन्यते ॥२७॥

*prakṛteḥ kriyamāṇāni guṇaiḥ karmāṇi sarvaśaḥ |*
*ahaṅkāravimūḍhātmā kartāhamiti manyate ||27||*

**27.** Actions of all types are done by the *guṇas* [qualities] of nature. One who has a deluded mind with a false notion of oneself believes: "I am the doer".

तत्त्ववित्तु महाबाहो गुणकर्मविभागयोः ।
गुणा गुणेषु वर्तन्त इति मत्वा न सज्जते ॥२८॥

*tattvavittu mahābāho guṇakarmavibhāgayoḥ |*
*guṇā guṇeṣu vartanta iti matvā na sajjate ||28||*

**28.** But one who knows the truth of *guṇas* and their functions remains detached upon the understanding that *guṇas* [sense organs] function with *guṇas* [sense objects], O *Mahābāhu* [*Arjuna*].

प्रकृतेर्गुणसंमूढाः सज्जन्ते गुणकर्मसु ।
तानकृत्स्नविदो मन्दान्कृत्स्नविन्न विचालयेत् ॥२९॥

*prakṛterguṇasaṁmūḍhāḥ sajjante guṇakarmasu |*
*tānakṛtsnavido mandānkṛtsnavinna vicālayet ||29||*

**29.** Those that are deluded by the *guṇas* [qualities] of nature are bound to the actions of the *guṇas*. One who has complete knowledge should not unsettle those who have incomplete knowledge and who are deluded.

मयि सर्वाणि कर्माणि सन्न्यस्याध्यात्मचेतसा ।
निराशीर्निर्ममो भूत्वा युध्यस्व विगतज्वरः ॥३०॥

*mayi sarvāṇi karmāṇi sannyasyādhyātmacetasā |*
*nirāśīrnirmamo bhūtvā yudhyasva vigatajvaraḥ ||30||*

**30.** With a discriminating mind, relinquish all actions to Me. May you fight without anxiety, without expectation, and without possessiveness.

ये मे मतमिदं नित्यमनुतिष्ठन्ति मानवाः ।
श्रद्धावन्तोऽनसूयन्तो मुच्यन्ते तेऽपि कर्मभिः ॥३१॥

*ye me matamidaṁ nityamanutiṣṭhanti mānavāḥ |*
*śraddhāvanto'nasūyanto mucyante te'pi karmabhiḥ ||31||*

**31.** Those who always follow my instruction [regarding how to conduct one's life], who have faith and do not reproach, are also freed from action.

ये त्वेतदभ्यसूयन्तो नानुतिष्ठन्ति मे मतम् ।
सर्वज्ञानविमूढांस्तान्विद्धि नष्टानचेतसः ॥३२॥

*ye tvetadabhyasūyanto nānutiṣṭhanti me matam |*
*sarvajñānavimūḍhāṁstānviddhi naṣṭānacetasaḥ ||32||*

**32.** But there are those who reproach [and] do not follow my instruction. They are filled with delusion in all forms of knowledge and without discernment. Know that they will be doomed.

सदृशं चेष्टते स्वस्याः प्रकृतेर्ज्ञान्वानपि ।
प्रकृतिं यान्ति भूतानि निग्रहः किं करिष्यति ॥३३॥

*sadṛśaṁ ceṣṭate svasyāḥ prakṛterjñānvānapi |*
*prakṛtiṁ yānti bhūtāni nigrahaḥ kiṁ kariṣyati ||33||*

**33.** Even a man of knowledge acts according to his own nature. Creatures follow [their] nature. How can one control [the flow of nature]?

इन्द्रियस्येन्द्रियस्यार्थे रागद्वेषौ व्यवस्थितौ ।
तयोर्न वशमागच्छेत्तौ ह्यस्य परिपन्थिनौ ॥३४॥

*indriyasyendriyasyārthe rāgadveṣau vyavasthitau |*
*tayorna vaśamāgacchettau hyasya paripanthinau ||34||*

**34.** Taste and aversion are fixed upon the object of each organ of perception. May one not fall under the spell of these two, for they are both one's enemies.

श्रेयान् स्वधर्मो विगुणः परधर्मात् स्वनुष्ठितात् ।
स्वधर्मे निधनं श्रेयः परधर्मो भयावहः ॥३५॥

*śreyān svadharmo viguṇaḥ paradharmāt svanuṣṭhitāt |*
*svadharme nidhanaṁ śreyaḥ paradharmo bhayāvahaḥ ||35||*

**35.** Better is one's own imperfectly performed duty than the well-performed duty of another. Better it is to die in one's own duty. Doing the duty of another brings fear [of not having fulfilled one's role in life].

अर्जुन उवाच
अथ केन प्रयुक्तोऽयं पापं चरति पूरुषः ।
अनिच्छन्नपि वार्ष्णेय बलादिव नियोजितः ॥३६॥

*arjuna uvāca*
*atha kena prayukto'yaṁ pāpaṁ carati pūruṣaḥ |*
*anicchannapi vārṣṇeya balādiva niyojitaḥ ||36||*

**36.** *Arjuna* spoke:
— Then, O *Vārṣṇeya* [*Kṛṣṇa*], why is it that one commits *pāpa* [an inappropriate action], even if unwilling, as if impelled by a force?

श्रीभगवानुवाच
काम एष क्रोध एष रजोगुणसमुद्भवः ।
महाशनो महापाप्मा विद्ध्येनमिह वैरिणम् ॥३७॥

*śrībhagavānuvāca*
*kāma eṣa krodha eṣa rajoguṇasamudbhavaḥ |*
*mahāśano mahāpāpmā viddhyenamiha vairiṇam ||37||*

**37.** the Lord [*Kṛṣṇa*] spoke:
— This is desire; this is anger, the great devourer and maker of *pāpa*, which is born of the *guṇa rajas*. Know that, here in this world, [desire] is the enemy.

धूमेनाव्रियते वह्निर्यथादर्शो मलेन च ।
यथोल्बेनावृतो गर्भस्तथा तेनेदमावृतम् ॥३८॥

*dhūmenāvriyate vahniryathādarśo malena ca |*
*yatholbenāvṛto garbhastathā tenedamāvṛtam ||38||*

**38.** Just as fire is covered by smoke; a mirror, dust; and the fetus, the womb; [knowledge] is shrouded by [desire] in the same way.

आवृतं ज्ञानमेतेन ज्ञानिनो नित्यवैरिणा ।
कामरूपेण कौन्तेय दुष्पूरेणानलेन च ॥३९॥

*āvṛtaṁ jñānametena jñānino nityavairiṇā |*
*kāmarūpeṇa kaunteya duṣpūreṇānalena ca ||39||*

**39.** This constant enemy obscures knowledge even for the wise, O *Kaunteya* [*Arjuna*]. Its form is insatiable desire, filled with suffering.

इन्द्रियाणि मनो बुद्धिरस्याधिष्ठानमुच्यते ।
एतैर्विमोहयत्येष ज्ञानमावृत्य देहिनम् ॥४०॥

*indriyāṇi mano buddhirasyādhiṣṭhānamucyate |*
*etairvimohayatyeṣa jñānamāvṛtya dehinam ||40||*

**40.** The senses, the mind and the intellect are said to be the base of this [desire]. Obscuring knowledge with these [sense, mind and intellect], it deludes the individual.

तस्मात्त्वमिन्द्रियाण्यादौ नियम्य भरतर्षभ ।
पाप्मानं प्रजहिह्येनं ज्ञानविज्ञाननाशनम् ॥४१॥

*tasmāttvamindriyāṇyādau niyamya bharatarṣabha |*
*pāpmānaṁ prajahihyenaṁ jñānavijñānanāśanam ||41||*

**41.** Therefore, O *Bharatarṣabha* [*Arjuna*], first put the senses under your control, and abandon this evil that destroys knowledge and wisdom.

इन्द्रियाणि पराण्याहुरिन्द्रियेभ्यः परं मनः ।
मनसस्तु परा बुद्धिर्यो बुद्धेः परतस्तु सः ॥४२॥

*indriyāṇi parāṇyāhurindriyebhyaḥ paraṁ manaḥ |*
*manasastu parā buddhiryo buddheḥ paratastu saḥ ||42||*

**42.** [The wise] say that the senses are superior [to objects]; the mind is superior to the senses; but the intellect is superior to the mind, whereas That [the *Ātman*] is superior to the intellect.

एवं बुद्धेः परं बुद्ध्वा संस्तभ्यात्मानमात्मना ।
जहि शत्रुं महाबाहो कामरूपं दुरासदम् ॥४३॥

*evaṁ buddheḥ paraṁ buddhvā saṁstabhyātmānamātmanā |*
*jahi śatruṁ mahābāho kāmarūpaṁ durāsadam ||43||*

**43.** Therefore, O *Mahābāhu* [*Arjuna*], knowing That [the *Ātman*] which is superior to the intellect, restrain the mind with the intellect [and] conquer the enemy in the form of desire, which is difficult to defeat.

ओं तत्सदिति श्रीमद्भगवद्गीतासूपनिषत्सु ब्रह्मविद्यायां योगशास्त्रे श्रीकृष्णार्जुनसंवादे कर्मयोगो नाम तृतीयोऽध्यायः ॥

*oṁ tatsaditi śrīmadbhagavadgītāsūpaniṣatsu*
*brahmavidyāyāṁ yogaśāstre śrīkṛṣṇārjunasaṁvāde*
*karmayogo nāma tṛtīyo'dhyāyaḥ ||*

*Oṁ*, this is the Truth. Thus is the third chapter, the subject [of which] is called "*Karma*", in the glorious *Bhagavadgītā*, [which is equivalent to] the *Upaniṣads*, [the subject of which is] the knowledge of *Brahman* [and] *yoga*, in the dialogue between *śrī Kṛṣṇa* and *Arjuna*.

# Chapter 4

## *Knowledge and the renunciation of action*

The teaching of *Śrī Kṛṣṇa* to *Arjuna* had not begun here; it is the same knowledge that has been available since the time of creation itself. It has been passed on from master to disciple in a continuous and unbroken lineage that is called *guru-śiṣya-paramparā*. This knowledge is of the absolute nature of the individual, of the creator, and of the universe. *Kṛṣṇa* and *Arjuna* are part of a tradition that had existed long before they did.

In order to facilitate the organization of society, four divisions of man were created, together with their respective activities, which were based on the *guṇas,* the three basic qualities of creation. Although the creator is solely responsible for all creation, he is completely exempt from action. He does nothing. The nature of action and inaction must be understood: the nature of action is movement and change; inaction, on the other hand, is not the opposite, which is merely the renunciation of action. Action is compelled by desire, and desire just does not simply disappear upon renouncing action: it only means that there is just no further expression or satisfaction of desire. There will always be action as long as there is an agent of action, even if the action itself may be repressed from expression.

Inaction, on the hand, is different: it is the nature of *Ātman,* the Self that is Consciousness, the witness of all action. Whereas action occurs due to the presence of Consciousness, the inverse is not true: Consciousness is by no means dependent upon action. Consciousness does nothing at all. Therefore, the wise see the inaction within action, and the action within inaction; the wise are aware of the body's actions, the senses, the mind and the intellect are made possible by Consciousness, and the wise are also aware that action exists in Consciousness - and that it is not subject to action.

This knowledge has the power to transform; it instantly liberates the individual from the limitation of action and its results.

Since it is very difficult to assimilate this knowledge, *Śrī Kṛṣṇa* speaks on the qualifications necessary to reach this goal, and then addresses *Arjuna* directly, encouraging him to use the weapons he has in his possession to banish his doubts and prepare his mind.

## Summary of the verses

Verses 1 to 3: *Śrī Kṛṣṇa* states that the knowledge transmitted by him in the *Gītā* is the same that had begun since creation, and that it is the same teaching of the *Vedas*.

Verse 4: *Arjuna* wants to know how the contemporary *Kṛṣṇa* can be the same one since the beginning of time.

Verses 5 to 8: *Kṛṣṇa* takes the moment to explain *avatāra*, which is one of the subjects covered in the *Vedas*. The *jīva* is born due to self-ignorance and past *karma*; the *avatāra* is a manifestation of the divine, which does not occur out of self-ignorance and *karma*, but out of the need within the universe to protect *dharma* and those that defend it.

Verses 9 to 15: *Śrī Kṛṣṇa* explains himself as *Īśvara* - That which is completely free of action and its results. The individual who is aware of the nature of *Īśvara* is freed from limitation, because the individual discovers the nature of *jīva* and *Īśvara* is in fact one and the same.

Everyone seeks *Īśvara* in one way or another and everyone gets that which one seeks.

Verses 16 to 24: *Śrī Kṛṣṇa* explains the difficulty in understanding the difference between action and inaction, and what both really are. Afterwards, he defines the wise insofar as action is concerned: which is a person who is aware of the inaction of the Self, which is actually Consciousness - even when aware of the action of the body and mind.

The wise are also aware of the potential action when the body and mind are still. Therefore, renunciation does not mean relinquishing action: it is having a complete awareness of the Self that is not subject to action. In other words, this kind of renunciation depends on one`s understanding of *Brahman* - and not on an action or inaction.

Verses 25 to 33: *Kṛṣṇa* explains the various *yajñas*, which are *sādhanas*, or disciplines that prepare an individual for self-knowledge. He cites *Brahma-yajña*, the discipline of the knowledge of *Brahman*, as the highest of all the *sādhanas*

Verse 34: For *Brahma-yajña*, one should search for a teacher to acquire self-knowledge - a *guru* who possesses such knowledge and methodology for such instruction. With humility, confidence and reverence, the seeker must request the *guru* to instruct him.

Verses 35 to 38: *Śrī Kṛṣṇa* explains the importance and the greatness of teaching that which completely liberates the individual from illusion - that which is the greatest agent of purification.

Verses 39 to 42: *Śrī Kṛṣṇa* states the qualifications that conduct an individual to self-knowledge and those which are contradictory. He ends the chapter by stating that no action affects one who has unwavering knowledge of the Self.

## अथ चतुर्थोऽध्यायः

***atha caturtho'dhyāyaḥ***

**Chapter four**

श्रीभगवानुवाच
इमं विवस्वते योगं प्रोक्तवानहमव्ययम् ।
विवस्वान्मनवे प्राह मनुरिक्ष्वाकवेऽब्रवीत् ॥१॥

*śrībhagavānuvāca*
*imaṁ vivasvate yogaṁ proktavānahamavyayam |*
*vivasvānmanave prāha manurikṣvākave'bravīt ||1||*

**1.** The Lord [*Kṛṣṇa*] spoke:
— I taught this imperishable *yoga* to *Vivasvat*. *Vivasvat* taught *Manu*, and *Manu* to *Ikṣvāku*.

एवं परम्पराप्राप्तमिमं राजर्षयो विदुः ।
स कालेनेह महता योगो नष्टः परन्तप ॥२॥

*evaṁ paramparāprāptamimaṁ rājarṣayo viduḥ |*
*sa kāleneha mahatā yogo naṣṭaḥ parantapa ||2||*

**2.** Handed down from generation to generation, the kings and *ṛṣis* thus knew *yoga*. With the passage of time, this [knowledge] has been lost here in this world, O *Parantapa* [*Arjuna*]!

स एवायं मया तेऽद्य योगः प्रोक्तः पुरातनः ।
भक्तोऽसि मे सखा चेति रहस्यं ह्येतदुत्तमम् ॥३॥

*sa evāyaṁ mayā te'dya yogaḥ proktaḥ purātanaḥ |*
*bhakto'si me sakhā ceti rahasyaṁ hyetaduttamam ||3||*

**3.** Today the same ancient *yoga* has been taught from me to you, who are my devotee and friend. Indeed, this [knowledge] is the greatest secret.

अर्जुन उवाच
अपरं भवतो जन्म परं जन्म विवस्वतः ।
कथमेतद्विजानीयां त्वमादौ प्रोक्तवानिति ॥४॥

*arjuna uvāca*
*aparaṁ bhavato janma paraṁ janma vivasvataḥ |*
*kathametadvijānīyāṁ tvamādau proktavāniti ||4||*

**4.** *Arjuna* spoke:
— Your birth was more recent; [whereas] the birth of *Vivasvat* was beforehand. How am I to understand that you taught this [*yoga*] in the beginning?

श्रीभगवानुवाच
बहूनि मे व्यतीतानि जन्मानि तव चार्जुन ।
तान्यहं वेद सर्वाणि न त्वं वेत्थ परन्तप ॥५॥

*śrībhagavānuvāca*
*bahūni me vyatītāni janmāni tava cārjuna |*
*tānyahaṁ veda sarvāṇi na tvaṁ vettha parantapa ||5||*

**5.** The Lord [*Kṛṣṇa*] spoke:
Many births of mine have come to pass, just as yours have, O *Arjuna*. I know them all; [however] you do not, O *Parantapa* [*Arjuna*]!

अजोऽपि सन्नव्ययात्मा भूतानामीश्वरोऽपि सन् ।
प्रकृतिं स्वामधिष्ठाय सम्भवाम्यात्ममायया ॥६॥

*ajo'pi sannavyayātmā bhūtānāmīśvaro'pi san |*
*prakṛtiṁ svāmadhiṣṭhāya sambhavāmyātmamāyayā ||6||*

**6.** Although birthless, of immutable nature [and] lord of all beings, I manifest myself by means of my own power to create, resorting to my *prakṛti* [the cause of all creation].

यदा यदा हि धर्मस्य ग्लानिर्भवति भारत ।
अभ्युत्थानमधर्मस्य तदात्मानं सृजाम्यहम् ॥७॥

*yadā yadā hi dharmasya glānirbhavati bhārata |*
*abhyutthānamadharmasya tadātmānaṁ sṛjāmyaham ||7||*

**7.** O *Bhārata* [*Arjuna*], whenever there is a decline in *dharma* and an increase of *adharma*, I shall certainly manifest.

परित्राणाय साधूनां विनाशाय च दुष्कृताम् ।
धर्मसंस्थापनार्थाय सम्भवामि युगे युगे ॥८॥

*paritrāṇāya sādhūnāṁ vināśāya ca duṣkṛtām |*
*dharmasaṁsthāpanārthāya sambhavāmi yuge yuge ||8||*

**8.** In order to protect those commited to *dharma*, and destroy those of *adharma*, in order to restore righteousness in each epoch, I am born.

जन्म कर्म च मे दिव्यमेवं यो वेत्ति तत्त्वतः ।
त्यक्त्वा देहं पुनर्जन्म नैति मामेति सोऽर्जुन ॥९॥

*janma karma ca me divyamevaṁ yo vetti tattvataḥ |*
*tyaktvā dehaṁ punarjanma naiti māmeti so'rjuna ||9||*

**9.** One who is thus aware of my divine birth and action when relinquishing the body does not ensue another birth. [That person] comes to me, O *Arjuna.*

वीतरागभयक्रोधा मन्मया मामुपाश्रिताः ।
बहवो ज्ञानतपसा पूता मद्भावमागताः ॥१०॥

*vītarāgabhayakrodhā manmayā māmupāśritāḥ |*
*bahavo jñānatapasā pūtā madbhāvamāgatāḥ ||10||*

**10.** Those who renounce attachment, fear and anger, who are the same as Me [in knowledge], who seek refuge in Me, many of whom have been purified by the discipline of self-knowledge, attain my nature.

ये यथा मां प्रपद्यन्ते तांस्तथैव भजाम्यहम् ।
मम वर्त्मानुवर्तन्ते मनुष्याः पार्थ सर्वशः ॥११॥

*ye yathā māṁ prapadyante tāṁstathaiva bhajāmyaham |*
*mama vartmānuvartante manuṣyāḥ pārtha sarvaśaḥ ||11||*

**11.** I bless people in the same manner they seek refuge in Me. People follow my path in many ways, O *Pārtha* [*Arjuna*].

काङ्क्षन्तः कर्मणां सिद्धिं यजन्त इह देवताः ।
क्षिप्रं हि मानुषे लोके सिद्धिर्भवति कर्मजा ॥१२॥

*kāṅkṣantaḥ karmaṇāṁ siddhiṁ yajanta iha devatāḥ |*
*kṣipraṁ hi mānuṣe loke siddhirbhavati karmajā ||12||*

**12.** Desiring the result of actions here and now, they revere gods, since results born of action come quickly in the world of mankind.

चातुर्वर्ण्यं मया सृष्टं गुणकर्मविभागशः ।
तस्य कर्तारमपि मां विद्ध्यकर्तारमव्ययम् ॥१३॥

*cāturvarṇyaṁ mayā sṛṣṭaṁ guṇakarmavibhāgaśaḥ |*
*tasya kartāramapi māṁ viddhyakartāramavyayam ||13||*

**13.** The four-fold division of society was created by Me, according to the *guṇas* [qualities] and duties. Though the author of this [division], know Me as the non-doer, the changeless.

न मां कर्माणि लिम्पन्ति न मे कर्मफले स्पृहा ।
इति मां योऽभिजानाति कर्मभिर्न स बध्यते ॥१४॥

*na māṁ karmāṇi limpanti na me karmaphale spṛhā |*
*iti māṁ yo'bhijānāti karmabhirna sa badhyate ||14||*

**14.** Actions do not affect Me. For Me, there is no craving the result of action. Therefore, one who clearly knows Me shall not be bound by action.

एवं ज्ञात्वा कृतं कर्म पूर्वैरपि मुमुक्षुभिः ।
कुरु कर्मैव तस्मात्त्वं पूर्वैः पूर्वतरं कृतम् ॥१५॥

*evaṁ jñātvā kṛtaṁ karma pūrvairapi mumukṣubhiḥ |*
*kuru karmaiva tasmāttvaṁ pūrvaiḥ pūrvataraṁ kṛtam ||15||*

**15.** Knowing [Me] in this manner, even seekers of ancient times performed action. Therefore, do perform action as those who had come before.

किं कर्म किमकर्मेति कवयोऽप्यत्र मोहिताः ।
तत्ते कर्म प्रवक्ष्यामि यज्ज्ञात्वा मोक्ष्यसेऽशुभात् ॥१६॥

*kiṁ karma kimakarmeti kavayo'pyatra mohitāḥ |*
*tatte karma pravakṣyāmi yajjñātvā mokṣyase'śubhāt ||16||*

**16.** Even scholars have been confused by this subject. "What is action? What is inaction?" Therefore, I shall speak to you about action. Understanding this, you shall be free from inauspiciousness [suffering].

कर्मणो ह्यपि बोद्धव्यं बोद्धव्यं च विकर्मणः ।
अकर्मणश्च बोद्धव्यं गहना कर्मणो गतिः ॥१७॥

*karmaṇo hyapi boddhavyaṁ boddhavyaṁ ca vikarmaṇaḥ |*
*akarmaṇaśca boddhavyaṁ gahanā karmaṇo gatiḥ ||17||*

**17.** Action [prescribed by the *Vedas*] must be understood. Prohibited actions, as well as inaction, must also be understood. The nature of action is difficult to comprehend.

कर्मण्यकर्म यः पश्येदकर्मणि च कर्म यः ।
स बुद्धिमान्मनुष्येषु स युक्तः कृत्स्नकर्मकृत् ॥१८॥

*karmaṇyakarma yaḥ paśyedakarmaṇi ca karma yaḥ |*
*sa buddhimānmanuṣyeṣu sa yuktaḥ kṛtsnakarmakṛt ||18||*

**18.** He who sees inaction in action and action in inaction is wise among men. He is yogi: he has done all there is to be done.

यस्य सर्वे समारम्भाः कामसङ्कल्पवर्जिताः ।
ज्ञानाग्निदग्धकर्माणं तमाहुः पण्डितं बुधाः ॥१९॥

*yasya sarve samārambhāḥ kāmasaṅkalpavarjitāḥ |*
*jñānāgnidagdhakarmāṇaṁ tamāhuḥ paṇḍitaṁ budhāḥ ||19||*

**19.** For one whom all endeavors are free of volition and desire, whose actions have been burned by the fire of knowledge, [even] the wise call him wise.

त्यक्त्वा कर्मफलासङ्गं नित्यतृप्तो निराश्रयः ।
कर्मण्यभिप्रवृत्तोऽपि नैव किञ्चित्करोति सः ॥२०॥

*tyaktvā karmaphalāsaṅgaṁ nityatṛpto nirāśrayaḥ |*
*karmaṇyabhipravṛtto'pi naiva kiñcitkaroti saḥ ||20||*

**20.** Abandoning attachment to the result of action, one who is always content, free from dependency – even when engaged in action – does nothing.

निराशीर्यतचित्तात्मा त्यक्तसर्वपरिग्रहः ।
शारीरं केवलं कर्म कुर्वन्नाप्नोति किल्बिषम् ॥२१॥

*nirāśīryatacittātmā tyaktasarvaparigrahaḥ |*
*śārīraṁ kevalaṁ karma kurvannāpnoti kilbiṣam ||21||*

**21.** One who is free of expectations, who has the mind and the organs of perception and action under control [and] whose possessions have all been abandoned, performing action only for the maintenance of the body, does not get an undesirable result.

यदृच्छालाभसन्तुष्टो द्वन्द्वातीतो विमत्सरः ।
समः सिद्धावसिद्धौ च कृत्वापि न निबध्यते ॥२२॥

*yadṛcchālābhasantuṣṭo dvandvātīto vimatsaraḥ |*
*samaḥ siddhāvasiddhau ca kṛtvāpi na nibadhyate ||22||*

**22.** Content with what comes by chance, unaffected by the opposites, free from envy, remaining the same before success and failure, one is not bound even when in action.

गतसङ्गस्य मुक्तस्य ज्ञानावस्थितचेतसः ।
यज्ञायाचरतः कर्म समग्रं प्रविलीयते ॥२३॥

*gatasaṅgasya muktasya jñānāvasthitacetasaḥ |*
*yajñāyācarataḥ karma samagraṁ pravilīyate ||23||*

**23.** Action [as well as its results] completely vanishes for one who is free from attachement, who is liberated, whose mind is rooted in self-knowledge, who acts with the attitude of *yajña* [that which must be done].

ब्रह्मार्पणं ब्रह्म हविर्ब्रह्माग्नौ ब्रह्मणा हुतम् ।
ब्रह्मैव तेन गन्तव्यं ब्रह्मकर्मसमाधिना ॥२४॥

*brahmārpaṇaṁ brahma havirbrahmāgnau brahmaṇā hutam |*
*brahmaiva tena gantavyaṁ brahmakarmasamādhinā ||24||*

**24.** The instrument [of sacrifice] is *Brahman*, the sacrifice is *Brahman*, sacrificed by *Brahman*, into the fire that is *Brahman*. *Brahman* is what truly must be reached by one who beholds *Brahman* within action.

दैवमेवापरे यज्ञं योगिनः पर्युपासते ।
ब्रह्माग्नावपरे यज्ञं यज्ञेनैवोपजुह्वति ॥२५॥

*daivamevāpare yajñaṁ yoginaḥ paryupāsate |*
*brahmāgnāvapare yajñaṁ yajñenaivopajuhvati ||25||*

**25.** Some *yogins* perform rituals only for the gods, others [*sannyāsins*] only offer themselves, by themselves, into the fire [that is the knowledge] of *Brahman*.

श्रोत्रादीनीन्द्रियाण्यन्ये संयमाग्निषु जुह्वति ।
शब्दादीन्विषयानन्य इन्द्रियाग्निषु जुह्वति ॥२६॥

*śrotrādīnīndriyāṇyanye saṁyamāgniṣu juhvati |*
*śabdādīnviṣayānanya indriyāgniṣu juhvati ||26||*

**26.** Others offer the senses, such as the ears, etc., into the fire of self-discipline. Others offer objects, such as sound, etc. into the fire of the senses.

सर्वाणीन्द्रियकर्माणि प्राणकर्माणि चापरे ।
आत्मसंयमयोगाग्नौ जुह्वति ज्ञानदीपिते ॥२७॥

*sarvāṇīndriyakarmāṇi prāṇakarmāṇi cāpare |*
*ātmasaṁyamayogāgnau juhvati jñānadīpite ||27||*

**27.** Others offer all the functions of the senses and the functions of the vital energy into the fire of self-discipline, which had been lit by discernment.

द्रव्ययज्ञास्तपोयज्ञा योगयज्ञास्तथापरे ।
स्वाध्यायज्ञानयज्ञाश्च यतयः संशितव्रताः ॥२८॥

*dravyayajñāstapoyajñā yogayajñāstathāpare |*
*svādhyāyajñānayajñāśca yatayaḥ saṁśitavratāḥ ||28||*

**28.** Others sacrifice wealth, practice austerities, practice *yoga*, and seek knowledge in study with intense vows and effort.

अपाने जुह्वति प्राणं प्राणेऽपानं तथापरे ।
प्राणापानगती रुद्ध्वा प्राणायामपरायणाः ॥२९॥

*apāne juhvati prāṇaṁ prāṇe'pānaṁ tathāpare |*
*prāṇāpānagatī ruddhvā prāṇāyāmaparāyaṇāḥ ||29||*

**29.** Yet others, followers of breath control, controlling the exhalation and the inhalation, sacrifice the exhalation in the inhalation and the inhalation in the exhalation.

अपरे नियताहाराः प्राणान्प्राणेषु जुह्वति ।
सर्वेऽप्येते यज्ञविदो यज्ञक्षपितकल्मषाः ॥३०॥

*apare niyatāhārāḥ prāṇānprāṇeṣu juhvati |*
*sarve'pyete yajñavido yajñakṣapitakalmaṣāḥ ||30||*

**30.** And yet others control [their] nourishment, sacrificing *prāṇas* [their desire to eat] in *prāṇas* [in the digestive fire]. All who follow these disciplines are liberated from impurities [of the mind] by these sacrifices.

यज्ञशिष्टामृतभुजो यान्ति ब्रह्म सनातनम् ।
नायं लोकोऽस्त्ययज्ञस्य कुतोऽन्यः कुरुसत्तम ॥३१॥

*yajñaśiṣṭāmṛtabhujo yānti brahma sanātanam |*
*nāyaṁ loko'styayajñasya kuto'nyaḥ kurusattama ||31||*

**31.** Those nourished by the nectar [the results] that remains from sacrifice reach the eternal *Brahman*. This world is not for one who does not sacrifice; so what about the other [world], O *Kurusattama* [*Arjuna*]?

एवं बहुविधा यज्ञा वितता ब्रह्मणो मुखे ।
कर्मजान्विद्धि तान्सर्वनेवं ज्ञात्वा विमोक्ष्यसे ॥३२॥

*evaṁ bahuvidhā yajñā vitatā brahmaṇo mukhe |*
*karmajānviddhi tānsarvanevaṁ jñātvā vimokṣyase ||32||*

**32.** Thus, many sacrifices are elaborately covered by the words of the *Vedas*. Know them all to be born of action. Knowing this, you shall be liberated.

श्रेयान्द्रव्यमयाद्यज्ञाज्ज्ञानयज्ञः परन्तप ।
सर्वं कर्माखिलं पार्थ ज्ञाने परिसमाप्यते ॥३३॥

*śreyāndravyamayādyajñājjñānayajñaḥ parantapa |*
*sarvaṁ karmākhilaṁ pārtha jñāne parisamāpyate ||33||*

**33.** O *Parantapa* [*Arjuna*], the discipline of self-knowledge is better than the discipline made of material [objects]. All action, without exception, O *Pārtha* [*Arjuna*], is included in self-knowledge.

तद्विद्धि प्रणिपातेन परिप्रश्नेन सेवया ।
उपदेक्ष्यन्ति ते ज्ञानं ज्ञानिनस्तत्त्वदर्शिनः ॥३४॥

*tadviddhi praṇipātena paripraśnena sevayā |*
*upadekṣyanti te jñānaṁ jñāninastattvadarśinaḥ ||34||*

**34.** Know that [this knowledge is gained] by paying respects, asking appropriate questions, [and] paying service. The wise - those who see the truth - shall teach you [this] self-knowledge.

यज्ज्ञात्वा न पुनर्मोहमेवं यास्यसि पाण्डव ।
येन भूतान्यशेषेण द्रक्ष्यस्यात्मन्यथो मयि ॥३५॥

*yajjñātvā na punarmohamevaṁ yāsyasi pāṇḍava |*
*yena bhūtānyaśeṣeṇa drakṣyasyātmanyatho mayi ||35||*

**35.** Knowing this, you shall not return to delusion again, O *Pāṇḍava* [*Arjuna*]. Through this [self-knowledge], you shall see all beings, without exception, in Me - as well as in you.

अपि चेदसि पापेभ्यः सर्वेभ्यः पापकृत्तमः ।
सर्वं ज्ञानप्लवेनैव वृजिनं सन्तरिष्यसि ॥३६॥

*api cedasi pāpebhyaḥ sarvebhyaḥ pāpakṛttamaḥ |*
*sarvaṁ jñānaplavenaiva vṛjinaṁ santariṣyasi ||36||*

**36.** Even if you were the greatest offender [of the law of *dharma*] among lawbreakers, only by the raft of self-knowledge shall you cross over [the ocean] of error.

यथैधांसि समिद्धोऽग्निर्भस्मसात्कुरुतेऽर्जुन ।
ज्ञानाग्निः सर्वकर्माणि भस्मसात्कुरुते तथा ॥३७॥

*yathaidhāṁsi samiddho'gnirbhasmasātkurute'rjuna |*
*jñānāgniḥ sarvakarmāṇi bhasmasātkurute tathā ||37||*

**37.** O *Arjuna*, just as a well-kindled fire reduces wood to ashes, so the fire of self-knowledge reduces all actions to ashes.

न हि ज्ञानेन सदृशं पवित्रमिह विद्यते ।
तत्स्वयं योगसंसिद्धः कालेनात्मनि विन्दति ॥३८॥

*na hi jñānena sadṛśaṁ pavitramiha vidyate |*
*tatsvayaṁ yogasaṁsiddhaḥ kālenātmani vindati ||38||*

**38.** Therefore, here in this world, there is no means of purification that is comparable to self-knowledge. After sometime, having prepared oneself through *yoga*, one naturally gains that [self-knowledge] in the mind.

श्रद्धावांल्लभते ज्ञानं तत्परः संयतेन्द्रियः ।
ज्ञानं लब्ध्वा परं शान्तिमचिरेणाधिगच्छति ॥३९॥

*śraddhāvāṁllabhate jñānaṁ tatparaḥ saṁyatendriyaḥ |*
*jñānaṁ labdhvā paraṁ śāntimacireṇādhigacchati ||39||*

**39.** One who has faith, who is dedicated, who has one's senses under one's command, attains knowledge. Once acquiring self-knowledge, one immediately attains supreme peace.

अज्ञश्चाश्रद्दधानश्च संशयात्मा विनश्यति ।
नायं लोकोऽस्ति न परो न सुखं संशयात्मनः ॥४०॥

*ajñaścāśraddadhānaśca saṁśayātmā vinaśyati |*
*nāyaṁ loko'sti na paro na sukhaṁ saṁśayātmanaḥ ||40||*

**40.** Constantly in doubt, one who is ignorant and faithless is destroyed. There is neither this world nor another, nor happiness, for one who doubts.

योगसंन्यस्तकर्माणं ज्ञानसंछिन्नसंशयम् ।
आत्मवन्तं न कर्माणि निबध्नन्ति धनञ्जय ॥४१॥

*yogasaṁnyastakarmāṇaṁ jñānasaṁchinnasaṁśayam |*
*ātmavantaṁ na karmāṇi nibadhnanti dhanañjaya ||41||*

**41.** O *Dhanañjaya* [*Arjuna*], action does not bind one who has renounced action through *yoga*, whose doubts have been eliminated through self-knowledge, one who has command of oneself.

तस्मादज्ञानसम्भूतं हृत्स्थं ज्ञानासिनात्मनः ।
छित्त्वैनं संशयं योगमातिष्ठोत्तिष्ठ भारत ॥४२॥

*tasmādajñānasambhūtaṁ hṛtsthaṁ jñānāsinātmanaḥ |*
*chittvainaṁ saṁśayaṁ yogamātiṣṭhottiṣṭha bhārata ||42||*

**42.** Therefore, by the sword of knowledge, slaying the self-doubt that is born of ignorance [and] residing in your mind, rise O *Bhārata* [*Arjuna*]! Follow *yoga*!

ओं तत्सदिति श्रीमद्भगद्गीतासूपनिषत्सु ब्रह्मविद्यायां योगशास्त्रे श्रीकृष्णार्जुनसंवादे ज्ञानकर्मसन्न्यासयोगो नाम चतुर्थोऽध्यायः॥

*oṁ tatsaditi śrīmadbhagadgītāsūpaniṣatsu brahmavidyāyāṁ yogaśāstre śrīkṛṣṇārjunasaṁvāde jñānakarmasannyāsayogo nāma caturtho'dhyāyaḥ ||*

*Oṁ*, this is the Truth. Thus is the fourth chapter, the subject [of which] is called "*Jñānakarmasannyāsa*" [the knowledge and the renunciation of action], in the glorious *Bhagavadgītā*, [which is equivalent to] the *Upaniṣads*, [the subject of which is] the knowledge of *Brahman* [and] *yoga*, in the dialogue between *śrī Kṛṣṇa* and *Arjuna*.

# Chapter 5

## *The renunciation of action*

From the beginning, *Arjuna* wishes to convince *Kṛṣṇa* to support him in renouncing action. *Kṛṣṇa* insists that he must act, since the problem is not in the action and its results, but in the impulse of tastes and aversions, which are by no means eliminated upon forfeiting action. Only actions performed with a comprehension of *karmayoga* will neutralize tastes and aversions.

*Śrī Kṛṣṇa* has already explained the importance of *karmayoga* and what is meant by renunciation; he has also described the wise as those who possess the knowledge of the Self, which is pure Consciousness - that which is free from action or any limitation whatsoever. *Kṛṣṇa* explains renunciation, or *sannyāsa*, as part of Vedic society.

Regardless of the society, people are subject to rights and obligations. Vedic society emphasized the obligations to be fulfilled by the various members of society in order to ensure the rights of all.

The *Vedas* divide society by the different functions and stages of life, in order to facilitate the understanding and fulfillment of these obligations. This division is made according to the stages of life, in which we have the student, the householder, the retiree, and finally the *sannyāsin*.

The obligations of each individual are for himself, for the members of the family, the society at large, and for nature itself.

By focusing on obligations and accepting the results of action with equanimity, the mental state changes: a space of relaxation opens up and allows the questions regarding the greater object of life to arise. Self-knowledge becomes important, and to reach it, there are two styles of life that may be followed: that of *karmayoga*, or participation in society; and that of *sannyāsa*, renunciation. However, in both cases, study and contemplation remain essential.

The *yogin* still has a productive role in society, whether it be in the family or in work, etc. The *sannyāsin* does not: his or her only obligation is that of study and contemplation. Regardless of the phase of life, the person who renounces is protected and respected in Vedic society, whether it be during the final phase or even as a young student.

*Sannyāsa* is therefore a way of life for the acquisition of self-knowledge. It is also a state of being for one who has already acquired - who is already aware of - the Self that is free from all action.

*Arjuna* does not understand that *karmayoga* prepares the mind for self-knowledge and also includes the study of the Self; he is not aware that renunciation is not necessary to acquire self-knowledge. He is especially unaware that when the tastes and aversions are strong and dominating, which make the mind react, a life of *karmayoga* is essential. Whenever in doubt, *karmayoga* is always a safer option than *sannyāsa*. Moreover, the wise renounce naturally, regardless of the way of life. It is for this reason that *Arjuna* once again asks which is better: *karmayoga* or *sannyāsa*. Actually, there is no way of determining which is better; it depends on the state of mental and emotional preparedness of each individual. Both ways lead to liberation, if accompanied by knowledge. However, *sannyāsa* is more difficult than *karmayoga*, since it requires a contemplative mind.

At the end of the chapter, anticipating the next theme, *Śrī Kṛṣṇa* begins instructions for meditation.

## Summary of the verses

Verse 1: *Arjuna* does not understand what *Kṛṣṇa* means by renunciation. He does not understand that renunciation means not identifying with the body and mind that perform action. He thinks *Kṛṣṇa* means renunciation is a life of reclusion, and thus he does not understand how it is possible to perform action and at the same time be free from action. Therefore, he asks *Kṛṣṇa* to tell him once again which is better: renunciation or action?

Verses 2 to 6: *Śrī Kṛṣṇa* speaks again about the two ways of life, *karmayoga* and *sannyāsa*, and says that both - together with knowledge - lead one to liberation. A relative freedom from the tastes and aversions is an important qualification, although a life of *yoga*, also called *karmayoga*, is more assured than renunciation, also called *sāṅkhya* in Chapter 3.

Verses 7 to 12: *Śrī Kṛṣṇa* instructs him on the vision of *karmayoga* and the various stages a person goes through. The *karmayogin* sacrifices all actions to *Īśvara* - with no expectation as to the result of action. This attitude disciplines the mind, and together with the teaching of a *guru*, it is possible to discover the true nature of the Self as being free from all action, thus becoming a *sannyāsin*. Hence, there are the *vividiṣasannyāsin*, the *vidvatsannyāsin*, and the *āpatsannyāsin*: the first renounciates the world in order to acquire knowledge; the second is a renunciant due to his knowledge of the Self that is free from all action; the third is a recourse at the time of death, in which one renounces from the world, since in the next life the individual will continue the process of self-knowledge.

Verses 8 to 9 describe the wise: those who spontaneously perform action while knowing they in fact do nothing.

Verses 10 to 11 describe the deliberate: those who do what must be done as a sacrifice to *Īśvara* in order to purify the mind.

Verse 12 describes the impulsive: those who act exclusively under the impulse of desire.

Verses 13 to 21: *Kṛṣṇa* describes the characteristics of the wise that neither act nor instigate action. All actions and their results belong to the body, the senses and the mind. The wise remain with *Brahman*: they neither rejoice upon acquiring that which is desired, nor are they afflicted by that which is undesirable; thus, they acquire unwavering happiness.

Verses 22 to 23: The discriminating individual is aware of the impermanence of pleasure, which arises out the contact of the sense with objects, and therefore does not become attached to them. This individual is capable of withstanding the impulses of desire and anger.

Verses 24 to 26: *Śrī Kṛṣṇa* states that the wise have attained an identity with *Brahman*, both while alive and after death.

Verses 27 to 29: *Kṛṣṇa* introduces meditation, a subject to be covered in the next chapter.

# अथ पञ्चमोऽध्यायः

***atha pañcamo'dhyāyaḥ***

**Fifth chapter**

अर्जुन उवाच
संन्यासं कर्मणां कृष्ण पुनर्योगं च शंससि ।
यच्छ्रेय एतयोरेकं तन्मे ब्रूहि सुनिश्चितम् ॥१॥

*arjuna uvāca*
*saṁnyāsaṁ karmaṇāṁ kṛṣṇa punaryogaṁ ca śaṁsasi |*
*yacchreya etayorekaṁ tanme brūhi suniścitam ||1||*

**1.** *Arjuna* spoke:
— O *Kṛṣṇa*, you exalt the renunciation from actions [*sannyāsa*] and, at the same time, performing action [*karma-yoga*]. Of the two, tell me definitively which is best.

श्रीभगवानुवाच
संन्यासः कर्मयोगश्च निःश्रेयसकरावुभौ ।
तयोस्तु कर्मसंन्यासात्कर्मयोगो विशिष्यते ॥२॥

*śrībhagavānuvāca*
*saṁnyāsaḥ karmayogaśca niḥśreyasakarāvubhau |*
*tayostu karmasaṁnyāsātkarmayogo viśiṣyate ||2||*

**2.** The Lord [*Kṛṣṇa*] spoke:
— Both renunciation and performing action as *yoga* lead to liberation. However, of the two, *karma-yoga* is better than *karma-sannyāsa* [performing action as *yoga* is better than renunciation of action].

ज्ञेयः स नित्यसंन्यासी यो न द्वेष्टि न काङ्क्षति ।
निर्द्वन्द्वो हि महाबाहो सुखं बन्धात्प्रमुच्यते ॥३॥

*jñeyaḥ sa nityasaṁnyāsī yo na dveṣṭi na kāṅkṣati |*
*nirdvandvo hi mahābāho sukhaṁ bandhātpramucyate ||3||*

**3.** One who neither hates nor desires should be known as a constant *sannyāsin*. Indeed, one who is free from the pairs of opposites is easily free from bondage, O *Mahābāhu* [*Arjuna*].

साङ्ख्ययोगौ पृथग्बालाः प्रवदन्ति न पण्डिताः ।
एकमप्यास्थितः सम्यगुभयोर्विन्दते फलम् ॥४॥

*sāṅkhyayogau pṛthagbālāḥ pravadanti na paṇḍitāḥ |*
*ekamapyāsthitaḥ samyagubhayorvindate phalam ||4||*

**4.** It is the childish, not the wise, who say that knowledge and *karma-yoga* are different. [But] he who follows just one [of the two] receives the fruit of both.

यत्साङ्ख्यैः प्राप्यते स्थानं तद्योगैरपि गम्यते ।
एकं साङ्ख्यं च योगं च यः पश्यति स पश्यति ॥५॥

*yatsāṅkhyaiḥ prāpyate sthānaṁ tadyogairapi gamyate |*
*ekaṁ sāṅkhyaṁ ca yogaṁ ca yaḥ paśyati sa paśyati ||5||*

**5.** That state is attained by *sannyāsins* and is also attained by *karmayogins*. He who see *sannyāsa* and *karmayoga* as one [truly] sees.

संन्यासस्तु महाबाहो दुःखमाप्तुमयोगतः ।
योगयुक्तो मुनिर्ब्रह्म न चिरेणाधिगच्छति ॥६॥

*saṁnyāsastu mahābāho duḥkhamāptumayogataḥ |*
*yogayukto munirbrahma na cireṇādhigacchati ||6||*

**6.** Although renunciation of action, O *Mahābāhu* [*Arjuna*], is difficult to attain without *karma-yoga*, the discriminating, who have surrendered to *karma-yoga*, attain *Brahman* without delay.

योगयुक्तो विशुद्धात्मा विजितात्मा जितेन्द्रियः ।
सर्वभूतात्मभूतात्मा कुर्वन्नपि न लिप्यते ॥७॥

*yogayukto viśuddhātmā vijitātmā jitendriyaḥ |*
*sarvabhūtātmabhūtātmā kurvannapi na lipyate ||7||*

**7.** One who is dedicated to [a life of] *karma-yoga*, whose mind has been purified, whose body and senses are under his command, who knows that one's self is the self of all beings, is not affected [by action] even when acting.

नैव किञ्चित्करोमीति युक्तो मन्येत तत्त्ववित् ।
पश्यञ्शृण्वन्स्पृशञ्जिघ्रन्नश्नन्गच्छन्स्वपञ्श्वसन् ॥८॥
प्रलपन्विसृजन्गृह्णन्नुन्मिषन्निमिषन्नपि ।
इन्द्रियाणीन्द्रियार्थेषु वर्तन्त इति धारयन् ॥९॥

*naiva kiñcitkaromīti yukto manyeta tattvavit |*
*paśyañśṛṇvanspṛśañjighrannaśnangacchansvapañśvasan ||8||*
*pralapanvisṛjangṛhṇannunmiṣannimiṣannapi |*
*indriyāṇīndriyārtheṣu vartanta iti dhārayan ||9||*

**8/9.** Clearly aware that it is the organs [mind, sense organs and action] that move among the objects, one who knows the truth, and is steadfast, is aware that "I never perform actions", even when seeing, hearing, touching, smelling, walking, sleeping, breathing, speaking, releasing, taking, opening and closing the eyes.

ब्रह्मण्याधाय कर्माणि सङ्गं त्यक्त्वा करोति यः ।
लिप्यते न स पापेन पद्मपत्रमिवाम्भसा ॥१०॥

*brahmaṇyādhāya karmāṇi saṅgaṁ tyaktvā karoti yaḥ |*
*lipyate na sa pāpena padmapatramivāmbhasā ||10||*

**10.** One who has abandoned attachment, sacrificing one's actions onto *Īśvara*, is no more tainted by the negative result of actions as the lotus flower is by water.

कायेन मनसा बुद्ध्या केवलैरिन्द्रियैरपि ।
योगिनः कर्म कुर्वन्ति सङ्गं त्यक्त्वात्मशुद्धये ॥११॥

*kāyena manasā buddhyā kevalairindriyairapi |*
*yoginaḥ karma kurvanti saṅgaṁ tyaktvātmaśuddhaye ||11||*

**11.** Having abandoned attachment, *karmayogins* perform action purely with the body, mind, intellect and also the senses, in order to purify the mind.

युक्तः कर्मफलं त्यक्त्वा शान्तिमाप्नोति नैष्ठिकीम् ।
अयुक्तः कामकारेण फले सक्तो निबध्यते ॥१२॥

*yuktaḥ karmaphalaṁ tyaktvā śāntimāpnoti naiṣṭhikīm |*
*ayuktaḥ kāmakāreṇa phale sakto nibadhyate ||12||*

**12.** The *karmayogin*, abandoning the fruit of actions, attains peace, which is the result of the dedication to a life of *yoga*. [Whereas] one who is not dedicated to *karmayoga*, [who] is under the impulse of desire [and] attached to the fruit of action, is imprisoned.

सर्वकर्माणि मनसा संन्यस्यास्ते सुखं वशी ।
नवद्वारे पुरे देही नैव कुर्वन्न कारयन् ॥१३॥

*sarvakarmāṇi manasā saṁnyasyāste sukhaṁ vaśī |*
*navadvāre pure dehī naiva kurvanna kārayan ||13||*

**13.** Renouncing all actions with a discriminative mind, he who is disciplined [and] inhabits the body, remains content within the city of nine gates[4]. He neither acts nor incites others to act.

न कर्तृत्वं न कर्माणि लोकस्य सृजति प्रभुः ।
न कर्मफलसंयोगं स्वभावस्तु प्रवर्तते ॥१४॥

*na kartṛtvaṁ na karmāṇi lokasya sṛjati prabhuḥ |*
*na karmaphalasaṁyogaṁ svabhāvastu pravartate ||14||*

4 The city of nine gates is the physical body, which has nine apertures that are called "gates". In this metaphor, the body is compared to a citadel with nine entrances; inside there is the lord of the citadel. When these entrances are opened anything can come inside; when closed, nothing enters. These nine apertures are two sockets of the eyes, two nostrils, two ears, a mouth and two lower apertures, which are the anus and the genital organ, whether masculine or feminine. *śrī Kṛṣṇa* states that the wise know that one is seated in the body; the ignorant think that the Self is the body.

**14.** The *Ātman* creates neither actions nor the feeling of being the agent of action, [and] not even the connection with the fruit of action. However, it is one's own nature that leads to action.

नादत्ते कस्यचित्पापं न चैव सुकृतं विभुः ।
अज्ञानेनावृतं ज्ञानं तेन मुह्यन्ति जन्तवः ॥१५॥

*nādatte kasyacitpāpaṁ na caiva sukṛtaṁ vibhuḥ |*
*ajñānenāvṛtaṁ jñānaṁ tena muhyanti jantavaḥ ||15||*

**15.** The *Ātman* does not withhold the negative result of action or the positive result of action from anyone. The intellect is shrouded by ignorance [and] because of this, people are deluded.

ज्ञानेन तु तदज्ञानं येषां नाशितमात्मनः ।
तेषामादित्यवज्ज्ञानं प्रकाशयति तत्परम् ॥१६॥

*jñānena tu tadajñānaṁ yeṣāṁ nāśitamātmanaḥ |*
*teṣāmādityavajjñānaṁ prakāśayati tatparam ||16||*

**16.** But for those whose ignorance of the *Ātman* has been destroyed by self-knowledge, [that] knowledge illuminates the absolute truth for them just like the sun.

तद्बुद्धयस्तदात्मानस्तन्निष्ठास्तत्परायणाः ।
गच्छन्त्यपुनरावृत्तिं ज्ञाननिर्धूतकल्मषाः ॥१७॥

*tadbuddhayastadātmānastanniṣṭhāstatparāyaṇāḥ |*
*gacchantyapunarāvṛttiṁ jñānanirdhūtakalmaṣāḥ ||17||*

**17.** For those whose mind is on That [*Brahman*], for those whom *Ātman* is That [*Brahman*], whom are unwavering in That [i.e., the knowledge of *Brahman*], for whom the only refuge is That [*Brahman*], whose impurities have been destroyed by self-knowledge, they go, never to return.

विद्याविनयसम्पन्ने ब्राह्मणे गवि हस्तिनि ।
शुनि चैव श्वपाके च पण्डिताः समदर्शिनः ॥१८॥

*vidyāvinayasampanne brāhmaṇe gavi hastini |*
*śuni caiva śvapāke ca paṇḍitāḥ samadarśinaḥ ||18||*

**18.** The wise see the same [*Brahman*] in a *brāhmaṇa* [a person dedicated to the spiritual life] who possesses knowledge and humility, as they do in a cow, in an elephant, in a dog, and even in a dog-eater [outcaste].

इहैव तैर्जितः सर्गो येषां साम्ये स्थितं मनः ।
निर्दोषं हि समं ब्रह्म तस्माद् ब्रह्मणि ते स्थिताः ॥१९॥

*ihaiva tairjitaḥ sargo yeṣāṁ sāmye sthitaṁ manaḥ |*
*nirdoṣaṁ hi samaṁ brahma tasmād brahmaṇi te sthitāḥ ||19||*

**19.** The cycle of births is overcome by those whose mind resides in the [vision of] identity [with *Brahman*] - even here in this life. Since *Brahman* is free from impurity [and] the same [in all beings], therefore they reside in *Brahman*.

न प्रहृष्येत्प्रियं प्राप्य नोद्विजेत्प्राप्य चाप्रियम् ।
स्थिरबुद्धिरसंमूढो ब्रह्मविद् ब्रह्मणि स्थितः ॥२०॥

*na prahṛṣyetpriyaṁ prāpya nodvijetprāpya cāpriyam |*
*sthirabuddhirasaṁmūḍho brahmavid brahmaṇi sthitaḥ ||20||*

**20.** One should neither rejoice upon attaining that which is desired, nor scorn having attained that which is undesired. With unwavering intellect, free from illusion, one who knows *Brahman* remains in *Brahman*.

बाह्यस्पर्शेष्वसक्तात्मा विन्दत्यात्मनि यत्सुखम् ।
स ब्रह्मयोगयुक्तात्मा सुखमक्षयमश्नुते ॥२१॥

*bāhyasparśeṣvasaktātmā vindatyātmani yatsukham |*
*sa brahmayogayuktātmā sukhamakṣayamaśnute ||21||*

**21.** One whose mind is unattached to external objects reaches the happiness that is oneself. One whose mind is unwavering in the knowledge of *Brahman* attains unwavering happiness.

ये हि संस्पर्शजा भोगा दुःखयोनय एव ते ।
आद्यन्तवन्तः कौन्तेय न तेषु रमते बुधः ॥२२॥

*ye hi saṁsparśajā bhogā duḥkhayonaya eva te |*
*ādyantavantaḥ kaunteya na teṣu ramate budhaḥ ||22||*

**22.** Indeed, the pleasures born of contact [between organs and objects] only create unhappiness, [because] they have a beginning and an end, O *Kaunteya* [*Arjuna*]. The wise are not amused by them.

शक्नोतीहैव यः सोढुं प्राक् शरीरविमोक्षणात् ।
कामक्रोधोद्भवं वेगं स युक्तः स सुखी नरः ॥२३॥

*śaknotīhaiva yaḥ soḍhuṁ prāk śarīravimokṣaṇāt |*
*kāmakrodhodbhavaṁ vegaṁ sa yuktaḥ sa sukhī naraḥ ||23||*

**23.** He who has the capacity to withstand the impulse born of desire and anger – here on earth – before the loss of the body [i.e., death], is a *karmayogin*; he is a content man.

योऽन्तःसुखोऽन्तरारामस्तथान्तर्ज्योतिरेव यः ।
स योगी ब्रह्मनिर्वाणं ब्रह्मभूतोऽधिगच्छति ॥२४॥

*yo'ntaḥsukho'ntarārāmastathāntarjyotireva yaḥ |*
*sa yogī brahmanirvāṇaṁ brahmabhūto'dhigacchati ||24||*

**24.** He whose happiness is within himself, he who delights in himself, whose mind illuminates himself, this *karmayogin* – identical to *Brahman* [while alive] – attains liberation in *Brahman*.

लभन्ते ब्रह्मनिर्वाणमृषयः क्षीणकल्मषाः ।
छिन्नद्वैधा यतात्मानः सर्वभूतहिते रताः ॥२५॥

*labhante brahmanirvāṇamṛṣayaḥ kṣīṇakalmaṣāḥ |*
*chinnadvaidhā yatātmānaḥ sarvabhūtahite ratāḥ ||25||*

**25.** The wise, for whom all impurity and doubt has been removed, who have command of their organs of action and perception, who delight in [promoting] the welfare of all beings, attain liberation.

कामक्रोधवियुक्तानां यतीनां यतचेतसाम् ।
अभितो ब्रह्मनिर्वाणं वर्तते विदितात्मनाम् ॥२६॥

*kāmakrodhaviyuktānāṁ yatīnāṁ yatacetasām |*
*abhito brahmanirvāṇaṁ vartate viditātmanām ||26||*

**26.** Liberation occurs in both cases [while dead or alive] for those free from desire and anger, for those who make an effort in the right direction, for those whose mind is under their command, [and] who know the *Ātman*.

स्पर्शान् कृत्वा बहिर्बाह्यान् चक्षुश्चैवान्तरे भ्रुवोः ।
प्राणापानौ समौ कृत्वा नासाभ्यन्तरचारिनौ ॥२७॥
यतेन्द्रियमनोबुद्धिर्मुनिर्मोक्षपरायणः ।
विगतेच्छाभयक्रोधो यः सदा मुक्त एव सः ॥२८॥

*sparśān kṛtvā bahirbāhyān cakṣuścaivāntare bhruvoḥ |*
*prāṇāpānau samau kṛtvā nāsābhyantaracārinau ||27||*
*yatendriyamanobuddhirmunirmokṣaparāyaṇaḥ |*
*vigatecchābhayakrodho yaḥ sadā mukta eva saḥ ||28||*

**27/28.** Keeping external objects external and his vision [as if focused] between the eyebrows; keeping the inhalation and exhalation movements of the nostrils calm; disciplining the sense organs and the organs of action, the mind and intellect; having the ability to reflect; aiming for liberation; being free from desire, fear and anger: one is always liberated.

भोक्तारं यज्ञतपसां सर्वलोकमहेश्वरम् ।
सुहृदं सर्वभूतानां ज्ञात्वा मां शान्तिमृच्छति ॥२९॥

*bhoktāraṁ yajñatapasāṁ sarvalokamaheśvaram |*
*suhṛdaṁ sarvabhūtānāṁ jñātvā māṁ śāntimṛcchati ||29||*

**29.** Knowing me as the guardian of the rituals and disciplines, as the Lord of all the world, as friend of all beings, one attains peace.

ओं तत्सदिति श्रीमद्भगवद्गीतासूपनिषत्सु ब्रह्मविद्यायां योगशास्त्रे
श्रीकृष्णार्जुनसंवादे कर्मसन्न्यासयोगो नाम पञ्चमोऽध्यायः॥

*oṁ tatsaditi śrīmadbhagavadgītāsūpaniṣatsu*
*brahmavidyāyāṁ yogaśāstre śrīkṛṣṇārjunasaṁvāde*
*karmasannyāsayogo nāma pañcamo'dhyāyaḥ ||*

*Oṁ*, this is the Truth. Thus is the fifth chapter, the subject [of which] is called "*karmasannyāsa*" [the renunciation of action], in the glorious *Bhagavadgītā*, [which is equivalent to] the *Upaniṣads*, [the subject of which is] the knowledge of *Brahman* [and] *yoga*, in the dialogue between *śrī Kṛṣṇa* and *Arjuna*.

# Chapter 6

## *Meditation*

In order to acquire knowledge, it is necessary to listen to the teaching that eliminates ignorance, to reflect in order to remove doubt, and to contemplate in order to eliminate errors, such as identifying oneself with the body and its qualities, or the mind and the intellect, as well as other errant identifications that are established by habit.

Contemplation, which is meditation on the nature of the subject, is not considered action, since it produces nothing new. It is the means by which knowledge becomes clear and present, free from obstacles.

There are two obstacles to knowledge: the reactions of the mind, due to tastes and aversions, which may be remedied by *karmayoga*; and the restlessness of the mind, the remedy for which is meditation.

Thus, meditation is a *sādhana* to discipline the mind, and contemplation is for consolidating knowledge.

A life of renunciation is more contemplative than active. When a mind becomes contemplative there is no more desire for action, and the person is then prepared for questioning the nature of the Self. It is this kind of mind that is fundamental for liberation.

Meditation is not a choice, since it is not an action, such as walking or speaking. A person without a meditative mind cannot decide to meditate; whereas a meditative person will naturally meditate.

If the mind is not prepared for meditation, *karmayoga* is necessary. By way of *karmayoga*, the extroverted mind becomes contemplative. Afterwards, a calmer life that is unattached to this world will become natural.

A yukta is a person whose mind has been disciplined by questioning and contemplation, who is free from the thirst for the objects of desire, and therefore resides in the Self.

At the end of the chapter, *Arjuna* complains that his mind is inconstant, perturbed, powerful and obstinate: he considers it too difficult to be controlled. *Śrī Kṛṣṇa* agrees that this is indeed the nature of the mind, and presents a method by which to control it: *abhyāsa*, repetition, and *vairāgya*, dispassion.

The mind has its own reason, its own logic. Furthermore, no reaction or emotion is without reason. We must comprehend the mind and accept it as it is. The practice of repetition is to see the mind as an instrument that is distinct from the Self - over and over again. Although I am thought, the Self is much more than thought. Seeing the mind from a certain distance allows one to recognize the nature of the Self, which is pure Consciousness, free from all thought.

Repetition also includes the practice of *japa*, which is the repetition of the same *mantra*, which allows the practitioner to understand the process of thinking, attachments, and the assets and liabilities of the mind itself, thereby becoming the conductor - the maestro - of the mind.

The second method, dispassion, begins with an objective awareness of the mind. The mind has a subjective perception of objects and situations, as if these things had the capacity to make one happy or sad. It is precisely for this reason that the mind is always running after the objects of its interest, whether it is out of love for an object, or out of the happiness it is thought to bring - or rejecting undesired objects, out of the suffering they are thought to cause. Both of these situations hijack the attention of the mind, which greatly desires either the presence or absence of objects in order to be content. The specific habit of the mind to superimpose the capacity of objects desired to make one content is called *śobhana-adhyāsa*. By means of observation and objectiveness, it is possible to see an object for what it is - just an object and nothing more - without the superimposed power of making anyone happy. This practice is called *vairāgya*.

Upon the knowledge of the Self, *śobhana-adhyāsa* is permanently dispelled, but until that happens, we must observe and distance ourselves from the projections of the mind.

Finally, *Arjuna* asks what happens to a person who dies before reaching the result of *yoga*. *Kṛṣṇa* assures him there is no such thing as losing in *yoga*: by going from one life to the next, the individual connects with the knowledge that had already been acquired in a previous life; then making more effort, and once free from obstacles, the individual reaches liberation.

## Summary of the verses

Verses 1 to 3: *Śrī Kṛṣṇa* states that *karmayoga*, a life of consciously choosing actions and being aware of the results of actions, is very important for meditation.

Verses 3 to 4: The renunciation of even the impulse that precedes desire, as well as its subsequent action, is a characteristic of a contemplative mind.

Verses 5 to 6: Two important values are mentioned: self-confidence and self-control, as the basis for any success.

Verses 7 to 9: The individual who has acquired self-knowledge remains unscathed by objects, people and situations in the world around.

Verses 10 to 13: *Śrī Kṛṣṇa* mentions the physical and preliminary preparations for meditation.

Verse 14: *Kṛṣṇa* states that the meditator - with a calm and focused mind - should meditate on *Īśvara*, which is indivisible with the Self.

Verse 15: *Śrī Kṛṣṇa* mentions the result of meditation.

Verses 16 to 17: Several disciplines that constitute a contemplative life are covered, such as moderation with regard to eating, sleeping, activity, and recreation.

Verses 18 to 26: *Śrī Kṛṣṇa* explains the nature of meditation. Every time the mind disperses the focus of meditation, it should be brought back slowly and gently.

Verses 27 to 32: Once again, the effects of meditation are mentioned. The best *yogin* is one whose knowledge of the Self is that it is the same in all beings.

Versos 33 to 34: *Arjuna* tells *Kṛṣṇa* that it is not easy to meditate and assimilate self-knowledge due to the restlessness of the mind.

Verses 35 to 36: *Kṛṣṇa* recognizes that restlessness is naturally a part of the mind and offers *Arjuna* two methods to solve this problem: repetition and detachment.

Verses 37 to 39: *Arjuna* thinks that it is not possible to attain liberation in one single lifetime, and asks what happens when one leaves meditation before attaining its fruits.

Verses 40 to 45: *Kṛṣṇa* assures *Arjuna* that anyone who begins the search for self-knowledge will never fall to bad fortune. A life of *yoga*, which is meditative, produces many merits that will lead to special births, and that it will lead to subsequent births that will be conducive to the spiritual search. The person will be compelled by the old *saṁskāras*, the tendencies from the past, and will eventually reach the final result.

Verses 46 to 47: *Śrī Kṛṣṇa* concludes this chapter by praising the person who meditates and encourages *Arjuna* to be a *yogin*, to meditate and to surrender his vision of himself to *Īśvara*.

# अथ षष्ठोऽध्यायः

***atha ṣaṣṭho'dhyāyaḥ***

**Sixth chapter**

श्रीभगवानुवाच
अनाश्रितः कर्मफलं कार्यं कर्म करोति यः ।
स संन्यासी च योगी च न निरग्निर्न चाक्रियः ॥१॥

*śrībhagavānuvāca*
*anāśritaḥ karmaphalaṁ kāryaṁ karma karoti yaḥ |*
*sa saṁnyāsī ca yogī ca na niragnirna cākriyaḥ ||1||*

**1.** The Lord [*Kṛṣṇa*] spoke:
— The *karmayogin* - who performs the action that must be done, free from attachment to the result of action - is a *sannyāsin*; [a *sannyāsin*] is not one who [merely] abandons the fire [the rituals and actions prescribed by the *Vedas*] and performs no action [such as offerings, disciplines and other activities of the world].

यं संन्यासमिति प्राहुर्योगं तं विद्धि पाण्डव ।
न ह्यसंन्यस्तसङ्कल्पो योगी भवति कश्चन ॥२॥

*yaṁ saṁnyāsamiti prāhuryogaṁ taṁ viddhi pāṇḍava |*
*na hyasaṁnyastasaṅkalpo yogī bhavati kaścana ||2||*

**2.** That which is known as renunciation, O *Pāṇḍava* [*Arjuna*], know it to be *karmayoga*, since no one becomes a *karmayogin* without abandoning desires [for the results of actions].

आरुरुक्षोर्मुनेर्योगं कर्म कारणमुच्यते ।
योगारूढस्य तस्यैव शमः कारणमुच्यते ॥३॥

*āruruksormuneryogaṁ karma kāraṇamucyate |*
*yogārūḍhasya tasyaiva śamaḥ kāraṇamucyate ||3||*

**3.** For one who possesses discernment [and] wishes to dominate *dhyānayoga* [the contemplative mind] *karmayoga* is considered the means. For one who dominates *dhyānayoga*, renunciation is considered the only means.

यदा हि नेन्द्रियार्थेषु न कर्मस्वनुषज्जते ।
सर्वसङ्कल्पसंन्यासी योगारूढस्तदोच्यते ॥४॥

*yadā hi nendriyārtheṣu na karmasvanuṣajjate |*
*sarvasaṅkalpasaṁnyāsī yogārūḍhastadocyate ||4||*

**4.** When one is no longer attached to either the objects of the senses or to actions, and has renounced the cause of all desire, it is then said that one has attained *yoga*.

उद्धरेदात्मनात्मानं नात्मानमवसादयेत् ।
आत्मैव ह्यात्मनो बन्धुरात्मैव रिपुरात्मनः ॥५॥

*uddharedātmanātmānaṁ nātmānamavasādayet |*
*ātmaiva hyātmano bandhurātmaiva ripurātmanaḥ ||5||*

**5.** May one uplift oneself by oneself. May one not look down upon oneself. Indeed, oneself is one's best friend; oneself [one's mind] is one's enemy.

बन्धुरात्मात्मनस्तस्य येनात्मैवात्मना जितः ।
अनात्मनस्तु शत्रुत्वे वर्तेतात्मैव शत्रुवत् ॥६॥

*bandhurātmātmanastasya yenātmaivātmanā jitaḥ |*
*anātmanastu śatrutve vartetātmaiva śatruvat ||6||*

**6.** The self is the friend of one who has mastered oneself by oneself. But, for one who has not mastered oneself, the self stays in the form of the enemy, exactly as an [external] enemy.

जितात्मनः प्रशान्तस्य परमात्मा समाहितः ।
शीतोष्णसुखदुःखेषु तथा मानापमानयोः ॥७॥

*jitātmanaḥ praśāntasya paramātmā samāhitaḥ |*
*śītoṣṇasukhaduḥkheṣu tathā mānāpamānayoḥ ||7||*

**7.** The unlimited Self is evident for one who has mastered the very self, whose mind is calm, [and] who is unwavering before cold and heat, pleasure and pain, and also before praise and ridicule.

ज्ञानविज्ञानतृप्तात्मा कूटस्थो विजितेन्द्रियः ।
युक्त इत्युच्यते योगी समलोष्टाश्मकाञ्चनः ॥८॥

*jñānavijñānatṛptātmā kūṭastho vijitendriyaḥ |*
*yukta ityucyate yogī samaloṣṭāśmakāñcanaḥ ||8||*

**8.** One whose mind is satisfied with knowledge and wisdom; who is unwavering; whose organs are under one's command; who is whole; who is same towards clay, a stone, and gold, is called a *yogin*.

सुहृन्मित्रार्युदासीनमध्यस्थद्वेष्यबन्धुषु ।
साधुष्वपि च पापेषु समबुद्धिर्विशिष्यते ॥९॥

*suhṛnmitrāryudāsīnamadhyasthadveṣyabandhuṣu |*
*sādhuṣvapi ca pāpeṣu samabuddhirviśiṣyate ||9||*

**9.** He who holds the same attitude toward a person who helps him for no particular reason, a friend, an enemy, a stranger, an acquaintance, someone who does not deserve to be loved, a relative, good people, and even those who consciously do what should not be done, is distinguished among men.

योगी युञ्जीत सततमात्मानं रहसि स्थितः ।
एकाकी यतचित्तात्मा निराशीरपरिग्रहः ॥१०॥

*yogī yuñjīta satatamātmānaṁ rahasi sthitaḥ |*
*ekākī yatacittātmā nirāśīraparigrahaḥ ||10||*

**10.** A *yogin* [who meditates], remaining alone, in an isolated place, with a disciplined mind and body, free from desire and possessions, should constantly concentrate his mind [on the object of meditation].

शुचौ देशे प्रतिष्ठाप्य स्थिरमासनमात्मनः ।
नात्युच्छ्रितं नातिनीचं चैलाजिनकुशोत्तरम् ॥११॥

*śucau deśe pratiṣṭhāpya sthiramāsanamātmanaḥ |*
*nātyucchritaṁ nātinīcaṁ cailājinakuśottaram ||11||*

**11.** Having established a firm seat in a clean place, not too high and not too low, covered by *kuśa* grass, animal skin and cloth,

तत्रैकाग्रं मनः कृत्वा यतचित्तेन्द्रियक्रियः ।
उपविश्यासने युञ्ज्याद्योगमात्मविशुद्धये ॥१२॥

*tatraikāgraṁ manaḥ kṛtvā yatacittendriyakriyaḥ |*
*upaviśyāsane yuñjyādyogamātmaviśuddhaye ||12||*

**12.** sitting there in [a] seat, having focused the mind on one point [and] controlling the activities of the mind and senses, one should surrender to *yoga* [to meditation] in order to purify the mind.

समं कायशिरोग्रीवं धारयन्नचलं स्थिरः ।
सम्प्रेक्ष्य नासिकाग्रं स्वं दिशश्चानवलोकयन् ॥१३॥

*samaṁ kāyaśirogrīvaṁ dhārayannacalaṁ sthiraḥ |*
*samprekṣya nāsikāgraṁ svaṁ diśaścānavalokayan ||13||*

**13.** Seated firmly, maintaining the trunk, head and neck aligned [and] motionless, looking [as if] to the point of the nose and not looking in [other] directions,

प्रशान्तात्मा विगतभीर्ब्रह्मचारिव्रते स्थितः ।
मनः संयम्य मच्चित्तो युक्त आसीत मत्परः ॥१४॥

*praśāntātmā vigatabhīrbrahmacārivrate sthitaḥ |*
*manaḥ saṁyamya maccitto yukta āsīta matparaḥ ||14||*

**14.** with a tranquil mind, free from fear, established in the *brahmacārya* vow, controlling the mind, the meditator should sit, holding Me in his mind as that which is most important.

युञ्जन्नेवं सदात्मानं योगी नियतमानसः ।
शान्तिं निर्वाणपरमां मत्संस्थामधिगच्छति ॥१५॥

*yuñjannevaṁ sadātmānaṁ yogī niyatamānasaḥ |*
*śāntiṁ nirvāṇaparamāṁ matsaṁsthāmadhigacchati ||15||*

**15.** Thus always focusing with a disciplined mind, the *yogin* attains peace: the permanence in my nature that is liberation.

नात्यश्नतस्तु योगोऽस्ति न चैकान्तमनश्नतः ।
न चातिस्वप्नशीलस्य जाग्रतो नैव चार्जुन ॥१६॥

*nātyaśnatastu yogo'sti na caikāntamanaśnataḥ |*
*na cātisvapnaśīlasya jāgrato naiva cārjuna ||16||*

**16.** O *Arjuna, yoga* is for neither one who eats too much nor one who eats nothing, nor for one who sleeps too much nor one who is always awake.

युक्ताहारविहारस्य युक्तचेष्टस्य कर्मसु ।
युक्तस्वप्नावबोधस्य योगो भवति दुःखहा ॥१७॥

*yuktāhāravihārasya yuktaceṣṭasya karmasu |*
*yuktasvapnāvabodhasya yogo bhavati duḥkhahā ||17||*

**17.** For one whose food and activity are measured, whose attitudes in action are controlled [and] whose sleep and waking are moderate, there is *yoga*, which destroys sorrow.

यदा विनियतं चित्तमात्मन्येवावतिष्ठते ।
निःस्पृहः सर्वकामेभ्यो युक्त इत्युच्यते तदा ॥१८॥

*yadā viniyataṁ cittamātmanyevāvatiṣṭhate |*
*niḥspṛhaḥ sarvakāmebhyo yukta ityucyate tadā ||18||*

**18.** Free from the thirst for the objects of desire, when the mind is disciplined [and] resides permanently in *Ātman*, one is then said to be fulfilled.

यथा दीपो निवातस्थो नेङ्गते सोपमा स्मृता ।
योगिनो यतचित्तस्य युञ्जतो योगमात्मनः ॥१९॥

*yathā dīpo nivātastho neṅgate sopamā smṛtā |*
*yogino yatacittasya yuñjato yogamātmanaḥ ||19||*

**19.** For example: just as a flame far from wind does not flicker, the *yogin*, who has a disciplined mind, is unwavering within himself.

यत्रोपरमते चित्तं निरुद्धं योगसेवया ।
यत्र चैवात्मनात्मानं पश्यन्नात्मनि तुष्यति ॥२०॥

*yatroparamate cittaṁ niruddhaṁ yogasevayā |*
*yatra caivātmanātmānaṁ paśyannātmani tuṣyati ||20||*

**20.** When the mind has been dominated by the discipline of meditation; when one beholds oneself by one's self, then one is satisfied with one's self.

सुखमात्यन्तिकं यत्तद्बुद्धिग्राह्यमतीन्द्रियम् ।
वेत्ति यत्र न चैवायं स्थितश्चलति तत्त्वतः ॥२१॥

*sukhamātyantikaṁ yattadbuddhigrāhyamatīndriyam |*
*vetti yatra na caivāyaṁ sthitaścalati tattvataḥ ||21||*

**21.** When one is aware of the infinite happiness that is beyond the perception of the senses [and] may [only] be apprehended by the intellect; [and] established [there], one does not deviate from the truth.

यं लब्ध्वा चापरं लाभं मन्यते नाधिकं ततः ।
यस्मिन् स्थितो न दुःखेन गुरुणापि विचाल्यते ॥२२॥

*yaṁ labdhvā cāparaṁ lābhaṁ manyate nādhikaṁ tataḥ |*
*yasmin sthito na duḥkhena guruṇāpi vicālyate ||22||*

**22.** And having reached this [truth], one comprehends that there is no greater gain than this; established in this, one does not sway [from this], not even for grave pain.

तं विद्याद् दुःखसंयोगवियोगं योगसंज्ञितम् ।
स निश्चयेन योक्तव्यो योगोऽनिर्विण्णचेतसा ॥२३॥

*taṁ vidyād duḥkhasaṁyogaviyogaṁ yogasaṁjñitam |*
*sa niścayena yoktavyo yogo'nirviṇṇacetasā ||23||*

**23.** Let it be known that the disconnection from the connection with pain is called *yoga*. This *yoga* is to be practiced with determination [and] with a mind that is not negligent.

सङ्कल्पप्रभवान्कामांस्त्यक्त्वा सर्वानशेषतः ।
मनसैवेन्द्रियग्रामं विनियम्य समन्ततः ॥२४॥

*saṅkalpaprabhavānkāmāṁstyaktvā sarvānaśeṣataḥ |*
*manasaivendriyagrāmaṁ viniyamya samantataḥ ||24||*

**24.** Having completely left behind all desires caused by volition, having completely disciplined the organs of perception and action with the mind,

शनैः शनैरुपरमेद्बुद्ध्या धृतिगृहीतया ।
आत्मसंस्थं मनः कृत्वा न किञ्चिदपि चिन्तयेत् ॥२५॥

*śanaiḥ śanairuparamedbuddhyā dhṛtigṛhītayā |*
*ātmasaṁsthaṁ manaḥ kṛtvā na kiñcidapi cintayet ||25||*

**25.** may one gently calm oneself with an intellect that is steady, [and] having the mind established in itself, may one think of nothing else.

यतो यतो निश्चरति मनश्चञ्चलमस्थिरम् ।
ततस्ततो नियम्यैतदात्मन्येव वशं नयेत् ॥२६॥

*yato yato niścarati manaścañcalamasthiram |*
*tatastato niyamyaitadātmanyeva vaśaṁ nayet ||26||*

**26.** For no matter what reason the unsteady, agitated mind is scattered, may one bring it back under his command after seizing [the mind] back from whatever reason.

प्रशान्तमनसं ह्येनं योगिनं सुखमुत्तमम् ।
उपैति शान्तरजसं ब्रह्मभूतमकल्मषम् ॥२७॥

*praśāntamanasaṁ hyenaṁ yoginaṁ sukhamuttamam |*
*upaiti śāntarajasaṁ brahmabhūtamakalmaṣam ||27||*

**27.** The highest bliss undoubtedly reaches the *yogin* [one who meditates] of tranquil mind, free from affliction and impurity, who has become *Brahman* [via self-knowledge].

युञ्जन्नेवं सदात्मानं योगी विगतकल्मषः ।
सुखेन ब्रह्मसंस्पर्शमत्यन्तं सुखमश्नुते ॥२८॥

*yuñjannevaṁ sadātmānaṁ yogī vigatakalmaṣaḥ |*
*sukhena brahmasaṁsparśamatyantaṁ sukhamaśnute ||28||*

**28.** Always yoking the mind in this way, the *yogin*, free of impurities, attains unlimited happiness effortlessly, which is born of the contact with [the knowledge of] *Brahman*.

सर्वभूतस्थमात्मानं सर्वभूतानि चात्मनि ।
ईक्षते योगयुक्तात्मा सर्वत्र समदर्शनः ॥२९॥

*sarvabhūtasthamātmānaṁ sarvabhūtāni cātmani |*
*īkṣate yogayuktātmā sarvatra samadarśanaḥ ||29||*

**29.** One whose mind is integrated by *yoga* [meditation], who sees the same Self in all beings, sees *Ātman* in all beings and all beings in *Ātman*.

योो मां पश्यति सर्वत्र सर्वं च मयि पश्यति ।
तस्याहं न प्रणश्यामि स च मे न प्रणश्यति ॥३०॥

*yo māṁ paśyati sarvatra sarvaṁ ca mayi paśyati |*
*tasyāhaṁ na praṇaśyāmi sa ca me na praṇaśyati ||30||*

**30.** For he who sees Me everywhere and sees everything in Me, I am not lost, nor is he lost to Me.

सर्वभूतस्थितं यो मां भजत्येकत्वमास्थितः ।
सर्वथा वर्तमानोऽपि स योगी मयि वर्तते ॥३१॥

*sarvabhūtasthitaṁ yo māṁ bhajatyekatvamāsthitaḥ |*
*sarvathā vartamāno'pi sa yogī mayi vartate ||31||*

**31.** He who, remaining with the vision of oneness, reaches Me, who is in all beings, this *yogin* is [thereby] in Me – no matter what his way of life.

आत्मौपम्येन सर्वत्र समं पश्यति योऽर्जुन ।
सुखं वा यदि वा दुःखं स योगी परमो मतः ॥३२॥

*ātmaupamyena sarvatra samaṁ paśyati yo'rjuna |*
*sukhaṁ vā yadi vā duḥkhaṁ sa yogī paramo mataḥ ||32||*

**32.** *Arjuna*, he who, considering himself as an example, sees [both] joy and sorrow equally in all beings, is considered the greatest *yogin*.

अर्जुन उवाच
योऽयं योगस्त्वया प्रोक्तः साम्येन मधुसूदन ।
एतस्याहं न पश्यामि चञ्चलत्वात् स्थितिं स्थिराम् ॥३३॥

*arjuna uvāca*
*yo'yaṁ yogastvayā proktaḥ sāmyena madhusūdana |*
*etasyāhaṁ na paśyāmi cañcalatvāt sthitiṁ sthirām ||33||*

**33.** *Arjuna* spoke:
— O *Madhusūdana* [*Kṛṣṇa*], this *yoga* has been explained by you as equanimity; I see no real existence of this [equanimity], due to the instability [of the mind].

चञ्चलं हि मनः कृष्ण प्रमाथि बलवद् दृढम् ।
तस्याहं निग्रहं मन्ये वायोरिव सुदुष्करम् ॥३४॥

*cañcalaṁ hi manaḥ kṛṣṇa pramāthi balavad dṛḍham |*
*tasyāhaṁ nigrahaṁ manye vāyoriva suduṣkaram ||34||*

**34.** Indeed the mind is unstable, tormenting, powerful, [and] obstinate, O *Kṛṣṇa*! I find it as difficult to control as the wind.

श्रीभगवानुवाच
असंशयं महाबाहो मनो दुर्निग्रहं चलम् ।
अभ्यासेन तु कौन्तेय वैराग्येण च गृह्यते ॥३५॥

*śrībhagavānuvāca*
*asaṁśayaṁ mahābāho mano durnigrahaṁ calam |*
*abhyāsena tu kaunteya vairāgyeṇa ca gṛhyate ||35||*

**35.** The Lord [*Kṛṣṇa*] spoke:
— Without doubt, O *Mahābāhu* [*Arjuna*], the mind is unstable [and] difficult to control. However, O *Kaunteya* [*Arjuna*], by repetition and detachment, it can be disciplined.

असंयतात्मना योगो दुष्प्राप इति मे मतिः ।
वश्यात्मना तु यतता शक्योऽवाप्तुमुपायतः ॥३६॥

*asaṁyatātmanā yogo duṣprāpa iti me matiḥ |*
*vaśyātmanā tu yatatā śakyo'vāptumupāyataḥ ||36||*

**36.** I consider *yoga* difficult to be attained by one whose mind is not disciplined, but [*yoga*] may be attained by one who makes an effort by proper means [and] whose mind is under one's command.

अर्जुन उवाच
अयतिः श्रद्धयोपेतो योगाच्चलितमानसः ।
अप्राप्य योगसंसिद्धिं कां गतिं कृष्ण गच्छति ॥३७॥

*arjuna uvāca*
*ayatiḥ śraddhayopeto yogāccalitamānasaḥ |*
*aprāpya yogasaṁsiddhiṁ kāṁ gatiṁ kṛṣṇa gacchati ||37||*

**37.** *Arjuna* spoke:
— O *Kṛṣṇa*, what end is reached by he whose effort was not enough, who trusts [*yoga* as a means of self-knowledge], [but] whose mind abandoned *yoga* without reaching *yoga* successfully?

कच्चिन्नोभयविभ्रष्टश्छिन्नाभ्रमिव नश्यति ।
अप्रतिष्ठो महाबाहो विमूढो ब्रह्मणः पथि ॥३८॥

*kaccinnobhayavibhraṣṭaśchinnābhramiva naśyati |*
*apratiṣṭho mahābāho vimūḍho brahmaṇaḥ pathi ||38||*

**38.** O *Mahābāhu*[*Kṛṣṇa*], he who lost himself on the road to *Brahman*, who has no base for himself [neither in action nor in knowledge] [and] has failed in both [*karmayoga* and in a life of renunciation], does he not destroy himself, as a cloud dispersed?

एतन्मे संशयं कृष्ण छेत्तुमर्हस्यशेषतः ।
त्वदन्यः संशयस्यास्य छेत्ता न ह्युपपद्यते ॥३९॥

*etanme saṁśayaṁ kṛṣṇa chettumarhasyaśeṣataḥ |*
*tvadanyaḥ saṁśayasyāsya chettā na hyupapadyate ||39||*

**39.** *Kṛṣṇa*, you are able to completely eliminate all my doubt. No one other than you can eliminate this doubt.

श्रीभगवानुवाच
पार्थ नैवेह नामुत्र विनाशस्तस्य विद्यते ।
न हि कल्याणकृत्कश्चिद्दुर्गतिं तात गच्छति ॥४०॥

*śrībhagavānuvāca*
*pārtha naiveha nāmutra vināśastasya vidyate |*
*na hi kalyāṇakṛtkaściddurgatiṁ tāta gacchati ||40||*

**40.** The Lord [*Kṛṣṇa*] spoke:
— O *Pārtha* [*Arjuna*], for this [person], there is no destruction either in this world or in the other. No one who performs action for liberation shall encounter misfortune, my son.

प्राप्य पुण्यकृतां लोकानुषित्वा शाश्वतीः समाः ।
शुचीनां श्रीमतां गेहे योगभ्रष्टोऽभिजायते ॥४१॥

*prāpya puṇyakṛtāṁ lokānuṣitvā śāśvatīḥ samāḥ |*
*śucīnāṁ śrīmatāṁ gehe yogabhraṣṭo'bhijāyate ||41||*

**41.** Having reached worlds through good actions, residing [there] for countless years, one who was not successful in *yoga*, is born again into a family of culture and wealth,

अथवा योगिनामेव कुले भवति धीमताम् ।
एतद्धि दुर्लभतरं लोके जन्म यदीदृशम् ॥४२॥

*athavā yogināmeva kule bhavati dhīmatām |*
*etaddhi durlabhataraṁ loke janma yadīdṛśam ||42||*

**42.** or is born into a family of discriminating *yogins*. Actually, a birth such as this is very difficult to be reached in this world.

तत्र तं बुद्धिसंयोगं लभते पौर्वदेहिकम् ।
यतते च ततो भूयः संसिद्धौ कुरुनन्दन ॥४३॥

*tatra taṁ buddhisaṁyogaṁ labhate paurvadehikam |*
*yatate ca tato bhūyaḥ saṁsiddhau kurunandana ||43||*

**43.** There [in this birth], he connects with the knowledge acquired in another body [another life] and further strives for liberation, O *Kurunandana* [*Arjuna*].

पूर्वाभ्यासेन तेनैव ह्रियते ह्यवशोऽपि सः ।
जिज्ञासुरपि योगस्य शब्दब्रह्मातिवर्तते ॥४४॥

*pūrvābhyāsena tenaiva hriyate hyavaśo'pi saḥ |*
*jijñāsurapi yogasya śabdabrahmātivartate ||44||*

**44.** Indeed, only by the previous impulse for self-knowledge – even without effort – he is led forward. Even he who only wishes to know of *yoga* surpasses the initial part of the *Vedas* [covering actions and their results].

प्रयत्नाद्यतमानस्तु योगी संशुद्धकिल्बिषः ।
अनेकजन्मसंसिद्धस्ततो याति परां गतिम् ॥४५॥

*prayatnādyatamānastu yogī saṁśuddhakilbiṣaḥ |*
*anekajanmasaṁsiddhastato yāti parāṁ gatim ||45||*

**45.** The *yogin*, striving appropriately, cleansed of impurities, successful after countless births, finally attains the highest goal.

तपस्विभ्योऽधिको योगी ज्ञानिभ्योऽपि मतोऽधिकः ।
कर्मिभ्यश्चाधिको योगी तस्माद्योगी भवार्जुन ॥४६॥

*tapasvibhyo'dhiko yogī jñānibhyo'pi mato'dhikaḥ |*
*karmibhyaścādhiko yogī tasmādyogī bhavārjuna ||46||*

**46.** The *yogin* is considered superior to those that practice austerities, superior even to the learned, and superior to those dedicated to action. Therefore, be a *yogin*, O *Arjuna*.

योगिनामपि सर्वेषां मद्गतेनान्तरात्मना ।
श्रद्धावान् भजते यो मां स मे युक्ततमो मतः ॥४७॥

*yogināmapi sarveṣāṁ madgatenāntarātmanā |*
*śraddhāvān bhajate yo māṁ sa me yuktatamo mataḥ ||47||*

**47.** Among all *yogins*, one who surrenders to Me, with the mind becoming one with Me – who has faith – is regarded by Me as the highest.

ओं तत्सदिति श्रीमद्भगवद्गीतासूपनिषत्सु ब्रह्मविद्यायां योगशास्त्रे
श्रीकृष्णार्जुनसंवादे ध्यानयोगो नाम षष्ठोऽध्यायः॥

*oṁ tatsaditi śrīmadbhagavadgītāsūpaniṣatsu*
*brahmavidyāyāṁ yogaśāstre śrīkṛṣṇārjunasaṁvāde*
*dhyānayogo nāma ṣaṣṭho'dhyāyaḥ ||*

*Oṁ*, this is the Truth. Thus is the sixth chapter, the subject [of which] is called "*dhyāna*" [meditation], in the glorious *Bhagavadgītā*, [which is equivalent to] the *Upaniṣads*, [the subject of which is] the knowledge of *Brahman* [and] *yoga*, in the dialogue between *śrī Kṛṣṇa* and *Arjuna*.

# Chapter 7

## *Knowledge and wisdom*

The knowledge of *Vedānta* can be summarized in the *mahāvākyam,* the phrase of instruction that is *tat tvam asi. Tvam,* "you", refers to the individual; *asi,* "are", indicates an identity; *tat,* "That", refers to *Īśvara,* That which is Everything, and at the same time, the cause of creation.

The first six chapters address the individual. In chapters seven to twelve, the *Gītā* refers to That which is Everything, *Īśvara.* The topic of the next six chapters is who *Īśvara* is and in what form, and what the relationship is between the individual, *jīva,* and *Īśvara.*

The cause of the universe is called *Īśvara* in Sanskrit. Any creation has two causes: an intelligent cause, *nimittakāraṇa,* an intelligent being who possesses the knowledge and capacity to produce an object; and a material cause, *upādānakāraṇa,* the material from which the object is made. *Śrī Kṛṣṇa* reveals the essential nature of *Īśvara, nirguṇabrahman,* and its form - from the standpoint of creation - *saguṇabrahman.*

There must be a cause for the universe, since there is a cause for everything that has a function. *Īśvara,* the cause of the universe, is not a question of faith: the fact that there is no such thing as an effect - a product - without a cause is a question of understanding; it is a question of knowledge and not one of belief. While we may not exactly know the nature of the cause of the universe, we know that one exists, just as there is no doubt about the existence of our great great grandfather, although we may not know him. Faith, or belief, creates a seed of doubt regarding the existence of something. Although saying "I believe it will rain today", it actually may or may not rain today. The same does not occur when I say "I believe I have a father", since there is absolutely no possibility of a person without parents. Therefore, it would be more correct to say, "I know I have a father, but I know neither where he is nor what he is like".

*Īśvara* is, at the same time, the intelligent and the material cause of the universe. We generally understand these two causes as separate; the way we understand the creation of a clay pot: there is the potter, who collects his material, the clay, from someplace. In the vision of the *Vedas*, *Īśvara* is not an intelligent being that takes hold of material that is separate from him in order to create the universe: just as a spider is both the intelligent and material cause of his spider web. *Īśvara* is the only cause of the universe: the intelligence behind creation, and at the same time, the universe itself that is not separate from *Īśvara*. In other words, the universe is the expression of *Īśvara*, just as a dream is an expression of the dreamer.

Therefore, it is not necessary to look for *Īśvara* in any place, since there is no place he cannot be found. He is space, air, fire, water, earth, and everything else. All that exists within time and space is *Īśvara*, including the body and mind, denominated as "my body" and "my mind", as will be explained in this chapter, in verse 6.

Analyzing the universe, we recognize that there is an order of cause and effect everywhere. And it is because of that order we can study various segments and occurrences in the universe and understand them from the research and analysis that constitute science. The various studies and sciences on the universe, such as physics, astrophysics, medicine, psychology, etc, are indeed made possible due to an infallible order that governs everything. This infallible order is called *Īśvara*.

When we recognize *Īśvara* as, at the same time, the cause and the expression of the universe, we may also conclude that the individual is not an entity separate from *Īśvara*, and therefore can further conclude that all that exists is in fact *Īśvara*. Nevertheless, *Īśvara* does not depend on the universe, although the universe depends on him in order to exist. Despite being the material cause of the universe, *Īśvara* is not just another object to be known. Were *Īśvara* an object, he would be distinct from the subject, the witness. Therefore, by definition as an object, he would be limited in time and space, with a beginning and an end. Essentially *Īśvara* is *Brahman*, completely free from time, space and form; he is the basis of all that exists - *sat*; he is the consciousness that always exists - *cit*; and he is free of any limitation and complete in himself - *pūrṇam*. His very nature is identical to that of *Ātman*. Thus, the *Vedas* state "*tat tvam asi*", "you are *Īśvara*". The understanding of this affirmation is in the upcoming chapters.

Chapter seven is called *jñāna vijñāna*. These two words refer to "knowledge", but when the two words are combined, we understand them differently. Here *jñāna* is the knowledge of *Īśvara*, but together with the prefix vi - which comes from *viśeṣa*, to be different - it refers to a unique and specific knowledge: the individual and That which is Everything - *jīva* and *Īśvara* - are one and the same.

In Sanskrit, we have the terms *pratyakṣa-jñānam*, knowledge that is perceived directly; *parokṣa jñānam*, indirect knowledge of an object that is distant from the subject; *aparokṣa jñānam*, the clear and present knowledge of something that is neither close nor far, but the very subject. Therefore, the partial knowledge of *Īśvara* - that He exists and is the cause of the universe - is called *jñāna*; complete knowledge of *Īśvara* - that He is indivisible from the individual and creation - is called *vijñāna*.

This knowledge of the indivisibility of the individual from That which is Everything is very difficult to comprehend, due to the illusory power of the three qualities, or *guṇas*, which govern the body, mind, and the entire universe.

The cause of *saṁsāra* - the life of endless changes, limitation and suffering - is ignorance of the nature of the Self that is none other than *Īśvara*.

All beings are deluded by the three *guṇas* and their constant fluctuations. This power of illusion that is constituted by the three *guṇas* is called *māyā*, and it belongs to *Īśvara*. It is extremely difficult, but not impossible, to see beyond *māyā*. In order to do so, one must seek *Īśvara* and come to know Him, thereby encountering *satyam*, that which is real, and discerning it from everything else which is only apparently real and subject to constant mutation.

The truth of *Īśvara* is *Brahman*. He, together with the power of *māyā*, becomes the universe. One must become aware of this truth, and it is for this reason that *Śrī Kṛṣṇa* unfolds this theme in this chapter. Also, in verse 16 of this chapter, *Śrī Kṛṣṇa* mentions four types of devotees: *ārta*, one who seeks *Īśvara* only in a moment of desperation; *arthārthin*, one who seeks Him to acquire something; and *jijñāsu*, one who desires to know *Īśvara*; only the fourth devotee, the *jñānin*, the wise, has *vijñāna*, which is the complete knowledge of Him. *Kṛṣṇa* states in verse 18 that this devotee is a sage and indivisible from Him.

## Summary of the verses

Verses 1 to 3: *Śrī Kṛṣṇa* tells *Arjuna* about how to come to know *Īśvara* and the importance of this knowledge. *Jñāna* is the awareness of *Īśvara*, and *vijñāna* is knowing the indivisible identity shared by *Īśvara* and *jīva*. The complete knowledge of *Īśvara* is the highest goal of life, since it is synonymous with self-knowledge. Among all people, few desire this knowledge; rare is the person who seeks it, rarer still is the person who acquires it.

Verses 4 to 7: *Kṛṣṇa* discusses the nature of *Īśvara* as *parā prakṛti* and *aparā prakṛti*, his superior and inferior nature. The inferior nature is described as being comprised of eight factors: the five subtle elements, the ego, the cosmic mind and the unmanifest. The nature denominated as *aparā*, or inferior, is under constant transformation; it is inert and limited. The superior nature, *parā*, is Consciousness, the truth of all living beings and the basis of the universe; it is called superior because it is unchanging, unlimited and omnipresent.

*Īśvara* is the cause of the entire universe - That from which all comes forth, That by which all is sustained, and That in which all is dissolved. All that exists is Him, and there is nothing that exists apart from Him. Just as beads are held by a string, the entire universe is sustained by *Īśvara*.

Verses 8 to 11: *Śrī Kṛṣṇa* identifies himself as *Īśvara* and states that He is the material cause of all that exists; He is the essence of everything, and therefore, all the greatness and glory of the universe is Him.

Verses 12 to 13: In these verses, *Śrī Kṛṣṇa* uses the term *bhāva*, signifying "objects" and "beings", but may also mean "mental states". In his *bhāṣya* (his commentary on the *Bhagavadgītā*), *Śrī Śaṅkarācārya* says that *bhāvāḥ* are *padārthāḥ* - objects. In verse 13, he explains that these *bhāvas*, which are constituted by the three *guṇas*, are in the form of *rāga, dveṣa, moha* etc.

All objects - regardless of whether they be living beings, people or objects of thought - are predominately composed of either *sattva* (related to satisfaction, peace and tranquility), or *rajas* (related to ambition and restlessness), or *tamas* (related to illusion and confusion) - all of which are born of *Īśvara*. Saying that one is born of the law of *karma* is the same as saying that one is born of *Īśvara*, since He is the Order that maintains the universe.

The entire universe is deluded by the mental states related to the three aforementioned *guṇas*. It is for this reason that people are not aware of *parameśvara*, which is beyond the three *guṇas* and is immutable. *Śrī Kṛṣṇa*, as *Īśvara*, states "I do not depend on them, but they depend on Me", thereby revealing the transcendental yet intrinsic nature of *Īśvara*.

Verse 14: In order to understand the nature of *Īśvara*, it is necessary to see beyond *māyā*, and the only way to do so is via *Īśvara*, seeking Him, desiring the awareness of Him.

Verses 15 to 16: *Kṛṣṇa* describes five types of people:

- Those which, deluded by *māyā*, do not recognize the existence of *Īśvara*, and compelled only by their desires, perform actions that they should not.

- Although the other four types are devout, holding *Īśvara* as existent and establishing a relationship with Him, they do so for different reasons, and therefore are distinct from one another: *ārtha* is one who is devout only in a moment of desperation; *arthārthin* is devout in order to acquire various material goods; *jijñāsu* is devout in order to obtain an awareness of the nature of *Īśvara*; and lastly, *jñānin* has discovered his indivisible identity with *Īśvara*.

Verses 17 to 19: *Śrī Kṛṣṇa* states that the devotion of *jñānin*, the wise, stands apart from the others, since it is based on knowledge. The wise are always united with *Īśvara*, and it is for this reason that they are distinct from the others, and there is no difference between the wise and *Īśvara*.

Verses 20 to 23: In these verses, those who are devout to different objects, such as wealth and power, are mentioned.

They are capable of great disciplines and receive the results of their actions. However, since their capacity of discernment is limited; they do not know how to seek that which would really make a difference in their lives.

Verses 24 to 26: The nature of *Īśvara* is revealed, but people without discernment do not recognize His immutable nature that is without form. These people, who are under the power of illusion, believe that *Īśvara* is subject to birth and changes. However, *Īśvara* is *māyāvī*, the illusionist - He who wields the power of illusion, who is all the knowledge of the past, present and future - and is therefore not subject to illusion at all.

Verses 27 to 30: Concluding the chapter, *Śrī Kṛṣṇa* mentions the obstacles to beholding the truth that is *Īśvara*. From very early in life, one possesses desires in the form of tastes and aversions due to the fundamental illusion about the truth of oneself. By way of *viveka* (discrimination or discernment) and *jijñāsā* (the desire to know the truth) the individual is liberated from the illusion regarding the objects in constant transformation, and begins the search for the knowledge of *Īśvara* with great dedication - thereby acquiring an awareness of *Brahman, karma, adhyātma, adhibhūta, adhidaiva* and *adhiyajña*. Once affirmed in this knowledge, the mind will naturally rest with this knowledge.

## अथ सप्तमोऽध्यायः

### *atha saptamo'dhyāyaḥ*

### Seventh chapter

श्रीभगवानुवाच
मय्यासक्तमनाः पार्थ योगं युञ्जन्मदाश्रयः ।
असंशयं समग्रं मां यथा ज्ञास्यसि तच्छृणु ॥१॥

*śrībhagavānuvāca*
*mayyāsaktamanāḥ pārtha yogaṁ yuñjanmadāśrayaḥ |*
*asaṁśayaṁ samagraṁ māṁ yathā jñāsyasi tacchṛṇu ||1||*

**1.** The Lord [*Kṛṣṇa*] spoke:
— O *Pārtha* [*Arjuna*], with [your] mind concentrated on Me, united in *yoga*, holding Me as your refuge, hear this [instruction] on how you, free of doubt, should know Me completely.

ज्ञानं तेऽहं सविज्ञानमिदं वक्ष्याम्यशेषतः ।
यज्ज्ञात्वा नेह भूयोऽन्यज्ज्ञातव्यमवशिष्यते ॥२॥

*jñānaṁ te'haṁ savijñānamidaṁ vakṣyāmyaśeṣataḥ |*
*yajjñātvā neha bhūyo'nyajjñātavyamavaśiṣyate ||2||*

**2.** I shall teach you this knowledge thoroughly, together with wisdom. Once acquired, there is nothing left here [in this life] to be known.

मनुष्याणां सहस्रेषु कश्चिद्यतति सिद्धये ।
यततामपि सिद्धानां कश्चिन्मां वेत्ति तत्त्वतः ॥३॥

*manuṣyāṇāṁ sahasreṣu kaścidyatati siddhaye |*
*yatatāmapi siddhānāṁ kaścinmāṁ vetti tattvataḥ ||3||*

**3.** One in a million makes an effort [for this knowledge]. Even among the seekers who make an effort, few really come to know Me.

भूमिरापोऽनलो वायुः खं मनो बुद्धिरेव च ।
अहङ्कार इतीयं मे भिन्ना प्रकृतिरष्टधा ॥४॥

*bhūmirāpo'nalo vāyuḥ khaṁ mano buddhireva ca |*
*ahaṅkāra itīyaṁ me bhinnā prakṛtiraṣṭadhā ||4||*

**4.** Earth, water, fire, air, space, the cosmic mind, the cosmic intellect, and also the unmanifest: this is my nature in eight parts.

अपरेयमितस्त्वन्यां प्रकृतिं विद्धि मे पराम् ।
जीवभूतां महाबाहो ययेदं धार्यते जगत् ॥५॥

*apareyamitastvanyāṁ prakṛtiṁ viddhi me parām |*
*jīvabhūtāṁ mahābāho yayedaṁ dhāryate jagat ||5||*

**5.** This [in eight parts] is [my] inferior [nature], but know my superior nature, which is different from that [and] is the essential nature of the individual, O *Mahābāhu* [*Arjuna*]. By this [nature], this creation is sustained.

एतद्योनीनि भूतानि सर्वाणीत्युपधारय ।
अहं कृत्स्नस्य जगतः प्रभवः प्रलयस्तथा ॥६॥

*etadyonīni bhūtāni sarvāṇītyupadhāraya |*
*ahaṁ kṛtsnasya jagataḥ prabhavaḥ pralayastathā ||6||*

**6.** Know that all beings are born of this [superior and inferior nature]. I am [the cause] of this creation and also the dissolution of the entire universe.

मत्तः परतरं नान्यत्किञ्चिदस्ति धनञ्जय ।
मयि सर्वमिदं प्रोतं सूत्रे मणिगणा इव ॥७॥

*mattaḥ parataraṁ nānyatkiñcidasti dhanañjaya |*
*mayi sarvamidaṁ protaṁ sūtre maṇigaṇā iva ||7||*

**7.** There is no other [cause] but Me, O *Dhanañjaya* [*Arjuna*]. In Me, all this [universe] is strung, just as beads on a string.

रसोऽहमप्सु कौन्तेय प्रभास्मि शशिसूर्ययोः ।
प्रणवः सर्ववेदेषु शब्दः खे पौरुषं नृषु ॥८॥

*raso'hamapsu kaunteya prabhāsmi śaśisūryayoḥ |*
*praṇavaḥ sarvavedeṣu śabdaḥ khe pauruṣaṁ nṛṣu ||8||*

**8.** O *Kaunteya* [*Arjuna*], in water, I am the flavor. I am the light in the Sun and the Moon. I am *Oṁ* in all the *Vedas*. In space, I am sound. In humans beings, I am [their] humanity.

पुण्यो गन्धः पृथिव्यां च तेजश्चास्मि विभावसौ ।
जीवनं सर्वभूतेषु तपश्चास्मि तपस्विषु ॥९॥

*puṇyo gandhaḥ pṛthivyāṁ ca tejaścāsmi vibhāvasau |*
*jīvanaṁ sarvabhūteṣu tapaścāsmi tapasviṣu ||9||*

**9.** And, on Earth, I am the pleasant fragrance; and in fire, I am heat. In all beings, I am life; and I am the austerity in all ascetics.

बीजं मां सर्वभूतानां विद्धि पार्थ सनातनम् ।
बुद्धिर्बुद्धिमतामस्मि तेजस्तेजस्विनामहम् ॥१०॥

*bījaṁ māṁ sarvabhūtānāṁ viddhi pārtha sanātanam |*
*buddhirbuddhimatāmasmi tejastejasvināmaham ||10||*

**10.** Know me, O *Pārtha* [*Arjuna*], as the eternal seed in all beings. I am the power of discernment for those that have the capacity to discriminate. I am the brilliance in the brilliant.

बलं बलवतां चाहं कामरागविवर्जितम् ।
धर्माविरुद्धो भूतेषु कामोऽस्मि भरतर्षभ ॥११॥

*balaṁ balavatāṁ cāhaṁ kāmarāgavivarjitam |*
*dharmāviruddho bhūteṣu kāmo'smi bharatarṣabha ||11||*

**11.** And, in the mighty, I am the might that is free from desire and attachment. In all beings, O *Bharatarṣabha* [*Arjuna*], I am the desire that does not oppose *dharma*.

ये चैव सात्त्विका भावा राजसास्तामसाश्च ये ।
मत्त एवेति तान्विद्धि न त्वहं तेषु ते मयि ॥१२॥

*ye caiva sāttvikā bhāvā rājasāstāmasāśca ye |*
*matta eveti tānviddhi na tvahaṁ teṣu te mayi ||12||*

**12.** And also comprehend that those beings and objects that are born of *sattva, rajas* and *tamas* come from Me. I am not in them, but they are in Me.

त्रिभिर्गुणमयैर्भावैरेभिः सर्वमिदं जगत् ।
मोहितं नाभिजानाति मामेभ्यः परमव्ययम् ॥१३॥

*tribhirguṇamayairbhāvairebhiḥ sarvamidaṁ jagat |*
*mohitaṁ nābhijānāti māmebhyaḥ paramavyayam ||13||*

**13.** Deluded by that which is produced by these three *guṇas* [qualities], the entire universe does not know Me [as] immutable [and] beyond these [qualities].

दैवी ह्येषा गुणमयी मम माया दुरत्यया ।
मामेव ये प्रपद्यन्ते मायामेतां तरन्ति ते ॥१४॥

*daivī hyeṣā guṇamayī mama māyā duratyayā |*
*māmeva ye prapadyante māyāmetāṁ taranti te ||14||*

**14.** Since my *māyā*[5], which is divine [and] composed of the *guṇas*, is difficult to overcome, only those who surrender to Me, cross over this *māyā*.

---

5 *Māyā* is the power by which *Brahman* becomes the Creator, *Īśvara*. *Māyā* has three *guṇas*, or characterisitcs, and therefore the universe, which is a projection on *Brahman* via *māyā*, also has three *guṇas*, which are: *sattva*, *rajas* and *tamas*. *Māyā*

न मां दुष्कृतिनो मूढाः प्रपद्यन्ते नराधमाः ।
माययापहृतज्ञाना आसुरं भावमाश्रिताः ॥१५॥

*na māṁ duṣkṛtino mūḍhāḥ prapadyante narādhamāḥ |*
*māyayāpahṛtajñānā āsuraṁ bhāvamāśritāḥ ||15||*

**15.** Those deluded and wrongful [are] the worst among men. Incapable of understanding, due to illusion, they seek refuge in malice [and] do not seek Me.

चतुर्विधा भजन्ते मां जनाः सुकृतिनोऽर्जुन ।
आर्तो जिज्ञासुरर्थार्थी ज्ञानी च भरतर्षभ ॥१६॥

*caturvidhā bhajante māṁ janāḥ sukṛtino'rjuna |*
*ārto jijñāsurarthārthī jñānī ca bharatarṣabha ||16||*

**16.** Four types of virtuous people worship Me, O *Arjuna*: the distressed; those who seek comfort and wealth; those who seek knowledge; and the wise, *Bharatarṣabha* [*Arjuna*].

तेषां ज्ञानी नित्ययुक्त एकभक्तिर्विशिष्यते ।
प्रियो हि ज्ञानिनोऽत्यर्थमहं स च मम प्रियः ॥१७॥

*teṣāṁ jñānī nityayukta ekabhaktirviśiṣyate |*
*priyo hi jñānino'tyarthamahaṁ sa ca mama priyaḥ ||17||*

---

belongs to *Īśvara*, and is therefore called *daivī*. The existence of *māyā* depends on *Brahman*. Here, *Kṛṣṇa* says that it is not easy to overcome *māyā*, since the mind is constantly under the power of the three *guṇas* and is not able to see the reality that is free from the *guṇas*. *Kṛṣṇa* says that the only means to overcome *māyā* is seek Him out. *śrī Śaṅkāra* states in his commentary on this verse that to seek *Īśvara* is to seek the reality that is the Self in all beings, *svātmabhūtam*.

**17.** Among them, it is the wise of unwavering knowledge and devotion to Oneness that are distinguished – for I am greatly loved by the wise, as they are loved by Me.

उदाराः सर्व एवैते ज्ञानी त्वात्मैव मे मतम् ।
आस्थितः स हि युक्तात्मा मामेवानुत्तमां गतिम् ॥१८॥

*udārāḥ sarva evaite jñānī tvātmaiva me matam |*
*āsthitaḥ sa hi yuktātmā māmevānuttamāṁ gatim ||18||*

**18.** All these are certainly noble, but the wise are none other than Me. This is my vision. Since with an unwavering mind, the wise have surrendered only to Me – the goal beyond which there is nothing.

बहूनां जन्मनामन्ते ज्ञानवान्मां प्रपद्यते ।
वासुदेवः सर्वमिति स महात्मा सुदुर्लभः ॥१९॥

*bahūnāṁ janmanāmante jñānavānmāṁ prapadyate |*
*vāsudevaḥ sarvamiti sa mahātmā sudurlabhaḥ ||19||*

**19.** At the end of many births, one who possesses the knowledge that "*Vāsudeva*[6] is everything" attains Me. Such a sage is very hard to find.

---

6 *Vāsudeva* refers to *Atman*, because *Vāsu* means that which is everywhere and *deva* means that which is brilliant, light, referring to Consciousness.

कामैस्तैस्तैर्हृतज्ञानाः प्रपद्यन्तेऽन्यदेवताः ।
तं तं नियममास्थाय प्रकृत्या नियताः स्वया ॥२०॥

*kāmaistaistairhṛtajñānāḥ prapadyante'nyadevatāḥ |*
*taṁ taṁ niyamamāsthāya prakṛtyā niyatāḥ svayā ||20||*

**20.** Driven by their own nature, those whose discernment has been stolen by desires look to other deities, according to the rules [of the rituals].

यो यो यां यां तनुं भक्तः श्रद्धयार्चितुमिच्छति ।
तस्य तस्याचलां श्रद्धां तामेव विदधाम्यहम् ॥२१॥

*yo yo yāṁ yāṁ tanuṁ bhaktaḥ śraddhayārcitumicchati |*
*tasya tasyācalāṁ śraddhāṁ tāmeva vidadhāmyaham ||21||*

**21.** Whomever worships whatever form [of deity] with faith, I make his faith unshakeable.

स तया श्रद्धया युक्तस्तस्या राधनमीहते ।
लभते च ततः कामान्मयैव विहितान् हि तान् ॥२२॥

*sa tayā śraddhayā yuktastasyā rādhanamīhate |*
*labhate ca tataḥ kāmānmayaiva vihitān hi tān ||22||*

**22.** Keeping the faith, one worships one's [deity] and receives from that [deity] the objects of [one's] desires, which are in fact granted by Me alone.

अन्तवत्तु फलं तेषां तद्भवत्यल्पमेधसाम् ।
देवान्देवयजो यान्ति मद्भक्ता यान्ति मामपि ॥२३॥

*antavattu phalaṁ teṣāṁ tadbhavatyalpamedhasām |*
*devāndevayajo yānti madbhaktā yānti māmapi ||23||*

**23.** However, for those of little discernment that result is finite. Those who worship deities go to those deities. Those who are my worshippers undoubtedly come to Me.

अव्यक्तं व्यक्तिमापन्नं मन्यन्ते मामबुद्धयः ।
परं भावमजानन्तो ममाव्ययमनुत्तमम् ॥२४॥

*avyaktaṁ vyaktimāpannaṁ manyante māmabuddhayaḥ |*
*paraṁ bhāvamajānanto mamāvyayamanuttamam ||24||*

**24.** Those without discernment – oblivious of my superior nature that is changeless, incomparable, unmanifest – think that I assume a manifestation.

नाहं प्रकाशः सर्वस्य योगमायासमावृतः ।
मूढोऽयं नाभिजानाति लोको मामजमव्ययम् ॥२५॥

*nāhaṁ prakāśaḥ sarvasya yogamāyāsamāvṛtaḥ |*
*mūḍho'yaṁ nābhijānāti loko māmajamavyayam ||25||*

**25.** Completely veiled by *yogamāyā* [*māyā* together with the three *guṇas*], I am evident to no one. Deluded, these people do not know Me, who is birthless and immutable.

वेदाहं समतीतानि वर्तमानानि चार्जुन ।
भविष्याणि च भूतानि मां तु वेद न कश्चन ॥२६॥

*vedāhaṁ samatītāni vartamānāni cārjuna |*
*bhaviṣyāṇi ca bhūtāni māṁ tu veda na kaścana ||26||*

**26.** O *Arjuna*, I know all the beings that existed in the past, those that exist today, and those that shall exist in the future – but no one knows Me.

इच्छाद्वेषसमुत्थेन द्वन्द्वमोहेन भारत ।
सर्वभूतानि सम्मोहं सर्गे यान्ति परन्तप ॥२७॥

*icchādveṣasamutthena dvandvamohena bhārata |*
*sarvabhūtāni sammohaṁ sarge yānti parantapa ||27||*

**27.** O *Parantapa* [*Arjuna*], all beings upon birth are deluded by the illusion of the pairs of opposites that are created by desire and aversion, O *Bhārata* [*Arjuna*].

येषां त्वन्तगतं पापं जनानां पुण्यकर्मणाम् ।
ते द्वन्द्वमोहनिर्मुक्ता भजन्ते मां दृढव्रताः ॥२८॥

*yeṣāṁ tvantagataṁ pāpaṁ janānāṁ puṇyakarmaṇām |*
*te dvandvamohanirmuktā bhajante māṁ dṛḍhavratāḥ ||28||*

**28.** However, those who do good actions – for whom *pāpa* [the result of inappropriate action] has come to an end, free from the illusion of the pairs of opposites [and] unwavering [in their] vows – worship Me.

जरामरणमोक्षाय मामाश्रित्य यतन्ति ये ।
ते ब्रह्म तद्विदुः कृत्स्नमध्यात्मं कर्म चाखिलम् ॥२९॥

*jarāmaraṇamokṣāya māmāśritya yatanti ye |*
*te brahma tadviduḥ kṛtsnamadhyātmaṁ karma cākhilam ||29||*

**29.** Sheltered in Me, those that strive for release from ageing and death, know Me by my complete form that is: *Brahman*, Oneself, and all action in its entirety.

साधिभूताधिदैवं मां साधियज्ञं च ये विदुः ।
प्रयाणकालेऽपि च मां ते विदुर्युक्तचेतसः ॥३०॥

*sādhibhūtādhidaivaṁ māṁ sādhiyajñaṁ ca ye viduḥ |*
*prayāṇakāle'pi ca māṁ te viduryuktacetasaḥ ||30||*

**30.** Those of disciplined mind, who know Me together with *adhibhūta*, *adhidaiva* and *adhiyajña* – even at the hour of death – know Me.

ओं तत्सदिति श्रीमद्भगवद्गीतासूपनिषत्सु ब्रह्मविद्यायां योगशास्त्रे
श्रीकृष्णार्जुनसंवादे ज्ञानविज्ञानयोगो नाम सप्तमोऽध्यायः॥

*oṁ tatsaditi śrīmadbhagavadgītāsūpaniṣatsu*
*brahmavidyāyāṁ yogaśāstre śrīkṛṣṇārjunasaṁvāde*
*jñānavijñānayogo nāma saptamo'dhyāyaḥ ||*

*Oṁ*, this is the Truth. Thus is the seventh chapter, the subject [of which] is called "*jñānavijñāna*" [Knowledge and Wisdom] in the glorious *Bhagavadgītā*, [which is equivalent to] the *Upaniṣads*, [the subject of which is] the knowledge of *Brahman* [and] *yoga*, in the dialogue between *śrī Kṛṣṇa* and *Arjuna*.

# Chapter 8

## *The imperishable Brahman*

There are two different names for chapter 8 of the *Bhagavadgītā*. One of them is *akṣarabrahman*, the imperishable *Brahman*, since that is exactly how the instruction of *Śrī Kṛṣṇa* to *Arjuna* begins in this chapter. The other name given to the chapter is *tāraka-brahman. Tāraka* means "that which helps to cross something". Here in the *Gītā*, the disciple *Arjuna* asks his *guru* for the means to cross *saṁsāra. Omkāra upāsanā*, the meditation on the syllable om, is then taught as a means to cross *saṁsāra*.

*Upāsanā* is defined as *saguṇabrahma-viṣaya-mānasa-vyāpāra*, a meditation, or a mental action by which the object is *saguṇabrahman*, which is *Īśvara. Upāsanā* is different from *nididhyāsana*, which is contemplation. Together with *śravaṇa* and *manana, nididhyāsana* is the means for acquiring self-knowledge, *ātmajñāna*, according to the teaching of the *Vedas*. The body of knowledge called *Veda*, subsequently divided into four parts: *ṛk, sāma, yajur, atharva*, is a means of knowledge, or *pramāṇa*, the topic of which is the subject, or *Ātman*, which is none other than *Brahman*, the imperishable cause of creation. *Upāsanā* and many forms of *dhyāna*, meditation, are mental actions that are *sādhana*, a discipline to prepare the mind to acquire self-knowledge, together with other actions. *Karmayoga* produces *antaḥkaraṇa-śuddhi*, a purification of the mind, and *dhyāna* (or *upāsanā*) produces *antaḥkaraṇa-naiścalya*, the steadiness of the mind. By means of these disciplines, the obstacles of the mind – such as attachment to the tastes and aversions, or *rāgadveṣa-mala*, and restlessness, or *vikṣepa* – will be diminished, and self-knowledge can be attained in a clear and consolidated form.

In order for meditation on *Īśvara* to become possible, some previous knowledge of *Īśvara* must be acquired, and this is precisely the objective of these chapters that form the second part of the *Gītā*.

*Śrī Kṛṣṇa* also tells us about another type of *mokṣa*, which is called *kramamukti*, liberation in steps.

A *mumukṣu*, an individual who desires liberation, does *upāsanā* in order to prepare the mind for self-knowledge. Others do *upāsanā*, since in the *Vedas* it is said that by doing specific *upāsanās*, people may go to a place called *brahmaloka*; afterwards, at the end of this cycle of creation, they will be taught by *Brahmājī* and will be liberated from the cycle of births and deaths. This means is called *brahmalokaprāpti*. The teaching received from *Brahmājī* is the same as *Vedānta*, which is the teaching that can be obtained here in this world from a *guru* capable of teaching *tat tvam asi*, "You are That", and make the disciple realize aham *Brahma asmi*, "I am *Brahman*". Between the two types of liberation – either here in this world, or in *brahmaloka* – the surest and fastest way to self-knowledge is right here and now.

At any rate, what leads the individual to overcome limitation and suffering is recognizing oneself as unlimited.

## Summary of the verses

*Śrī Kṛṣṇa*, at the end of chapter 7, verses 29 and 30, praises the wise who are devout, describes their knowledge using many new words, and states that one who knows *Īśvara* never loses self-knowledge – not even upon the hour of death. These two verses comprise the basis for the question of *Arjuna* at the beginning of chapter 8.

Verses 1 and 2: *Arjuna* poses seven questions to *Śrī Kṛṣṇa*;

six refer to the terms he had just heard, and the last is regarding a person's thought at the hour of death.

Verse 3: *Śrī Kṛṣṇa* responds to the first three questions. He states that *Brahman* is the imperishable and unlimited reality; that *adhyātma* is *Brahman*, or the Self in each body; that *karma*, besides meaning "any action", refers to a ritual or sacrifice mentioned in the *Vedas*. *Karma* and their results are the cause of subsequent births. *Karma* is also inseparable from *Brahman*, that which is real, *satyam*.

Verse 4: The other three questions are answered. *Adhibhūta* is all the universe that is perishable, meaning all that is born, grows, transforms, declines and dies. *Adhidaiva* is *Īśvara* that – as far as actions are concerned – is *karmaphaladātṛ*, or the order that governs the result of actions made by individuals. These three aspects exist in *Brahman* and, just like the other three, they are the objects of the previous question of *Arjuna*; they depend on *Brahman*, which is the immutable base of all that exists.

Verses 5 to 7: Lord *Kṛṣṇa* responds in detail to the final part of the question posed by *Arjuna* regarding the hour of death and how reality may be considered at that time.

Verses 5 to 8: *Kṛṣṇa* says that what is thought upon the hour of death shall determine the conditions of the following birth. One who thinks about *Īśvara*, also called *Parameśvara*, at the hour of death, becomes one with Him. He concludes that one who continues performing actions and collecting their results must keep *Īśvara* in mind: although such a practice may seem difficult, it is possible if maintaining a constant discipline.

Verse 9: In order for anyone to think about anything, the thing must be known. Therefore, the nature of *Puruṣa* is described.

Verses 10 to 13: These verses describe the way a *yogin*

directs his mind at the moment of death in order to go to *brahmaloka*, where he shall reach final liberation. So that a series of practices may me done at the hour of death, they have to be practiced beforehand, during the life of the *yogin*. These practices include the control of the senses and of the *prāṇa*; which should be directed to the top of the head, between the eyebrows. While controlling the mind and repeating the syllable *Oṁ*, the *yogin* leaves the body and obtains the highest objective.

Verse 14: *Kṛṣṇa* states that the *yogin* who has disciplined his mind may easily attain *Īśvara*.

Verses 15 to 19: *Śrī Kṛṣṇa* explains what it means to obtain absolute success: the final liberation that comes from acknowledging one's own indivisible identity with *Īśvara*, thereby obtaining success in the world of objects, within a cycle of future births and deaths.

Better births, with bodies that are more able to bring pleasure in worlds or dimensions that are better than this one of humans, do not end the cycle of births and deaths called *saṁsāra*: the continuous cycle of the unmanifest to the manifest, which is birth, and then from the manifest to the unmanifest, which is death – which includes all the happiness and suffering that is part of this process.

Verses 20 to 22: In verse 13, the syllable *Oṁ* was mentioned, by the repetition of which the *yogin* attains *brahmaloka*, where one will obtain the final knowledge and be liberated from the cycle of births and deaths. The syllable *Oṁ*, called *oṁkāra*, is the name, *vācya*, of *Brahman*. In verses 20 to 22, the *vācya* of *Oṁ* is mentioned, or rather, that which is denominated by this syllable.

Verses 23 to 26: There are two types of devotees or seekers of *Brahman*: those that desire the knowledge of *Brahman*, the only reality and the truth of *jīva* and *Īśvara*; and those that meditate on *Oṁ*, *oṁkāra*-upāsakas, which go to *brahmaloka*, where they receive the teaching of *Brahmājī*, the Creator himself, and thereby attain liberation by taking the path of *uttara-mārga* after death.

There are yet others that perform rituals and actions in the service of humanity and desire a better life. These people take the path of *dakṣiṇā-marga* upon death, and then return to this world. The south, *dakṣiṇā*, symbolizes *saṁsāra*; the north, *uttara*, symbolizes *mokṣa*. The northern path, *uttara mārga* or *uttarāyaṇa*, is also called the path of light, *śukla gati*, which is presided by the deities of fire, the day, and the bright lunar fortnight. The southern path, *dakṣiṇā-marga* or *dakṣiṇāyaṇa*, is called the dark path, *kṛṣṇa gati*, and it is presided by the deities of smoke, the night, and the dark lunar fortnight. All of these are mentioned to indicate the knowledge of *Brahman* is the easiest and most direct path to liberation for individual here in this world.

Verse 27: *Upāsanā* directs the individual to *brahmaloka*, where there will be liberation. This process is called *kramamukti*. *Upāsanā* also prepares the mind of whoever desires liberation, and it directs them to their teacher and to self-knowledge.

*Kṛṣṇa* states that the *yogin* who knows both paths is aware that one leads to liberation while the other keeps the person in *saṁsāra*. Upon this understanding, there will be no more illusion that going to heaven or to a better birth will bring final liberation.

Verse 28: Finally, the knowledge of the answers to the questions of *Arjuna* is praised. The *sādhana*, the means, and the final objective, *sādhya*, which is *mokṣa*, becomes clear to the *yogin*. Upon acquiring the knowledge of *Brahman*, the *yogin* attains the highest state possible, *paraṁ sthānam*, *aiṣvaraṁ sthānam*, which is identical to that of *Īśvara*.

# अथाष्टमोऽध्यायः

***athāṣṭamo'dhyāyaḥ***

**Eighth chapter**

अर्जुन उवाच
किं तद्ब्रह्म किमध्यात्मं किं कर्म पुरुषोत्तम ।
अधिभूतं च किं प्रोक्तमधिदैवं किमुच्यते ॥१॥

*arjuna uvāca*
*kiṁ tadbrahma kimadhyātmaṁ kiṁ karma puruṣottama |*
*adhibhūtaṁ ca kiṁ proktamadhidaivaṁ kimucyate ||1||*

**1.** *Arjuna* spoke:
— What is that *Brahman*? What is *adhyātma*? What is *karma*, O *Puruṣottama* [*Kṛṣṇa*]? What is called *adhibhūta*? And what is called *adhidaiva*?

अधियज्ञः कथं कोऽत्र देहेऽस्मिन्मधुसूदन ।
प्रयाणकाले च कथं ज्ञेयोऽसि नियतात्मभिः ॥२॥

*adhiyajñaḥ kathaṁ ko'tra dehe'sminmadhusūdana |*
*prayāṇakāle ca kathaṁ jñeyo'si niyatātmabhiḥ ||2||*

**2.** What is *adhiyajña* [and] how is it [that it stays] here in this body, O *Madhusūdana* [*Kṛṣṇa*]? And, upon the hour of death, how are You to be known by those who are disciplined?

श्रीभगवानुवाच
अक्षरं ब्रह्म परमं स्वभावोऽध्यात्ममुच्यते ।
भूतभावोद्भवकरो विसर्गः कर्मसंज्ञितः ॥३॥

*śrībhagavānuvāca*
*akṣaraṁ brahma paramaṁ svabhāvo'dhyātmamucyate |*
*bhūtabhāvodbhavakaro visargaḥ karmasaṁjñitaḥ ||3||*

**3.** The Lord [*Kṛṣṇa*] spoke:
— *Brahman* is immutable [and] unlimited. The nature of the Self is called *adhyātma*. Offerings which are the cause of creation of all beings is called *karma*.

अधिभूतं क्षरो भावः पुरुषश्चाधिदैवतम् ।
अधियज्ञोऽहमेवात्र देहे देहभृतां वर ॥४॥

*adhibhūtaṁ kṣaro bhāvaḥ puruṣaścādhidaivatam |*
*adhiyajño'hamevātra dehe dehabhṛtāṁ vara ||4||*

**4.** O *dehabhṛtām vara* [*Arjuna*], [all] perishable beings are *adhibhūta*. *Hiraṇyagarbha* [the total subtle body] is *adhidaivata*. And *adhiyajña* is Me in this body.

अन्तकाले च मामेव स्मरन्मुक्त्वा कलेवरम् ।
यः प्रयाति स मद्भावं याति नास्त्यत्र संशयः ॥५॥

*antakāle ca māmeva smaranmuktvā kalevaram |*
*yaḥ prayāti sa madbhāvaṁ yāti nāstyatra saṁśayaḥ ||5||*

**5.** And, abandoning the body at the hour of death, one who departs while remembering Me goes to my being. As far as this is concerned, there is no doubt.

यं यं वापि स्मरन्भावं त्यजत्यन्ते कलेवरम् ।
तं तमेवैति कौन्तेय सदा तद्भावभावितः ॥६॥

*yaṁ yaṁ vāpi smaranbhāvaṁ tyajatyante kalevaram |*
*taṁ tamevaiti kaunteya sadā tadbhāvabhāvitaḥ ||6||*

**6.** Thinking about a specific object, one abandons the body at the moment of death; that same [object] is reached by focusing one's thought on that object, O *Kaunteya* [*Arjuna*].

तस्मात्सर्वेषु कालेषु मामनुस्मर युध्य च ।
मय्यर्पितमनोबुद्धिर्मामेवैष्यस्यसंशयः ॥७॥

*tasmātsarveṣu kāleṣu māmanusmara yudhya ca |*
*mayyarpitamanobuddhirmāmevaiṣyasyasaṁśayaḥ ||7||*

**7.** Therefore, remember Me and fight at all times. With the mind and intellect as an offering to Me, you shall undoubtedly come to Me alone.

अभ्यासयोगयुक्तेन चेतसा नान्यगामिना ।
परमं पुरुषं दिव्यं याति पार्थानुचिन्तयन् ॥८॥

*abhyāsayogayuktena cetasā nānyagāminā |*
*paramaṁ puruṣaṁ divyaṁ yāti pārthānucintayan ||8||*

**8.** O *Pārtha* [*Arjuna*], reflecting [on this teaching] with a mind that is undistracted due to the practice of meditation, one attains the unlimited Being, full of light.

कविं पुराणमनुशासितारम्-
अणोरणीयांसमनुस्मरेद्यः ।
सर्वस्य धातारमचिन्त्यरूपम्-
आदित्यवर्णं तमसः परस्तात् ॥९॥

*kaviṁ purāṇamanuśāsitāram*
*aṇoraṇīyāṁsamanusmaredyaḥ |*
*sarvasya dhātāramacintyarūpam*
*ādityavarṇaṁ tamasaḥ parastāt ||9||*

**9.** One who meditates on That which possesses all knowledge, which is eternal, which governs everything, which is more subtle than the subtle, which sustains everything, whose form cannot be imagined, which is as bright as the light of the sun, which is above ignorance [attains the limitless Being].

प्रयाणकाले मनसाचलेन
भक्त्या युक्तो योगबलेन चैव ।
भ्रुवोर्मध्ये प्राणमावेश्य सम्यक्
स तं परं पुरुषमुपैति दिव्यम् ॥१०॥

*prayāṇakāle manasācalena*
*bhaktyā yukto yogabalena caiva |*
*bhruvormadhye prāṇamāveśya samyak*
*sa taṁ paraṁ puruṣamupaiti divyam ||10||*

**10.** Upon the hour of death, with an unwavering mind, having devotion and fixing the *prāṇa* between the eyebrows with the power of [the pratice] of *yoga*, one reaches the supreme [and] shining Being.

यदक्षरं वेदविदो वदन्ति
　　विशन्ति यद्यतयो वीतरागाः ।
यदिच्छन्तो ब्रह्मचर्यं चरन्ति
　　तत्ते पदं सङ्ग्रहेण प्रवक्ष्ये ॥११॥

*yadakṣaraṁ vedavido vadanti*
*viśanti yadyatayo vītarāgāḥ |*
*yadicchanto brahmacaryaṁ caranti*
*tatte padaṁ saṅgraheṇa pravakṣye ||11||*

**11.** Those that know the *Vedas* speak about this [*Brahman*] that is imperishable; the renunciants, free from desire, attain this [*Brahman*]; and those that desire this [*Brahman*] live a life of study. I shall explain to you briefly about this objective.

सर्वद्वाराणि संयम्य मनो हृदि निरुध्य च ।
मूर्ध्न्याधायात्मनः प्राणमास्थितो योगधारणाम् ॥१२॥

*sarvadvārāṇi saṁyamya mano hṛdi nirudhya ca |*
*mūrdhnyādhāyātmanaḥ prāṇamāsthito yogadhāraṇām ||12||*

**12.** Closing all the gates of the body [the sense organs], fixing the mind in the heart and the *prāṇa* at the top of the head, remaining concentrated in *yoga*,

ओमित्येकाक्षरं ब्रह्म व्याहरन्मामनुस्मरन् ।
यः प्रयाति त्यजन्देहं स याति परमां गतिम् ॥१३॥

*omityekākṣaraṁ brahma vyāharanmāmanusmaran |*
*yaḥ prayāti tyajandehaṁ sa yāti paramāṁ gatim ||13||*

**13.** pronouncing "*Oṁ*", which has one syllable [and] is [the name of] *Brahman*, [and] remembering Me, one that departs, abandoning the body, reaches the highest goal.

अनन्यचेताः सततं यो मां स्मरति नित्यशः ।
तस्याहं सुलभः पार्थ नित्ययुक्तस्य योगिनः ॥१४॥

*ananyacetāḥ satataṁ yo māṁ smarati nityaśaḥ |*
*tasyāhaṁ sulabhaḥ pārtha nityayuktasya yoginaḥ ||14||*

**14.** O *Pārtha* [*Arjuna*], I am easily reached by the *yogin* who is always disciplined [and] remembers Me with an undistracted mind.

मामुपेत्य पुनर्जन्म दुःखालयमशाश्वतम् ।
नाप्नुवन्ति महात्मानः संसिद्धिं परमां गताः ॥१५॥

*māmupetya punarjanma duḥkhālayamaśāśvatam |*
*nāpnuvanti mahātmānaḥ saṁsiddhiṁ paramāṁ gatāḥ ||15||*

**15.** Once attaining Me, the wise have no further birth, which is ephemeral [and] the cause of suffering. They reach the highest goal.

आब्रह्मभुवनाल्लोकाः पुनरावर्तिनोऽर्जुन ।
मामुपेत्य तु कौन्तेय पुनर्जन्म न विद्यते ॥१६॥

*ābrahmabhuvanāllokāḥ punarāvartino'rjuna |*
*māmupetya tu kaunteya punarjanma na vidyate ||16||*

**16.** O *Arjuna*, all worlds – even the world of *Brahmā* [the Creator] – are subject to return. Attaining Me, however, O *Kaunteya* [*Arjuna*], there is no further birth.

सहस्रयुगपर्यन्तमहर्यद्ब्रह्मणो विदुः ।
रात्रिं युगसहस्रान्तां तेऽहोरात्रविदो जनाः ॥१७॥

*sahasrayugaparyantamaharyadbrahmaṇo viduḥ |*
*rātriṁ yugasahasrāntāṁ te'horātravido janāḥ ||17||*

**17.** Those that know day and night know that [just] one day of *Brahmā* lasts one thousand *yugas* [and] the night, one thousand *yugas*.

अव्यक्ताद्व्यक्तयः सर्वाः प्रभवन्त्यहरागमे ।
रात्र्यागमे प्रलीयन्ते तत्रैवाव्यक्तसंज्ञके ॥१८॥

*avyaktādvyaktayaḥ sarvāḥ prabhavantyaharāgame |*
*rātryāgame pralīyante tatraivāvyaktasaṁjñake ||18||*

**18.** From the unmanifest, all manifestations are born at dawn. At dusk, all is dissolved there, in that which is called the unmanifest.

भूतग्रामः स एवायं भूत्वा भूत्वा प्रलीयते ।
रात्र्यागमेऽवशः पार्थ प्रभवत्यहरागमे ॥१९॥

*bhūtagrāmaḥ sa evāyaṁ bhūtvā bhūtvā pralīyate |*
*rātryāgame'vaśaḥ pārtha prabhavatyaharāgame ||19||*

**19.** This multitude of beings, having been born several times, are dissolved at dusk, O *Pārtha* [*Arjuna*], [and] appear again at dawn.

परस्तस्मात्तु भावोऽन्योऽव्यक्तोऽव्यक्तात्सनातनः ।
यः स सर्वेषु भूतेषु नश्यत्सु न विनश्यति ॥२०॥

*parastasmāttu bhāvo'nyo'vyakto'vyaktātsanātanaḥ |*
*yaḥ sa sarveṣu bhūteṣu naśyatsu na vinaśyati ||20||*

**20.** However, besides the unmanifest, there is another unmanifest Being that is eternal [and] not destroyed when all other beings are destroyed.

अव्यक्तोऽक्षर इत्युक्तस्तमाहुः परमां गतिम् ।
यं प्राप्य न निवर्तन्ते तद्धाम परमं मम ॥२१॥

*avyakto'kṣara ityuktastamāhuḥ paramāṁ gatim |*
*yaṁ prāpya na nivartante taddhāma paramaṁ mama ||21||*

**21.** The unmanifest is called Imperishable; [the *Vedas*] say that It [unmanifest and imperishable] is the highest goal. [People] do not return after reaching That which is the highest place of existence.

पुरुषः स परः पार्थ भक्त्या लभ्यस्त्वनन्यया ।
यस्यान्तःस्थानि भूतानि येन सर्वमिदं ततम् ॥२२॥

*puruṣaḥ sa paraḥ pārtha bhaktyā labhyastvananyayā |*
*yasyāntaḥsthāni bhūtāni yena sarvamidaṁ tatam ||22||*

**22.** That Supreme Being is attained by undivided devotion. [All] beings are within Him, all of this is pervaded by Him, O *Pārtha* [*Arjuna*]!

यत्र काले त्वनावृत्तिमावृत्तिं चैव योगिनः ।
प्रयाता यान्ति तं कालं वक्ष्यामि भरतर्षभ ॥२३॥

*yatra kāle tvanāvṛttimāvṛttiṁ caiva yoginaḥ |*
*prayātā yānti taṁ kālaṁ vakṣyāmi bharatarṣabha ||23||*

**23.** The *yogins* that depart go, at a certain time, either to return or not to return. I shall speak on this [specific] time, O *Bharatarṣabha* [*Arjuna*]!

अग्निर्ज्योतिरहः शुक्लः षण्मासा उत्तरायणम् ।
तत्र प्रयाता गच्छन्ति ब्रह्म ब्रह्मविदो जनाः ॥२४॥

*agnirjyotirahaḥ śuklaḥ ṣaṇmāsā uttarāyaṇam |*
*tatra prayātā gacchanti brahma brahmavido janāḥ ||24||*

**24.** Departing in that moment [governed by the deity] of fire, of light, of day, of the bright fortnight of the moon [and] of the six months of the Northern solstice, those that meditate on [*saguṇa*] *Brahman* go to *Brahman* [*brahmaloka*].

धूमो रात्रिस्तथा कृष्णः षण्मासा दक्षिणायनम् ।
तत्र चान्द्रमसं ज्योतिर्योगी प्राप्य निवर्तते ॥२५॥

*dhūmo rātristathā kṛṣṇaḥ ṣaṇmāsā dakṣiṇāyanam |*
*tatra cāndramasaṁ jyotiryogī prāpya nivartate ||25||*

**25.** [Departing] in that moment [governed by the deities] of smoke, of night, the dark fortnight of the moon, and the six months of the Southern solstice, the *yogin*, reaching the light of the moon, returns.

शुक्लकृष्णे गती ह्येते जगतः शाश्वते मते ।
एकया यात्यनावृत्तिमन्ययावर्तते पुनः ॥२६॥

*śuklakṛṣṇe gatī hyete jagataḥ śāśvate mate |*
*ekayā yātyanāvṛttimanyayāvartate punaḥ ||26||*

**26.** As one knows, these two paths of the world - *śukla*, of light; and *Kṛṣṇa*, of darkness - are considered eternal [as continuous as *saṁsāra*]. By one, [the *yogin*] goes never to return; by the other, [the *yogin*] goes and returns again.

नैते सृती पार्थ जानन्योगी मुह्यति कश्चन ।
तस्मात्सर्वेषु कालेषु योगयुक्तो भवार्जुन ॥२७॥

*naite sṛtī pārtha jānanyogī muhyati kaścana |*
*tasmātsarveṣu kāleṣu yogayukto bhavārjuna ||27||*

**27.** O *Pārtha* [*Arjuna*], knowing these two paths, no *yogin* diludes himself. Therefore, O *Arjuna*, always be one who is united in *yoga*.

वेदेषु यज्ञेषु तपःसु चैव
दानेषु यत्पुण्यफलं प्रदिष्टम् ।
अत्येति तत्सर्वमिदं विदित्वा
योगी परं स्थानमुपैति चाद्यम् ॥२८॥

*vedeṣu yajñeṣu tapaḥsu caiva*
*dāneṣu yatpuṇyaphalaṁ pradiṣṭam |*
*atyeti tatsarvamidaṁ viditvā*
*yogī paraṁ sthānamupaiti cādyam ||28||*

**28.** The *yogin*, knowing this [the answers to the questions of *Arjuna*], goes beyond any positive result of actions indicated [by the *Vedas*] regarding [the study of] *Vedas*, any [enactment of] rituals, any [practice of] austerities, and also any [offerings of] donation. And he attains the highest place that is the cause [of the entire universe].

ओं तत्सदिति श्रीमद्भगवद्गीतासूपनिषत्सु ब्रह्मविद्यायां योगशास्त्रे श्रीकृष्णार्जुनसंवादे अक्षरब्रह्मयोगो नामाष्टमोऽध्यायः ॥

*oṁ tatsaditi śrīmadbhagavadgītāsūpaniṣatsu brahmavidyāyāṁ yogaśāstre śrīkṛṣṇārjunasaṁvāde akṣarabrahmayogo nāmāṣṭamo'dhyāyaḥ ||*

*Oṁ*, this is the Truth. Thus is the eighth chapter, the subject [of which] is called "*akṣarabrahma*" [the imperishable *Brahman*], in the glorious *Bhagavadgītā*, [which is equivalent to] the *Upaniṣads*, [the subject of which is] the knowledge of *Brahman* [and] *yoga*, in the dialogue between *śrī Kṛṣṇa* and *Arjuna*.

# Chapter 9

## *King of knowledge, king of secrets*

In the previous chapter, *Śrī Kṛṣṇa* explains *upāsanā* (the meditation on *saguṇabrahman*, or *Īśvara*, which may lead to *kramamukti*) but the main objective of *Kṛṣṇa* is immediate liberation by way of self-knowledge here in this life. *Upāsanā* becomes a way of preparing the mind for the knowledge of *nirguṇabrahman*, the truth of *Īśvara* and *jīva*.

In chapter 9, the awareness of the indivisible identity between the individual and *Īśvara* is called *rājavidyā*, the king of knowledge. There are so many fields of knowledge: physics, medicine, psychology, engineering, botany, and many others. However, among all fields of knowledge, one has the utmost importance: the knowledge of the Self.

The awareness of the objects in the universe and the subsequent relationship between the individual and these objects depends on the vision that one has of oneself. It is for this reason that self-knowledge is paramount, and thus called the king of all other forms of knowledge.

An erroneous or confused vision of oneself will affect one's relationship with the world. Therefore, the *Vedas* say that self-knowledge is the objective of human life: to know oneself as eternal and free of limitation completely changes one's relationship with the world around. The knowledge of the Self is the essential nature of the subject, which is *Brahman*. For example, there is gold and ornaments made of gold, such as a ring, a necklace, or a bracelet. Before the creation of such ornaments, there was gold, after the destruction of the same ornaments, there will still be gold. Along the way, there are forms we call ring, necklace, and bracelet: these forms have a name (*nāma rūpa*); they are creation. They are not real; real is unchanging - real is the gold. Forms do not exist by themselves; hence they are called *mithyā*: only apparently real. That which is only apparently real naturally depends on that which is real -*satya* - which in this case is gold. *Brahman* is *satya*, and the universe is *mithyā*, which is created as if by magic!

The Consciousness that is always present is the essential truth of the individual, the universe, and *Īśvara*.

This knowledge is also called *rājaguhya*, the great secret, because it is so difficult to comprehend. Even when taught, it may remain unknown.

*Brahman*, the cause of all existence, is not subject to any kind of transformation, whatsoever, in order to become the universe. Were He to transform, his absolute and limitless nature would cease to exist. Therefore, it is said that *Brahman* is real, while the universe is not - it is only apparently real. In fact, it is none other than That which is real, or *Brahman*, that actually exists.

In verses 4 and 5, *Śrī Kṛṣṇa* says that all that exists is pervaded by Consciousness, That which is real. Since this concept is very difficult to comprehend, *Śrī Kṛṣṇa* says that, although one does not understand the teaching, there is still something that can be done to facilitate its comprehension. The main obstacles to this knowledge are the tastes and aversions that imprison the mind. One should perform actions as an offering to *Īśvara* and prepare for the result of the action - come what may. By recognizing *Īśvara* as That which governs action - and hence, That which "gives" the result of such action - it becomes much easier to deal with tastes and aversions. With this attitude and the desire to understand *Īśvara*, all one's *yoga* and *kṣema* (the desire to acquire and maintain) will be satisfied, as mentioned in verse 22.

This attitude to receive whatever may come, since it comes from *Īśvara*, which is the Order which governs actions and results, neutralizes the power of the tastes and aversions, thereby freeing the mind for the comprehension of the indivisible identity that is between *jīva* and *Īśvara*. It is for this reason that this knowledge is called *rājavidyā*, the king of knowledge, or *rājaguhya*, the king of secrets, since the individual is hidden from himself. Despite all instruction, this concept is very difficult to comprehend. The secret is that you are already that which you wish to be. That is why the instruction of *Vedānta* may be summarized in *tat tvam asi*, "You are *Īśvara*".

It is paramount to point out that whenever *Śrī Kṛṣṇa* says "I" or "Me", as in verses 7 and 16, among so many others, he is identifying himself as *Īśvara*. Therefore, we must read both "I" and "Me" as "*Īśvara*".

## Summary of the verses

Verses 1 to 3: In the first three verses, *Kṛṣṇa* introduces the subject of the knowledge of *Īśvara*, which is called *jñāna* and is accompanied by the word *vijñāna*, intimate knowledge that is clear, since there is no difference between *Īśvara* and *jīva*. On this understanding, there is an immediate comprehension of the Self. This knowledge is called the king of knowledge or the king of secrets. It is a secret, because even by listening, it will not be understood unless the listener has some special qualifications, such as a basic trust in this body of knowledge and the person teaching it, the desire to learn, and mental preparedness.

Verses 4 to 5: These verses reveal the nature of *Īśvara* with the paradoxical language that is typical of the *Upaniṣads*. He pervades the entire universe, but does not depend on the universe, but in reality there is no universe separate from Him: the universe is not separate from *Īśvara*, but, at the same time, due to the power of *māyā*, there appears to be a separate universe.

Verse 6: In order to better explain the last two verses, *Kṛṣṇa* gives us an example.

Verses 7 to 10: On the universe, *Śrī Kṛṣṇa* says that it is actually He - who is *Īśvara* - that is the basis of the three moments of any created object: *sṛṣṭi*, the creation; *sthiti*, its maintenance; and *laya*, its dissolution. The power of *Īśvara*, which is his *Prakṛti*, is inseparable from Him and is responsible for the cycles of creation, which are in constant movement. Although *Īśvara* is responsible for the universe and his movement is constant, He is not involved in action: He neither performs actions, nor does He receive the result of action.

Verses 11 and 12: However, due to ignorance and its consequence, which is illusion, people do not know the nature of *Īśvara*. They think that He is creator, responsible for the act of creation, and further conclude that the *Ātman*, the Self, is the agent of action. People feel guilty for their acts and desire to produce specific results via actions, by which, out of delusion, they think such acquistions will make them happy.

It is due to this ignorance and illusion that beings are imprisoned in *saṁsāra*.

Ignorance is universal, but there are those that do not even question that which they seek, or their desires. They simply remain under this illusion and live a life in vain.

Verses 13 and 14: However, there are those that carry a discriminating attitude towards reality; they discover this most basic of ignorance and seek the knowledge of *Īśvara*, which is the same as self-knowledge. They seek *Īśvara* to be freed from this prison, and this search becomes a commitment that is expressed throughout their entire life. When one discovers the value for the knowledge of *Īśvara*, there is no effort in occupying one's mind with this search; what has value for one person becomes an object of love - and the mind will naturally run in the direction of the object of love whenever possible.

Verse 15: There are different ways that people seek *Īśvara*: as something singular, identical to themselves, or as something apart from them, which may exist in one of many forms.

Verses 16 to 19: In these verses, *Īśvara* is described as the creator, the potential for creation and all that is created; it is also described as limitless - the basic and immutable truth.

Verses 20 to 22: *Śrī Kṛṣṇa* covers *kāmakāma*, one who is ignorant of reality and seeks various objects of desire. In order to reach them, this person acts and performs Vedic rituals, and may even reach other worlds, such as a type of heaven, *svargaloka*, described in the *Vedas*. However, just actions are limited, so are their results: thus this person returns to this world and desires yet more objects. On the other hand, all those free from the objects of desire, *niṣkāma*, seeking the knowledge of *Īśvara*, address only Him. Such people are given - as the result of their actions - *yoga* and *kṣema*, all that they seek and protect. Verse 22 refers to the wise, who desire nothing, as well as *mumukṣu*, who desire a comprehension of *Īśvara*. Both are protected. This verse marks the exact middle of the *Bhagavadgītā*.

Verses 23 to 29: *Kṛṣṇa* says that all those devout to *devatās* - the different aspects of *Īśvara* - are in fact devoted to *Īśvara*. All acts of devotion go to Him, despite the ignorance of the devout regarding Him. Therefore, each and every one receives that which they desire by means of their act of devotion. Anything can be offered, most important is the attitude behind such offering.

One who is devout is a *karmayogin*, or a *sannyāsin*, an ascetic, and all one's action should be mentally offered to *Īśvara*. That said, due to the attitude behind such offering, the devout attain *antaḥkaraṇa-śuddhi*, the preparation of the mind. Tastes and aversions become second place, and *dharma*, or righteous action and that which must be done, becomes the first priority. The devout understand that *dharma* is *Īśvara* and makes every effort possible for liberation, which is nothing more than their identity as *Īśvara*. Offering an action to *Īśvara* is to act according to *dharma*, which in fact has two aspects: to do that which must be done, and to act according to universal values. The devout who act accordingly will go to *Īśvara*, who is accessible to all; however, it is the devout that desire Him, seek Him and reach Him.

Verses 30 to 34: In the following verses, the greatness of devotion is emphasized. The declaration that even a person with neither the qualifications for knowledge, nor *karmayoga* – although devout – may reach *Īśvara*, seems a bit exaggerated. What is in fact meant by such a declaration is that, by way of devotion, a person will reach the means for knowledge. *Kṛṣṇa* says that the devout are never destroyed. This declaration of *Śrī Kṛṣṇa* is well-known. The devout are those that recognize the existence of *Īśvara* and desire the awareness of Him; even if, for any reason, their conduct has been inappropriate, devotion will transform this conduct in no time, aligning their minds with *dharma*, and finally reaching the peace that is their essential nature – the highest of objectives.

## अथ नवमोऽध्यायः

***atha navamo'dhyāyaḥ***

**Ninth chapter**

श्रीभगवानुवाच
इदं तु ते गुह्यतमं प्रवक्ष्याम्यनसूयवे ।
ज्ञानं विज्ञानसहितं यज्ज्ञात्वा मोक्ष्यसेऽशुभात् ॥१॥

*śrībhagavānuvāca*
*idaṁ tu te guhyatamaṁ pravakṣyāmyanasūyave |*
*jñānaṁ vijñānasahitaṁ yajjñātvā mokṣyase'śubhāt ||1||*

**1.** The Lord [*Kṛṣṇa*] spoke:
— Thus I shall tell you, who is free from jealousy, about the greatest of all secrets. This is knowledge together with wisdom. Acquiring this knowledge, you shall be free from suffering.

राजविद्या राजगुह्यं पवित्रमिदमुत्तमम् ।
प्रत्यक्षावगमं धर्म्यं सुसुखं कर्तुमव्ययम् ॥२॥

*rājavidyā rājaguhyaṁ pavitramidamuttamam |*
*pratyakṣāvagamaṁ dharmyaṁ susukhaṁ kartumavyayam ||2||*

**2.** This is the king of knowledge, the king of secrets, the greatest of purifiers. That which is perceived directly, which is not contrary to *dharma*, easily reached [and] imperishable.

अश्रद्दधानाः पुरुषा धर्मस्यास्य परन्तप ।
अप्राप्य मां निवर्तन्ते मृत्युसंसारवर्त्मनि ॥३॥

*aśraddadhānāḥ puruṣā dharmasyāsya parantapa |*
*aprāpya māṁ nivartante mṛtyusaṁsāravartmani ||3||*

**3.** Those who do not trust this *dharma* [teaching], O *Parantapa* [*Arjuna*], not reaching Me, most certainly stay in *saṁsāra*, where there is death.

मया ततमिदं सर्वं जगदव्यक्तमूर्तिना ।
मत्स्थानि सर्वभूतानि न चाहं तेष्ववस्थितः ॥४॥

*mayā tatamidaṁ sarvaṁ jagadavyaktamūrtinā |*
*matsthāni sarvabhūtāni na cāhaṁ teṣvavasthitaḥ ||4||*

**4.** The entire universe is pervaded by Me, by [my] unmanifest form. All beings are in Me [but] I am not in them.

न च मत्स्थानि भूतानि पश्य मे योगमैश्वरम् ।
भूतभृन्न च भूतस्थो ममात्मा भूतभावनः ॥५॥

*na ca matsthāni bhūtāni paśya me yogamaiśvaram |*
*bhūtabhṛnna ca bhūtastho mamātmā bhūtabhāvanaḥ ||5||*

**5.** Yet those beings are not in Me. See my divine *yoga* [the power of *Īśvara*]. I myself am the cause of [all] beings and that which sustains all beings, [but] I am not in them.

यथाकाशस्थितो नित्यं वायुः सर्वत्रगो महान् ।
तथा सर्वाणि भूतानि मत्स्थानीत्युपधारय ॥६॥

*yathākāśasthito nityaṁ vāyuḥ sarvatrago mahān |*
*tathā sarvāṇi bhūtāni matsthānītyupadhāraya ||6||*

**6.** Just like the vast wind that everywhere goes, which is always in space, know that all beings are in Me.

सर्वभूतानि कौन्तेय प्रकृतिं यान्ति मामिकम् ।
कल्पक्षये पुनस्तानि कल्पादौ विसृजाम्यहम् ॥७॥

*sarvabhūtāni kaunteya prakṛtiṁ yānti māmikam |*
*kalpakṣaye punastāni kalpādau visṛjāmyaham ||7||*

**7.** O *Kaunteya* [*Arjuna*], at the end of the cycle of creation, all beings go to my *Prakṛti*. [And] at the beginning of the [next] cycle of creation, I shall create them again.

प्रकृतिं स्वामवष्टभ्य विसृजामि पुनः पुनः ।
भूतग्राममिमं कृत्स्नमवशं प्रकृतेर्वशात् ॥८॥

*prakṛtiṁ svāmavaṣṭabhya visṛjāmi punaḥ punaḥ |*
*bhūtagrāmamimaṁ kṛtsnamavaśaṁ prakṛtervaśāt ||8||*

**8.** Maintaining my *Prakṛti* under control, I create all this group of beings again and again, without any will on my part, [but] due to the will of *Prakṛti*.

न च मां तानि कर्माणि निबध्नन्ति धनञ्जय ।
उदासीनवदासीनमसक्तं तेषु कर्मसु ॥९॥

*na ca māṁ tāni karmāṇi nibadhnanti dhanañjaya |*
*udāsīnavadāsīnamasaktaṁ teṣu karmasu ||9||*

**9.** However these actions do not imprison Me, O *Dhanañjaya* [*Arjuna*], since I remain as a bystander, free from attachment to these actions.

मयाध्यक्षेण प्रकृतिः सूयते सचराचरम् ।
हेतुनानेन कौन्तेय जगद्विपरिवर्तते ॥१०॥

*mayādhyakṣeṇa prakṛtiḥ sūyate sacarācaram |*
*hetunānena kaunteya jagadviparivartate ||10||*

**10.** Presided by Me, *Prakṛti* creates all that moves and all that is inert. For this reason, O *Kaunteya* [*Arjuna*], the world turns.

अवजानन्ति मां मूढा मानुषीं तनुमाश्रितम् ।
परं भावमजानन्तो मम भूतमहेश्वरम् ॥११॥

*avajānanti māṁ mūḍhā mānuṣīṁ tanumāśritam |*
*paraṁ bhāvamajānanto mama bhūtamaheśvaram ||11||*

**11.** The deluded, ignoring my superior nature [as] the Lord of [all] beings, are indifferent to Me, [although] I am in the human body.

मोघाशा मोघकर्माणो मोघज्ञाना विचेतसः ।
राक्षसीमासुरीं चैव प्रकृतिं मोहिनीं श्रिताः ॥१२॥

*moghāśā moghakarmāṇo moghajñānā vicetasaḥ |*
*rākṣasīmāsurīṁ caiva prakṛtiṁ mohinīṁ śritāḥ ||12||*

**12.** Those without discernment, whose hopes are futile, whose actions are unproductive [and] whose knowledge is useless, submit themselves to the nature of illusion of the *rākṣasas* and *asuras* [those of demonic nature].

महात्मानस्तु मां पार्थ दैवीं प्रकृतिमाश्रिताः ।
भजन्त्यनन्यमनसो ज्ञात्वा भूतादिमव्ययम् ॥१३॥

*mahātmānastu māṁ pārtha daivīṁ prakṛtimāśritāḥ |*
*bhajantyananyamanaso jñātvā bhūtādimavyayam ||13||*

**13.** However, O *Pārtha* [*Arjuna*], those whose mind is discriminating submit themselves to the nature of the *devas* [and], knowing Me [as the] imperishable cause of all beings, they seek Me with the mind focused on Me alone.

सततं कीर्तयन्तो मां यतन्तश्च दृढव्रताः ।
नमस्यन्तश्च मां भक्त्या नित्ययुक्ता उपासते ॥१४॥

*satataṁ kīrtayanto māṁ yatantaśca dṛḍhavratāḥ |*
*namasyantaśca māṁ bhaktyā nityayuktā upāsate ||14||*

**14.** Those that always behold my glories, those that make a concerted effort, those that surrender to Me with devotion and [are] always disciplined, seek Me.

ज्ञानयज्ञेन चाप्यन्ये यजन्तो मामुपासते ।
एकत्वेन पृथक्त्वेन बहुधा विश्वतोमुखम् ॥१५॥

*jñānayajñena cāpyanye yajanto māmupāsate |*
*ekatvena pṛthaktvena bahudhā viśvatomukham ||15||*

**15.** And there are others that revere [Me] by way of ritual of knowledge. They seek Me in various ways: as identical [to them], as different [from them], [or] as That of many forms.

अहं क्रतुरहं यज्ञः स्वधाहमहमौषधम् ।
मन्त्रोऽहमहमेवाज्यमहमग्निरहं हुतम् ॥१६॥

*ahaṁ kraturahaṁ yajñaḥ svadhāhamahamauṣadham |*
*mantro'hamahamevājyamahamagnirahaṁ hutam ||16||*

**16.** I am the Vedic rituals. I am the rituals prescribed by *smṛti*. I am the food offered to ancestors. I am the food [for all beings]. I am the *mantra*. I am the ghee [that is sacrificed]. I am the fire. I am the sacrifice.

पिताहमस्य जगतो माता धाता पितामहः ।
वेद्यं पवित्रमोङ्कार ऋक्साम यजुरेव च ॥१७॥

*pitāhamasya jagato mātā dhātā pitāmahaḥ |*
*vedyaṁ pavitramoṅkāra ṛksāma yajureva ca ||17||*

**17.** I am the father, the mother, the grandfather [and] the sustainer of this creation. I am also That which must be known, the purifier, the syllable *Oṁ*. I am *Ṛk Veda*, the *Sāma Veda*, the *Yajur Veda*.

गतिर्भर्ता प्रभुः साक्षी निवासः शरणम् सुहृत् ।
प्रभवः प्रलयः स्थानं निधानं बीजमव्ययम् ॥१८॥

*gatirbhartā prabhuḥ sākṣī nivāsaḥ śaraṇam suhṛt |*
*prabhavaḥ pralayaḥ sthānaṁ nidhānaṁ bījamavyayam ||18||*

**18.** I am the final objective. I am That which sustains everything. I am the Lord. I am the witness. I am the home. I am protection. I am the friend. I am the creation, the dissolution [and] the foundation. I am the trove [of all that will be lived in the future and]. I am the imperishable seed.

तपाम्यहमहं वर्षं निगृह्णाम्युत्सृजामि च ।
अमृतं चैव मृत्युश्च सदसच्चाहमर्जुन ॥१९॥

*tapāmyahamahaṁ varṣaṁ nigṛhṇamyutsṛjāmi ca |*
*amṛtaṁ caiva mṛtyuśca sadasaccāhamarjuna ||19||*

**19.** I illuminate and I heat. I withhold and send rain. I am immortality and also death. I am the manifest and the unmanifest, O *Arjuna*.

त्रैविद्या मां सोमपाः पूतपापा
यज्ञैरिष्ट्वा स्वर्गतिं प्रार्थयन्ते ।
ते पुण्यमासाद्य सुरेन्द्रलोकम्-
अश्नन्ति दिव्यान्दिवि देवभोगान् ॥२०॥

*traividyā māṁ somapāḥ pūtapāpā*
*yajñairiṣṭvā svargatiṁ prārthayante |*
*te puṇyamāsādya surendralokam*
*aśnanti divyāndivi devabhogān ||20||*

**20.** Those who know the three *Vedas*, those that drink *soma* [as part of the Vedic ritual], those who are purified from the negative results of their actions, having performed rituals, ask to go to *svarga* [heaven]. Once acquiring the positive effects of their actions, [and therefore] the world of *Indra*, they enjoy heaven and the celestial pleasures of celestial beings.

ते तं भुक्त्वा स्वर्गलोकं विशालं
क्षीणे पुण्ये मर्त्यलोकं विशन्ति ।
एवं त्रयीधर्ममनुप्रपन्नाः
गतागतं कामकामा लभन्ते ॥२१॥

*te taṁ bhuktvā svargalokaṁ viśālaṁ*
*kṣīṇe puṇye martyalokaṁ viśanti |*
*evaṁ trayīdharmamanuprapannāḥ*
*gatāgataṁ kāmakāmā labhante ||21||*

**21.** Once enjoying the vast *svargaloka* [heaven], once [their] merit ends, they [re]enter the world of mortals. Thus, desirous of various objects, following the rituals prescribed in the three *Vedas*, they reach the state of going and coming.

अनन्याश्चिन्तयन्तो मां ये जनाः पर्युपासते ।
तेषां नित्याभियुक्तानां योगक्षेमं वहाम्यहम् ॥२२॥

*ananyāścintayanto māṁ ye janāḥ paryupāsate |*
*teṣāṁ nityābhiyuktānāṁ yogakṣemaṁ vahāmyaham ||22||*

**22.** Those people who think of Me as not being different [from them], attain Me. For those united with Me, I take care of what they want to acquire (*yoga*) and protect (*kṣema*).

येऽप्यन्यदेवताभक्ता यजन्ते श्रद्धयान्विताः ।
तेऽपि मामेव कौन्तेय यजन्त्यविधिपूर्वकम् ॥२३॥

*ye'pyanyadevatābhaktā yajante śraddhayānvitāḥ |*
*te'pi māmeva kaunteya yajantyavidhipūrvakam ||23||*

**23.** Even those who worship other gods [and] revere them with faith, in fact revere Me in ignorance, O *Kaunteya* [*Arjuna*].

अहं हि सर्वयज्ञानां भोक्ता च प्रभुरेव च ।
न तु मामभिजानन्ति तत्त्वेनातश्च्यवन्ति ते ॥२४॥

*ahaṁ hi sarvayajñānāṁ bhoktā ca prabhureva ca |*
*na tu māmabhijānanti tattvenātaścyavanti te ||24||*

**24.** For I am the enjoyer and Lord of all the rituals, although they in fact do not know Me. Hence, they fail.

यान्ति देवव्रता देवान्पितॄन्यान्ति पितृव्रताः ।
भूतानि यान्ति भूतेज्या यान्ति मद्याजिनोऽपि माम् ॥२५॥

*yānti devavratā devānpitṝnyānti pitṛvratāḥ |*
*bhūtāni yānti bhūtejyā yānti madyājino'pi mām ||25||*

**25.** Those who worship gods go to [those] gods. Those who worship ancestors go to [their] ancestors. Those who worship spirits go to [those] spirits. And those who worship Me come to Me.

पत्रं पुष्पं फलं तोयं यो मे भक्त्या प्रयच्छति ।
तदहं भक्त्युपहृतमश्नामि प्रयतात्मनः ॥२६॥

*patraṁ puṣpaṁ phalaṁ toyaṁ yo me bhaktyā prayacchati |*
*tadahaṁ bhaktyupahṛtamaśnāmi prayatātmanaḥ ||26||*

**26.** [If] someone offers me, with devotion, a leaf, a flower, a fruit [or] water, I receive that which has been given with devotion by one who has a purified mind.

यत्करोषि यदश्नासि यज्जुहोषि ददासि यत् ।
यत्तपस्यसि कौन्तेय तत्कुरुष्व मदर्पणम् ॥२७॥

*yatkaroṣi yadaśnāsi yajjuhoṣi dadāsi yat |*
*yattapasyasi kaunteya tatkuruṣva madarpaṇam ||27||*

**27.** Whatever you sacrifice, whatever you do, whatever you eat, whatever you sacrifice in a ritual [or] as a donation, O son of *Kuntī* [*Arjuna*], do it as an offering to Me.

शुभाशुभफलैरेवं मोक्ष्यसे कर्मबन्धनैः ।
सन्न्यासयोगयुक्तात्मा विमुक्तो मामुपैष्यसि ॥२८॥

*śubhāśubhaphalairevaṁ mokṣyase karmabandhanaiḥ |*
*sannyāsayogayuktātmā vimukto māmupaiṣyasi ||28||*

**28.** You will thereby be liberated by the bonds of actions that produce the results desired and undesired. With the mind surrendered to *sannyāsa* and *karmayoga*, you are liberated [and] shall come to Me.

समोऽहं सर्वभूतेषु न मे द्वेष्योऽस्ति न प्रियः ।
ये भजन्ति तु मां भक्त्या मयि ते तेषु चाप्यहम् ॥२९॥

*samo'haṁ sarvabhūteṣu na me dveṣyo'sti na priyaḥ |*
*ye bhajanti tu māṁ bhaktyā mayi te teṣu cāpyaham ||29||*

**29.** I am the same in all beings. There is no one either hated or loved more [than another] by Me. However, for those that seek Me with devotion, they are in Me, and I am also in them.

अपि चेत्सुदुराचारो भजते मामनन्यभाक् ।
साधुरेव स मन्तव्यः सम्यग्व्यवसितो हि सः ॥३०॥

*api cetsudurācāro bhajate māmananyabhāk |*
*sādhureva sa mantavyaḥ samyagvyavasito hi saḥ ||30||*

**30.** [Someone who] worships Me, seeking nothing else, is deemed a righteous person - even if someone of bad conduct - since this person possesses clear knowledge.

क्षिप्रं भवति धर्मात्मा शश्वच्छान्तिं निगच्छति ।
कौन्तेय प्रतिजानीहि न मे भक्तः प्रणश्यति ॥३१॥

*kṣipraṁ bhavati dharmātmā śaśvacchāntiṁ nigacchati |*
*kaunteya pratijānīhi na me bhaktaḥ praṇaśyati ||31||*

**31.** He quickly becomes righteous [and] attains eternal peace. O *Kaunteya* [*Arjuna*], know that no devotee of mine is [ever] destroyed.

मां हि पार्थ व्यपाश्रित्य येऽपि स्युः पापयोनयः ।
स्त्रियो वैश्यास्तथा शुद्रास्तेऽपि यान्ति परां गतिम् ॥३२॥

*māṁ hi pārtha vyapāśritya ye'pi syuḥ pāpayonayaḥ |*
*striyo vaiśyāstathā śudrāste'pi yānti parāṁ gatim ||32||*

**32.** O *Pārtha* [*Arjuna*], seeking refuge in Me, even women, *vaiśyas*, *śudras*, and also those that are born [primarily from] *pāpa* [the negative result of action], attain the highest objective[7].

---

7 This verse often generates misunderstanding due what is apparently blatant prejudice. This verse has often been translated as "O *Pārtha* [*Arjuna*], even *pāpayonayaḥ* [those that are born primarily from *pāpa*, the negative result of actions], such as women, the *vaiśyas* and the *śudras*, seeking refuge in Me, attain the highest objective." With this translation, it seems that criminals, women and people of these two social divisions have been disdainfully grouped together. My guru Swami Dayananda Saraswati does not agree with this common translation: he explains that the word *tathā* ("and also") brings another meaning to the verse by separating women, *vaiśyas* and *śudras* from *pāpayonayaḥ*. It is this translation from Swamiji we use in this book. Nevertheless, the question still remains as to why women and these two castes have even been specified. We can only offer the following context to explain such a citation: In the case of women, the feminine mind has often been associated as being more emotional than rational; *vaiśya* and *śudra* are two of the four Vedic social divisions: as the caste responsible for commerce, *vaiśyas* have been seen as naturally and appropriately attached to objects as part of their role in life; It has been said that it is natural for *śudras* to work by receiving orders, and preferring to receive orders than to take decisions, this group was seen as having a natural tendency not to practice analysis. Regardless of such contextualization, it is our interpretation that emotion, attachment, and lack of analysis have been identified as obstacles to the highest objective.

किं पुनर्ब्राह्मणाः पुण्या भक्ता राजर्षयस्तथा ।
अनित्यमसुखं लोकमिमं प्राप्य भजस्व माम् ॥३३॥

*kiṁ punarbrāhmaṇāḥ puṇyā bhaktā rājarṣayastathā |*
*anityamasukhaṁ lokamimaṁ prāpya bhajasva mām ||33||*

**33.** And what can be said of the *brāhmaṇas* [those of a discriminating and clear mind] who have *puṇya* [the positive result of actions] as the cause of their birth, and also of the wise kings? Having attained this perishable and unhappy world, devote yourself to Me.

मन्मना भव मद्भक्तो मद्याजी मां नमस्कुरु ।
मामेवैष्यसि युक्त्वैवमात्मानं मत्परायणः ॥३४॥

*manmanā bhava madbhakto madyājī māṁ namaskuru |*
*māmevaiṣyasi yuktvaivamātmānaṁ matparāyaṇaḥ ||34||*

**34.** Be one whose mind is committed to Me, be devout to Me, be one who offers [prayers and rituals] to Me, who surrenders to Me. Thusly disciplined, holding Me as the objective, you shall certainly reach Me, the Self [of all beings].

ओं तत्सदिति श्रीमद्भगवद्गीतासूपनिषत्सु ब्रह्मविद्यायां योगशास्त्रे श्रीकृष्णार्जुनसंवादे राजविद्याराजगुह्ययोगो नाम नवमोऽध्यायः॥

*oṁ tatsaditi śrīmadbhagavadgītāsūpaniṣatsu brahmavidyāyāṁ yogaśāstre śrīkṛṣṇārjunasaṁvāde rājavidyārājaguhyayogo nāma navamo'dhyāyaḥ ||*

*Oṁ*, this is the Truth. Thus is the ninth chapter, the subject [of which] is called the "*rājavidyārājaguhya*" [the king of knowledge, the king of secrets], in the glorious *Bhagavadgītā*, [which is equivalent to] the *Upaniṣads*, [the subject of which is] the knowledge of *Brahman* [and] *yoga*, in the dialogue between *śrī Kṛṣṇa* and *Arjuna*.

# Chapter 10

## *The glories*

In this chapter, *Śrī Kṛṣṇa* identifies himself as *Īśvara* and says that all that can be found in the universe belongs to Him, since He is the material cause of creation. All glory and greatness belongs to Him. Thus, this chapter is called *vibhūti*, the glories of *Īśvara*.

Although individuals believe that they possess objects - believing themselves to be the author or creator of this or that, of something different or original, of an idea or object - all the wonders in wonders in this universe that enchant people really belong to Him. The concept of "I" and "me", *ahaṅkāra* and *mamakāra*, is just an illusion. Nothing in this universe was completely created by anyone; rather, something may have indeed been organized differently by an individual, within the possibilities already inherent in the universe, which is *Īśvara*. Everything is *Īśvara* and belongs to Him. The conclusion that "I invented" is nothing more than a partial and illusory vision. *Īśvara* is the cause, the manifestation and the possibilities, including the body, mind, and intellect of the individual.

*Arjuna* wants to know how he may behold *Īśvara*, and *Kṛṣṇa* says that *Īśvara* may be seen in the entire universe, particularly where there is something wondrous. When beholding beauty, both *jīva* and *Īśvara* become one, because beholding beauty dissolves the ego - momentarily - and the individual sees himself as part of that experience and finds himself in a moment without any desires, completely satisfied once other cravings vanish.

He says "I am the wind that blows, the sun that shines,

the wisdom of the wise, the power of the mighty". All glory belongs to *Īśvara*. And when a person discovers that everything belongs to the cosmic being and comes from Him, the person's mind transforms. The person understands that there is an Order that governs the universe. If there is suffering, there is also a way to deal with it. There is always a solution for any situation, since there is an Order that does not err.

By comprehending *Īśvara* this way, there is an automatic relaxation of the mind. This relaxation gives room for questioning and the search for liberation from limitation.

## Summary of the verses

Verses 1 to 3: Awareness of the glory of *Īśvara* is not accessible for just anyone; one who acquires it is free from all suffering.

Verses 4 to 7: The physical and subtle universe is presented as being born of *Īśvara*. By recognizing the fact that everything belongs to Him, the concepts of "I" and "me", *ahaṅkāra* and *mamakāra*, regarding the universe, diminish.

With a better understanding of the nature of *Īśvara*, it becomes possible to understand the phrase from *Upaniṣad* "I am *Brahman*" and comprehend that all qualities belong to *Īśvara*, although manifested in different measures by people and objects. Thus, there will be no more room for jealousy, competition, pride, or the feeling of inferiority, since everything pertains to Him.

Verse 8: The wise that clearly know reality attain an identity with *Īśvara*.

Verses 9 to 11: The wise are complete with the vision of *Īśvara*; however, the devout who have some knowledge of *Īśvara* also share their knowledge with others as they study and dedicate their entire lives to worshiping *Īśvara*. Due to this dedication, those who are devout to *saguṇabrahman*, which is *Īśvara*, attain the means for the final knowledge.

Verses 12 to 18: *Arjuna* shows that he has acquired some understanding of everything he has just heard. He knows that he must prepare the mind in order to behold *Īśvara*, and *upāsanā*, which is the meditation on Him, is the best way to purify the mind. With this perspective, the *jīva* is not separate from *Īśvara*, and the *jīvatva*, the state of being *jīva*, is seen as only apparent.

*Arjuna* asks *Kṛṣṇa* to explain in detail the expression and glories of *Īśvara*.

Verses 19 to 42: In these verses, *Śrī Kṛṣṇa* describes his glories. As there are many and it is impossible to describe them all, the most important ones are mentioned. To begin with, *Kṛṣṇa* says that to know *Īśvara* is to know *Ātman* and all glory belongs to *Ātman*! Each object described becomes an object of meditation on *Īśvara*. Finally, in verse 39, *Kṛṣṇa* states that He is the material cause of all beings, and that there is nothing mobile or immobile, conscious or inert that is separate from Him. Anything of any greatness, of value or any power is an expression of Him and part of the glory of *Īśvara*. It is for this reason that He is called *bhagavat*, he who possesses wealth, *bhagas*. There are six *bhagas*: knowledge, wealth, supremacy, power, fame and detachment.

All the greatness of *Īśvara* is mentioned for the meditation on Him – and not to define Him – since there are countless unmentioned aspects, but as they form part of creation, they also naturally belong to *Īśvara*.

All qualities of greatness are motives for the pride and envy of *jīva*, and thus, such qualities should be understood as only pertaining to *Īśvara* and none other. Pride and envy are caused by illusion and confusion. Everything that is only belongs to *Īśvara*; the entire universe is part of His infinite greatness.

# अथ दशमोऽध्यायः

***atha daśamo'dhyāyaḥ***

**TENTH CHAPTER**

श्रीभगवानुवाच
भूय एव महाबाहो शृणु मे परमं वचः ।
यत्तेऽहं प्रीयमाणाय वक्ष्यामि हितकाम्यया ॥१॥

*śrībhagavānuvāca*
*bhūya eva mahābāho śṛṇu me paramaṁ vacaḥ |*
*yatte'haṁ prīyamāṇāya vakṣyāmi hitakāmyayā ||1||*

**1.** The Lord [*Kṛṣṇa*] spoke:
— Once again, O *Mahābāhu* [*Arjuna*], hear my word on that which is Highest, which I, wishing your well-being, shall tell you, who delights [in this knowledge].

न मे विदुः सुरगणाः प्रभवं न महर्षयः ।
अहमादिर्हि देवानां महर्षीणां च सर्वशः ॥२॥

*na me viduḥ suragaṇāḥ prabhavaṁ na maharṣayaḥ |*
*ahamādirhi devānāṁ maharṣīṇāṁ ca sarvaśaḥ ||2||*

**2.** Neither the gods nor the great sages know my origin, since I am the cause of all gods and the wise.

योमामजमनादिं च वेत्ति लोकमहेश्वरम् ।
असंमूढः स मर्त्येषु सर्वपापैः प्रमुच्यते ॥३॥

*yo māmajamanādiṁ ca vetti lokamaheśvaram |*
*asaṁmūḍhaḥ sa martyeṣu sarvapāpaiḥ pramucyate ||3||*

**3.** Having dispelled illusion, one who knows Me as not-born, with no beginning, and the great Lord of the universe, is freed from all *pāpa* [the negative effect of actions] among mortals.

बुद्धिर्ज्ञानमसंमोहः क्षमा सत्यं दमः शमः ।
सुखं दुःखं भवोऽभावो भयं चाभयमेव च ॥४॥
अहिंसा समता तुष्टिस्तपो दानं यशोऽयशः ।
भवन्ति भावा भूतानां मत्त एव पृथग्विधाः ॥५॥

*buddhirjñānamasaṁmohaḥ kṣamā satyaṁ damaḥ śamaḥ |*
*sukhaṁ duḥkhaṁ bhavo'bhāvo bhayaṁ cābhayameva ca ||4||*
*ahiṁsā samatā tuṣṭistapo dānaṁ yaśo'yaśaḥ |*
*bhavanti bhāvā bhūtānāṁ matta eva pṛthagvidhāḥ ||5||*

**4/5.** Intellect, knowledge, the absence of illusion, patience, truth, discipline of the organs of perception and action, discipline of the mind, happiness, dissatisfaction, birth, destruction, fear, fearlessness, non-violence, equanimity, satisfaction, asceticism, generosity, fame, disrepute, [all] these different types of expressions of beings come from Me alone.

महर्षयः सप्त पूर्वे चत्वारो मनवस्तथा ।
मद्भावा मानसा जाता येषां लोक इमाः प्रजाः ॥६॥

*maharṣayaḥ sapta pūrve catvāro manavastathā |*
*madbhāvā mānasā jātā yeṣāṁ loka imāḥ prajāḥ ||6||*

**6.** The seven great sages of the past, as well as the four *Manus*, all of whom are of my nature, were born of my mind, and from them were born the beings of this world.

एतां विभूतिं योगं च मम यो वेत्ति तत्त्वतः ।
सोऽविकम्पेन योगेन युज्यते नात्र संशयः ॥७॥

*etāṁ vibhūtiṁ yogaṁ ca mama yo vetti tattvataḥ |*
*so'vikampena yogena yujyate nātra saṁśayaḥ ||7||*

**7.** One who truly knows my glory and power is blessed with unwavering knowledge - of this there is no doubt.

अहं सर्वस्य प्रभवो मत्तः सर्वं प्रवर्तते ।
इति मत्वा भजन्ते मां बुधा भावसमन्विताः ॥८॥

*ahaṁ sarvasya prabhavo mattaḥ sarvaṁ pravartate |*
*iti matvā bhajante māṁ budhā bhāvasamanvitāḥ ||8||*

**8.** "I am the origin of everything; Everything manifests from Me", thusly aware [and] having devotion, the wise reach Me.

मच्चित्ता मद्गतप्राणा बोधयन्तः परस्परम् ।
कथयन्तश्च मां नित्यं तुष्यन्ति च रमन्ति च ॥९॥

*maccittā madgataprāṇā bodhayantaḥ parasparam |*
*kathayantaśca māṁ nityaṁ tuṣyanti ca ramanti ca ||9||*

**9.** Those who are mindful of Me, who have surrendered their organs of action and perception to Me, who teach one another [about Me] and always speak of Me, are always satisfied and remain content.

तेषां सततयुक्तानां भजतां प्रीतिपूर्वकम् ।
ददामि बुद्धियोगं तं येन मामुपयान्ति ते ॥१०॥

*teṣāṁ satatayuktānāṁ bhajatāṁ prītipūrvakam |*
*dadāmi buddhiyogaṁ taṁ yena māmupayānti te ||10||*

**10.** To these [people] who are always devout to Me, who worship me with love, I give [them] the clear knowledge by which they can reach Me.

तेषामेवानुकम्पार्थमहमज्ञानजं तमः ।
नाशयाम्यात्मभावस्थो ज्ञानदीपेन भास्वता ॥११॥

*teṣāmevānukampārthamahamajñānajaṁ tamaḥ |*
*nāśayāmyātmabhāvastho jñānadīpena bhāsvatā ||11||*

**11.** Out of compassion for them, I, dwelling in their intellects, destroy the darkness born of ignorance with the shining light of knowledge.

अर्जुन उवाच
परं ब्रह्म परं धाम पवित्रं परमं भवान् ।
पुरुषं शाश्वतं दिव्यमादिदेवमजं विभुम् ॥१२॥

*arjuna uvāca*
*paraṁ brahma paraṁ dhāma pavitraṁ paramaṁ bhavān |*
*puruṣaṁ śāśvataṁ divyamādidevamajaṁ vibhum ||12||*

**12.** *Arjuna* spoke:
— You are the limitless *Brahman*, the greatest of lights, the greatest purifier, the eternal Self, divine, not-born, the origin of the Gods, He who pervades everything.

आहुस्त्वामृषयः सर्वे देवर्षिर्नारदस्तथा ।
असितो देवलो व्यासः स्वयं चैव ब्रवीषि मे ॥१३॥

*āhustvāmṛṣayaḥ sarve devarṣirnāradastathā |*
*asito devalo vyāsaḥ svayaṁ caiva bravīṣi me ||13||*

**13.** [Thus] all the seers, the divine sage *Nārada* and also *Asita, Devala* and *Vyāsa* speak of You, as You have also told me [about You].

सर्वमेतदृतं मन्ये यन्मां वदसि केशव ।
न हि ते भगवन्व्यक्तिं विदुर्देवा न दानवाः ॥१४॥

*sarvametadṛtaṁ manye yanmāṁ vadasi keśava |*
*na hi te bhagavanvyaktiṁ vidurdevā na dānavāḥ ||14||*

**14.** I consider all You have told me to be the truth, O *Keśava* [*Kṛṣṇa*]. Indeed, neither gods nor demons know your manifestation, O *Bhagavat* [*Kṛṣṇa*].

स्वयमेवात्मनात्मानं वेत्थ त्वं पुरुषोत्तम ।
भूतभावन भूतेश देवदेव जगत्पते ॥१५॥

*svayamevātmanātmānaṁ vettha tvaṁ puruṣottama |*
*bhūtabhāvana bhūteśa devadeva jagatpate ||15||*

**15.** O Supreme Being, O Creator of all beings, O Governor of all beings, O God of gods, O Protector of the universe! You alone know Yourself by Yourself!

वक्तुमर्हस्यशेषेण दिव्या ह्यात्मविभूतयः ।
याभिर्विभूतिभिर्लोकानिमांस्त्वं व्याप्य तिष्ठसि ॥१६॥

*vaktumarhasyaśeṣeṇa divyā hyātmavibhūtayaḥ |*
*yābhirvibhūtibhirlokānimāṁstvaṁ vyāpya tiṣṭhasi ||16||*

**16.** You alone should entirely recount your extraordinary glories. You pervade the universe by these glories.

कथं विद्यामहं योगिंस्त्वां सदा परिचिन्तयन् ।
केषु केषु च भावेषु चिन्त्योऽसि भगवन्मया ॥१७॥

*kathaṁ vidyāmahaṁ yogiṁstvāṁ sadā paricintayan |*
*keṣu keṣu ca bhāveṣu cintyo'si bhagavanmayā ||17||*

**17.** O Lord of all powers, always mindful of You, how may I know You? And by what objects should I meditate on You, O Lord?

विस्तरेणात्मनो योगं विभूतिं च जनार्दन ।
भूयः कथय तृप्तिर्हि शृण्वतो नास्ति मेऽमृतम् ॥१८॥

*vistareṇātmano yogaṁ vibhūtiṁ ca janārdana |*
*bhūyaḥ kathaya tṛptirhi śṛṇvato nāsti me'mṛtam ||18||*

**18.** Once again [and] in detail, O *Janārdana* [*Kṛṣṇa*], explain your power and glory. I am never satiated from hearing [this] nectar [in the form of words].

श्रीभगवानुवाच
हन्त ते कथयिष्यामि दिव्या ह्यात्मविभूतयः ।
प्राधान्यतः कुरुश्रेष्ठ नास्त्यन्तो विस्तरस्य मे ।।१९।।

*śrībhagavānuvāca*
*hanta te kathayiṣyāmi divyā hyātmavibhūtayaḥ |*
*prādhānyataḥ kuruśreṣṭha nāstyanto vistarasya me ||19||*

**19.** The Lord [*Kṛṣṇa*] spoke:
— Here! I shall tell you about the most prominent of my divine glories, O *Kuruśreṣṭha* [*Arjuna*], since my glories are endless.

अहमात्मा गुडाकेश सर्वभूताशयस्थितः ।
अहमादिश्च मध्यं च भूतानामन्त एव च ।।२०।।

*ahamātmā guḍākeśa sarvabhūtāśayasthitaḥ |*
*ahamādiśca madhyaṁ ca bhūtānāmanta eva ca ||20||*

**20.** O *Guḍākeśa* [*Arjuna*], I am the Self that is in the heart of all beings; I am the beginning, the middle and also the end of all beings.

आदित्यानामहं विष्णुर्ज्योतिषां रविरंशुमान् ।
मरीचिर्मरुतामस्मि नक्षत्राणामहं शशी ॥२१॥

*ādityānāmahaṁ viṣṇurjyotiṣāṁ raviraṁśumān |*
*marīcirmarutāmasmi nakṣatrāṇāmahaṁ śaśī ||21||*

**21.** Of all the *ādityas*, I am *Viṣṇu*; among lights, I am the radiant sun; among *maruts*, I am *Marīci*; among all that shines at night, I am the moon.

वेदानां सामवेदोऽस्मि देवानामस्मि वासवः ।
इन्द्रियाणां मनश्चास्मि भूतानामस्मि चेतना ॥२२॥

*vedānāṁ sāmavedo'smi devānāmasmi vāsavaḥ |*
*indriyāṇāṁ manaścāsmi bhūtānāmasmi cetanā ||22||*

**22.** Among the *Vedas*, I am *Sāma Veda*; among the Gods, I am *Indra*; among the organs, I am the mind. And I am the intelligence among living beings.

रुद्राणां शङ्करश्चास्मि वित्तेशो यक्षरक्षसाम् ।
वसूनां पावकश्चास्मि मेरुः शिखरिणामहम् ॥२३॥

*rudrāṇāṁ śaṅkaraścāsmi vitteśo yakṣarakṣasām |*
*vasūnāṁ pāvakaścāsmi meruḥ śikhariṇāmaham ||23||*

**23.** Among *rudras*, I am *Śaṅkara* and among *yakṣas* and *rakṣasas*, I am *Kubera*. Among the *vasus*, I am fire; and among peaks, I am *Meru* [Everest].

पुरोधसां च मुख्यं मां विद्धि पार्थ बृहस्पतिम् ।
सेनानीनामहं स्कन्दः सरसामस्मि सागरः ॥२४॥

*purodhasāṁ ca mukhyaṁ māṁ viddhi pārtha bṛhaspatim |*
*senānīnāmahaṁ skandaḥ sarasāmasmi sāgaraḥ ||24||*

**24.** Among priests, know Me, O *Pārtha* [*Arjuna*], as none other than *Bṛhaspati*. Among generals, I am *Skanda*. Among bodies of water, I am the ocean.

महर्षीणां भृगुरहं गिरामस्म्येकमक्षरम् ।
यज्ञानां जपयज्ञोऽस्मि स्थावराणां हिमालयः ॥२५॥

*maharṣīṇāṁ bhṛguraham̐ girāmasmyekamakṣaram |*
*yajñānāṁ japayajño'smi sthāvarāṇāṁ himālayaḥ ||25||*

**25.** Among the wise, I am *Bhṛgu*. Among words, I am the single syllable [*oṁ*]. Among rituals, I am *japa*. Among mountains, I am the Himalayas.

अश्वत्थः सर्ववृक्षाणां देवर्षीणां च नारदः ।
गन्धर्वाणां चित्ररथः सिद्धानां कपिलो मुनिः ॥२६॥

*aśvatthaḥ sarvavṛkṣāṇāṁ devarṣīṇāṁ ca nāradaḥ |*
*gandharvāṇāṁ citrarathaḥ siddhānāṁ kapilo muniḥ ||26||*

**26.** Among trees, I am the pipal; among celestial sages, I am *Nārada*. Among the *gandharvas*, I am *Citraratha*. Among those that attain perfection, I am the sage *Kapila*.

उच्चैःश्रवसमश्वानां विद्धि माममृतोद्भवम् ।
ऐरावतं गजेन्द्राणां नराणां च नराधिपम् ॥२७॥

*uccaiḥśravasamaśvānāṁ viddhi māmamṛtodbhavam |*
*airāvataṁ gajendrāṇāṁ narāṇāṁ ca narādhipam ||27||*

**27.** Know that I am *Uccaihśravas* among horses, born of nectar. Among elephants, I am *Airāvata*; and among men, I am king.

आयुधानामहं वज्रं धेनूनामस्मि कामधुक् ।
प्रजनश्चास्मि कन्दर्पः सर्पाणामस्मि वासुकिः ॥२८॥

*āyudhānāmahaṁ vajraṁ dhenūnāmasmi kāmadhuk |*
*prajanaścāsmi kandarpaḥ sarpāṇāmasmi vāsukiḥ ||28||*

**28.** Among weapons, I am *vajra* [the thunderbolt of *Indra*]. Among the cows, I am *Kāmadhenu* [the wish-fulfilling cow]. I am the procreator, the god of love. Among poison snakes, I am *Vāsuki*.

अनन्तश्चास्मि नागानां वरुणो यादसामहम् ।
पितृणामर्यमा चास्मि यमः सम्यमतामहम् ॥२९॥

*anantaścāsmi nāgānāṁ varuṇo yādasāmaham |*
*pitṝṇāmaryamā cāsmi yamaḥ samyamatāmaham ||29||*

**29.** Among serpents, I am *Ananta*. Among deities of water, I am *Varuṇa*. Among the ancestors, I am *Aryamā*. And among those that subdue, I am *Yama*.

प्रह्लादश्चास्मि दैत्यानां कालः कलयतामहम् ।
मृगाणां च मृगेन्द्रोऽहं वैनतेयश्च पक्षिणाम् ॥३०॥

*prahlādaścāsmi daityānāṁ kālaḥ kalayatāmaham |*
*mṛgāṇāṁ ca mṛgendro'haṁ vainateyaśca pakṣiṇām ||30||*

**30.** Among the daityas, I am *Prahlāda*. Among all that can be counted, I am time. Among beasts, I am the lion. And among birds, I am *Garuḍa*.

पवनः पवतामस्मि रामः शस्त्रभृतामहम् ।
झषाणां मकरश्चास्मि स्रोतसामस्मि जाह्नवी ॥३१॥

*pavanaḥ pavatāmasmi rāmaḥ śastrabhṛtāmaham |*
*jhaṣāṇāṁ makaraścāsmi srotasāmasmi jāhnavī ||31||*

**31.** Of all that purifies, I am the Wind. Among those that bear arms, I am *Rāma*. Among fish, I am the shark. And among rivers, I am the Ganges.

सर्गाणामादिरन्तश्च मध्यं चैवाहमर्जुन ।
अध्यात्मविद्या विद्यानां वादः प्रवदतामहम् ॥३२॥

*sargāṇāmādirantaśca madhyaṁ caivāhamarjuna |*
*adhyātmavidyā vidyānāṁ vādaḥ pravadatāmaham ||32||*

**32.** Of creations, I am the beginning, the middle and the end, O *Arjuna*. Of all knowledge, I am the knowledge of the Self. Of all arguments, I am *vāda* [the comprehesion of truth between debaters].

अक्षराणामकारोऽस्मि द्वन्द्वः सामासिकस्य च ।
अहमेवाक्षयः कालो धाताऽहं विश्वतोमुखः ॥३३॥

*akṣarāṇāmakāro'smi dvandvaḥ sāmāsikasya ca |*
*ahamevākṣayaḥ kālo dhātā'haṁ viśvatomukhaḥ ||33||*

**33.** Among all letters, I am the letter "*a*". Of all compound words, I am *dvandva*[8]. I am infinite time and I alone grant the result of action in all directions.

मृत्युः सर्वहरश्चाहमुद्भवश्च भविष्यताम् ।
कीर्तिः श्रीर्वाक् च नारीणां स्मृतिर्मेधा धृतिः क्षमा ॥३४॥

*mṛtyuḥ sarvaharaścāhamudbhavaśca bhaviṣyatām |*
*kīrtiḥ śrīrvāk ca nārīṇāṁ smṛtirmedhā dhṛtiḥ kṣamā ||34||*

**34.** I am death that everything destroys, and I am the source of all that is to be. Among the words of feminine gender, I am fame, wealth, words, memory, intelligence, courage and patience.

बृहत्साम तथा साम्नां गायत्री छन्दसामहम् ।
मासानां मार्गशीर्षोऽहमृतूनां कुसुमाकरः ॥३५॥

*bṛhatsāma tathā sāmnāṁ gāyatrī chandasāmaham |*
*māsānāṁ mārgaśīrṣo'hamṛtūnāṁ kusumākaraḥ ||35||*

---

8 *Dvandva* is a compound word in which two nouns have equal value, such as the Sanskrit words for "teacher (*ācārya*) and student (*śiṣyaḥ*)", whereby two become one, *ācāryaśiṣyaḥ*, just as *jiva* and *Īśvara*.

**35.** And also among *sāmas* chants, I am *bṛhatsāma*. Of meters, I am *gāyatrī*. Of months, I am *mārgaśīrṣa* [November-December]. Of the seasons, I am spring.

द्यूतं छलयतामस्मि तेजस्तेजस्विनामहम् ।
जयोऽस्मि व्यवसायोऽस्मि सत्त्वं सत्त्ववतामहम् ॥३६॥

*dyūtaṁ chalayatāmasmi tejastejasvināmaham |*
*jayo'smi vyavasāyo'smi sattvaṁ sattvavatāmaham ||36||*

**36.** Of trickery, I am the game of dice. Among brilliant men, I am that which shines. I am victory; I am effort. In those who are contemplative, I am the power of contemplation.

वृष्णीनां वासुदेवोऽस्मि पाण्डवानां धनञ्जयः ।
मुनीनामप्यहं व्यासः कवीनामुशना कविः ॥३७॥

*vṛṣṇīnāṁ vāsudevo'smi pāṇḍavānāṁ dhanañjayaḥ |*
*munīnāmapyahaṁ vyāsaḥ kavīnāmuśanā kaviḥ ||37||*

**37.** Of all *Vṛṣṇis*, I am *Vāsudeva* [*Kṛṣṇa*]. Of all *Pāṇḍavas*, I am *Dhanañjaya* [*Arjuna*]. Of all sages, I am *Vyāsa*, and among seers, I am *Śukra*.

दण्डो दमयतामस्मि नीतिरस्मि जिगीषताम् ।
मौनं चैवास्मि गुह्यानां ज्ञानं ज्ञानवतामहम् ॥३८॥

*daṇḍo damayatāmasmi nītirasmi jigīṣatām |*
*maunaṁ caivāsmi guhyānāṁ jñānaṁ jñānavatāmaham ||38||*

**38.** Among punishments, I am the stick. Among those that desire victory, I am justice. Among secrets, I am silence. And also, I am the knowledge in those who are wise.

यच्चापि सर्वभूतानां बीजं तदहमर्जुन ।
न तदस्ति विना यत्स्यान्मया भूतं चराचरम् ॥३९॥

*yaccāpi sarvabhūtānāṁ bījaṁ tadahamarjuna |*
*na tadasti vinā yatsyānmayā bhūtaṁ carācaram ||39||*

**39.** And, *Arjuna*, I am that which is the seed of all beings. There is nothing mobile or immobile that exists without Me.

नान्तोऽस्ति मम दिव्यानां विभूतीनां परन्तप ।
एष तूद्देशतः प्रोक्तो विभूतेर्विस्तरो मया ॥४०॥

*nānto'sti mama divyānāṁ vibhūtīnāṁ parantapa |*
*eṣa tūddeśataḥ prokto vibhūtervistaro mayā ||40||*

**40.** O *Parantapa* [*Arjuna*], there is no end to my extraordinary glories. However, these details of [my] glory have been declared by me as a mere illustration.

यद्यद्विभूतिमत्सत्त्वं श्रीमदूर्जितमेव वा ।
तत्तदेवावगच्छ त्वं मम तेजोऽंशसम्भवम् ॥४१॥

*yadyadvibhūtimatsattvaṁ śrīmadūrjitameva vā |*
*tattadevāvagaccha tvaṁ mama tejo'ṁśasambhavam ||41||*

**41.** Know that whatever exists, which is glorious, which has wealth or power, is born of my splendor.

अथवा बहुनैतेन किं ज्ञातेन तवार्जुन ।
विष्टभ्याहमिदं कृत्स्नमेकांशेन स्थितो जगत् ॥४२॥

*athavā bahunaitena kiṁ jñātena tavārjuna |*
*viṣṭabhyāhamidaṁ kṛtsnamekāṁśena sthito jagat ||42||*

**42.** But what is all this knowledge to you, O *Arjuna*, [when] I remain sustaining the entire universe with just a single fraction [of Myself]?

ओं तत्सदिति श्रीमद्भगवद्गीतासूपनिषत्सु ब्रह्मविद्यायां योगशास्त्रे श्रीकृष्णार्जुनसंवादे विभूतियोगो नाम दशमोऽध्यायः॥

*oṁ tatsaditi śrīmadbhagavadgītāsūpaniṣatsu*
*brahmavidyāyāṁ yogaśāstre śrīkṛṣṇārjunasaṁvāde*
*vibhūtiyogo nāma daśamo'dhyāyaḥ ||*

*Oṁ*, this is the Truth. Thus is the tenth chapter, the subject [of which] is called "*vibhūti*" [the glories], in the glorious *Bhagavadgītā*, [which is equivalent to] the *Upaniṣads*, [the subject of which is] the knowledge of *Brahman* [and] *yoga*, in the dialogue between *śrī Kṛṣṇa* and *Arjuna*.

# Chapter 11

## *The cosmic vision*

The last verse of the previous chapter motivates the question of *Arjuna* that gives rise to this chapter. Carefully, *Arjuna* makes a request to *Śrī Kṛṣṇa* in four verses, saying that he has understood what has been taught to him until now, but that he would like to see His cosmic form. Since *Arjuna* knows that this is not an experience for just anyone, he requests that, if he is indeed worthy, that *Kṛṣṇa* bless him by satisfying this desire.

Naturally, *Arjuna* has not really completely understood the teaching. He insists on seeing the universe as something separate from him. He still has not understood that seeing or understanding *Īśvara* is to recognize His essential nature, which is the Consciousness that is the same truth of the individual and the universe. *Arjuna* is not seeing that he is already one with *Īśvara*.

The power to manifest the universe, called *māyā*, and the universe itself, do not have a reality separate from *Īśvara*. The power of creation and creation itself do not exist on their own, therefore they are called *mithyā*, a term that is translated as "not real" or "apparent". However, not being real does not mean something does not exist, since the universe is obviously an object of our experience. Nevertheless, both the power of creation and creation itself are completely dependent upon the absolute, *Brahman*, the only reality.

In *Vedānta*, we define that which is real as *deśa-kāla-vastu-pariccheda-śūnyam nityam*: 'that which always exists and is totally free from the limits of space, time and any object whatsoever'. That which is apparent, *mithyā*, is called *anirvacanīyam*, or 'that which is experienced but cannot be defined', since it depends on another thing to exist and to be defined; just as all objects in this universe, it is constantly under transformation. That which is real is unchanging, immutable, ever-present; that which is apparent only seems real. It is the same when we analyze a shirt: we note it is made of fabric, which is made of thread, which is made of cotton, etc. Therefore, what is it? A shirt? Thread? Or cotton? Each object depends upon another to exist. When one thing depends upon another to exist, it is called apparent. When it exists by itself, it is called real. We therefore conclude that shirt is not a real entity; it is only apparent. That which is absolute, however, is not dependent upon anything.

The Absolute is called *Brahman*, which is *sat-cit-ānanda*: the Consciousness that is always present and limitless. The universe is *mithyā*, which is under constant change and where nothing exists alone. The universe depends upon *Brahman*. *Brahman*, as the cause of the universe, is called *Īśvara*. Actually, the universe is an apparent manifestation and not a creation within time and space. Time and space are part of "creation". What allows for the manifestation of *Brahman* in the form of the universe is *māyā-śakti*, the power to make the universe appear while causing no transformation in *Brahman*, the cause of the universe.

The cosmic form is called *viśvarūpa* or *virāṭsvarūpa*, the Consciousness in the form of the physical universe. The *Vedas* state that the universe is *Īśvara*, which is Consciousness, and which is at the same time both the cause and the manifestation of the universe, while undergoing no transformation whatsoever, *vivarta-upādāna-kārana*. Therefore, the vision of *Īśvara*, which is the cosmic form, is to see the entire universe and to comprehend that all is but an apparent manifestation of the immutable *Brahman*. Thus, in this moment, *Arjuna* wishes to see all that exists in all directions and requests to see the cosmic form, the form of *Īśvara*. This request can only be granted by a special power that is conceded in that very moment.

After hearing of *Īśvara* and his glories in Chapter 10, *Arjuna* says that he would like to be able to behold the entire cosmic form with his own eyes. *Arjuna* asks to be granted the power to see the entire universe with human eyes. Although *Śrī Kṛṣṇa* explains that this is not a normal and possible experience for either humans or celestial beings, He grants him the experience. *Arjuna* then sees all creation before him in the body of *Kṛṣṇa*; he sees things of great beauty and others horrific. He sees himself, his brothers and cousins united for war; he sees the war happening; he sees the grandfather *Bhiṣma*, the master *Droṇa* and so many others at the "mouth of death". By seeing everything at the same time happening quickly, he becomes aghast. He describes all he sees, and his fear and terror grow until he cannot stand it any longer, and asks *Kṛṣṇa* to return to his prior and familiar form.

Upon returning to the pleasing and familiar form of *Kṛṣṇa*, *Arjuna* realizes that the individual is not separate from *Īśvara*. He sees that all the glory and greatness of the universe - as well as the senses, mind and intellect - belong to *Īśvara*. The more one is able to behold *Īśvara* and identify oneself with Him, the more one is able to remain content and understand the order and beauty that is *Īśvara*.

In sum, in this chapter we see the description of the cosmic form in the words of *Arjuna* and *Sañjaya*. It is enchanting and at the same time terrifying - since nothing of the cosmos is left out! Seeing the universe as a whole, *Arjuna* perceives the Order that maintains everything in movement. He is scared when he sees what he had not expected: the war in progress, death, and the destruction of loved ones. He sees time running very quickly, and everything running to dissolution. He does not comprehend what he sees and becomes terrified. It is then that *Arjuna* asks *Kṛṣṇa* to assume his prior familiar form - and *Kṛṣṇa* does so smiling! It is for this reason that this chapter is called the cosmic vision.

## Summary of the verses

Verse 1: *Arjuna* states that he is free from delusion, due to the teaching of *Kṛṣṇa* on the *Ātman*, or the Absolute.

Verse 2: He also states that he has understood *Īśvara* and His glories.

Verses 3 and 4: Finally, *Arjuna* asks to see His divine form, if *Kṛṣṇa* believes he is capable of beholding It.

Verses 5 to 7: *Śrī Kṛṣṇa* agrees to give *Arjuna* a view of the cosmic form and that he shall see all that he desires.

Verse 8: ...but he will need special eyes! Therefore, *Śrī Kṛṣṇa* grants him the capacity to see much more than common human eyes can see: he will see the entire universe that is *Īśvara*.

Verses 9 to 14: *Sañjaya* describes His cosmic form. All creation is a decoration of *Īśvara*, which is by nature *arūpa*, without form. The cosmic form is extraordinary and enchanting: it extends in all directions and includes all possible and existing forms. *Arjuna* is in awe, and with his hands together, he salutes the Lord of the universe.

Verses 15 to 17: *Arjuna* describes what he sees, a magnificent form that includes all things, is everywhere, and very brilliant.

Verses 18 to 20: He recognizes *Īśvara* as the imperishable, That which must be known, the support of the universe and protector of the universal order: the heavens, the Earth, and the space between, exist in Him. *Arjuna* says that the cosmos is wonderful, but at the same time, terrifying!

Verses 21 and 22: Various groups admire Him, others fear Him. *Arjuna* shows his enchantment with the cosmos in these verses.

Verses 23 to 30: Afterwards, *Arjuna* says that all fear Him, seeing the immeasurable form of *Īśvara* in which he also resides. His eyes focus on the cosmic expression of death; he speaks of what is called the "mouth of death" and how people are attracted to it. *Arjuna* feels fear and confusion about the nature of *Īśvara*, which before had been so enchanting.

Verse 31: Finally, *Arjuna* asks about *Īśvara*, since he does not know Him, and neither does he understand his expression.

Verses 32 to 34: *Śrī Kṛṣṇa* responds that He is everything, including time, the terrible death and the destruction of the universe. When the hour of death arrives, it happens by a means. In this moment of war, *Arjuna* is this means, an instrument of death as determined by *Īśvara*, the Order of the universe. For this reason, *Kṛṣṇa* says that *Arjuna* should get up and decide for war and thereby conquer his enemies, who are already condemned to death by the very cosmic order, *Īśvara*. In verse 33, he says: "Be merely an instrument, *Arjuna*!".

Verse 35: *Sañjaya* tells of the condition of *Arjuna* who shakes out of fear with palms together saluting *Kṛṣṇa* in his cosmic form. He is of mixed emotions; he is both fearful and enchanted. His attitude is respectful, but his voice cracks and stammers.

Verses 36 to 44: *Arjuna* is now taken by devotion and reverences from having beheld the greatness of *Īśvara*. In verses 41 and 42, *Arjuna* asks for forgiveness for the colloquial way in which he had treated *Kṛṣṇa* all these years. This is because it is only now that *Arjuna* clearly sees that he is beholding an *avatāra*, a divine manifestation to fulfill a specific objective, who is without original ignorance or *karma* that had resulted in his birth.

Verses 45 and 46: *Arjuna* tells *Kṛṣṇa* that he is in awe of the vision of the cosmic form; however, at the same time, his mind has been taken by fear and asks that He return to his pleasing and familiar form as *Kṛṣṇa*!

Verses 47 to 49: Lord *Kṛṣṇa* reassumes his form and says that his brilliant and limitless cosmic form has been shown to no other, since it cannot be reached by means of rituals, nor studies, nor discipline or sacrifice.

The desire of *Arjuna* was satisfied, and *Kṛṣṇa* now tells him that he has no reason for fear, and should be calm and content seeing his familiar form as *Kṛṣṇa*.

Verses 50 and 51: *Sañjaya* tells king *Dhṛtarāṣṭra* that *Kṛṣṇa* returned to his original form and *Arjuna* is satisfied, as he himself has declared.

Verses 52 to 55: *Śrī Kṛṣṇa* says that His form cannot be seen by any other means, except by total devotion that is without the duality of worshipper and worshipped. Only the devout, who perform action for *Īśvara*, are free from attachment and enmity, and seeking *Īśvara* as the final objective, they reach Him.

# अथैकादशोऽध्यायः

## *athaikādaśo'dhyāyaḥ*

## Eleventh chapter

अर्जुन उवाच
मदनुग्रहाय परमं गुह्यमध्यात्मसंज्ञितम् ।
यत्त्वयोक्तं वचस्तेन मोहोऽयं विगतो मम ॥१॥

*arjuna uvāca*
*madanugrahāya paramaṁ guhyamadhyātmasaṁjñitam |*
*yattvayoktaṁ vacastena moho'yaṁ vigato mama ||1||*

**1.** *Arjuna* spoke:
— Your teaching on the Self has banished my delusion. It is the highest secret taught by you to bless me.

भवाप्ययौ हि भूतानां श्रुतौ विस्तरशो मया ।
त्वत्तः कमलपत्राक्ष माहात्म्यमपि चाव्ययम् ॥२॥

*bhavāpyayau hi bhūtānāṁ śrutau vistaraśo mayā |*
*tvattaḥ kamalapatrākṣa māhātmyamapi cāvyayam ||2||*

**2.** O *Kamalapatrākṣa* [*Kṛṣṇa*], I have certainly heared in detail from You about creation and the destruction of beings, and also of your unending glory.

एवमेतद्यथात्थ त्वमात्मानं परमेश्वर ।
द्रष्टुमिच्छामि ते रूपमैश्वरं पुरुषोत्तम ॥३॥

*evametadyathāttha tvamātmānaṁ parameśvara |*
*draṣṭumicchāmi te rūpamaiśvaraṁ puruṣottama ||3||*

**3.** O *Parameśvara* [*Kṛṣṇa*], just as you have spoken on your nature, I thus wish to see your form as *Īśvara*, O *Puruṣottama* [*Kṛṣṇa*].

मन्यसे यदि तच्छक्यं मया द्रष्टुमिति प्रभो ।
योगेश्वर ततो मे त्वं दर्शयात्मानमव्ययम् ॥४॥

*manyase yadi tacchakyaṁ mayā draṣṭumiti prabho |*
*yogeśvara tato me tvaṁ darśayātmānamavyayam ||4||*

**4.** O *Prabhu* [*Kṛṣṇa*], if you think it possible for me to see this [your form as *Īśvara*], then show me, O *Yogeśvara* [*Kṛṣṇa*], show me your endless Self.

श्रीभगवानुवाच
पश्य मे पार्थ रूपाणि शतशोऽथ सहस्रसः ।
नानाविधानि दिव्यानि नानावर्णाकृतीनि च ॥५॥

*śrībhagavānuvāca*
*paśya me pārtha rūpāṇi śataśo'tha sahasrasaḥ |*
*nānāvidhāni divyāni nānāvarṇākṛtīni ca ||5||*

**5.** The Lord [*Kṛṣṇa*] spoke:
— O *Pārtha* [*Arjuna*], behold my hundreds and thousands of forms of various extraordinary kinds of different colors and shapes.

पश्यादित्यान्वसून् रुद्रानश्विनौ मरुतस्तथा ।
बहून्यदृष्टपूर्वाणि पश्याश्चर्याणि भारत ॥६॥

*paśyādityānvasūn rudrānaśvinau marutastathā |*
*bahūnyadṛṣṭapūrvāṇi paśyāścaryāṇi bhārata ||6||*

**6.** See the *Ādityas*, the *Vasus*, the *Rudras*, the two *Aśvinis* and the *Maruts*. Behold the many wonders never before seen, O *Bhārata* [*Arjuna*].

इहैकस्थं जगत्कृत्स्नं पश्याद्य सचराचरम् ।
मम देहे गुडाकेश यच्चान्यद्द्रष्टुमिच्छसि ॥७॥

*ihaikasthaṁ jagatkṛtsnaṁ paśyādya sacarācaram |*
*mama dehe guḍākeśa yaccānyaddraṣṭumicchasi ||7||*

**7.** Now behold here the entire universe, moving and motionless, established as one in my body, O *Guḍākeśa* [*Arjuna*]. And whatever else you wish to see.

न तु मां शक्यसे द्रष्टुमनेनैव स्वचक्षुषा ।
दिव्यं ददामि ते चक्षुः पश्य मे योगमैश्वरम् ॥८॥

*na tu māṁ śakyase draṣṭumanenaiva svacakṣuṣā |*
*divyaṁ dadāmi te cakṣuḥ paśya me yogamaiśvaram ||8||*

**8.** Although you may not see Me with your own eyes. I give you extraordinary eyes. Behold the power of *Īśvara*!

सञ्जय उवाच
एवमुक्त्वा ततो राजन्महायोगेश्वरो हरिः ।
दर्शयामास पार्थाय परमं रूपमैश्वरम् ॥९॥

*sañjaya uvāca*
*evamuktvā tato rājanmahāyogeśvaro hariḥ* |
*darśayāmāsa pārthāya paramaṁ rūpamaiśvaram* ||9||

**9.** *Sañjaya* spoke:
— Having spoken thus, O King, *Hari* [*Kṛṣṇa*], the great Lord of *yoga*, revealed to *Pārtha* [*Arjuna*] the supreme form of *Īśvara*.

अनेकवक्त्रनयनमनेकाद्भुतदर्शनम् ।
अनेकदिव्याभरणं दिव्यानेकोद्यतायुधम् ॥१०॥

*anekavaktranayanamanekādbhutadarśanam* |
*anekadivyābharaṇaṁ divyānekodyatāyudham* ||10||

**10.** [He showed] countless mouths and eyes, countless wonderous visions, countless unimaginable ornaments, countless and extraordinary raised weapons.

दिव्यमाल्याम्बरधरं दिव्यगन्धानुलेपनम् ।
सर्वाश्चर्यमयं देवमनन्तं विश्वतोमुखम् ॥११॥

*divyamālyāmbaradharaṁ divyagandhānulepanam* |
*sarvāścaryamayaṁ devamanantaṁ viśvatomukham* ||11||

**11.** [He showed a form] wearing divine flowers and garments, anointed with divine perfumes, filled with wonders, brilliant, endless, facing all directions.

दिवि सूर्यसहस्रस्य भवेद्युगपदुत्थिता ।
यदि भाः सदृशी सा स्याद्भासस्तस्य महात्मनः ॥१२॥

*divi sūryasahasrasya bhavedyugapadutthitā |*
*yadi bhāḥ sadṛśī sā syādbhāsastasya mahātmanaḥ ||12||*

**12.** Should a thousand suns rise all at once in the sky, its splendor would be the same as that great Lord.

तत्रैकस्थं जगत्कृत्स्नं प्रविभक्तमनेकधा ।
अपश्यद्देवदेवस्य शरीरे पाण्डवस्तदा ॥१३॥

*tatraikasthaṁ jagatkṛtsnaṁ pravibhaktamanekadhā |*
*apaśyaddevadevasya śarīre pāṇḍavastadā ||13||*

**13.** There, in the body of the Lord of Lords, the son of *Pāṇḍu* [*Arjuna*] then beheld the entire universe established in one [and also] divided in various ways.

ततः स विस्मयाविष्टो हृष्टरोमा धनञ्जयः ।
प्रणम्य शिरसा देवं कृताञ्जलिरभाषत ॥१४॥

*tataḥ sa vismayāviṣṭo hṛṣṭaromā dhanañjayaḥ |*
*praṇamya śirasā devaṁ kṛtāñjalirabhāṣata ||14||*

**14.** Then he, *Dhanañjaya* [*Arjuna*], in awe, with his hair on end, bowing his head with his palms joined, said to the Lord:

अर्जुन उवाच
पश्यामि देवांस्तव देव देहे
सर्वांस्तथा भूतविशेषसङ्घान् ।
ब्रह्माणमीशं कमलासनस्थं
ऋषींश्च सर्वानुरगांश्च दिव्यान् ॥१५॥

*arjuna uvāca*
*paśyāmi devāṁstava deva dehe*
*sarvāṁstathā bhūtaviśeṣasaṅghān |*
*brahmāṇamīśaṁ kamalāsanasthaṁ*
*ṛṣīṁśca sarvānuragāṁśca divyān ||15||*

**15.** *Arjuna* spoke:
— O Lord [*Kṛṣṇa*], in your body I see all the Gods and beings assembled, the Lord *Brahmā* seated on a lotus, all the *ṛṣis* and various celestial serpents.

अनेकबाहूदरवक्त्रनेत्रं
पश्यामि त्वां सर्वतोऽनन्तरूपम् ।
नान्तं न मध्यं न पुनस्तवादिं
पश्यामि विश्वेश्वर विश्वरूप ॥१६॥

*anekabāhūdaravaktranetraṁ*
*paśyāmi tvāṁ sarvato'nantarūpam |*
*nāntaṁ na madhyaṁ na punastavādiṁ*
*paśyāmi viśveśvara viśvarūpa ||16||*

**16.** I see your infinite form in all directions, with many arms, bellies, mouths and eyes. I do not see your end, nor your middle, nor your beginning, o Lord of the universe, O cosmos!

किरीटिनं गदिनं चक्रिणं च
तेजोराशिं सर्वतो दीप्तिमन्तम् ।
पश्यामि त्वां दुर्निरीक्ष्यं समन्ताद्-
दीप्तानलार्कद्युतिमप्रमेयम् ॥१७॥

*kirīṭinaṁ gadinaṁ cakriṇaṁ ca*
*tejorāśiṁ sarvato dīptimantam |*
*paśyāmi tvāṁ durnirīkṣyaṁ samantād-*
*dīptānalārkadyutimaprameyam ||17||*

**17.** I see you as a brilliant mass of light in every direction, with crown, club and disc. I see you as difficult to be seen, with all sides shining as the light of fire and the sun, and whose limits are incomprehensible.

त्वमक्षरं परमं वेदितव्यं
त्वमस्य विश्वस्य परं निधानम् ।
त्वमव्ययः शाश्वतधर्मगोप्ता
सनातनस्त्वं पुरुषो मतो मे ॥१८॥

*tvamakṣaraṁ paramaṁ veditavyaṁ*
*tvamasya viśvasya paraṁ nidhānam |*
*tvamavyayaḥ śāśvatadharmagoptā*
*sanātanastvaṁ puruṣo mato me ||18||*

**18.** You are imperishable, limitless, That which is to be known; You are That which sustains the entire universe, immutable; You are the One who protects the eternal law; my perception is that you are eternal.

अनादिमध्यान्तमनन्तवीर्यम्-
अनन्तबाहुं शशिसूर्यनेत्रम् ।
पश्यामि त्वां दीप्तहुताशवक्त्रं
स्वतेजसा विश्वमिदं तपन्तम् ॥१९॥

*anādimadhyāntamanantavīryam*
*anantabāhuṁ śaśisūryanetram |*
*paśyāmi tvāṁ dīptahutāśavaktraṁ*
*svatejasā viśvamidaṁ tapantam ||19||*

**19.** I behold You as that which has no beginning, no middle, no end, as the infinite power, with an infinite number of arms, whose eyes are the sun and the moon, whose mouth is as the burning fire that heats the universe with your light.

द्यावापृथिव्योरिदमन्तरं हि
व्याप्तं त्वयैकेन दिशश्च सर्वाः ।
दृष्ट्वाद्भुतं रूपमुग्रं तवेदं
लोकत्रयं प्रव्यथितं महात्मन् ॥२०॥

*dyāvāpṛthivyoridamantaraṁ hi*
*vyāptaṁ tvayaikena diśaśca sarvāḥ |*
*dṛṣṭvādbhutaṁ rūpamugraṁ tavedaṁ*
*lokatrayaṁ pravyathitaṁ mahātman ||20||*

**20.** The space between heaven and Earth is truly pervaded in all directions by You. Upon seeing your marvelous and terrible form, the three worlds tremble, *Mahātman* [*Kṛṣṇa*]!

अमी हि त्वां सुरसङ्घा विशन्ति
केचिद्भीताः प्राञ्जलयो गृणन्ति ।
स्वस्तीत्युक्त्वा महर्षिसिद्धसङ्घाः
स्तुवन्ति त्वां स्तुतिभिः पुष्कलाभिः ॥२१॥

*amī hi tvāṁ surasaṅghā viśanti*
*kecidbhītāḥ prāñjalayo gṛṇanti |*
*svastītyuktvā maharṣisiddhasaṅghāḥ*
*stuvanti tvāṁ stutibhiḥ puṣkalābhiḥ ||21||*

**21.** Those groups of gods truly enter into You, some in terror with their palms together in reverence. Groups of wisemen and *siddhas*[9] glorify You with songs full of meaning, reverberating "let there be Peace".

रुद्रादित्या वसवो ये च साध्याः
विश्वेऽश्विनौ मरुतश्चोष्मपाश्च ।
गन्धर्वयक्षासुरसिद्धसङ्घाः
वीक्षन्ते त्वां विस्मिताश्चैव सर्वे ॥२२॥

*rudrādityā vasavo ye ca sādhyāḥ*
*viśve'śvinau marutaścoṣmapāśca |*
*gandharvayakṣāsurasiddhasaṅghāḥ*
*vīkṣante tvāṁ vismitāścaiva sarve ||22||*

**22.** All the *rudras, ādityas, vasus, sādhyas, viśvadevas*, the two *aśvins*, the *maruts*, the *uṣmapas* and also the groups of *gandharvas, yakṣas, asuras* and *siddhas* behold You in awe.

---

9 *Siddhas* are *yogins* that have acquired powers and, at the same time, have acquired self-knowledge.

रूपं महत्ते बहुवक्त्रनेत्रं
महाबाहो बहुबाहूरुपादम् ।
बहूदरं बहुदंष्ट्राकरालं
दृष्ट्वा लोकाः प्रव्यथितास्तथाहम् ॥२३॥

*rūpaṁ mahatte bahuvaktranetraṁ*
*mahābāho bahubāhūrupādam |*
*bahūdaraṁ bahudaṁṣṭrākarālaṁ*
*dṛṣṭvā lokāḥ pravyathitāstathāham ||23||*

**23.** O *Mahābāhu* [*Kṛṣṇa*], upon seeing Your vast form with many mouths and eyes, with many arms, legs and feet, with many bellies [and] tusks, people tremble in fear, and I also.

नभःस्पृशं दीप्तमनेकवर्णं
व्यात्ताननं दीप्तविशालनेत्रम् ।
दृष्ट्वा हि त्वां प्रव्यथितान्तरात्मा
धृतिं न विन्दामि शमं च विष्णो ॥२४॥

*nabhaḥspṛśaṁ dīptamanekavarṇaṁ*
*vyāttānanaṁ dīptaviśālanetram |*
*dṛṣṭvā hi tvāṁ pravyathitāntarātmā*
*dhṛtiṁ na vindāmi śamaṁ ca viṣṇo ||24||*

**24.** Having really seen You touching the sky, shining with countless colors and shapes, with gaping mouths [and] brilliant eyes, my mind is in terror, and I find no courage nor Peace, O *Viṣṇu* [*Kṛṣṇa*]!

दंष्ट्राकरालानि च ते मुखानि
दृष्ट्वैव कालानलसन्निभानि ।
दिशो न जाने न लभे च शर्म
प्रसीद देवेश जगन्निवास ॥२५॥

*daṁṣṭrākarālāni ca te mukhāni*
*dṛṣṭvaiva kālānalasannibhāni |*
*diśo na jāne na labhe ca śarma*
*prasīda deveśa jagannivāsa ||25||*

**25.** Indeed, seeing your mouths with tusks bearing the flames of time, I lose my sense of direction and I find no comfort. Have mercy, O *Deveśa* [*Kṛṣṇa*], O *Jagannivāsa* [*Kṛṣṇa*]!

अमी च त्वां धृतराष्ट्रस्य पुत्राः
सर्वे सहैवावनिपालसङ्घैः ।
भीष्मो द्रोणः सूतपुत्रस्तथासौ
सहास्मदीयैरपि योधमुख्यैः ॥२६॥

*amī ca tvāṁ dhṛtarāṣṭrasya putrāḥ*
*sarve sahaivāvanipālasaṅghaiḥ |*
*bhīṣmo droṇaḥ sūtaputrastathāsau*
*sahāsmadīyairapi yodhamukhyaiḥ ||26||*

**26.** And all the sons of *Dhṛtarāṣṭra*, along with groups of kings, as well as *Bhīṣma*, *Droṇa*, the son of the charioteer [*Karṇa*], together with our chief warriors, [enter] into You.

वक्त्राणि ते त्वरमाणा विशन्ति
    दंष्ट्राकरालानि भयानकानि ।
केचिद्विलग्ना दशनान्तरेषु
    सन्दृश्यन्ते चूर्णितैरुत्तमाङ्गैः ॥२७॥

*vaktrāṇi te tvaramāṇā viśanti*
    *daṁṣṭrākarālāni bhayānakāni |*
*kecidvilagnā daśanāntareṣu*
    *sandṛśyante cūrṇitairuttamāṅgaiḥ ||27||*

**27.** They quickly enter you fearful and terrible gaping mouths, some cling to your teeth with their heads smashed.

यथा नदीनां बहवोऽम्बुवेगाः
    समुद्रमेवाभिमुखा द्रवन्ति ।
तथा तवामी नरलोकवीराः
    विशन्ति वक्त्राण्यभिविज्वलन्ति ॥२८॥

*yathā nadīnāṁ bahavo'mbuvegāḥ*
    *samudramevābhimukhā dravanti |*
*tathā tavāmī naralokavīrāḥ*
    *viśanti vaktrāṇyabhivijvalanti ||28||*

**28.** Just as the many running waters of rivers naturally flow towards the ocean, these heroes of the world flow into [your, *Kṛṣṇa*] mouth of flames.

यथा प्रदीप्तं ज्वलनं पतङ्गाः
विशन्ति नाशाय समृद्धवेगाः ।
तथैव नाशाय विशन्ति लोकास्-
तवापि वक्त्राणि समृद्धवेगाः ॥२९॥

*yathā pradīptaṁ jvalanaṁ pataṅgāḥ*
*viśanti nāśāya samṛddhavegāḥ |*
*tathaiva nāśāya viśanti lokās-*
*tavāpi vaktrāṇi samṛddhavegāḥ ||29||*

**29.** Just as a moth speeds quickly to the blazing flame of destruction, people hurriedly enter your mouths to their destruction.

लेलिह्यसे ग्रसमानः समन्ताल्-
लोकान्समग्रान्वदनैर्ज्वलद्भिः ।
तेजोभिरापूर्य जगत्समग्रं
भासस्तवोग्राः प्रतपन्ति विष्णो ॥३०॥

*lelihyase grasamānaḥ samantāl-*
*lokānsamagrānvadanairjvaladbhiḥ |*
*tejobhirāpūrya jagatsamagraṁ*
*bhāsastavogrāḥ pratapanti viṣṇo ||30||*

**30.** Swallowing everyone in all directions with mouths of flames, You taste [them]. Filling the universe ablaze, your terrible flame [everyone] burns, O *Viṣṇu* [*Kṛṣṇa*]!

आख्याहि मे को भवानुग्ररूपो
नमोऽस्तु ते देववर प्रसीद ।
विज्ञातुमिच्छामि भवन्तमाद्यं
न हि प्रजानामि तव प्रवृत्तिम् ॥३१॥

*ākhyāhi me ko bhavānugrarūpo*
*namo'stu te devavara prasīda |*
*vijñātumicchāmi bhavantamādyaṁ*
*na hi prajānāmi tava pravṛttim ||31||*

**31.** Tell me, who are You of such terrifying form? Salutations to you, O *Devavara* [*Kṛṣṇa*]! Have mercy! I wish to know You, who is the origin of everything, since I do not comprehend your actions.

श्रीभगवानुवाच
कालोऽस्मि लोकक्षयकृत्प्रवृद्धो
लोकान्समाहर्तुमिह प्रवृत्तः ।
ऋतेऽपि त्वां न भविष्यन्ति सर्वे
येऽवस्थिताः प्रत्यनीकेषु योधाः ॥३२॥

*śrībhagavānuvāca*
*kālo'smi lokakṣayakṛtpravṛddho*
*lokānsamāhartumiha pravṛttaḥ |*
*ṛte'pi tvāṁ na bhaviṣyanti sarve*
*ye'vasthitāḥ pratyanīkeṣu yodhāḥ ||32||*

**32.** The Lord [*Kṛṣṇa*] spoke:
— I am time, the great destroyer of worlds. I am here to annihilate [these] people. Regardless of you, all the warriors from both armies shall cease to exist.

तस्मात्त्वमुत्तिष्ठ यशो लभस्व
जित्वा शत्रून् भुङ्क्ष्व राज्यं समृद्धम् ।
मयैवैते निहताः पूर्वमेव
निमित्तमात्रं भव सव्यसाचिन् ॥३३॥

*tasmāttvamuttiṣṭha yaśo labhasva*
*jitvā śatrūn bhuṅkṣva rājyaṁ samṛddham |*
*mayaivaite nihatāḥ pūrvameva*
*nimittamātraṁ bhava savyasācin ||33||*

**33.** Therefore, stand up [and] attain glory! Having conquered the enemies, enjoy a prosperous kingdom. These [enemies] have already been slain by Me. Be the mere instrument, O *Savyasācin* [*Arjuna*]!

द्रोणं च भीष्मं च जयद्रथं च
कर्णं तथान्यानपि योधवीरान् ।
मया हतांस्त्वं जहि मा व्यथिष्ठाः
युध्यस्व जेतासि रणे सपत्नान् ॥३४॥

*droṇaṁ ca bhīṣmaṁ ca jayadrathaṁ ca*
*karṇaṁ tathānyānapi yodhavīrān |*
*mayā hatāṁstvaṁ jahi mā vyathiṣṭhāḥ*
*yudhyasva jetāsi raṇe sapatnān ||34||*

**34.** Slay *Droṇa, Bhīṣma, Jayadratha, Karṇa* and other brave warriors who have [already] been slain by Me. Have no fear. Fight! You shall conquer the enemy in battle.

सञ्जय उवाच
एतच्छ्रुत्वा वचनं केशवस्य
कृताञ्जलिर्वेपमानः किरीटी ।
नमस्कृत्वा भूय एवाह कृष्णं
सगद्गदं भीतभीतः प्रणम्य ॥३५॥

*sañjaya uvāca*
*etacchrutvā vacanaṁ keśavasya*
*kṛtāñjalirvepamānaḥ kirīṭī |*
*namaskṛtvā bhūya evāha kṛṣṇaṁ*
*sagadgadaṁ bhītabhītaḥ praṇamya ||35||*

**35.** *Sañjaya* spoke:
— Having heard the words of *Keśava* [*Kṛṣṇa*], the crowned-one [*Arjuna*], trembling in terror, with his palms joined, prostrated himself, bowed once again and spoke chokingly to *Kṛṣṇa*:

अर्जुन उवाच
स्थाने हृषीकेश तव प्रकीर्त्या
जगत्प्रहृष्यत्यनुरज्यते च ।
रक्षांसि भीतानि दिशो द्रवन्ति
सर्वे नमस्यन्ति च सिद्धसङ्घाः ॥३६॥

*arjuna uvāca*
*sthāne hṛṣīkeśa tava prakīrtyā*
*jagatprahṛṣyatyanurajyate ca |*
*rakṣāṁsi bhītāni diśo dravanti*
*sarve namasyanti ca siddhasaṅghāḥ ||36||*

**36.** *Arjuna* spoke:
— O *Hṛṣīkeśa* [*Kṛṣṇa*], people are rightly rejoiced and in awe of your glory, and the demons flee in terror in all directions, and all the groups of *siddhas* bow [to You].

कस्माच्च ते न नमेरन्महात्मन्
गरीयसे ब्रह्मणोऽप्यादिकर्त्रे ।
अनन्त देवेश जगन्निवास
त्वमक्षरं सदसत्तत्परं यत् ॥३७॥

*kasmācca te na nameranmahātman*
*garīyase brahmaṇo'pyādikartre |*
*ananta deveśa jagannivāsa*
*tvamakṣaraṁ sadasattatparaṁ yat ||37||*

**37.** And why should they not bow to You, O *Mahātman* [*Kṛṣṇa*], who is superior, who is the cause of even the Creator? O *Ananta* [*Kṛṣṇa*]! O *Deveśa* [*Kṛṣṇa*]! O *Jagannivāsa* [*Kṛṣṇa*]! You are immutable, beyond cause and effect.

त्वमादिदेवः पुरुषः पुराणस्-
त्वमस्य विश्वस्य परं निधानम् ।
वेत्तासि वेद्यं च परं च धाम
त्वया ततं विश्वमनन्तरूप ॥३८॥

*tvamādidevaḥ puruṣaḥ purāṇas-*
*tvamasya viśvasya paraṁ nidhānam |*
*vettāsi vedyaṁ ca paraṁ ca dhāma*
*tvayā tataṁ viśvamanantarūpa ||38||*

**38.** You are the first among gods, the eldest of beings, and the supreme resting place for the dissolution of this universe; You are That which everything knows, That which must be known, the highest abode. Creation is pervaded by you, O *anantarūpa* [*Kṛṣṇa*]!

वायुर्यमोऽग्निर्वरुणः शशाङ्कः
　　प्रजापतिस्त्वं प्रपितामहश्च ।
नमो नमस्तेऽस्तु सहस्रकृत्वः
　　पुनश्च भूयोऽपि नमो नमस्ते ॥३९॥

*vāyuryamo'gnirvaruṇaḥ śaśāṅkaḥ*
　　*prajāpatistvaṁ prapitāmahaśca |*
*namo namaste'stu sahasrakṛtvaḥ*
　　*punaśca bhūyo'pi namo namaste ||39||*

**39.** You are *Vāyu, Yama, Agni, Varuṇa,* the moon, *Prajāpati,* and also the grandfather and great-grandfather [of creation]. A thousand salutations to You. Over and over again, salutations, salutations to You.[10]

10 *Arjuna* mentions, in this verse, special characteristics of *Īśvara* that he recognizes. He comprehends *Īśvara* as the grandfather and great-grandfather of creation, which means that He is the Creator and also the ultimate Cause of Creation, known as *Param Brahman*. He also declares that all the expressions of the universe are Him, whether it be air, fire, water, and also deat

नमः पुरस्तादथ पृष्ठतस्ते
　　नमोऽस्तु ते सर्वत एव सर्व ।
अनन्तवीर्यामितविक्रमस्त्वं
　　सर्वं समाप्नोषि ततोऽसि सर्वः ॥४०॥

*namaḥ purastādatha pṛṣṭhataste*
*namo'stu te sarvata eva sarva |*
*anantavīryāmitavikramastvaṁ*
*sarvaṁ samāpnoṣi tato'si sarvaḥ ||40||*

**40.** Salutations to You from in front and behind; salutations to You in all directions, O That which Everything is! You pervade everything with profound courage and infinite power. For this reason, You are everything.

सखेति मत्वा प्रसभं यदुक्तं
　　हे कृष्ण हे यादव हे सखेति ।
अजानता महिमानं तवेदं
　　मया प्रमादात्प्रणयेन वापि ॥४१॥

*sakheti matvā prasabhaṁ yaduktaṁ*
*he kṛṣṇa he yādava he sakheti |*
*ajānatā mahimānaṁ tavedaṁ*
*mayā pramādātpraṇayena vāpi ||41||*

**41.** These impertinent [interjections]: "O *Kṛṣṇa*, O *Yādava*, O friend", came from me out of friendship, in ignorance of your glory, by negligence or familiarity.

यच्चावहासार्थमसत्कृतोऽसि
विहारशय्यासनभोजनेषु ।
एकोऽथवाप्यच्युत तत्समक्षं
तत्क्षामये त्वामहमप्रमेयम् ॥४२॥

*yaccāvahāsārthamasatkṛto'si*
*vihāraśayyāsanabhojaneṣu |*
*eko'thavāpyacyuta tatsamakṣaṁ*
*tatkṣāmaye tvāmahamaprameyam ||42||*

**42.** Furthermore, you have been mockingly disrespected [by me] at play, while resting, seated or eating, alone or before the eyes of others, O *Acyuta* [*Kṛṣṇa*]. For this I ask your forgiveness, He who cannot be known.

पितासि लोकस्य चराचरस्य
त्वमस्य पूज्यश्च गुरुर्गरीयान् ।
न त्वत्समोऽस्त्यभ्यधिकः कुतोऽन्यो
लोकत्रयेऽप्यप्रतिमप्रभाव ॥४३॥

*pitāsi lokasya carācarasya*
*tvamasya pūjyaśca gururgarīyān |*
*na tvatsamo'styabhyadhikaḥ kuto'nyo*
*lokatraye'pyapratimaprabhāva ||43||*

**43.** You are the Father of the universe, of all things moving and motionless. You are adored by this [universe] and are the primordial *guru*. There is no other equal to You. How can there be another greater [than you] in the three worlds, O Lord of incomparable greatness?

तस्मात्प्रणम्य प्रणिधाय कायं
प्रसादये त्वामहमीशमीड्यम् ।
पितेव पुत्रस्य सखेव सख्युः
प्रियः प्रियायार्हसि देव सोढुम् ॥४४॥

*tasmātpraṇamya praṇidhāya kāyaṁ*
*prasādaye tvāmahamīśamīḍyam |*
*piteva putrasya sakheva sakhyuḥ*
*priyaḥ priyāyārhasi deva soḍhum ||44||*

**44.** Therefore, bowing, prostrating [my] body, I ask forgiveness from You who is the Lord of Praise. O Lord [*Kṛṣṇa*], may you tolerate [my offenses] as a father to a son, as a friend to a friend, as a lover to the beloved!

अदृष्टपूर्वं हृषितोऽस्मि दृष्ट्वा
भयेन च प्रव्यथितं मनो मे ।
तदेव मे दर्शय देव रूपं
प्रसीद देवेश जगन्निवास ॥४५॥

*adṛṣṭapūrvaṁ hṛṣito'smi dṛṣṭvā*
*bhayena ca pravyathitaṁ mano me |*
*tadeva me darśaya deva rūpaṁ*
*prasīda deveśa jagannivāsa ||45||*

**45.** Having seen that which has never before been seen, I am delighted, and yet my mind trembles with fear. O *deva* [*Kṛṣṇa*], show me that [original] form, O *Deveśa* [*Kṛṣṇa*], bless me, O *Jagannivāsa* [*Kṛṣṇa*]!

किरीटिनं गदिनं चक्रहस्तम्
इच्छामि त्वां द्रष्टुमहं तथैव ।
तेनैव रूपेण चतुर्भुजेन
सहस्रबाहो भव विश्वमूर्ते ॥४६॥

*kirīṭinaṁ gadinaṁ cakrahastam*
*icchāmi tvāṁ draṣṭumahaṁ tathaiva |*
*tenaiva rūpeṇa caturbhujena*
*sahasrabāho bhava viśvamūrte ||46||*

**46.** I wish to see You just as before; with a crown, with a club, with a disc in hand. Become the same four-armed one, O *Sahasrabāhu* [*Kṛṣṇa*]! O *Viśvamūrti* [*Kṛṣṇa*]!

श्रीभगवानुवाच
मया प्रसन्नेन तवार्जुनेदं
रूपं परं दर्शितमात्मयोगात् ।
तेजोमयं विश्वमनन्तमाद्यं
यन्मे त्वदन्येन न दृष्टपूर्वम् ॥४७॥

*śrībhagavānuvāca*
*mayā prasannena tavārjunedaṁ*
*rūpaṁ paraṁ darśitamātmayogāt |*
*tejomayaṁ viśvamanantamādyaṁ*
*yanme tvadanyena na dṛṣṭapūrvam ||47||*

**47.** The Lord [*Kṛṣṇa*] spoke:
— By my power, O *Arjuna*, this limitless form has been shown [to you] by Me who is content with you. This form of mine is splendorous, complete, limitless, the origin [of everything and] never before seen by anyone other than you.

न वेदयज्ञाध्ययनैर्न दानैर्-
न च क्रियाभिर्न तपोभिरुग्रैः ।
एवंरूपः शक्य अहं नृलोके
द्रष्टुं त्वदन्येन कुरुप्रवीर ॥४८॥

*na vedayajñādhyayanairna dānair-*
*na ca kriyābhirna tapobhirugraiḥ |*
*evaṁrūpaḥ śakya ahaṁ nṛloke*
*draṣṭuṁ tvadanyena kurupravīra ||48||*

**48.** Not by the study of the *Vedas* nor sacrifices, nor by acts of charity, nor by performing rituals, not even by severe austerities, may I be seen in such a form in the world of men by any other than you, O *Kurupravīra* [*Arjuna*].

मा ते व्यथा मा च विमूढभावो
दृष्ट्वा रूपं घोरमीदृङ्ममेदम् ।
व्यपेतभीः प्रीतमनाः पुनस्त्वं
तदेव मे रूपमिदं प्रपश्य ॥४९॥

*mā te vyathā mā ca vimūḍhabhāvo*
*dṛṣṭvā rūpaṁ ghoramīdṛṅmamedam |*
*vyapetabhīḥ prītamanāḥ punastvaṁ*
*tadeva me rūpamidaṁ prapaśya ||49||*

**49.** May you have neither fear nor confusion upon seeing such a frightful form as mine. Fearless [and] content, once again, behold my [previous] form.

सञ्जय उवाच
इत्यर्जुनं वासुदेवस्तथोक्त्वा
स्वकं रूपं दर्शयामास भूयः ।
आश्वासयामास च भीतमेनं
भूत्वा पुनः सौम्यवपुर्महात्मा ॥५०॥

*sañjaya uvāca*
*ityarjunaṁ vāsudevastathoktvā*
*svakaṁ rūpaṁ darśayāmāsa bhūyaḥ |*
*āśvāsayāmāsa ca bhītamenaṁ*
*bhūtvā punaḥ saumyavapurmahātmā ||50||*

**50.** *Sañjaya* spoke:
— Thus, *Vāsudeva* [*Kṛṣṇa*], having thereby spoken to *Arjuna*, once again revealed His [previous] form. And the great Lord calmed [*Arjuna*], who was terrified, by once again assuming [His] pleasing form.

अर्जुन उवाच
दृष्ट्वेदं मानुषं रूपं तव सौम्यं जनार्दन ।
इदानीमस्मि संवृत्तः सचेताः प्रकृतिं गतः ॥५१॥

*arjuna uvāca*
*dṛṣṭvedaṁ mānuṣaṁ rūpaṁ tava saumyaṁ janārdana |*
*idānīmasmi saṁvṛttaḥ sacetāḥ prakṛtiṁ gataḥ ||51||*

**51.** *Arjuna* spoke:
— Seeing your pleasant human form, O *Janārdana* [*Kṛṣṇa*], I have recovered my tranquil mind [and] have been restored to my normal state.

श्रीभगवान् उवाच
सुदुर्दर्शमिदं रूपं दृष्टवानसि यन्मम ।
देवा अप्यस्य रूपस्य नित्यं दर्शनकाङ्क्षिणः ॥५२॥

*śrībhagavān uvāca*
*sudurdarśamidaṁ rūpaṁ dṛṣṭavānasi yanmama |*
*devā apyasya rūpasya nityaṁ darśanakāṅkṣinaḥ ||52||*

**52.** The Lord [*Kṛṣṇa*] spoke:
— This form of Mine that you have seen is very difficult to behold. Even the gods have always longed to see it.

नाहं वेदैर्न तपसा न दानेन न चेज्यया ।
शक्य एवंविधो द्रष्टुं दृष्टवानसि मां यथा ॥५३॥

*nāhaṁ vedairna tapasā na dānena na cejyayā |*
*śakya evaṁvidho draṣṭuṁ dṛṣṭavānasi māṁ yathā ||53||*

**53.** The way in which you have seen Me, I may not be seen, not even by the *Vedas*, nor by austerities or charities, not even by rituals.

भक्त्या त्वनन्यया शक्य अहमेवंविधोऽर्जुन ।
ज्ञातुं द्रष्टुं च तत्त्वेन प्रवेष्टुं च परन्तप ॥५४॥

*bhaktyā tvananyayā śakya ahamevaṁvidho'rjuna |*
*jñātuṁ draṣṭuṁ ca tattvena praveṣṭuṁ ca parantapa ||54||*

**54.** Therefore, O *Arjuna*, [only] by exclusive devotion may I be known in such a form, may I be seen and reached as I am, O *Parantapa* [*Arjuna*].

मत्कर्मकृन्मत्परमो मद्भक्तः सङ्गवर्जितः ।
निर्वैरः सर्वभूतेषु यः स मामेति पाण्डव ॥५५॥

*matkarmakṛnmatparamo madbhaktaḥ saṅgavarjitaḥ |*
*nirvairaḥ sarvabhūteṣu yaḥ sa māmeti pāṇḍava ||55||*

**55.** He who dedicates his actions to Me, he who holds Me as supreme, he who is devoted to Me, he who is free from attachment [and] without animosity toward any being, he comes to Me, O *Pāṇḍava* [*Arjuna*].

ओं तत्सदिति श्रीमद्भगवद्गीतासूपनिषत्सु ब्रह्मविद्यायां योगशास्त्रे
श्रीकृष्णार्जुनसंवादे विश्वरूपदर्शनयोगो नामैकादशोऽध्यायः॥

*oṁ tatsaditi śrīmadbhagavadgītāsūpaniṣatsu*
*brahmavidyāyāṁ yogaśāstre śrīkṛṣṇārjunasaṁvāde*
*viśvarūpadarśanayogo nāmaikādaśo'dhyāyaḥ ||*

*Oṁ*, this is the Truth. Thus is the eleventh chapter, the subject [of which] is called "*viśvarūpadarśana*" [the cosmic vision], in the glorious *Bhagavadgītā*, [which is equivalent to] the *Upaniṣads*, [the subject of which is] the knowledge of *Brahman* [and] *yoga*, in the dialogue between *śrī Kṛṣṇa* and *Arjuna*.

# Chapter 12

## *Devotion*

The theme of this chapter is devotion. The devout are those that recognize the nature of *Īśvara* and act according to *dharma*, avoiding *adharma*.

*Dharma* is an ensemble of universal values, as well as that which must be done by each individual in a given situation. It is also known as svadharma. To act while obeying *dharma* is to respect *dharma*; therefore, in the event there is a conflict or antagonism between one's desires and *dharma*, to forfeit such desires in order to uphold *dharma* is to respect *dharma*.

This conflict is due to *rāgas* - that which one likes to do and has a taste for; and *dveṣas* - that which one dislikes and avoids. As long as what one likes to do is aligned with what one should do, there is no conflict and *dharma* reigns. However, there is often an antagonism between desire and *dharma*. If the individual opts to do what should be done, *dharma*, while disregarding tastes and aversions, there will be no conflict. On the contrary, if the individual is not able to disregard tastes and aversions in order to do what must be done, conflict is then inevitable. This is an internal conflict, because the human being already has an innate sense of that which is appropriate and inappropriate behavior, and at the same time has a feeling for that which is desirable and undesirable - not only for himself but for others as well. Therefore, that which is against *dharma* is in opposition to *Īśvara*, the cosmic order of *dharma*. The devout perform action for *Īśvara*, which means acting according to *dharma*. This is a choice, since the free will of man may opt for the contrary.

This chapter begins with yet another question from *Arjuna*, not unlike the others he has already made. *Arjuna* wishes to renounce action, thinking erroneously that doing so is the way to liberation. His *guru* asks him to do the opposite, to perform action, but changing only his attitude when doing so.

In reality, there is actually no choice between *sannyāsa* and *karmayoga*. *Sannyāsa* demands the maturity that a life of *karmayoga* brings. If an individual already has the preparedness to renounce, there will be neither conflict nor doubt about which choice is better. *Kṛṣṇa* states that there is renouncement in *karmayoga* and requests that *Arjuna* perform his actions with an appropriate attitude.

Thus, once again, *Arjuna* makes the same question that he has asked since the beginning of the *Bhagavadgītā*, but he has now placed the question a little differently. He wants to know which is better: those that seek *nirguṇabrahman* via the knowledge of *Ātman*, the Self that is *Brahman*; or those that seek *saguṇabrahman*, *Īśvara*. The former are on their way to renouncement, *nivṛtti-mārga*; the latter have chosen *pravṛtti-mārga*, the road of action. The *karmayogin* has obligations with family, society, the country, and with *Īśvara*; he meditates on *saguṇabrahman*, which is *Īśvara*. For those that have renounced, there are no more obligations. Such an individual may dedicate himself solely to self-knowledge, and meditate on *nirguṇabrahman*, That which has no form, the truth of *jīva*, the individual, and *Īśvara*.

The question appears different, since *Arjuna* does not specifically ask about *sannyāsa* or *karmayoga*, but in essence the question is quite the same. He asks about those that meditate on the Imperishable via *nirguṇabrahma-upāsanā* (the contemplation of *Brahman* that is *Ātman*) and the devout that meditate on *Īśvara* via *saguṇabrahma-upāsanā*.

Always being mindful of *Īśvara* and acting accordingly makes a person a devotee and also a *karmayogin* - the two of which are not different, says *Śrī Kṛṣṇa*. Furthermore, devotion demands knowledge, since it is impossible to love someone or something without comprehending it. Loving that which is unknown to us is to love only our image of an object and not really the object itself. Devotion, on the other hand, is love without limits, without any conditions or demands. Unconditional love requires a complete comprehension of the other. Only when the object of love is immutable may love be unconditional. Therefore, this unconditional love that is devotion to *Īśvara* requires a complete comprehension of His absolute and immutable nature. Hence, the devotee is also wise, and also a *karmayogin*.

It is a mistake to think that one may choose among three or more options for liberation: *karmayoga, bhaktiyoga* or *jñānayoga* - meaning the paths of action, devotion, or knowledge. This is a mistaken perspective on the means or path to liberation. In fact, all three practices work jointly as a means to an end. However, among the three, *jñānayoga* is simply not a choice because knowledge is undoubtedly the direct means to liberation, since the very feeling of being limited is due to an error regarding oneself - the ignorance of one's true nature that can only be revealed by knowledge. Knowledge is a direct means to *mokṣa*.

The other two paths are choices that one can make to help gain the necessary qualifications for *mokṣa*. In the event the individual's mind is reactive, agitated and attached to concepts and beliefs, *karmayoga* is applied. And for *karmayoga*, the understanding of and surrender to *Īśvara* - which is *bhakti* - is essential. Surrender and love demand a prior knowledge of the person or object to which such devotion will be dedicated. Were it any other way, the love dedicated will not be for a specific person or object, but rather for what one imagines them to be. Hence, there is no option among the three paths as a means for liberation, but each one is directly linked to the other. For the wise who possess knowledge, the attitude of *karmayoga* and devotion are natural; for those seeking knowledge, *karmayoga* and devotion are disciplines practiced while acquiring knowledge.

The individual may be seen as different from *Īśvara* since the former has a body - a form - and the latter includes all forms. However, the form of the individual is included in the cosmic form; therefore, there is actually no difference between them. Moreover, from the perspective of the Absolute, the individual and *Īśvara* are the same *sat-cit-ānanda Brahman*. Just as the waves and the ocean, although different in form, the wave is at the same time part of the ocean, and they are essentially the same reality: water.

Nevertheless, as an individual, a person must relate with different people. In each relationship, a person is different, assuming a different role, which changes according to the way others also change. For a father, the individual may be a son; for the son, the individual may be the father - and his language, attitude and thought may completely modify accordingly. However, there is one relationship that is constant and fundamental: the one between the creature and the Creator. As a creature of the Universe, the individual necessarily relates to the Creator in the form of the Universe and its laws, whether recognizing this fact or not. It is the awareness of this relationship between the creature and the Creator that makes one devout. However, for some people, this fundamental relationship still has not been realized, and it is only recognized in specific acts of worship, such as before an altar, in which an individual has an apparent bout of temporary devotion.

While a person still does not yet recognize the devotee inside oneself, or one's relationship with the Creator, some actions to make the devotee inside more apparent are indicated. These devotional actions are called worship, because they bring the devotee inside to the surface of the mind. Only the devout that recognize the reality of *Īśvara* discover their identity with Him.

In this chapter, *Śrī Kṛṣṇa* says that devotion is not a special act of worship, but the attitude behind a given action, which is the meaning behind verse 6 of this chapter.

Thus we see that devotion is not quite as simple as it is said to be. It is not just an act of worship, but an entire attitude that starts upon an understanding. In many cases, devotion is impossible due to the ego of a person, the *ahaṅkāra*, which means the exaggerated vision of oneself and the false sensation of being the center of the Universe. Imprisoned by one's tastes and aversions, this individual suffers and feels isolated from the world without recognizing the Order that is *Īśvara*. Only the devout - with a mind free from the prison of the tastes and aversions - are capable of accommodating the entire universe and beholding the truth as taught by the *guru*: the indivisible identity between the individual and *Īśvara*. Such is the devotion of the wise: it is the absolute love that exists once the ego that had previously separated the individual from *Īśvara* is debased and recognized as unreal. Thus, the duality of jiva and *Īśvara* is dissolved, and there remains the oneness in which the only thing that exists is *Īśvara*, which is *Brahman*.

## Summary of the verses

Verse 1: *Arjuna* wants to know which is better: to be a devotee of *saguṇabrahman*, whose form has been described, or to be a devotee of *nirguṇabrahman*, the imperishable and unmanifest.

Verse 2: Although those that meditate on the Imperishable are identical to *Īśvara*, *Kṛṣṇa* says that *karmayogins* are better, because He knows it is safer for *Arjuna* to be a *karmayogin*, following the life of a *karmayogin*.

In fact, one only reaches liberation with knowledge of *nirguṇabrahman*, but meditation on *saguṇabrahman* is important.

Verses 3 to 5: *Kṛṣṇa* says that one who controls one's senses and one's mind, and meditates on the indestructible, attains *Īśvara*. This person who contemplates *akṣarabrahman* already has his or her mind disciplined and relates to the world objectively.

It is important to note how *Śrī Kṛṣṇa* says that *karmayogins* are better and special, but never affirms that the *karmayogin* attains final liberation, since in fact it is the teaching and contemplation of *nirguṇabrahman* that constitute the means to reach indivisibility with *Brahman*!

He also points out that contemplation of *nirguṇabrahman* is simply not possible for people without discipline and who are attached to the body and things related to the body.

Verses 6 to 8: *Śrī Kṛṣṇa* says that people dedicated to seeking *saguṇabrahman*, the devout, and *karmayogins* who focus the mind on *Īśvara*, are helped in leaving the ocean that is *saṁsāra*. The dedication and commitment of these people - as expressed in all their actions and way of life - will lead them to opportunities to encounter an appropriate teacher and instruction.

There is a misconception regarding verse 7. The word *samuddhartā* is translated as "savior" and it is said that *Īśvara* saves his worshippers (and only these!) from *saṁsāra*. Such prejudice is an obvious contradiction to everything that has been taught in the *Gītā*! Moreover: exactly what kind of salvation would this be referring to anyway?

This confusion is due to a mistaken presupposition that the individual is limited and that liberation, *mokṣa*, is a process in which the individual will transform from what one is now to another state in the future. Much to the contrary: *mokṣa* is attained by the knowledge that the essential nature of *jīva*, the individual, is eternal and unlimited. Therefore, the liberation that actually takes place is one of freedom from the ignorance and the mistaken or false references of oneself.

The so-called "blessing of *Īśvara*" comes in the form of the result of one's action. A person is blessed due to one's effort, whether in the form of the qualifications necessary for liberation or liberation itself. Such a blessed person is clear of mind and has the means to acquire knowledge. This blessed person becomes clearly aware of the indivisible identity between *jīva*, the individual, and *Īśvara*, That which is Everything.

Therefore, effort, commitment and sincerity directed to *Īśvara* lead the devout to their oneness with Him.

Verse 9: *Kṛṣṇa* says that if it is not possible to focus the mind on *saguṇabrahman*, there is yet one thing that can be done: *abhyāsa*, discipline in the form of mindful - and not mechanical - repetition. *Śrī Kṛṣṇa* says that *abhyāsa* is to constantly return the mind to the same object of meditation and fix it there (*cittasya ekasmin ālambane sarvataḥ samāhṛtya punaḥ punaḥ sthāpana abhyāsaḥ*). There are many disciplines that can lead the mind to focus on *saguṇabrahman*: *japa, dhāraṇā, dhyāna* and *upāsanā* - all of which will thereby lead to an awareness of *nirguṇabrahman*.

Verse 10: However, in case not even such mindful repetition is possible, one must do one's daily obligations and disciplines dedicated to *Īśvara*, as a *karmayogin*, without focusing on the result of action, but rather dedicating it as an offering.

Verse 11: Nonetheless, if even this is too difficult, because one has too many desires and is practicing *kāma-karma*, or actions stimulated by desire, one should remember *Īśvara*, who is *karmaphala-dātṛ* – He that governs action and its results – and receive such results as coming from Him, and do so without reacting.

Both attitudes as mentioned by *Śrī Kṛṣṇa* in verses 10 and 11 are *karmayoga*. In verse 10, the focus is on action; in verse 11, the focus is on receiving the result of action. The *karmayogin* prepares for the awareness of *nirguṇabrahman*.

Verse 12: *Kṛṣṇa*, praising the renunciation of the fruit of action as a way to prepare the mind for knowledge, says that knowledge is superior to meditation without knowledge; however, meditation with knowledge is superior to knowledge with obstacles (such as doubt and lack of clarity); renouncing the result of action (which is *karmayoga*) is superior to meditation. Renunciation is praised, since it brings immediate peace. Receiving the result of action as *prasāda*, a present from *Īśvara*, brings immediate peace of mind: this attitude is called *prasāda-buddhi*.

Verse 13 to 20: The characteristics of the wise become the inspiration and disciplines of the ignorant. The devout to *saguṇabrahman* are also *karmayogin*; they see *Īśvara* as separate from them. This devotion, *bhakti*, is not a higher form of devotion. The greatest devotion of all is that of the wise who recognize the indivisibility between *jīva* and *Īśvara*.

*Nārada*, in his *bhaktisūtra*, calls the first form of devotion *aparā bhakti*, and the second, *parā bhakti*: inferior and superior devotion. In these verses, *Śrī Kṛṣṇa* describes the devout, who are also wise. The wise are described as possessing various characteristics, such as being friendly, compassionate, balanced, accommodating, satisfied, calm, self-controlled, knowledgeable, devoted, subtle, pure, efficient and impartial; while at the same time, they are described as being free from aversion, the notion of "mine", the false notion of "I", euphoria, intolerance, fear, anxiety, dependence on others, egotistical action, sadness, ambition, and attachment to the pairs of opposites.

Finally, in verse 20, *Śrī Kṛṣṇa* tells *Arjuna*, in response to his question, that those who follow His instruction on *dharma* and the Absolute, with faith in the teaching, holding *Īśvara* as the highest objective, are much loved by Him.

## अथ द्वादशोऽध्यायः

***atha dvādaśo'dhyāyaḥ***

**Chapter twelve**

अर्जुन उवाच
एवं सततयुक्ता ये भक्तास्त्वां पर्युपासते ।
ये चाप्यक्षरमव्यक्तं तेषां के योगवित्तमाः ॥१॥

*arjuna uvāca*
*evaṁ satatayuktā ye bhaktāstvāṁ paryupāsate |*
*ye cāpyakṣaramavyaktaṁ teṣāṁ ke yogavittamāḥ ||1||*

**1.** *Arjuna* spoke:
— Then, between the dedicated devout who meditate on You and those that meditate on the Imperishable and Unmanifest, which are the best *yogins*?

श्रीभगवानुवाच
मय्यावेश्य मनो ये मां नित्ययुक्ता उपासते ।
श्रद्धया परयोपेतास्ते मे युक्ततमा मताः ॥२॥

*śrībhagavānuvāca*
*mayyāveśya mano ye māṁ nityayuktā upāsate |*
*śraddhayā parayopetāste me yuktatamā matāḥ ||2||*

**2.** The Lord [*Kṛṣṇa*] spoke:
— Those who have fixed their minds on Me, who are always committed to Me, who meditate on Me [and] are endowed with great Faith, these [people] are considered the best *yogins* by Me.

ये त्वक्षरमनिर्देश्यमव्यक्तं पर्युपासते ।
सर्वत्रगमचिन्त्यं च कूटस्थमचलं ध्रुवम् ॥३॥

*ye tvakṣaramanirdeśyamavyaktaṁ paryupāsate |*
*sarvatragamacintyaṁ ca kūṭasthamacalaṁ dhruvam ||3||*

3. However, those that meditate on the Imperishable that everything pervades, the undefinable, the unmanifest, the unimaginable, the immutable, the unmoving, the eternal,

सन्नियम्येन्द्रियग्रामं सर्वत्र समबुद्धयः ।
ते प्राप्नुवन्ति मामेव सर्वभूतहिते रताः ॥४॥

*sanniyamyendriyagrāmaṁ sarvatra samabuddhayaḥ |*
*te prāpnuvanti māmeva sarvabhūtahite ratāḥ ||4||*

**4.** these [people], having disciplined the organs of perception and action, even-minded on all occasions, rejoicing in the welfare of all beings, they truly reach Me.

क्लेशोऽधिकतरस्तेषामव्यक्तासक्तचेतसाम् ।
अव्यक्ता हि गतिर्दुःखं देहवद्भिरवाप्यते ॥५॥

*kleśo'dhikatarasteṣāmavyaktāsaktacetasām |*
*avyaktā hi gatirduḥkhaṁ dehavadbhiravāpyate ||5||*

**5.** The difficulty is much greater for those whose minds are focused on the Unmanifest, since the target that is the Unmanifest can hardly be reached by those attached to the body.

ये तु सर्वाणि कर्माणि मयि सन्न्यस्य मत्पराः ।
अनन्येनैव योगेन मां ध्यायन्त उपासते ॥६॥

*ye tu sarvāṇi karmāṇi mayi sannyasya matparāḥ |*
*ananyenaiva yogena māṁ dhyāyanta upāsate ||6||*

**6.** However, those that seek Me, holding Me as the highest objective, renouncing all their action to Me, [and] meditating with complete surrender,

तेषामहं समुद्धर्ता मृत्युसंसारसागरात् ।
भवामि न चिरात्पार्थ मय्यावेशितचेतसाम् ॥७॥

*teṣāmahaṁ samuddhartā mṛtyusaṁsārasāgarāt |*
*bhavāmi na cirātpārtha mayyāveśitacetasām ||7||*

**7.** for these [people], who have turned their minds to Me, I thus become the liberator from the ocean of *saṁsāra*, which is characterized by death, O *Pārtha* [*Arjuna*].

मय्येव मन आधत्स्व मयि बुद्धिं निवेशय ।
निवसिष्यसि मय्येव अत ऊर्ध्वं न संशयः ॥८॥

*mayyeva mana ādhatsva mayi buddhiṁ niveśaya |*
*nivasiṣyasi mayyeva ata ūrdhvaṁ na saṁśayaḥ ||8||*

**8.** Turn the mind to Me. Make the intellect penetrate Me. And afterwards, there is no doubt that you shall remain with Me.

अथ चित्तं समाधातुं न शक्नोषि मयि स्थिरम् ।
अभ्यासयोगेन ततो मामिच्छाप्तुं धनञ्जय ॥९॥

*atha cittaṁ samādhātuṁ na śaknoṣi mayi sthiram |*
*abhyāsayogena tato māmicchāptuṁ dhanañjaya ||9||*

**9.** If you cannot firmly fix the mind on Me, then try to reach Me by the discipline of repetition, O *Dhanañjaya* [*Arjuna*].

अभ्यासेऽप्यसमर्थोऽसि मत्कर्मपरमो भव ।
मदर्थमपि कर्माणि कुर्वन् सिद्धिमवाप्स्यसि ॥१०॥

*abhyāse'pyasamartho'si matkarmaparamo bhava |*
*madarthamapi karmāṇi kurvan siddhimavāpsyasi ||10||*

**10.** [If] you are incapable of the practice of repetition, become one for whom actions dedicated to Me are the utmost important. Even by doing mere actions, [if] dedicated to Me, you shall be successful.

अथैतदप्यशक्तोऽसि कर्तुं मद्योगमाश्रितः ।
सर्वकर्मफलत्यागं ततः कुरु यतात्मवान् ॥११॥

*athaitadapyaśakto'si kartuṁ madyogamāśritaḥ |*
*sarvakarmaphalatyāgaṁ tataḥ kuru yatātmavān ||11||*

**11.** If even this you are unable to do, then renounce the fruit of all actions, dedicating yourself to perform actions for Me, with a disciplined mind.

श्रेयो हि ज्ञानमभ्यासाज्ज्ञानाद्ध्यानं विशिष्यते ।
ध्यानात्कर्मफलत्यागस्त्यागाच्छान्तिरनन्तरम् ॥१२॥

*śreyo hi jñānamabhyāsājjñānāddhyānaṁ viśiṣyate |*
*dhyānātkarmaphalatyāgastyāgācchāntiranantaram ||12||*

**12.** Knowledge is indeed better than the practice of repetition. Meditation [with knowledge] is better than knowledge [alone]. Renouncing the results of actions is better than meditation, since from renunciation comes peace.

अद्वेष्टा सर्वभूतानां मैत्रः करुण एव च ।
निर्ममो निरहङ्कारः समदुःखसुखः क्षमी ॥१३॥

*adveṣṭā sarvabhūtānāṁ maitraḥ karuṇa eva ca |*
*nirmamo nirahaṅkāraḥ samaduḥkhasukhaḥ kṣamī ||13||*

**13.** One who has no aversions, who is friendly with all beings and truly wields compassion, who is free of the notions of "mine" and "I", who is the same in both situations pleasant and unpleasant, who is accommodating,

सन्तुष्टः सततं योगी यतात्मा दृढनिश्चयः ।
मय्यर्पितमनोबुद्धिर्यो मद्भक्तः स मे प्रियः ॥१४॥

*santuṣṭaḥ satataṁ yogī yatātmā dṛḍhaniścayaḥ |*
*mayyarpitamanobuddhiryo madbhaktaḥ sa me priyaḥ ||14||*

**14.** one who is always content, who is a *yogin* [who has an unwavering mind], who is self-controlled, whose knowledge is firm, who has surrendered the mind and intellect to me, this my devotee is loved by Me.

यस्मान्नोद्विजते लोको लोकान्नोद्विजते च यः ।
हर्षामर्षभयोद्वेगैर्मुक्तो यः स च मे प्रियः ॥१५॥

*yasmānnodvijate loko lokānnodvijate ca yaḥ |*
*harṣāmarṣabhayodvegairmukto yaḥ sa ca me priyaḥ ||15||*

**15.** One who neither disturbs the world nor is disturbed by the world, who is free from euphoria, intolerance, fear and anxiety, this [person] is loved by Me.

अनपेक्षः शुचिर्दक्ष उदासीनो गतव्यथः ।
सर्वारम्भपरित्यागी यो मद्भक्तः स मे प्रियः ॥१६॥

*anapekṣaḥ śucirdakṣa udāsīno gatavyathaḥ |*
*sarvārambhaparityāgī yo madbhaktaḥ sa me priyaḥ ||16||*

**16.** One who is free from dependence [on others and things], who is pure, competent, impartial, free of fear, who has abandoned all egotistical action, this my devotee is loved by Me.

यो न हृष्यति न द्वेष्टि न शोचति न काङ्क्षति ।
शुभाशुभपरित्यागी भक्तिमान्यः स मे प्रियः ॥१७॥

*yo na hṛṣyati na dveṣṭi na śocati na kāṅkṣati |*
*śubhāśubhaparityāgī bhaktimānyaḥ sa me priyaḥ ||17||*

**17.** One who neither rejoices, nor hates, nor grieves, nor desires, one who has abandoned [actions] good and evil, one who has devotion, this [person] is loved by Me.

समः शत्रौ च मित्रे च तथा मानापमानयोः ।
शीतोष्णसुखदुःखेषु समः सङ्गविवर्जितः ।।१८।।

*samaḥ śatrau ca mitre ca tathā mānāpamānayoḥ |*
*śītoṣṇasukhaduḥkheṣu samaḥ saṅgavivarjitaḥ ||18||*

**18.** One who remains the same before a friend or foe, before honor or disgrace, who remains the same in cold or heat, in happiness and sadness, free from attachment,

तुल्यनिन्दास्तुतिर्मौनी सन्तुष्टो येन केनचित् ।
अनिकेतः स्थिरमतिर्भक्तिमान्मे प्रियो नरः ।।१९।।

*tulyanindāstutirmaunī santuṣṭo yena kenacit |*
*aniketaḥ sthiramatirbhaktimānme priyo naraḥ ||19||*

**19.** One who remains the same before blame or praise, who measures words, content with anything, homeless [without attachment to place and objects] with unwavering knowledge, who has devotion, [this] person is loved by Me.

ये तु धर्म्यामृतमिदं यथोक्तं पर्युपासते ।
श्रद्दधाना मत्परमा भक्तास्तेऽतीव मे प्रियाः ।।२०।।

*ye tu dharmyāmṛtamidaṁ yathoktaṁ paryupāsate |*
*śraddadhānā matparamā bhaktāste'tīva me priyāḥ ||20||*

**20.** As has been spoken, the devout that follow this [knowledge] on what is righteous and leads to immortality, with Faith [in this instruction and in the *guru*], holding Me as the highest objective, are much loved by Me.

ओं तत्सदिति श्रीमद्भगवद्गीतासूपनिषत्सु ब्रह्मविद्यायां योगशास्त्रे
श्रीकृष्णार्जुनसंवादे भक्तियोगो नाम द्वादशोऽध्यायः ॥

*oṁ tatsaditi śrīmadbhagavadgītāsūpaniṣatsu*
*brahmavidyāyāṁ yogaśāstre śrīkṛṣṇārjunasaṁvāde*
*bhaktiyogo nāma dvādaśo'dhyāyaḥ ||*

*Oṁ*, this is the Truth. Thus is the twelfth chapter, the subject [of which] is called "*bhakti*" [devotion], in the glorious *Bhagavadgītā*, [which is equivalent to] the *Upaniṣads*, [the subject of which is] the knowledge of *Brahman* [and] *yoga*, in the dialogue between *śrī Kṛṣṇa* and *Arjuna*.

# Chapter 13

## *The distinction between the field and one who knows the field*

The main theme of the first six last chapters of the *Bhagavadgītā* is the indivisible identity of *jīva* (the individual) and *Īśvara*. This identity is revealed in the phrase "*tat tvam asi*": "you are That". "You" is *jīva*, "That" is *Īśvara*, and the verb to be, "are", indicates this identity.

At first, this realization seems preposterous, but it is explained in many texts of *Vedānta*, primarily in the *Upaniṣads* and in the *Bhagavadgītā*.

Recognizing the fact that this identity is quite difficult to comprehend, *Kṛṣṇa* offers *Arjuna* - and all of us - some help regarding the qualification of the mind for this understanding, in the form of values and attitudes.

There are some values that contribute to the awareness of the absolute Self, and also to distinguishing that which is apparently real but is in fact false.

Chapter 13 begins with a request from *Arjuna* to explain six terms. It is said that verse 1 was not part of the *Gītā* that *Śrī Śaṅkara* had in hand, since he made absolutely no reference to it; however, this verse presents the topics to be covered in the chapter. The terms are *kṣetra* (the field), *kṣetrajña* (he who knows the field), *jñāna* (the qualifications that lead to knowledge), *jñeya* (That which is to be known), *Puruṣa* (the Self) and *Prakṛti* (the cause of the relative world).

There has always been much confusion regarding this terminology; therefore, it is understandable why *Arjuna* requested clarification.

Although the verse presents the words in another order,

we have chosen to group them accordingly, since they can be divided into three pairs.

*Kṣetra* means "a place or field that is cultivated, where something is planted and its result is harvested".

*Śrī Kṛṣṇa* says that *kṣetra* is the entire universe, beginning with the body. He mentions the body, since we consider ourselves to be the body, which is one of the meanings of "I". All that which is experienced is *kṣetra*.

*Kṣetrajña* is the consciousness by which all the *kṣetra* is known and which is present in all bodies.

*Jñāna* means "knowledge"; however, here it is defined as the values or qualifications of the mind that collaborate to comprehend the absolute Self. These values are listed in verses 8 to 12.

*Jñeya* is That which is to be known, mentioned in verses 13 to 18. *Kṛṣṇa* says that by knowing this *jñeya,* which is in fact *Brahman,* one attains immortality. *Brahman* is defined as That which has no beginning; That which may not be called as existent (as an object) or nonexistent; That which sustains all beings, as well as the creator and destroyer of all things. *Brahman* is the light of all lights, the Consciousness of consciousness that illuminates even ignorance; it is the Consciousness that is present in all minds.

Therefore, our *guru Kṛṣṇa* gives us a beautiful explanation via paradoxes: although apparently divided into creator, sustainer, and destroyer of the universe, *Brahman,* That which is to be known, is indivisible; it is That which experiences all qualities while at the same time is exempt from any qualities whatsoever; *Brahman* becomes manifest via the organs while not possessing any organs; *Brahman* is both inside and outside all beings in the universe; *Brahman* is to be known as distinct from both the body and the universe, although it is due to Him that the body and universe exist. Furthermore, since *Brahman* has no form, He cannot be known as would an object.

Finally, *Prakṛti* and *Puruṣa* are explained. *Śrī Kṛṣṇa* states that both have no beginning. Due to *Prakṛti*, *Īśvara* becomes the Cause of the universe. The multitude in the universe exists because of *Prakṛti*, which is not independent from *Puruṣa*. It is due to *Puruṣa* that the individual comes to experience things. *Puruṣa* is another word for *kṣetrajña*.

Together, *Puruṣa* and *Prakṛti* are the cause of *saṁsāra*; however, the two cannot be joined to create anything, since the former is absolute and the latter is relative. The connection between the two is only apparent, since the entire universe is merely superimposed on the Absolute.

*Saṁsāra* is the experience of *sukha* and *duḥkha*, joy and pain; one who experiences *saṁsāra* is a *saṁsārin*. Within this definition, it appears that *Puruṣa* is *saṁsārin*; however, this cannot be true: because if the Self, which is *Puruṣa*, were subjugated to *saṁsāra*, it would be limited as all objects, and thus liberation, or *mokṣa*, would not be possible. Therefore, the sense of being a *saṁsārin*, of being limited, is just a feeling and not a reality - because that which is real is immutable and absolute, which is the Self.

*Śrī Kṛṣṇa* presents a solution for this problem, this enigma: the state of *saṁsārin* is only due to ignorance. It is a problem created by the inadequate interpretation of individual experience. The fact that one feels limited, as a *saṁsārin*, is a mistaken conclusion. Although *asaṅga* by nature, and free from all attachment or association, the *Puruṣa* is often identified as *Prakṛti*, which is limited just as the physical body, the mind and senses; this association is not real or true or a reality and is caused by the ignorance of one's own true nature. There is no other cause for *saṁsāra*!

Therefore, *Śrī Kṛṣṇa* says that awareness of the *Puruṣa*

is necessary for the liberation from *saṁsāra*. A person who sees *Īśvara* in all beings – who sees that which is indestructible even when things perish – sees the one true reality, and is thereby liberated from delusion and suffering.

In order to attain this knowledge with clarity, some practices, such as questioning, contemplation, and *karmayoga* are necessary, as well as following the instruction of qualified gurus.

Only an individual who has prepared the mind and who has listened to the teachings will be capable of recognizing oneself as the one true reality that performs no action and is neither subject to its results, just as space is always pure and is affected by nothing.

Just as the sun illuminates everything, *Puruṣa* (which is *kṣetrajña*, the *Ātman*) illuminates the *kṣetra*, since its very nature is the light, Consciousness, which is but one.

*Śrī Kṛṣṇa* ends the chapter by stating that those who recognize the difference between *kṣetra* and *kṣetrajña* shall reach the ultimate objective: liberation.

## Summary of the verses

Verse 1: This verse is not part of the *Bhagavadgītā* as *Śrī Śaṅkara* would have had in hand, since he made no mention of it. However, this verse that is the question of *Arjuna* is useful in presenting the three pairs of words that are explained throughout the chapter.

Verses 2 and 3: *Śrī Kṛṣṇa* begins to respond and reorganize the words mentioned. He begins with *kṣetra* and *kṣetrajña*, which are synonyms for *Prakṛti* and *Puruṣa*. He states that *kṣetra*, which means the "field", is the body. The pronouns "this" and "it" refer to objects. The body is a place where action is done and the results are acquired. The body is specifically mentioned, since it is most often mistaken as being the subject, rather than being correctly perceived as yet another object that is part of the Universe.

*Kṣetrajña* is that which recognizes the *kṣetra*. It is the true subject, and afterwards *Śrī Kṛṣṇa* defines it as *parameśvara*, the Consciousness in all bodies.

Since *kṣetrajña* is *jīva* and also *parameśvara*, these two verses disclose the teaching of the *mahāvākya*: "*tat tvam asi*", "you are That"; the individual is That which is Everything; *jīva* is *Īśvara*.

*Śaṅkara*'s commentary, called the *Śaṅkara bhāṣya*, on verse 3, is an extensive and elaborate analysis of the vision of non-duality, *advaita* - which refers to the indivisible identity of *jīva* and *Īśvara* - by which one is liberated from the feeling of limitation.

Verses 4 and 5: *Śrī Kṛṣṇa* presents the theme of this chapter, *kṣetra* and *kṣetrajña*, which are explained in many hymns and in much discourse by the wise and in the words of the *Vedas*.

Verses 6 and 7: These verses define *kṣetra*, which went by the name of *Prakṛti* in chapter 7, verse 4. *Prakṛti* has eight aspects: the five subtle elements, *samaṣṭi-ahaṅkāra* (or *hiraṇyagarbha*), *buddhi* (or *mahat*) and *avyakta*.

The combination of the five subtle elements are the cause of the five gross elements (space, air, fire, water, and earth) and of the cosmic-ego, which is also called *hiraṇyagarbha* or *Brahmājī*, the origin of all creation; *mahat*, also called *samaṣṭi-buddhi*, is the initial impulse for creation, the cause of the cosmic ego; and finally, *avyakta* is the unmanifest state of all creation, the potential for the manifestation of the universe. This *avyakta* is *māyā śakti*, the power of *Īśvara* to manifest the universe.

The second line of verse 6 and verse 7 cover *vikṛti* or *vikāra*, the modifications of *Prakṛti*.

All these eight aspects and their respective modification are *kṣetra*. The physical, subtle and causal bodies have been included, along with the senses, the objects of the senses and the mind with its various thoughts.

Verses 8 to 12: In these verses, *Kṛṣṇa* has given us the qualifications necessary for the acquisition of knowledge, which is herein called *jñāna*. When the mind possesses a value for these twenty values[11], and these values are present in the mind of the seeker, this mind is acknowledged as being prepared for the acquisition of self-knowledge.

Verses 13 to 18: *Kṛṣṇa* tells us what is *jñeya*, That which is to be known, which is called *Brahman*: That which has no beginning, cannot be heralded as neither existent nor non-existent; That which is both inside and outside of all beings; That which is motionless, but at the same time, That which moves; That which is far from those that seek It as an object, and so close to those who know that *Brahman* is aham, one's own Self.

*Brahman* is That which is the most subtle, even more subtle than space. *Brahman* has no specific form, qualities or parts. *Brahman* pervades everything and is in every place. Both time and space exist in *Brahman*. Therefore, since *Brahman* is not a specific object, there is no way that it may be discovered by means of knowledge. It may only be recognized as the subject itself, the Self, which is Consciousness, *caitanya*.

*Brahman* is indivisible, but appears to be divided by the *upādhis*, the conditioning factors of various bodies. Although many people, *jīvas*, experience feelings of separation, there is in fact no such separation from *Brahman*, which is the one

---

11 Swami Dayananda explains each one of these 20 values in his book DAYANANDA, S. The Value of Values, Arsha Vidya Research and Publication Trust. Chennai, India.

true reality that pervades everything. Thus, there is no need for trying to end such divisions or separation when in fact they do not exist. What is essentially needed is to eliminate the ignorance, confusion and mistaken identity regarding this one true reality.

With regard to the Universe, *Brahman* is the creator, its sustainer, and its destroyer.

*Brahman* is the light in all sources of light and beyond the reach of the darkness that is ignorance, since Consciousness is capable of illuminating even ignorance. An awareness of *Brahman*, which is present in the mind of all beings, may be achieved by way of a *vṛtti*, an insightful thought.

The method of teaching is specific and unique. Only by following the traditional teaching may an awareness of *Brahman*, which is *Ātman*, be achieved. One of the methods is the use of paradoxes; *Brahman* is explained by use of *upādhis*, superimposed conditioning factors that are immediately contradicted as not pertaining to *Brahman* (such as a clear, colorless crystal appearing as a red stone due to a red cloth near it; the red cloth is an *upādhi*). This method is called *adhyāropa-apavāda* (superimposition-negation), meaning the negation of that which is superimposed.

The method is used by *Śrī Kṛṣṇa*, especially in verses 14 and 15, to teach *Arjuna*. First *Brahman* is cited with *upādhis*, with apparent conditioning factors and afterwards, correctly restated as free of any *upādhis*, thereby rendering the *upādhis* as *mithyā*: not pertaining to *Brahman* in fact, but only apparently. When the *upādhis* are hence negated, when the *śruti* (the Vedic texts) state that *Brahman* is neither *sat* nor *asat*, neither something nor its opposite, it may suggest that *Brahman* is *śūnya*, a zero or emptiness. Therefore, to negate such zero or emptiness, *Brahman* is given characteristics and presented as 'That which has hands and feet on all sides, and also ears; That which pervades all that exists'. *Brahman* appears with *upādhis* and their characteristics; however, *Brahman* is essentially free of all *upādhis*. What is not real is called *mithyā* and is dependent on *Brahman*.

*Brahman* appears with the qualities of the senses, but is free of all senses; free of any associations, despite the fact that *Brahman* upholds everything; *Brahman* experiences all qualities, the *guṇas*, but remains completely free from them.

Verse 19: in this verse, *Śrī Kṛṣṇa* summarizes what has already been covered - *kṣetra, kṣetrajña, jñāna* and *jñeya* - responding to part of the question from *Arjuna*. Then, *Kṛṣṇa* praises the person that dedicates himself to this learning, saying that an individual attains an identity with *Īśvara* once comprehending all that has been taught. The qualification necessary for this goal is dedication, devotion to *Īśvara* and the awareness of Him that is, in fact, self-knowledge.

Verses 20 to 24: *Śrī Kṛṣṇa* responds to the final part of the question from *Arjuna* - what is *Puruṣa* and *Prakṛti*? Both have no beginning. *Prakṛti* creates everything due to *Puruṣa*; therefore, both are the cause of everything.

*Prakṛti* is the cause of the body, the mind and its activities; *Puruṣa* is the cause of all experiences, whether positive or negative, joy or pain. In the physical body, *Puruṣa* appears to be *kartṛ* (the agent of action) and *bhoktṛ* (that which receives the result of action and experiences it). Although free from any bond, *Puruṣa* is stuck in *saṁsāra*, due to the attachment and identity with the body, mind and senses and their qualities. The cause of this attachment is ignorance of one's true nature. The cause of *saṁsāra* is neither in *Puruṣa*, nor in *Prakṛti*, but in the identity that arises from this combination, which is *jīva*. In fact, neither *saṁsāra* nor *jīva* are real. For liberation from *saṁsāra*, self-knowledge is fundamental, which means the awareness that *Puruṣa* is *Ātman*.The individual who fully comprehends *Puruṣa* and *Prakṛti* will no longer be born.

Verses 25 and 26: Some *upāyas* are presented, which are means to help acquire *ātma-darśana*, the vision of the Self, such as *dhyāna* (meditation), etc.

Besides listening to the discourse on the Self, contemplation is important; for some, besides contemplation, analysis is necessary; and yet for others, *karmayoga* is paramount.

Others need more qualifications and are instructed by their gurus to follow various disciplines.

Verse 27: The reason for which the knowledge of the indivisible identity between *kṣetrajña* (*Ātman*) and *Īśvara* leads to *mokṣa* is explained: the union between *kṣetra* and *kṣetrajña*, although experienced, is indeed impossible, since *kṣetrajña* is *Ātman* and *kṣetra* is *anātman*. This union is in fact superimposed, just as the illustration of the snake and the rope: they cannot be united into one, but one is confused for the other, since the characteristics of one - such as long, thin, flexibe - may be mistaken for the other. Therefore, we have an *adhyāsa*, an untruth superimposed on that which is real, due to ignorance. By the study of *Vedānta*, these two things, *Ātman* and *anātman*, which are often confused, are duly separated upon understanding the one true nature of the Self, the Universe, and the cause of creation.

Verses 28 to 32: One that truly sees this reality sees That which must be known and reaches the highest objective of life, *mokṣa*.

In verse 29, *Śrī Kṛṣṇa* says that only the person who sees *Īśvara* in every place and everywhere does not "destroy himself by himself". Although all people wish to live, *Śrī Śaṅkara* explains that all those ignorant of *Ātman* are indifferent to *Ātman*, and thereby destroy themselves. Ignorance is denial. It is due to this ignorance that a person remains as if destroyed; one's true nature is denied as if it did not exist, since that which is ignored has the status of nonexistent.

Verses 33 and 34: These verses present illustrations to facilitate the comprehension of *Ātman*. In verse 33, *Ātman* is compared to space, which pervades everything and is affected by nothing. In verse 34, it is compared to the sun that is the only thing that illuminates everything.

Verse 35: This verse concludes the chapter on *kṣetra* and *kṣetrajña*. Understanding the paradox that these two are different and opposites, and at the same time neither distinct nor separate is the knowledge that liberates.

# अथ त्रयोदशोऽध्यायः

## *atha trayodaśo'dhyāyaḥ*

## Chapter thirteen

अर्जुन उवाच
प्रकृतिं पुरुषं चैव क्षेत्रं क्षेत्रज्ञमेव च ।
एतद् वेदितुमिच्छामि ज्ञानं ज्ञेयं च केशव ॥१॥

*arjuna uvāca*
*prakṛtiṁ puruṣaṁ caiva kṣetraṁ kṣetrajñameva ca |*
*etad veditumicchāmi jñānaṁ jñeyaṁ ca keśava ||1||*

**1.** *Arjuna* spoke:
— O *Keśava* [*Kṛṣṇa*], I wish to know this: [what is] *prakṛti, puruṣa, kṣetra, kṣetrajña, jñāna* and also *jñeya*?

श्रीभगवानुवाच
इदं शरीरं कौन्तेय क्षेत्रमित्यभिधीयते ।
एतद्यो वेत्ति तं प्राहुः क्षेत्रज्ञ इति तद्विदः ॥२॥

*śrībhagavānuvāca*
*idaṁ śarīraṁ kaunteya kṣetramityabhidhīyate |*
*etadyo vetti taṁ prāhuḥ kṣetrajña iti tadvidaḥ ||2||*

**2.** The Lord [*Kṛṣṇa*] spoke:
— This body, O *Kaunteya* [*Arjuna*], is called *kṣetra*. Those that know it say that one who knows this [*kṣetra*] is the *kṣetrajña*.

क्षेत्रज्ञं चापि मां विद्धि सर्वक्षेत्रेषु भारत ।
क्षेत्रक्षेत्रज्ञयोर्ज्ञानं यत्तज्ज्ञानं मतं मम ॥३॥

*kṣetrajñaṁ cāpi māṁ viddhi sarvakṣetreṣu bhārata |*
*kṣetrakṣetrajñayorjñānaṁ yattajjñānaṁ mataṁ mama ||3||*

**3.** Know me also as *kṣetrajña* in all *kṣetras* [bodies], O *Bhārata* [*Arjuna*]. The knowledge of *kṣetra* and *kṣetrajña* is considered by Me as the knowledge.

तत्क्षेत्रं यच्च यादृक् च यद्विकारि यतश्च यत् ।
स च यो यत्प्रभावश्च तत्समासेन मे शृणु ॥४॥

*tatkṣetraṁ yacca yādṛk ca yadvikāri yataśca yat |*
*sa ca yo yatprabhāvaśca tatsamāsena me śṛṇu ||4||*

**4.** What is that *kṣetra*? What is [its] nature? And what are its modifications? Which is born from what? Who is he [*kṣetrajña*]? And what is his glory? Hear me succinctly:

ऋषिभिर्बहुधा गीतं छन्दोभिर्विविधैः पृथक् ।
ब्रह्मसूत्रपदैश्चैव हेतुमद्भिर्विनिश्चितैः ॥५॥

*ṛṣibhirbahudhā gītaṁ chandobhirvividhaiḥ pṛthak |*
*brahmasūtrapadaiścaiva hetumadbhirviniścitaiḥ ||5||*

**5.** [This] has been sung in various ways by the sages, in various ways with several Vedic meters with words that reveal *Brahman* with reason and clarity.

महाभूतान्यहङ्कारो बुद्धिरव्यक्तमेव च ।
इन्द्रियाणि दशैकं च पञ्च चेन्द्रियगोचराः ॥६॥

*mahābhūtānyahaṅkāro buddhiravyaktameva ca |*
*indriyāṇi daśaikaṁ ca pañca cendriyagocarāḥ ||6||*

**6.** The [five] subtle elements, the *ahaṅkāra*, *Mahat*, the Unmanifest, the ten organs and one [the mind] and the five objects of the senses–

इच्छा द्वेषः सुखं दुःखं सङ्घातश्चेतना धृतिः ।
एतत्क्षेत्रं समासेन सविकारमुदाहृतम् ॥७॥

*icchā dveṣaḥ sukhaṁ duḥkhaṁ saṅghātaścetanā dhṛtiḥ |*
*etatkṣetraṁ samāsena savikāramudāhṛtam ||7||*

**7.** desire, hatred, pleasure, pain, the group [of mind and body], intelligence, courage – this has been described briefly as *kṣetra*, with its modifications.

अमानित्वमदम्भित्वमहिंसा क्षान्तिरार्जवम् ।
आचार्योपासनं शौचं स्थैर्यमात्मविनिग्रहः ॥८॥

*amānitvamadambhitvamahiṁsā kṣāntirārjavam |*
*ācāryopāsanaṁ śaucaṁ sthairyamātmavinigrahaḥ ||8||*

**8.** Absence of pride, absence of pretension, non-violence, accommodation, rectitude, dedication to the teacher, purity, persistence, self-control;

इन्द्रियार्थेषु वैराग्यमनहङ्कार एव च ।
जन्ममृत्युजराव्याधिदुःखदोषानुदर्शनम् ॥९॥

*indriyārtheṣu vairāgyamanahaṅkāra eva ca |*
*janmamṛtyujarāvyādhiduḥkhadoṣānudarśanam ||9||*

**9.** unattachment to the objects of the senses, absence of egotism and the perception of pain as inherent to birth, death, old age and disease;

असक्तिरनभिष्वङ्गः पुत्रदारगृहादिषु ।
नित्यं च समचित्तत्वमिष्टानिष्टोपपत्तिषु ॥१०॥

*asaktiranabhiṣvaṅgaḥ putradāragṛhādiṣu |*
*nityaṁ ca samacittatvamiṣṭāniṣṭopapattiṣu ||10||*

**10.** non-dependence, absence of attachment to son, wife, home, etc., maintenance of constant even-mindedness in acquiring that which is desired and undesired;

मयि चानन्ययोगेन भक्तिरव्यभिचारिणी ।
विविक्तदेशसेवित्वमरतिर्जनसंसदि ॥११॥

*mayi cānanyayogena bhaktiravyabhicāriṇī |*
*viviktadeśasevitvamaratirjanasaṁsadi ||11||*

**11.** and unwavering devotion to Me, [knowing that] there is no other [than *Īśvara*], frequenting secluded places, absence of the need for the company of others;

अध्यात्मज्ञाननित्यत्वं तत्त्वज्ञानार्थदर्शनम् ।
एतज्ज्ञानमिति प्रोक्तमज्ञानं यदतोऽन्यथा ॥१२॥

*adhyātmajñānanityatvaṁ tattvajñānārthadarśanam |*
*etajjñānamiti proktamajñānaṁ yadato'nyathā ||12||*

**12.** constantly seeking the knowledge of *Ātman*, insight into the knowledge of the truth, this is called *jñāna*, knowledge – that which is contrary to this is *ajñāna*, ignorance.

ज्ञेयं यत्तत्प्रवक्ष्यामि यज्ज्ञात्वामृतमश्नुते ।
अनादिमत्परं ब्रह्म न सत्तन्नासदुच्यते ॥१३॥

*jñeyaṁ yattatpravakṣyāmi yajjñātvāmṛtamaśnute |*
*anādimatparaṁ brahma na sattannāsaducyate ||13||*

**13.** I shall explain *jñeya*. Having known this, one reaches immortality. It is the limitless *Brahman* that has no beginning. It is said that He is neither *sat* [an effect] nor *asat* [the cause].

सर्वतः पाणिपादं तत्सर्वतोऽक्षिशिरोमुखम् ।
सर्वतः श्रुतिमल्लोके सर्वमावृत्य तिष्ठति ॥१४॥

*sarvataḥ pāṇipādaṁ tatsarvato'kṣiśiromukham |*
*sarvataḥ śrutimalloke sarvamāvṛtya tiṣṭhati ||14||*

**14.** He has hands and feet in all directions; he has eyes, heads, and mouths in all directions [and also] ears. He remains pervading the entire world.

सर्वेन्द्रियगुणाभासं सर्वेन्द्रियविवर्जितम् ।
असक्तं सर्वभृच्चैव निर्गुणं गुणभोक्तृ च ॥१५॥

*sarvendriyaguṇābhāsaṁ sarvendriyavivarjitam |*
*asaktaṁ sarvabhṛccaiva nirguṇaṁ guṇabhoktṛ ca ||15||*

**15.** [He is] manifest by the functions of all the organs, yet free from all the organs. Sustaining everything, [yet] He is independent. And [it is] He who experiences the qualities, although free from the qualities.

बहिरन्तश्च भूतानामचरं चरमेव च ।
सूक्ष्मत्वात्तदविज्ञेयं दूरस्थं चान्तिके च तत् ॥१६॥

*bahirantaśca bhūtānāmacaraṁ carameva ca |*
*sūkṣmatvāttadavijñeyaṁ dūrasthaṁ cāntike ca tat ||16||*

**16.** He is inside and outside all beings; He is motionless and moving; because He is the most subtle, He is not an object of knowledge; and He is the farthest and the closest.

अविभक्तं च भूतेषु विभक्तमिव च स्थितम् ।
भूतभर्तृ च तज्ज्ञेयं ग्रसिष्णु प्रभविष्णु च ॥१७॥

*avibhaktaṁ ca bhūteṣu vibhaktamiva ca sthitam |*
*bhūtabhartṛ ca tajjñeyaṁ grasiṣṇu prabhaviṣṇu ca ||17||*

**17.** And He is not divided, but remains as if divided into beings. That which is to be known [*Brahman*] is the creator, sustainer, and destroyer of all beings.

ज्योतिषामपि तज्ज्योतिस्तमसः परमुच्यते ।
ज्ञानं ज्ञेयं ज्ञानगम्यं हृदि सर्वस्य विष्ठितम् ॥१८॥

*jyotiṣāmapi tajjyotistamasaḥ paramucyate |*
*jñānaṁ jñeyaṁ jñānagamyaṁ hṛdi sarvasya viṣṭhitam ||18||*

**18.** He is also the light of all lights; it is said that He is something beyond darkness. He is knowledge – That which is to be known [and] That which is the goal of knowledge [liberation] – present in the hearts of all.

इति क्षेत्रं तथा ज्ञानं ज्ञेयं चोक्तं समासतः ।
मद्भक्त एतद्विज्ञाय मद्भावायोपपद्यते ॥१९॥

*iti kṣetraṁ tathā jñānaṁ jñeyaṁ coktaṁ samāsataḥ |*
*madbhakta etadvijñāya madbhāvāyopapadyate ||19||*

**19.** Thus, *kṣetra*, *jñāna* and *jñeya* have been briefly explained. Knowing this, my devotee attains my nature.

प्रकृतिं पुरुषं चैव विद्ध्यनादी उभावपि ।
विकारांश्च गुणांश्चैव विद्धि प्रकृतिसम्भवान् ॥२०॥

*prakṛtiṁ puruṣaṁ caiva viddhyanādī ubhāvapi |*
*vikārāṁśca guṇāṁścaiva viddhi prakṛtisambhavān ||20||*

**20.** Know that *Prakṛti* and *Puruṣa* have no beginning. Know that the modifications and the *guṇas* [the qualities] are born of *Prakṛti*.

कार्यकरणकर्तृत्वे हेतुः प्रकृतिरुच्यते ।
पुरुषः सुखदुःखानां भोक्तृत्वे हेतुरुच्यते ॥२१॥

*kāryakaraṇakartṛtve hetuḥ prakṛtirucyate |*
*puruṣaḥ sukhaduḥkhānāṁ bhoktṛtve heturucyate ||21||*

**21.** The cause of the creation of the physical and subtle body is called *Prakṛti*. The cause of the experience of pleasure and pain is called *Puruṣa*.

पुरुषः प्रकृतिस्थो हि भुङ्क्ते प्रकृतिजान् गुणान् ।
कारणं गुणसङ्गोऽस्य सदसद्योनिजन्मसु ॥२२॥

*puruṣaḥ prakṛtistho hi bhuṅkte prakṛtijān guṇān |*
*kāraṇaṁ guṇasaṅgo'sya sadasadyonijanmasu ||22||*

**22.** *Puruṣa*, remaining in *Prakṛti*, experiences the *guṇas* [the qualities] that are born of *Prakṛti*. For that [*Puruṣa*], the attachment to the *guṇas* is the cause of better and worse births [depending on the predominance of *puṇya* or *pāpa*].

उपद्रष्टानुमन्ता च भर्ता भोक्ता महेश्वरः ।
परमात्मेति चाप्युक्तो देहेऽस्मिन् पुरुषः परः ॥२३॥

*upadraṣṭānumantā ca bhartā bhoktā maheśvaraḥ |*
*paramātmeti cāpyukto dehe'smin puruṣaḥ paraḥ ||23||*

**23.** The limitless *Puruṣa* in this body is said to be the witness, that which consents [to everything], the sustainer, the experiencer, the great lord, and also the limitless one.

य एवं वेत्ति पुरुषं प्रकृतिं च गुणैः सह ।
सर्वथा वर्तमानोऽपि न स भूयोऽभिजायते ॥२४॥

*ya evaṁ vetti puruṣaṁ prakṛtiṁ ca guṇaiḥ saha |*
*sarvathā vartamāno'pi na sa bhūyo'bhijāyate ||24||*

**24.** One who thusly knows *Puruṣa* and *Prakṛti* together with the *guṇas* [the qualities] – regardless of one's way of life – is not born again.

ध्यानेनात्मनि पश्यन्ति केचिदात्मानमात्मना ।
अन्ये साङ्ख्येन योगेन कर्मयोगेन चापरे ॥२५॥

*dhyānenātmani paśyanti kecidātmānamātmanā |*
*anye sāṅkhyena yogena karmayogena cāpare ||25||*

**25.** Some perceive the Self in the mind, with the mind, by way of meditation. Others, by way of studying and questioning; and others, by way of *karmayoga*.

अन्ये त्वेवमजानन्तः श्रुत्वान्येभ्य उपासते ।
तेऽपि चातितरन्त्येव मृत्युं श्रुतिपरायणाः ॥२६॥

*anye tvevamajānantaḥ śrutvānyebhya upāsate |*
*te'pi cātitarantyeva mṛtyuṁ śrutiparāyaṇāḥ ||26||*

**26.** Yet others, not knowing this, seek [the Self] listening to others. And even these [who listen], [and] who are dedicated to the teaching, certainly overcome death.

यावत्सञ्जायते किञ्चित्सत्त्वं स्थावरजङ्गमम् ।
क्षेत्रक्षेत्रज्ञसंयोगात्तद्विद्धि भरतर्षभ ॥२७॥

*yāvatsañjāyate kiñcitsattvaṁ sthāvarajaṅgamam |*
*kṣetrakṣetrajñasaṁyogāttadviddhi bharatarṣabha ||27||*

**27.** Know that any object that is born, moving or motionless, is due to the union of *kṣetra* and *kṣetrajña*, O *Bharatarṣabha* [*Arjuna*].

समं सर्वेषु भूतेषु तिष्ठन्तं परमेश्वरम् ।
विनश्यत्स्वविनश्यन्तं यः पश्यति स पश्यति ॥२८॥

*samaṁ sarveṣu bhūteṣu tiṣṭhantaṁ parameśvaram |*
*vinaśyatsvavinaśyantaṁ yaḥ paśyati sa paśyati ||28||*

**28.** One who sees the supreme Lord, who remains the same in all beings [and] is indestructible among the destructible, this one [truly] sees.

समं पश्यन् हि सर्वत्र समवस्थितमीश्वरम् ।
न हिनस्त्यात्मनात्मानं ततो याति परां गतिम् ॥२९॥

*samaṁ paśyan hi sarvatra samavasthitamīśvaram |*
*na hinastyātmanātmānaṁ tato yāti parāṁ gatim ||29||*

**29.** Indeed, seeing *Īśvara*, who remains the same in all beings, one does not destroy himself by himself, [and] therefore reaches the highest objective [liberation].

प्रकृत्यैव च कर्माणि क्रियमाणानि सर्वशः ।
यः पश्यति तथात्मानमकर्तारं स पश्यति ॥३०॥

*prakṛtyaiva ca karmāṇi kriyamāṇāni sarvaśaḥ |*
*yaḥ paśyati tathātmānamakartāraṁ sa paśyati ||30||*

**30.** One who sees all actions as being performed in all ways by *Prakṛti* – and the Self as not being the agent of action – this one [truly] sees.

यदा भूतपृथग्भावमेकस्थमनुपश्यति ।
तत एव च विस्तारं ब्रह्म सम्पद्यते तदा ॥३१॥

*yadā bhūtapṛthagbhāvamekasthamanupaśyati |*
*tata eva ca vistāraṁ brahma sampadyate tadā ||31||*

**31.** When seeing the multitude of beings residing in one being [the *Ātman*] and seeing that creation [comes] from That [*Ātman*], one then becomes *Brahman*.

अनादित्वान्निर्गुणत्वात्परमात्मायमव्ययः ।
शरीरस्थोऽपि कौन्तेय न करोति न लिप्यते ॥३२॥

*anāditvānnirguṇatvātparamātmāyamavyayaḥ |*
*śarīrastho'pi kaunteya na karoti na lipyate ||32||*

**32.** The limitless Self is immutable, since it has no beginning and no qualities, O *Kaunteya* [*Arjuna*]; This [Self], although residing in the body, neither performs action nor is affected [by the fruit of action].

यथा सर्वगतं सौक्ष्म्यादाकाशं नोपलिप्यते ।
सर्वत्रावस्थितो देहे तथात्मा नोपलिप्यते ॥३३॥

*yathā sarvagataṁ saukṣmyādākāśaṁ nopalipyate |*
*sarvatrāvasthito dehe tathātmā nopalipyate ||33||*

**33.** Just as space that pervades everything is not affected due to its subtlety, the Self that pervades the entire body is not affected.

यथा प्रकाशयत्येकः कृत्स्नं लोकमिमं रविः ।
क्षेत्रं क्षेत्री तथा कृत्स्नं प्रकाशयति भारत ॥३४॥

*yathā prakāśayatyekaḥ kṛtsnaṁ lokamimaṁ raviḥ |*
*kṣetraṁ kṣetrī tathā kṛtsnaṁ prakāśayati bhārata ||34||*

**34.** Just as the sun illuminates this entire world, so the kṣetrī [the *Ātman*] illuminates the *kṣetra*, O *Bhārata* [*Arjuna*]!

क्षेत्रक्षेत्रज्ञयोरेवमन्तरं ज्ञानचक्षुषा ।
भूतप्रकृतिमोक्षं च ये विदुर्यान्ति ते परम् ॥३५॥

*kṣetrakṣetrajñayorevamantaraṁ jñānacakṣuṣā |*
*bhūtaprakṛtimokṣaṁ ca ye viduryānti te param ||35||*

**35.** Thus, with the eye of knowledge, those that know the distinction between *kṣetra* and *kṣetrajña*, as well as the elimination of ignorance in beings, attain the Absolute.

ओं तत्सदिति श्रीमद्भगवद्गीतासूपनिषत्सु ब्रह्मविद्यायां योगशास्त्रे श्रीकृष्णार्जुनसंवादे क्षेत्रक्षेत्रज्ञविभागयोगो नाम त्रयोदशोऽध्यायः ॥

*oṁ tatsaditi śrīmadbhagavadgītāsūpaniṣatsu brahmavidyāyāṁ yogaśāstre śrīkṛṣṇārjunasaṁvāde kṣetrakṣetrajñavibhāgayogo nāma trayodaśo'dhyāyaḥ ||*

*Oṁ*, this is the Truth. Thus is the thirteenth chapter, the subject [of which] is called "*kṣetrakṣetrajñavibhāga*" [the distinction between the field and the knower of the field], in the glorious *Bhagavadgītā*, [which is equivalent to] the *Upaniṣads*, [the subject of which is] the knowledge of *Brahman* [and] *yoga*, in the dialogue between *śrī Kṛṣṇa* and *Arjuna*.

# Chapter 14

## *The division of the three qualities*

In chapter 13, verse 22, *Śrī Kṛṣṇa* says that the entire universe manifests due to the union between *kṣetra* and *kṣetrajña*. He also mentions that the process of *saṁsāra* - the constant flow of births and deaths of *jīvas* - is due to the attachment to the *guṇas* of *Prakṛti*, which is also called *kṣetra*.

Introducing chapter 14, *Śrī Śaṅkara*, in his commentary, or *bhāṣya*, states that it is here that the union between *kṣetra* and *kṣetrajña*, *Prakṛti* and *Puruṣa*, and the attachment to the *guṇas* should be explained.

Besides these topics, *Śrī Kṛṣṇa* demonstrates how a person can free himself from the bondage of these three *guṇas*.

*Śrī Śaṅkara* reaffirms that the cause of the universe is *Puruṣa* and *Prakṛti*. *Prakṛti* alone does not create: *Prakṛti* is dependent upon *Puruṣa*; however, *Puruṣa* is always *asaṅga*, dependent upon nothing.

The cause of the manifestation of the universe, which includes *saṁsāra*, is the union of *Puruṣa* and *Prakṛti*; however, this union is in fact only apparent, due to *avidyā*, ignorance.

Opening chapter 14, our commentator on the *Bhagavadgītā*, *Śrī Śaṅkara*, places some questions to be answered throughout the twenty-seven verses, or *ślokas*, which comprise this chapter: "How does one become attached to the *guṇas*? What are the *guṇas*? How do they bind someone? How does one become free from *guṇas*? What characteristics does a person free from the *guṇas* have?"

In the first two verses, *Śrī Kṛṣṇa* praises knowledge, calling it *uttama*, the most important, and *para*, meaning that the topic is the Absolute.

There are many branches of knowledge, since there are indeed many objects to be known; however, the most important of all knowledge is self-knowledge, the object of which is in fact the subject: the Self that is limitless. This knowledge is the instrument for liberating one from suffering and from the process of births and deaths. Self-knowledge is the way to *mokṣa*.

The next topic covered is the creation of the universe. *Puruṣa* and *Prakṛti* are mentioned as the father and mother, the universal parents of all that exists, the intelligent cause and the material cause of the universe. *Prakṛti* is the mother, the uterus for the entire universe. In this uterus, *Puruṣa* deposits the seed, which is the intelligent cause of the universe. This means that *Puruṣa, Brahman,* gives existence and consciousness to *Prakṛti* and, therefore *Prakṛti* can create. It is for this reason that we say that *Brahman*, together with *māyā*, is *Īśvara*: the cause of the universe.

*Prakṛti* has three *guṇas* or qualities that are seen in everything that exists: *sattva, rajas* and *tamas*. These three *guṇas* characterize and also imprison the individual. How each *guṇa* imprisons is described as follows:

*Sattva* is clarity and the absence of suffering. It imprisons the individual with an attachment to pleasure and knowledge. The nature of *rajas* is that of passion and desire, imprisoning one with an attachment to action. *Tamas* is born of ignorance and is caused by delusion and error. It imprisons one with indifference, indolence and lethargy.

The three *guṇas* are always present; however, when one of the three becomes more prevalent, it dominates the other two. Signs of the prevalence of one of the three can always be observed: when attention and clarity predominate, *sattva* reigns; when physical or mental restlessness predominate, *rajas* reigns; with obscurity, indifference, idleness or lethargy predominate, *tamas* reigns.

Subsequent births are determined by the *guṇa* that predominates at the end of one's life. Finally, it is also said that the result of an action predominated by each of the three *guṇas* is also different. Therefore, for the person predominately bound to *sattva*, the result of one's life and action will be one of clarity and the absence of suffering; the results of *rajas* are of discomfort; and for the person predominated by *tamas*, the results are of ignorance and delusion.

When analyzing the effects of these three *guṇas*, a person naturally desires *sattva* and is bound by it. Therefore, the *guru* says that, although *sattva* facilitates comprehension and mental preparedness, it must be understood that *Ātman* is free from the three *guṇas* - including *sattva*. Thus, there is no agent of action other than the *guṇas* and, furthermore, if the individual recognizes his or her own nature beyond the *guṇas*, one's indivisible identity with *Īśvara* will be discovered.

All action is done by the *guṇas*; Consciousness does nothing. Action is done by the body, by the senses and the mind-intellect - all of which is born of the *Prakṛti* that has three *guṇas*. The *Ātman* does not perform any action whatsoever. By recognizing the nature of *Ātman*, which is pure Consciousness and possesses neither *guṇas* nor performs action, the wise see that the *guṇas* are the only ones responsible for action. And for the person that discovers one's nature that is free from the *guṇas*, there is no further birth, death, old age or suffering: this person attains liberation.

It is for this reason that *Arjuna* asks about *guṇātīta*, one that goes beyond the *guṇas*, asking how is the conduct of such a person, and also what must be done to go beyond the *guṇas*.

This question from *Arjuna* on the characteristics of the

*guṇātīta* reflects the question in chapter 2, verse 54, on the characteristics of *sthitaprajña*, one who has an unwavering knowledge of oneself.

The *Gītā* teaches us that the wise do not judge others, do not criticize, and do not desire the characteristics of the *guṇas*. When seeing their body or mind in one of these characteristics - clarity, restlessness, or confusion - the wise know that it is due to the three *guṇas* and are neither perturbed by nor identify with these characteristics.

Finally, after answering the first two questions, *Kṛṣṇa* indicates *bhakti*, or devotion, as a means to go beyond the *guṇas*. *Śaṅkara* states that *bhakti* is *yoga*, and that *bhaktiyoga* is the equivalent of *vivekavijñāna*, discernment and clear knowledge. A person dedicated to the questioning of one's true nature is indeed seeking *Īśvara*, seeking to comprehend *Īśvara* and one's identity with Him. This search is called *bhakti*. It is the power of this search and the power of the commitment to this search that leads to self-knowledge - and in doing so, one becomes qualified to become *Brahman*, since *Brahman* is the same as *Ātman*, the same as the Self.

## Summary of the verses

Verses 1 and 2: In these initial verses, *Śrī Kṛṣṇa* covers the importance of this knowledge to attract the attention of the listener - namely, *Arjuna* - on what will follow. Among all forms of knowledge, this self-knowledge is paramount, since its result is the liberation of suffering and the sensation of limitation and imprisonment. This subject matter, and mainly the result it yields, makes this knowledge special and distinguished among all other forms.

Verses 3 and 4: *Kṛṣṇa* explains creation by saying that *Prakṛti* creates the Universe due to the presence of *Puruṣa*, as if they were the mother and father of the Universe.

Verses 5 to 9: *Prakṛti*, is the material cause of creation, and has three *guṇas* or basic characteristics. These three *guṇas* are responsible for all expressions of the Universe and they have the capacity to imprison individuals. This bondage is not real, but, as in the words of *Śrī Śaṅkarācārya* in his commentary, it is an apparent bondage, *nibadhnanti iva*. It is bondage due to confusion and attachment only; if it were real, liberation would not be possible.

Verses 11 to 13: In these verses, *Kṛṣṇa* describes the *liṅgas*, the signs of the presence of each one of the three *guṇas*.

Verses 14 to 16: The destiny of an individual after death, *gati*, is covered. During the life of an individual, the *guṇas* can modify; the *guṇa* that predominates upon the hour of death leads the person to follow a path that matches with the same *guṇa*.

Verses 17 and 18: *Kṛṣṇa* summarizes what has already been said in previous verses and elaborates on *phala*: the fruit of action acquired by each *guṇa*, as both a result in this life and the next.

Verses 19 and 20: *Kṛṣṇa* instructs on how to go beyond the *guṇas*. This transcendence is accomplished via the knowledge of the Self as free from *guṇas*. The *Ātman* is free from *guṇas* and their characteristics. Due to an individual's mistaken identity with *Prakṛti*, one considers oneself to be the agent of action, or *kartṛ*; and the one who receives results, or *bhoktṛ*. By discovering the nature of the one true Self, the individual recognizes and identifies himself or herself with *Īśvara*.

Verse 21: *Arjuna* asks *Kṛṣṇa* about the characteristics of a *guṇātīta*, or one that has gone beyond the *guṇas*: what is this individual's behavior, or *ācāra*? And how does this person go beyond the *guṇas*? This question is not unlike the question placed in chapter 2, verse 54.

Verses 22 to 25: *Kṛṣṇa* responds to the first part of the question placed by *Arjuna* on who would be *guṇātīta*. This individual would desire neither the presence nor absence of the qualities of *Prakṛti*, the three *guṇas*, nor would he criticize or judge others due to the *guṇas*. Such an individual would simply recognize that all movement is due to the attraction and repulsion of the *guṇas*, and thus remain neutral and neither react to nor be affected by the pleasant or unpleasant experiences that are merely a part of the constant movement of *Prakṛti*. This neutrality becomes possible when the individual discovers the Self that is complete and exempt of want: needing to do nothing to be happy and feeling that nothing is missing. This is the natural composure of the *guṇātīta*, describing his *ācāra*, his conduct, which is the object of *Arjuna*'s question.

Verse 26: *Kṛṣṇa* responds to the final part of the question: what is the *sādhana*? What should be done in order for a person to go beyond the *guṇas*?

*Kṛṣṇa* says that *bhakti*, devotion, is the means. Devotion is an unwavering, unbreakable commitment to seeking *Īśvara*. This search is for the knowledge of the indivisible identity between the individual and Everything, and it is this self-knowledge that leads the individual to become *Brahman*, or rather, to know oneself as *Brahman* who is indestructible, immutable and ever-existing.

# अथ चतुर्दशोऽध्यायः

## *atha caturdaśo'dhyāyaḥ*

## Chapter fourteen

श्रीभगवानुवाच
परं भूयः प्रवक्ष्यामि ज्ञानानां ज्ञानमुत्तमम् ।
यज्ज्ञात्वा मुनयः सर्वे परां सिद्धिमितो गताः ॥१॥

*śrībhagavānuvāca*
*paraṁ bhūyaḥ pravakṣyāmi jñānānāṁ jñānamuttamam |*
*yajjñātvā munayaḥ sarve parāṁ siddhimito gatāḥ ||1||*

**1.** The Lord [*Kṛṣṇa*] spoke:
— Once again I shall speak on the knowledge of the Absolute, which is the most important of all knowledge; acquiring this [knowledge], all the wise, after this [life], attain final liberation.

इदं ज्ञानमुपाश्रित्य मम साधर्म्यमागताः ।
सर्गेऽपि नोपजायन्ते प्रलये न व्यथन्ति च ॥२॥

*idaṁ jñānamupāśritya mama sādharmyamāgatāḥ |*
*sarge'pi nopajāyante pralaye na vyathanti ca ||2||*

**2.** Surrendering to this knowledge, [they] attain my nature. They are neither reborn in creation nor perish upon dissolution.

मम योनिर्महद्ब्रह्म तस्मिन् गर्भं दधाम्यहम् ।
संभवः सर्वभूतानां ततो भवति भारत ॥३॥

*mama yonirmahadbrahma tasmin garbhaṁ dadhāmyaham |*
*saṁbhavaḥ sarvabhūtānāṁ tato bhavati bhārata ||3||*

**3.** My uterus is *Prakṛti*. In it I deposit the seed, thus occurs the origin of all beings, O *Bhārata* [*Arjuna*].

सर्वयोनिषु कौन्तेय मूर्तयः सम्भवन्ति याः ।
तासां ब्रह्म महद्योनिरहं बीजप्रदः पिता ॥४॥

*sarvayoniṣu kaunteya mūrtayaḥ sambhavanti yāḥ |*
*tāsāṁ brahma mahadyoniraham̐ bījapradaḥ pitā ||4||*

**4.** O *Kaunteya* [*Arjuna*], *Prakṛti* is the womb for the forms that are born in all wombs. I am the father that sows the seed.

सत्त्वं रजस्तम इति गुणाः प्रकृतिसम्भवाः ।
निबध्नन्ति महाबाहो देहे देहिनमव्ययम् ॥५॥

*sattvaṁ rajastama iti guṇāḥ prakṛtisambhavāḥ |*
*nibadhnanti mahābāho dehe dehinamavyayam ||5||*

**5.** *Sattva, rajas, tamas* are the qualities born from *Prakṛti*, O *Mahābāhu* [*Arjuna*]. They bind the immutable Self in the body.

तत्र सत्त्वं निर्मलत्वात्प्रकाशकमनामयम् ।
सुखसङ्गेन बध्नाति ज्ञानसङ्गेन चानघ ॥६॥

*tatra sattvaṁ nirmalatvātprakāśakamanāmayam |*
*sukhasaṅgena badhnāti jñānasaṅgena cānagha ||6||*

**6.** Among them, O *Anagha* [*Arjuna*], *sattva*, being free from impurity, has the nature of light [and] is free from suffering. It imprisons with attachment to pleasure and to knowledge.

रजो रागात्मकं विद्धि तृष्णासङ्गसमुद्भवम् ।
तन्निबध्नाति कौन्तेय कर्मसङ्गेन देहिनम् ॥७॥

*rajo rāgātmakaṁ viddhi tṛṣṇāsaṅgasamudbhavam |*
*tannibadhnāti kaunteya karmasaṅgena dehinam ||7||*

**7.** Know that *rajas* is the nature of passion [and] the cause of desire and attachment. It imprisons the Self with attachment to action, O *Kaunteya* [*Arjuna*].

तमस्त्वज्ञानजं विद्धि मोहनं सर्वदेहिनाम् ।
प्रमादालस्यनिद्राभिस्तन्निबध्नाति भारत ॥८॥

*tamastvajñānajaṁ viddhi mohanaṁ sarvadehinām |*
*pramādālasyanidrābhistannibadhnāti bhārata ||8||*

**8.** Know indeed that *tamas* is born of ignorance [and] deludes all beings. It imprisons with indifference, indolence [and] sleepiness, O *Bhārata* [*Arjuna*].

सत्त्वं सुखे सञ्जयति रजः कर्मणि भारत ।
ज्ञानमावृत्य तु तमः प्रमादे सञ्जयत्युत ॥९॥

*sattvaṁ sukhe sañjayati rajaḥ karmaṇi bhārata |*
*jñānamāvṛtya tu tamaḥ pramāde sañjayatyuta ||9||*

**9.** *Sattva* binds one to pleasure [and] *rajas* to action; whereas *tamas*, obscuring discernment, binds one to negligence, O *Bhārata* [*Arjuna*].

रजस्तमश्चाभिभूय सत्त्वं भवति भारत ।
रजः सत्त्वं तमश्चैव तमः सत्त्वं रजस्तथा ॥१०॥

*rajastamaścābhibhūya sattvaṁ bhavati bhārata |*
*rajaḥ sattvaṁ tamaścaiva tamaḥ sattvaṁ rajastathā ||10||*

**10.** There is *Sattva* [when] prevailing over *rajas* and *tamas*, O *Bhārata* [*Arjuna*]; There is *rajas* [when] prevailing over *sattva* and *tamas*; There is *tamas* [when] prevailing over *sattva* and *rajas*.

सर्वद्वारेषु देहेऽस्मिन् प्रकाश उपजायते ।
ज्ञानं यदा तदा विद्याद्विवृद्धं सत्त्वमित्युत ॥११॥

*sarvadvāreṣu dehe'smin prakāśa upajāyate |*
*jñānaṁ yadā tadā vidyādvivṛddhaṁ sattvamityuta ||11||*

**11.** When the light of knowledge shines through all the senses in the body, know indeed that *sattva* is predominate.

लोभः प्रवृत्तिरारम्भः कर्मणामशमः स्पृहा ।
रजस्येतानि जायन्ते विवृद्धे भरतर्षभ ॥१२॥

*lobhaḥ pravṛttirārambhaḥ karmaṇāmaśamaḥ spṛhā |*
*rajasyetāni jāyante vivṛddhe bharatarṣabha ||12||*

**12.** Greed, activity, undertaking actions, restlessness, desire: these appear when *rajas* is predominate, O *Bharatarṣabha* [*Arjuna*].

अप्रकाशोऽप्रवृत्तिश्च प्रमादो मोह एव च ।
तमस्येतानि जायन्ते विवृद्धे कुरुनन्दन ॥१३॥

*aprakāśo'pravṛttiśca pramādo moha eva ca |*
*tamasyetāni jāyante vivṛddhe kurunandana ||13||*

**13.** Darkness, idleness, indifference, and also illusion: these appear when *tamas* is predominate, O *Kurunandana* [*Arjuna*].

यदा सत्त्वे प्रवृद्धे तु प्रलयं याति देहभृत् ।
तदोत्तमविदां लोकानमलान् प्रतिपद्यते ॥१४॥

*yadā sattve pravṛddhe tu pralayaṁ yāti dehabhṛt |*
*tadottamavidāṁ lokānamalān pratipadyate ||14||*

**14.** If one dies when *sattva* is predominate, one then reaches places free from impurity, where there are those that meditate.

रजसि प्रलयं गत्वा कर्मसङ्गिषु जायते ।
तथा प्रलीनस्तमसि मूढयोनिषु जायते ॥१५॥

*rajasi pralayaṁ gatvā karmasaṅgiṣu jāyate |*
*tathā pralīnastamasi mūḍhayoniṣu jāyate ||15||*

**15.** Upon death when *rajas* [is predominate], one is born among those attached to action. Similarly, when one is dead when *tamas* [is predominate], one is born in the wombs of the deluded.

कर्मणः सुकृतस्याहुः सात्त्विकं निर्मलं फलम् ।
रजसस्तु फलं दुःखमज्ञानं तमसः फलम् ॥१६॥

*karmaṇaḥ sukṛtasyāhuḥ sāttvikaṁ nirmalaṁ phalam |*
*rajasastu phalaṁ duḥkhamajñānaṁ tamasaḥ phalam ||16||*

**16.** [The wise] say the *sattva* fruit of action is pure merit. The *rajas* fruit of action is suffering, whereas the *tamas* fruit of action is ignorance.

सत्त्वात्सञ्जायते ज्ञानं रजसो लोभ एव च ।
प्रमादमोहौ तमसो भवतोऽज्ञानमेव च ॥१७॥

*sattvātsañjāyate jñānaṁ rajaso lobha eva ca |*
*pramādamohau tamaso bhavato'jñānameva ca ||17||*

**17.** Knowledge is born from *sattva*, and greed from *rajas*. Negligence and illusion come from *tamas*, and ignorance too.

ऊर्ध्वं गच्छन्ति सत्त्वस्था मध्ये तिष्ठन्ति राजसाः ।
जघन्यगुणवृत्तस्था अधो गच्छन्ति तामसाः ॥१८॥

*ūrdhvaṁ gacchanti sattvasthā madhye tiṣṭhanti rājasāḥ |*
*jaghanyaguṇavṛttasthā adho gacchanti tāmasāḥ ||18||*

**18.** People with predominance of *sattva* go upward; people with predominance of *rajas* remain in the middle; those with predominance of *tamas*, which remain with activities of the lowest *guṇa*, go downward.

नान्यं गुणेभ्यः कर्तारं यदा द्रष्टानुपश्यति ।
गुणेभ्यश्च परं वेत्ति मद्भावं सोऽधिगच्छति ॥१९॥

*nānyaṁ guṇebhyaḥ kartāraṁ yadā draṣṭānupaśyati |*
*guṇebhyaśca paraṁ vetti madbhāvaṁ so'dhigacchati ||19||*

**19.** When one who [truly] sees realizes the agent of action is none other than the *guṇas* and knows [the Self] as beyond the *guṇas*, one reaches my nature.

गुणानेतानतीत्य त्रीन्देही देहसमुद्भवान् ।
जन्ममृत्युजरादुःखैर्विमुक्तोऽमृतमश्नुते ॥२०॥

*guṇānetānatītya trīndehī dehasamudbhavān |*
*janmamṛtyujarāduḥkhairvimukto'mṛtamaśnute ||20||*

**20.** Having transcended the *guṇas*, which are the cause of the body [and of another birth], the person is free from birth, death, old age, misery [and] reaches immortality.

अर्जुन उवाच
कैर्लिङ्गैस्त्रीन् गुणानेतानतीतो भवति प्रभो ।
किमाचारः कथं चैतांस्त्रीन् गुणानतिवर्तते ॥२१॥

*arjuna uvāca*
*kairliṅgaistrīn guṇānetānatīto bhavati prabho |*
*kimācāraḥ kathaṁ caitāṁstrīn guṇānativartate ||21||*

**21.** *Arjuna* spoke:
— O Lord, what are the characteristics of he who has gone beyond these three *guṇas*? How is his conduct? How does he go beyond these three *guṇas*?

श्रीभगवानुवाच
प्रकाशं च प्रवृत्तिं च मोहमेव च पाण्डव ।
न द्वेष्टि सम्प्रवृत्तानि न निवृत्तानि काङ्क्षति ॥२२॥

*śrībhagavānuvāca*
*prakāśaṁ ca pravṛttiṁ ca mohameva ca pāṇḍava |*
*na dveṣṭi sampravṛttāni na nivṛttāni kāṅkṣati ||22||*

**22.** The Lord [*Kṛṣṇa*] spoke:
— O *Pāṇḍava* [*Arjuna*], he neither hates nor desires the presence or absence of clarity or activity or delusion.

उदासीनवदासीनो गुणैर्यो न विचाल्यते ।
गुणा वर्तन्त इत्येव योऽवतिष्ठति नेङ्गते ॥२३॥

*udāsīnavadāsīno guṇairyo na vicālyate |*
*guṇā vartanta ityeva yo'vatiṣṭhati neṅgate ||23||*

**23.** He remains as if indifferent; he is not disturbed by the *guṇas* [and] does not waver. He remains steady [with the understanding that] "only the *guṇas* act".

समदुःखसुखः स्वस्थः समलोष्टाश्मकाञ्चनः ।
तुल्यप्रियाप्रियो धीरस्तुल्यनिन्दात्मसंस्तुतिः ॥२४॥

*samaduḥkhasukhaḥ svasthaḥ samaloṣṭāśmakāñcanaḥ |*
*tulyapriyāpriyo dhīrastulyanindātmasaṁstutiḥ ||24||*

**24.** Residing in the Self, wise is one who remains the same in pleasure and pain; who remains the same before clay, a stone [and] gold; who remains the same before the desirable and undesirable; who remains the same in blame and praise;

मानापमानयोस्तुल्यस्तुल्यो मित्रारिपक्षयोः ।
सर्वारम्भपरित्यागी गुणातीतः स उच्यते ॥२५॥

*mānāpamānayostulyastulyo mitrāripakṣayoḥ |*
*sarvārambhaparityāgī guṇātītaḥ sa ucyate ||25||*

**25.** who remains the same in honor and dishonor; who remains the same with friend and foe; [and] renouncing all actions, he is called "one who has gone beyond the *guṇas*".

मां च योऽव्यभिचारेण भक्तियोगेन सेवते ।
स गुणान्समतीत्यैतान्ब्रह्मभूयाय कल्पते ॥२६॥

*māṁ ca yo'vyabhicāreṇa bhaktiyogena sevate |*
*sa guṇānsamatītyaitānbrahmabhūyāya kalpate ||26||*

**26.** And he who seeks Me with undivided devotion, having transcended these *guṇas*, is prepared for the state of being [that is] *Brahman*.

ब्रह्मणो हि प्रतिष्ठाहममृतस्याव्ययस्य च ।
शाश्वतस्य च धर्मस्य सुखस्यैकान्तिकस्य च ॥२७॥

*brahmaṇo hi pratiṣṭāhamamṛtasyāvyayasya ca |*
*śāśvatasya ca dharmasya sukhasyaikāntikasya ca ||27||*

**27.** For I am the basis of *Brahman*, which is immortal, immutable, the eternal *dharma* [the knowledge that sustains the universe] and absolute plenitude.

ओं तत्सदिति श्रीमद्भगवद्गीतासूपनिषत्सु ब्रह्मविद्यायां योगशास्त्रे श्रीकृष्णार्जुनसंवादे गुणत्रयविभागयोगो नाम चतुर्दशोऽध्यायः॥

*oṁ tatsaditi śrīmadbhagavadgītāsūpaniṣatsu brahmavidyāyāṁ yogaśāstre śrīkṛṣṇārjunasaṁvāde guṇatrayavibhāgayogo nāma caturdaśo'dhyāyaḥ ||*

*Oṁ*, this is the Truth. Thus is the fourteenth chapter, the subject [of which] is called "*guṇatrayavibhāga*" [the division of the three qualities], in the glorious *Bhagavadgītā*, [which is equivalent to] the *Upaniṣads*, [the subject of which is] the knowledge of *Brahman* [and] *yoga*, in the dialogue between *śrī Kṛṣṇa* and *Arjuna*.

# Chapter 15

## *The greater self*

The objective of chapter 15 is to develop *vairāgya*, or dispassion, in order to seek and understand *Īśvara* and the identity with Him in order to attain *mokṣa*, or liberation. It is essential for the *mumukṣu*, one seeking liberation, to understand what *saṁsāra* is, and thereby remain unattached to it. In order to meet this end, *Śrī Kṛṣṇa* describes *saṁsāra* with the image of a tree whose roots are from above.

Dispassion is the pre-requisite, or *adhikāra*, to go beyond *saṁsāra*. Without dispassion, self-knowledge will not be attained.

*Śrī Śaṅkara* explains that liberation is reached by means of a process of acquiring self-knowledge, *jñānaprāptikrameṇa*, due to the blessings of this very knowledge itself, *prasādāt*. The blessings of this knowledge are the results of actions done by the individual seeking self-knowledge. There is a series of practices to prepare the mind since it is in the mind where knowledge occurs. The preparation of the mind, *antaḥkaraṇa-śuddhi*, and the means necessary for study, depend on the blessing of *Īśvara*.

This chapter covers *saṁsāra*, the indivisible identity of *jīva* and *Īśvara* – the comprehension of which frees the individual from *saṁsāra* – and the qualifications needed for this comprehension.

The singular identity between *jīva* and *Īśvara* is the main theme of the *Gītā* and of *Vedānta*. This identity is explained in all the chapters of the *Gītā*, but particularly in chapters 13 to 18. Chapter 15 is exceptional in its coverages of this topic.

Right in the beginning of the chapter, *Kṛṣṇa* speaks of

the sacred-fig tree - the *aśvattha* - which is an allegory of *saṁsāra*. This tree perpetuates itself, spreading out aerial roots which become new tree trunks, and new trees. It transforms itself continuously with a long-life due to the continual roots - just like *saṁsāra*, which is vast and not easily destroyed.

*Saṁsāra* appears impossible to destroy, but analyzing it better, we see that it is as a dream - *mithyā* - and only apparent, not real. The only reality it has is its root, *Brahman*: the only thing that is real. For this reason, *saṁsāra* can only be cut by "the strong arm of dispassion". Other qualifications are also mentioned.

Free from delusion, the abode from where there is no return is reached. It is a place described as the source of all light, and that which cannot be illuminated by any of the common sources of light: neither the sun of day, nor the moon of night, nor fire on Earth. Having reached this state of self-knowledge, one does not return, since it is that which is real, the source of all light, *caitanya*. It is *Brahma-caitanya* that exists as *jīva* and also *jagat*. Therefore, it is clear that the *jīva* attains *Īśvara* via self-knowledge, without any transformation, without needing to go anywhere.

Thus, *Kṛṣṇa* poetically says that the universe is an expression of *Īśvara*. The sun, the light and the fire are forms of Him. He is manifested on Earth as the sustenance and power that feeds all beings. It becomes the digestive fire in the body of living beings, transforming, burning food so that it may be digested and assimilated. He is seated in the hearts and minds of all living beings. He is the author of the *Vedas*, That which is to be known by the *Vedas*, as well as the student and knower of the *Vedas*. Thus, *Brahman* is *Īśvara*, *jīva* and *jagat* - all that exists - and it is this that must be understood.

*Brahman* in the form of the Universe is *kṣara-puruṣa*; as

the Unmanifest, He is called *akṣara-puruṣa*. Besides these two, there is also the *uttama-puruṣa*, which is the Absolute; He is called the *puruṣottama*, because He is beyond that which is manifested and unmanifested: That which is free from all that exists, but upon which all things depend.

In the end, *Kṛṣṇa* says that the person who knows *Ātman* as *puruṣottama* fulfills his or her life, by having used one's intellect to its maximum potential to acquire the self-knowledge that is difficult to be acquired.

## Summary of the verses

Verses 1 to 3: *Kṛṣṇa* describes *saṁsāra* by using the image of the sacred-fig tree - both of which are vast and imperishable, although one day they will have an end despite the constant transformation.

*Saṁsāra* is indeed mysterious: it is not easily revealed. Its roots are up high in that which is eternal and free from time; its branches are below and spread out among various births within time and space. The person who truly knows this tree of *saṁsāra*, knows the *Vedas*, since it is in the *Vedas* that essentially state that the root of *saṁsāra* is *Brahman*, which is *Ātman*, the Subject.

*Kṛṣṇa* further adds that it is not easy to destroy the tree of *saṁsāra*, since its roots are strong. It is well-rooted in the ignorance of the reality of *saṁsāra*, which is none other than *Brahman*. All its forms, which is its manifestation, are not real; they are in constant transformation. Ignorance of That which is real keeps *saṁsāra* alive, and dispassion is the only weapon capable of destroying it. Dispassion is cultivated by the constant analysis of what is real and what is only apparently real. In other words, the questioning of what is *satya* and what is *mithyā*.

Verse 4: With dispassion comes a disinterest in the world

of objects, conquests, recognitions, and then the final objective is sought. The finalization of this search means the surrender of the Self to *Brahman*. The false "I", the ego, or the *ahaṅkāra*, is surrendered: what remains is that which is real, or *Puruṣa*, which is *Brahman*.

Verse 5: Mentioned here are the qualifications of the individual that surrenders the *ahaṅkāra*, seeks *Puruṣa* and reaches the final objective from which there is no return.

Verse 6: The final objective, pada, is explained. This is *Brahman*, which is the Consciousness that lights everything, even itself, and not illuminated by the common forms of light that are the Sun, the Moon and fire.

Verses 7 and 8: Those that reach the highest objective – the indivisible identity with *Brahman* – do not return to *saṁsāra*, since they discover their being that is *Brahman*. Reaching the highest objective involves no movement whatsoever: it is a question of knowledge. For this reason, it is said that there is no return, since there was indeed no voyage, but rather recognition of one's true nature. *Kṛṣṇa* says that *jīva* is part of *Brahman*: a simple part of That which is everything in the form of an individual. *Jīva* is *Brahman* reflected in *upādhi*, an individual conditioning. Despite appearing as only a part, due to *upādhi*, the individual is indeed *Brahman*. The *jīva* conducts the senses and the mind externally from the physical body upon the hour of death and enter the physical body upon birth.

Verse 9: *Jīva* experiences all objects via the five senses and the mind.

Verse 10: Therefore, *Īśvara* has the apparent form of *jīva*. Only those with the eye of self-knowledge can see this truth; others, who are deluded, simply do not.

Verse 11: Only those with a content mind and the maturity cultivated by a life of *yoga*, those who make the effort in the right direction, recognize the presence of *Ātman* in the intellect. Despite all effort, if there is no maturity or discernment, one will not be able to see *Ātman*.

Verses 12 to 15: With these verses, *Śrī Kṛṣṇa* reveals *sarvātmatva*, which is *Ātman* - the Self that is in all that exists, *sarvavyavahārāspadatva* - and the base of all transaction with the world. In summary, the greatness of *Brahman* is once again resounded, or His expressions in the form of the Universe: He is the light in the Sun and Moon and fire; He enters Earth and sustains all beings; just like the digestive fire, He digests the food consumed by all beings; He is eaten by those that eat; He is that which is behind all mental functions, such as memory, forgetfulness, and knowledge. He is the author of the *Vedas*, He is That which is to be known by the *Vedas* and also He who knows the *Vedas*.

Verses 16 to 18: Thus, *Brahman* is *jīva*, *Īśvara* and is also *jagat*. To reach Him is to know Him. *Brahman* is *kṣara-puruṣa*, all the perishable Universe, and *akṣara-puruṣa*, the Imperishable, the cause of the Universe. These two, *kṣara-puruṣa* and *akṣara-puruṣa*, are called *Puruṣa*. There is another that is called *uttama-puruṣa*, the highest *Puruṣa*, the Absolute, which is also called *paramātman* and *puruṣottama*: That which sustains everything and is beyond *kṣara* and *akṣara-puruṣa*.

Verses 19 to 20: Finally, the fruit of the awareness of *Puruṣa* is pronounced: one who knows that which everything attains the Self of everything - becoming wise, reaching all that can be reached and thereby contented.

## अथ पञ्चदशोऽध्यायः

### *atha pañcadaśo'dhyāyaḥ*

### Chapter fifteen

श्रीभगवानुवाच
ऊर्ध्वमूलमधःशाखमश्वत्थं प्राहुरव्ययम् ।
छन्दांसि यस्य पर्णानि यस्तं वेद स वेदवित् ॥१॥

*śrībhagavānuvāca*
*ūrdhvamūlamadhaḥśākhamaśvatham prāhuravyayam |*
*chandāṁsi yasya parṇāni yastaṁ veda sa vedavit ||1||*

**1.** The Lord [*Kṛṣṇa*] spoke:
— They speak of the eternal sacred-fig, [the tree] that has root upward [and] branches downward [and] whose leaves are the *Vedas*. Who knows it, knows the *Vedas*.

अधश्चोर्ध्वं प्रसृतास्तस्य शाखाः
गुणप्रवृद्धा विषयप्रवालाः ।
अधश्च मूलान्यनुसन्ततानि
कर्मानुबन्धीनि मनुष्यलोके ॥२॥

*adhaścordhvaṁ prasṛtāstasya śākhāḥ*
*guṇapravṛddhā viṣayapravālāḥ |*
*adhaśca mūlānyanusantatāni*
*karmānubandhīni manuṣyaloke ||2||*

**2.** Its branches, fortified by the *guṇas*, [and] its shoots, the objects [of the senses], are spread above and below. And also [its] roots are extended downwards, causing actions in the world of men.

न रूपमस्येह तथोपलभ्यते
नान्तो न चादिर्न च सम्प्रतिष्ठा ।
अश्वत्थमेनं सुविरूढमूलम्-
असङ्गशस्त्रेण दृढेन छित्त्वा ॥३॥

*na rūpamasyeha tathopalabhyate*
*nānto na cādirna ca sampratiṣṭhā |*
*aśvatthamenaṁ suvirūḍhamūlam*
*asaṅgaśastreṇa dṛḍhena chittvā ||3||*

**3.** The form of this [tree] is such that is it is not perceptible here. [It] has no beginning, middle or end. One must cut this sacred-fig tree, which is well-rooted, with the strong arm of dispassion.

ततः पदं तत्परिमार्गितव्यं
यस्मिन् गता न निवर्तन्ति भूयः ।
तमेव चाद्यं पुरुषं प्रपद्ये
यतः प्रवृत्तिः प्रसृता पुराणी ॥४॥

*tataḥ padaṁ tatparimārgitavyaṁ*
*yasmin gatā na nivartanti bhūyaḥ |*
*tameva cādyaṁ puruṣaṁ prapadye*
*yataḥ pravṛttiḥ prasṛtā purāṇī ||4||*

**4.** Then that higher goal must be sought [and], reaching it, from there one does not return. [The attitude should be the following:] I seek refuge in that original Self from which came the primordial process of manifestation.

निर्मानमोहा जितसङ्गदोषाः
अध्यात्मनित्या विनिवृत्तकामाः ।
द्वन्द्वैर्विमुक्ताः सुखदुःखसञ्ज्ञैर्-
गच्छन्त्यमूढाः पदमव्ययं तत् ॥५॥

*nirmānamohā jitasaṅgadoṣāḥ*
*adhyātmanityā vinivṛttakāmāḥ |*
*dvandvairvimuktāḥ sukhaduḥkhasañjñair-*
*gacchantyamūḍhāḥ padamavyayaṁ tat ||5||*

**5.** Those that are free of pride and delusion – having defeated the error of attachment, always committed to the [knowledge of] the Self, free from desires, free from the opposites known as pleasure and pain, [and] free from delusion – reach the object [that is] imperishable.

न तद्भासयते सूर्यो न शशाङ्को न पावकः ।
यद्गत्वा न निवर्तन्ते तद्धाम परमं मम ॥६॥

*na tadbhāsayate sūryo na śaśāṅko na pāvakaḥ |*
*yadgatvā na nivartante taddhāma paramaṁ mama ||6||*

**6.** Neither sun, nor moon, nor fire illuminates it – that is my highest abode – reaching it, no one returns.

ममैवांशो जीवलोके जीवभूतः सनातनः ।
मनः षष्ठानीन्द्रियाणि प्रकृतिस्थानि कर्षति ॥७॥

*mamaivāṁśo jīvaloke jīvabhūtaḥ sanātanaḥ |*
*manaḥ ṣaṣṭhānīndriyāṇi prakṛtisthāni karṣati ||7||*

**7.** In the world of the living, one part of Me is indeed in the form of the eternal *jīva*, which assumes the [five] organs of perception, plus the mind that is the sixth, which are in the physical body.

शरीरं यदवाप्नोति यच्चाप्युत्क्रामतीश्वरः ।
गृहीत्वैतानि संयाति वायुर्गन्धानिवाशयात् ॥८॥

*śarīraṁ yadavāpnoti yaccāpyutkrāmatīśvaraḥ |*
*gṛhītvaitāni saṁyāti vāyurgandhānivāśayāt ||8||*

**8.** And when the living one departs [the body] and acquires [another] body, he carries these [organs of perception and the mind], just as the wind carries fragrances from whence they came.

श्रोत्रं चक्षुः स्पर्शनं च रसनं घ्राणमेव च ।
अधिष्ठाय मनश्चायं विषयानुपसेवते ॥९॥

*śrotraṁ cakṣuḥ sparśanaṁ ca rasanaṁ ghrāṇameva ca |*
*adhiṣṭhāya manaścāyaṁ viṣayānupasevate ||9||*

**9.** This [*jīva*], resides in the ear, the eye, the skin, the tongue, the nose and also the mind, experiencing objects.

उत्क्रामन्तं स्थितं वापि भुञ्जानं वा गुणान्वितम् ।
विमूढा नानुपश्यन्ति पश्यन्ति ज्ञानचक्षुषः ॥१०॥

*utkrāmantaṁ sthitaṁ vāpi bhuñjānaṁ vā guṇānvitam |*
*vimūḍhā nānupaśyanti paśyanti jñānacakṣuṣaḥ ||10||*

**10.** The deluded do not see He who departs [the body] or who remains [in the body], who experiences [objects] or is associated with the *guṇas*; [however] those with the eye of knowledge can.

यतन्तो योगिनश्चैनं पश्यन्त्यात्मन्यवस्थितम् ।
यतन्तोऽप्यकृतात्मानो नैनं पश्यन्त्यचेतसः ॥११॥

*yatanto yoginaścainaṁ paśyantyātmanyavasthitam |*
*yatanto'pyakṛtātmāno nainaṁ paśyantyacetasaḥ ||11||*

**11.** And the *yogins* who make an effort see this Self, who is in the intellect. Those who have not prepared the mind with discernment do not see this Self, despite [all] efforts.

यदादित्यगतं तेजो जगद्भासयतेऽखिलम् ।
यच्चन्द्रमसि यच्चाग्नौ तत्तेजो विद्धि मामकम् ॥१२॥

*yadādityagataṁ tejo jagadbhāsayate'khilam |*
*yaccandramasi yaccāgnau tattejo viddhi māmakam ||12||*

**12.** Know that my light that is in the Sun, which illuminates the entire Universe, is the [same] light in the Moon and in fire.

गामाविश्य च भूतानि धारयाम्यहमोजसा ।
पुष्णामि चौषधीः सर्वाः सोमो भूत्वा रसात्मकः ॥१३॥

*gāmāviśya ca bhūtāni dhārayāmyahamojasā |*
*puṣṇāmi cauṣadhīḥ sarvāḥ somo bhūtvā rasātmakaḥ ||13||*

**13.** And entering the Earth, I sustain all beings with [my] energy. Becoming the nourishing moon, I give sustenance to all plants.

अहं वैश्वानरो भूत्वा प्राणिनां देहमाश्रितः ।
प्राणापानसमायुक्तः पचाम्यन्नं चतुर्विधम् ॥१४॥

*ahaṁ vaiśvānaro bhūtvā prāṇināṁ dehamāśritaḥ |*
*prāṇāpānasamāyuktaḥ pacāmyannaṁ caturvidham ||14||*

**14.** [and] residing in the living as the digestive fire, together with *prāṇa* and *apāna* [the respiratory and eliminatory systems], I digest the four kinds of food.

सर्वस्य चाहं हृदि संनिविष्टो
मत्तः स्मृतिर्ज्ञानमपोहनं च ।
वेदैश्च सर्वैरहमेव वेद्यो
वेदान्तकृद्वेदविदेव चाहम् ॥१५॥

*sarvasya cāhaṁ hṛdi saṁniviṣṭo*
*mattaḥ smṛtirjñānamapohanaṁ ca |*
*vedaiśca sarvairahameva vedyo*
*vedāntakṛdvedavideva cāham ||15||*

**15.** And I am seated in the hearts of all. From Me, memory, knowledge and forgetfulness come forth. I am That which is to be know by the *Vedas*. I am the author of *Vedānta* and He who knows the *Vedas*.

द्वाविमौ पुरुषौ लोके क्षरश्चाक्षर एव च ।
क्षरः सर्वाणि भूतानि कूटस्थोऽक्षर उच्यते ॥१६॥

*dvāvimau puruṣau loke kṣaraścākṣara eva ca |*
*kṣaraḥ sarvāṇi bhūtāni kūṭastho'kṣara ucyate ||16||*

**16.** In the world, there are two *puruṣas*: the perishable and the imperishable. Perishable are all beings. The Immutable is called imperishable.

उत्तमः पुरुषस्त्वन्यः परमात्मेत्युदाहृतः ।
यो लोकत्रयमाविश्य बिभर्त्यव्यय ईश्वरः ॥१७॥

*uttamaḥ puruṣastvanyaḥ paramātmetyudāhṛtaḥ |*
*yo lokatrayamāviśya bibhartyavyaya īśvaraḥ ||17||*

**17.** But the highest *Puruṣa* is different, called the Highest Self: that immutable *Īśvara* that, by entering the three worlds, sustains [both the perishable and imperishable *Puruṣa*].

यस्मात्क्षरमतीतोऽहमक्षरादपि चोत्तमः ।
अतोऽस्मि लोके वेदे च प्रथितः पुरुषोत्तमः ॥१८॥

*yasmātkṣaramatīto'hamakṣarādapi cottamaḥ |*
*ato'smi loke vede ca prathitaḥ puruṣottamaḥ ||18||*

**18.** Since I am beyond perishable and also imperishable, thus I am rightly known as *Puruṣottama* [the highest Self] in the world and in the *Vedas*.

यो मामेवमसम्मूढो जानाति पुरुषोत्तमम् ।
स सर्वविद्भजति मां सर्वभावेन भारत ॥१९॥

*yo māmevamasammūḍho jānāti puruṣottamam |*
*sa sarvavidbhajati māṁ sarvabhāvena bhārata ||19||*

**19.** One who, undeluded, knows Me as *Puruṣottama*, this all-knowing [person] reaches Me as the truth of all beings, O *Bhārata* [*Arjuna*].

इति गुह्यतमं शास्त्रमिदमुक्तं मयानघ ।
एतद्बुद्ध्वा बुद्धिमान् स्यात्कृतकृत्यश्च भारत ॥२०॥

*iti guhyatamaṁ śāstramidamuktaṁ mayānagha |*
*etadbuddhvā buddhimān syātkṛtakṛtyaśca bhārata ||20||*

**20.** Thus, this knowledge that is the highest secret has been taught by Me, O *Anagha* [*Arjuna*] – the knowledge of which one becomes wise and fulfills all duties, O *Bhārata* [*Arjuna*].

ओं तत्सदिति श्रीमद्भगवद्गीतासूपनिषत्सु ब्रह्मविद्यायां योगशास्त्रे
श्रीकृष्णार्जुनसंवादे पुरुषोत्तमयोगो नाम पञ्चदशोऽध्यायः॥

*oṁ tatsaditi śrīmadbhagavadgītāsūpaniṣatsu*
*brahmavidyāyāṁ yogaśāstre śrīkṛṣṇārjunasaṁvāde*
*puruṣottamayogo nāma pañcadaśo'dhyāyaḥ ||*

*Oṁ*, this is the Truth. Thus is the fifteenth chapter, the subject [of which] is called "*puruṣottama*" [the Highest Self], in the glorious *Bhagavadgītā*, [which is equivalent to] the *Upaniṣads*, [the subject of which is] the knowledge of *Brahman* [and] *yoga*, in the dialogue between *śrī Kṛṣṇa* and *Arjuna*.

# Chapter 16

## *The distinction between positive and negative characteristics*

Chapter 16 of the *Bhagavadgītā* describes two natures of people: those that have the mental characteristics for self-knowledge and those that have the mental characteristics that hold them deluded and impassioned. These characteristics are called *daivī-sampat* and *āsurī-sampat*, respectively. The *sattva* characteristics belong to *daivī-sampat*; the *rajas* and *tamas* characteristics belong to *āsurī-sampat*.

All people can be put into one group or the other. Although the *daivī* characteristics contribute to self-knowledge, they alone are not enough for liberation; awareness of the Self that is eternal, limitless, and the cause of the Universe must be assimilated via a means of knowledge that is *Vedānta*.

In chapter 9, the *daivī, āsurī* and *rākṣasī* natures were mentioned in verses 12 and 13. Here in this chapter, these characteristics are mentioned in detail.

A mind of *daivī* nature, predominated by *sattva*, is clear and discerning, as well as committed to the highest values. This kind of mind is free from the power of the tastes and aversions, *rāgas* and *dveṣas*, which imprison the *āsurī* and *rākṣasī* minds. When *rāga* - desire and ambition - is strong in the mind, this impulsive individual cannot share with others and takes from others, be it wealth, ideas, position or power. Furthermore, an individual dominated by *dveṣa* - aversion and hatred - is capable of cruel, aggressive and destructive acts.

Only a person of the *daivī* nature will seek knowledge of

the truth and liberation from *saṁsāra*.

Those of *āsurī* and *rākṣasī* nature shall remain in *saṁsāra*.

The characteristics herein called *daivī-sampat* are natural to people of discernement and emotional maturity. Anyone can develop them as long as one understands that what one truly wants is in fact peace and also to be free from limitation.

In this chapter, the characteristics that lead one and divert one from peace and self-knowledge are mentioned separately. The qualities mentioned here are not intended to be instruments for either judging or criticizing oneself or others. As long as each habit or behavior present in oneself is identified as useless or contrary to self-knowledge, they will surely be abandoned in order to obtain the highest of objectives: liberation. These habits and behaviors will be left behind for a higher goal: *paramapuruṣārtha*, or *mokṣa*.

*Śrī Kṛṣṇa* gives us a list of values to be developed, and afterwards, a description of the characterisitcs that must be left behind, since they are damaging to oneself and contrary to self-knowledge. *Kṛṣṇa* further states that, in other future births, people remain with these same qualities, until they are shed by discernment. It is therefore not only in this life that people suffer and cause suffering. The three characteristics that lead to suffering are *kāma*, desire, *krodha*, anger, and *lobha*, greed. They remain strong due to a lack of discrimination, or discernment. Closing the chapter *Kṛṣṇa* says that *śāstra*, which are the *Vedas*, is a *pramāṇa*, a means of knowledge by which to determine what one should and should not do. The discriminating individual does not only follow desires, or in other words, doing only what is convenient in detriment to what is appropriate. Instead, this individual employs discernment with each step and opportunity in order to do what must be done in the best way possible.

This individual attains freedom in action.

## Summary of the verses

Verses 1 to 3: *Kṛṣṇa* gives a list of characteristics to be cultivated, since they lead to liberation. These characteristics are called *daivī-sampat*, the wealth of the *devas*, predominated by *sattva*.

Verse 4: A list of the *āsurī-sampat* characteristics are summarized, the wealth of the *asuras*, predominated by *rajas* and *tamas*.

Verse 5: *Kṛṣṇa* speaks on the destiny of the two groups of people: those with the wealth of the *devas* and those with the wealth of the *asuras*. The characteristics of the former lead to liberation, and the latter lead to bondage.

Verse 6: *Śrī Kṛṣṇa* says that He shall speak about the second group so that we know what should be avoided when the objective is liberation.

Verses 7 to 20: In detail, the characteristics of the *asuras* are listed.

According to this description, we can see how this kind of individual thinks, how this group is deluded, worrisome, anxious, desirous and angry. For this reason, says *Kṛṣṇa*, these people are pressured by their own desires, anger, etc, to act without any concern for *dharma*, or that which is correct - thereby accumulating *pāpa*, the negative result of action - and are reborn again and again in situations of suffering and ignorance.

Verse 21: Finally, *Kṛṣṇa* states that the three main characteristics of the *asura* are: desire, anger and greed. These characteristics can destroy a person and must be avoided.

Verse 22: The person who avoids these "three doors to darkness" and follows that which is good, *śreyas* - making the choice for virtue - reaches the highest goal.

Verses 23 to 24: In the last two verses, *Kṛṣṇa* states that the *śāstra*, the *Vedas*, is the means of knowledge by which to determine what should and should not be done – and it is with this knowledge that actions should be exacted.

# अथ षोडशोऽध्यायः

## *atha ṣoḍaśo'dhyāyaḥ*

## Chapter sixteen

श्रीभगवानुवाच
अभयं सत्त्वसंशुद्धिर्ज्ञानयोगव्यवस्थितिः ।
दानं दमश्च यज्ञश्च स्वाध्यायस्तप आर्जवम् ॥१॥

*śrībhagavānuvāca*
*abhayaṁ sattvasaṁśuddhirjñānayogavyavasthitiḥ |*
*dānaṁ damaśca yajñaśca svādhyāyastapa ārjavam ||1||*

**1.** The Lord [*Kṛṣṇa*] spoke:
— Fearlessness, purity of mind, perseverance in knowledge and discipline, the capacity for giving, control of the senses, daily prayers, study and repetition of the *Vedas*, austerity and rectitude,

अहिंसा सत्यमक्रोधस्त्यागः शान्तिरपैशुनम् ।
दया भूतेष्वलोलुप्त्वं मार्दवं ह्रीरचापलम् ॥२॥

*ahiṁsā satyamakrodhastyāgaḥ śāntirapaiśunam |*
*dayā bhūteṣvaloluptvaṁ mārdavaṁ hrīracāpalam ||2||*

**2.** non-violence, truthfulness, absence of anger, renunciation, tranquility, absence of calumny, compassion for all beings, absence of delusion regarding temptation, gentleness, modesty, absence of restlessness,

तेजः क्षमा धृतिः शौचमद्रोहो नातिमानिता ।
भवन्ति सम्पदं दैवीमभिजातस्य भारत ॥३॥

*tejaḥ kṣamā dhṛtiḥ śaucamadroho nātimānitā |*
*bhavanti sampadaṁ daivīmabhijātasya bhārata ||3||*

**3.** brilliance, patience, fortitude, purity, absence of the desire to hurt others, [and] absence of vanity are for those born with the characteristics of *deva*, O *Bhārata* [*Arjuna*].

दम्भो दर्पोऽभिमानश्च क्रोधः पारुष्यमेव च ।
अज्ञानं चाभिजातस्य पार्थ सम्पदमासुरीम् ॥४॥

*dambho darpo'bhimānaśca krodhaḥ pāruṣyameva ca |*
*ajñānaṁ cābhijātasya pārtha sampadamāsurīm ||4||*

**4.** Hipocrisy, arrogance, pride, anger, insolence and ignorance [are] for those born with characteristics of *asura*, O *Pārtha* [*Arjuna*].

दैवी संपद्विमोक्षाय निबन्धायासुरी मता ।
मा शुचः संपदं दैवीमभिजातोऽसि पाण्डव ॥५॥

*daivī saṁpadvimokṣāya nibandhāyāsurī matā |*
*mā śucaḥ saṁpadaṁ daivīmabhijāto'si pāṇḍava ||5||*

**5.** It is said that the characteristics of the *devas* are for liberation [and] the characteristics of the *asuras* are for bondage. Do not grieve, O *Pāṇḍava* [*Arjuna*]! You were born with the characteristics of *deva*.

द्वौ भूतसर्गौ लोकेऽस्मिन्दैव आसुर एव च ।
दैवो विस्तरशः प्रोक्त आसुरं पार्थ मे शृणु ॥६॥

*dvau bhūtasargau loke'smindaiva āsura eva ca |*
*daivo vistaraśaḥ prokta āsuraṁ pārtha me śṛṇu ||6||*

**6.** In this world [there are] two types of beings: *daiva* [related to *devas*, divine], [and] *āsura* [related to *āsuras*, demonic]. *Daiva* has been explained in detail. [On the nature of] *āsura*, hear me, O *Pārtha* [*Arjuna*]!

प्रवृत्तिं च निवृत्तिं च जना न विदुरासुराः ।
न शौचं नापि चाचारो न सत्यं तेषु विद्यते ॥७॥

*pravṛttiṁ ca nivṛttiṁ ca janā na vidurāsurāḥ |*
*na śaucaṁ nāpi cācāro na satyaṁ teṣu vidyate ||7||*

**7.** *Āsura* people do not know what should and should not be done. For them there is neither purity, nor appropriate conduct, nor truthfulness.

असत्यमप्रतिष्ठं ते जगदाहुरनीश्वरम् ।
अपरस्परसम्भूतं किमन्यत्कामहैतुकम् ॥८॥

*asatyamapratiṣṭhaṁ te jagadāhuranīśvaram |*
*aparasparasambhūtaṁ kimanyatkāmahaitukam ||8||*

**8.** They say: "The world has no truth, no [ethical] basis, no lord; it is born from the union between a man and a woman, caused by desire and nothing else".

एतां दृष्टिमवष्टभ्य नष्टात्मानोऽल्पबुद्धयः ।
प्रभवन्त्युग्रकर्माणः क्षयाय जगतोऽहिताः ॥९॥

*etāṁ dṛṣṭimavaṣṭabhya naṣṭātmāno'lpabuddhayaḥ |*
*prabhavantyugrakarmāṇaḥ kṣayāya jagato'hitāḥ ||9||*

**9.** Holding this viewpoint, lost in their search, with little discernment [and] of cruel actions, [these men are] enemies of the world; they exist for destruction.

काममाश्रित्य दुष्पूरं दम्भमानमदान्विताः ।
मोहाद्गृहीत्वासद्ग्राहान् प्रवर्तन्तेऽशुचिव्रताः ॥१०॥

*kāmamāśritya duṣpūraṁ dambhamānamadānvitāḥ |*
*mohādgṛhītvāsadgrāhān pravartante'śucivratāḥ ||10||*

**10.** Based on insatiable desires, full of hipocrisy, vanity [and] pride, bound to false conclusions due to delusion, they act with unclean motives.

चिन्तामपरिमेयां च प्रलयान्तामुपाश्रिताः ।
कामोपभोगपरमा एतावदिति निश्चिताः ॥११॥

*cintāmaparimeyāṁ ca pralayāntāmupāśritāḥ |*
*kāmopabhogaparamā etāvaditi niścitāḥ ||11||*

**11.** Preoccupied with countless worries until death, and committed to the gratification from objects, they conclude: "that is all".

आशापाशशतैर्बद्धाः कामक्रोधपरायणाः ।
ईहन्ते कामभोगार्थमन्यायेनार्थसञ्चयान् ॥१२॥

*āśāpāśaśatairbaddhāḥ kāmakrodhaparāyaṇāḥ |
īhante kāmabhogārthamanyāyenārthasañcayān ||12||*

**12.** Bound by a hundred straps of hope, surrendering to lust and to anger, they seek gratification from objects by hoarding wealth by improper means.

इदमद्य मया लब्धमिमं प्राप्स्ये मनोरथम् ।
इदमस्तीदमपि मे भविष्यति पुनर्धनम् ॥१३॥

*idamadya mayā labdhamimaṁ prāpsye manoratham |
idamastīdamapi me bhaviṣyati punardhanam ||13||*

**13.** "This has been obtained by me today. I will get that [other] desire. There is this wealth, and in the future that [other] wealth shall be mine also."

असौ मया हतः शत्रुर्हनिष्ये चापरानपि ।
ईश्वरोऽहमहं भोगी सिद्धोऽहं बलवान्सुखी ॥१४॥

*asau mayā hataḥ śatrurhaniṣye cāparānapi |
īśvaro'hamahaṁ bhogī siddho'haṁ balavānsukhī ||14||*

**14.** "That enemy has been destroyed by me. And I shall destroy others as well. I am the lord. I am the one who has pleasure. I am successful, powerful, happy."

आढ्योऽभिजनवानस्मि कोऽन्योऽस्ति सदृशो मया ।
यक्ष्ये दास्यामि मोदिष्य इत्यज्ञानविमोहिताः ॥१५॥

*āḍhyo'bhijanavānasmi ko'nyo'sti sadṛśo mayā |*
*yakṣye dāsyāmi modiṣya ityajñānavimohitāḥ ||15||*

**15.** "I am rich. I come from a noble family. Who else is equal to me? I shall sacrifice. I shall donate. I shall rejoice", thus [think] those lacking discernment due to ignorance.

अनेकचित्तविभ्रान्ता मोहजालसमावृताः ।
प्रसक्ताः कामभोगेषु पतन्ति नरकेऽशुचौ ॥१६॥

*anekacittavibhrāntā mohajālasamāvṛtāḥ |*
*prasaktāḥ kāmabhogeṣu patanti narake'śucau ||16||*

**16.** Fooled by many thoughts, enshrouded by the net of delusion, attached to the gratification from objects, they fall into vile hell.

आत्मसंभाविताः स्तब्धा धनमानमदान्विताः ।
यजन्ते नामयज्ञैस्ते दम्भेनाविधिपूर्वकम् ॥१७॥

*ātmasaṁbhāvitāḥ stabdhā dhanamānamadānvitāḥ |*
*yajante nāmayajñaiste dambhenāvidhipūrvakam ||17||*

**17.** Praised by their own selves, arrogant, full of vanity and pride from wealth, they perform merely apparent rituals with hypocrisy, [and] not following what is prescribed.

अहङ्कारं बलं दर्पं कामं क्रोधं च संश्रिताः ।
मामात्मपरदेहेषु प्रद्विषन्तोऽभ्यसूयकाः ॥१८॥

*ahaṅkāraṁ balaṁ darpaṁ kāmaṁ krodhaṁ ca saṁśritāḥ |*
*māmātmaparadeheṣu pradviṣanto'bhyasūyakāḥ ||18||*

**18.** Tied to egotism, to power, to arrogance, to lust, and to anger, [these] envious ones despise me in their own bodies and in those of others.

तानहं द्विषतः क्रूरान् संसारेषु नराधमान् ।
क्षिपाम्यजस्रमशुभानासुरीष्वेव योनिषु ॥१९॥

*tānahaṁ dviṣataḥ krūrān saṁsāreṣu narādhamān |*
*kṣipāmyajasramaśubhānāsurīṣveva yoniṣu ||19||*

**19.** I continually hurl these hateful and cruel ones – who act viciously, the lowest of men – into the wombs of *asura* in *saṁsāra* [the cycle of birth and death].

आसुरीं योनिमापन्ना मूढा जन्मनि जन्मनि ।
मामप्राप्यैव कौन्तेय ततो यान्त्यधमां गतिम् ॥२०॥

*āsurīṁ yonimāpannā mūḍhā janmani janmani |*
*māmaprāpyaiva kaunteya tato yāntyadhamāṁ gatim ||20||*

**20.** Deluded, having attained *āsura* wombs, without ever attaining Me in birth after birth, they go to an even lower condition, O *Kaunteya* [*Arjuna*].

त्रिविधं नरकस्येदं द्वारं नाशनमात्मनः ।
कामः क्रोधस्तथा लोभस्तस्मादेतत्त्रयं त्यजेत् ॥२१॥

*trividhaṁ narakasyedaṁ dvāraṁ nāśanamātmanaḥ |*
*kāmaḥ krodhastathā lobhastasmādetattrayaṁ tyajet ||21||*

**21.** Threefold is the gate to hell, which is [the means to] self-destruction: desire, anger and greed; therefore, one should abandon these three.

एतैर्विमुक्तः कौन्तेय तमोद्वारैस्त्रिभिर्नरः ।
आचरत्यात्मनः श्रेयस्ततो याति परां गतिम् ॥२२॥

*etairvimuktaḥ kaunteya tamodvāraistribhirnaraḥ |*
*ācaratyātmanaḥ śreyastato yāti parāṁ gatim ||22||*

**22.** O *Kaunteya* [*Arjuna*], released from these three gates to darkness, a man does what is best for himself [and] thereby goes to the highest goal.

यः शास्त्रविधिमुत्सृज्य वर्तते कामकारतः ।
न स सिद्धिमवाप्नोति न सुखं न परां गतिम् ॥२३॥

*yaḥ śāstravidhimutsṛjya vartate kāmakārataḥ |*
*na sa siddhimavāpnoti na sukhaṁ na parāṁ gatim ||23||*

**23.** Having abandoned the prescription of the *Vedas*, one that acts on the impulse of desire attains neither maturity nor happiness, nor the highest goal.

तस्माच्छास्त्रं प्रमाणं ते कार्याकार्यव्यवस्थितौ ।
ज्ञात्वा शास्त्रविधानोक्तं कर्म कर्तुमिहार्हसि ॥२४॥

*tasmācchāstraṁ pramāṇaṁ te kāryākāryavyavasthitau |*
*jñātvā śāstravidhānoktaṁ karma kartumihārhasi ||24||*

**24.** Therefore, for you the *Vedas* are the means for knowledge to determine what should and should not be done. Knowing what is prescribed by the *Vedas*, you should perform action in this world.

ओं तत्सदिति श्रीमद्भगवद्गीतासूपनिषत्सु ब्रह्मविद्यायां योगशास्त्रे श्रीकृष्णार्जुनसंवादे दैवासुरसम्पद्विभागयोगो नाम षोडशोऽध्यायः ॥

*oṁ tatsaditi śrīmadbhagavadgītāsūpaniṣatsu brahmavidyāyāṁ yogaśāstre śrīkṛṣṇārjunasaṁvāde daivāsurasampadvibhāgayogo nāma ṣoḍaśo'dhyāyaḥ ||*

*Oṁ*, this is the Truth. Thus is the sixteenth chapter, the subject [of which] is the called "*daivāsurasaṁpadvibhāga*" [the distinction between positive and negative characteristics], in the glorious *Bhagavadgītā*, [which is equivalent to] the *Upaniṣads*, [the subject of which is] the knowledge of *Brahman* [and] *yoga*, in the dialogue between *śrī Kṛṣṇa* and *Arjuna*.

# Chapter 17

## *The distinction among the three kinds of faith*

In the end of chapter 16, *Kṛṣṇa* says that the *śāstra*, the *Vedas*, is the means of knowledge for determining what should and should not be done. Having heard this, *Arjuna* places the question that opens chapter 17: what is the *niṣṭhā*, the basis of a person who performs rituals and prayers with faith, *śraddhā*, although not following the rule of the *śāstra* on exactly how to perform the ritual? Is this person of *sattva*, *rajas* or *tamas*?

What should and should not be done is primarily a question of common sense. Thus, anyone should be able to determine what must be done. However, due to the delusion caused by the attachment to tastes and aversions that imprison the mind of individuals, it often becomes difficult to know what should be done and what should be avoided.

A better decision can be made with the help of the *śāstra*, the *Veda*, as a means of knowledge for analyzing action and its consequences.

An action may bring immediate gratification, but if the consequences of such an action are seen as undesirable or may cause suffering, then it is clear that the action should not to be done.

The free choice of action must include awareness of its consequences. A suitable course of action produces a positive result, whereas an unsuitable course of action produces a negative result - even if it immediately gratifies by satisfying a desire. It is for this reason that *Kṛṣṇa* says that *śāstra* must be the instrument for choosing what shall and shall not be done - and not permitting desire to make the choice!

With the terminology of the *guṇas* - *sattva*, *rajas* and

*tamas* - *Arjuna* asks what is the basis for the person who does not perform rituals according to the rules.

To answer his question, *Kṛṣṇa* analyzes faith and the three types of faith.

In verse 3, *Kṛṣṇa* says that faith, *śraddhā*, is determined by the nature of the mind of the person, since one is nothing more than one's faith - *yaḥ yacchraddhaḥ sa eva saḥ*, one is as one's faith be - and the faith may be of *sattva*, *rajas* or *tamas*.

*Arjuna* specifically asks about the ritual that is performed with faith, although not as prescribed. *Śrī Kṛṣṇa* could easily give a direct answer, but responds by elaborating this theme and including other factors, such as the choice of food, of ritual, of austerity and of devotion. Regarding austerity, he says that it may be physical, oral or mental. *Kṛṣṇa* points out that the *sattva* choice always leads to self-knowledge, and the choice for *rajas* or *tamas* keeps the person deluded.

As in chapter 16, *Kṛṣṇa* helps us to understand our choices and desires so that we may have more freedom in choosing our actions in our daily lives as *mumukṣu*, seekers of liberation, thus qualifying us daily for self-knowledge.

Finally, *Kṛṣṇa* states the importance of om *tat sat*, three words that denominate *Brahman*, as per the *Vedas* and as is repeated by people that know and follow the *Vedas*. Upon practicing rituals, austerities and offerings, these words are pronounced by those seeking *mokṣa*. Pronouncing them purifies one's actions and makes them *sattva*. *Kṛṣṇa* says that *śraddhā* is a very important factor in performing any action as a discipline for self-knowledge - without *śraddhā* the action loses its value.

## Summary of the verses

Verses 1: *Arjuna* places a question considering the statement of *Kṛṣṇa* at the end of the last chapter: In what category does a person belong who performs rituals and prayers with faith, although without following the prescription of the *Vedas* of how to do so? "Is it *sattva, rajas* or *tamas*?" he asks.

Verses 2 to 4: *Kṛṣṇa* could respond directly, but he decides to analyze the three types of faith that are according to the nature of the mind of the person.

Worship is conducted according to one's faith, according to what a person believes.

Verses 5 and 6: There are those that have practices considered religious, but in fact are terrible and cause suffering. Such practices involve untruths and egotism, desire and passion, as well as lack of discernment.

Such people are to be seen as *āsura*, predominated by *rajas* and *tamas*.

Verses 7 to 22: *Śrī Kṛṣṇa* introduces other topics that will also be analyzed for their predominance of *sattva, rajas* and *tamas*: such as food, rituals, austerities and offerings. Upon examining *tapas*, austerities, *Kṛṣṇa* states the three kinds, which may be physical, oral or mental, and analyzes each one.

Verses 23 to 27: *Kṛṣṇa* says that any action may include error or omission. Therefore, the *mantra "oṁ tat sat"*, pronounced by the Creator at the moment of creation is of great importance. Upon pronouncing this *mantra,* any error or mistake committed will be neutralized. Therefore, at the beginning of any activity, the person who knows the *Vedas* pronounces "*oṁ*", the person that desires liberation pronounces "*tat*", which is the name of *Brahman,* and the word "*sat*" is used to accompany an auspicious action.

Verse 28: At the end of the chapter, *Śrī Kṛṣṇa* highlights the importance of faith, *śraddhā* when performing a ritual, an austerity or an action. Without faith, the action will be designated as *asat*: that which has no purpose and does not produce the desired result.

## अथ सप्तदशोऽध्यायः

### *atha saptadaśo'dhyāyaḥ*

### Chapter seventeen

अर्जुन उवाच
ये शास्त्रविधिमुत्सृज्य यजन्ते श्रद्धयान्विताः ।
तेषां निष्ठा तु का कृष्ण सत्त्वमाहो रजस्तमः ॥१॥

*arjuna uvāca*
*ye śāstravidhimutsṛjya yajante śraddhayānvitāḥ |*
*teṣāṁ niṣṭhā tu kā kṛṣṇa sattvamāho rajastamaḥ ||1||*

**1.** *Arjuna* spoke:
— What is the basic characteristic of those that – abandoning the rule of scripture – perform rituals with faith? Is it *sattva, rajas* or *tamas,* O *Kṛṣṇa*!?

श्रीभगवानुवाच
त्रिविधा भवति श्रद्धा देहिनां सा स्वभावजा ।
सात्त्विकी राजसी चैव तामसी चेति तां शृणु ॥२॥

*śrībhagavānuvāca*
*trividhā bhavati śraddhā dehināṁ sā svabhāvajā |*
*sāttvikī rājasī caiva tāmasī ceti tāṁ śṛṇu ||2||*

**2.** The Lord [*Kṛṣṇa*] spoke:
— Faith – natural to mankind – is of three types: *sāttvikī, rājasī* and also *tāmasī*. Now hear this:

सत्त्वानुरूपा सर्वस्य श्रद्धा भवति भारत ।
श्रद्धामयोऽयं पुरुषो यो यच्छ्रद्धः स एव सः ॥३॥

*sattvānurūpā sarvasya śraddhā bhavati bhārata |*
*śraddhāmayo'yaṁ puruṣo yo yacchraddhaḥ sa eva saḥ ||3||*

**3.** One's faith is according to one's mind, O *Bhārata* [*Arjuna*]. One is as one's faith be. According to one's faith, so shall a person truly be.

यजन्ते सात्त्विका देवान् यक्षरक्षांसि राजसाः ।
प्रेतान्भूतगणांश्चान्ये यजन्ते तामसा जनाः ॥४॥

*yajante sāttvikā devān yakṣarakṣāṁsi rājasāḥ |*
*pretānbhūtagaṇāṁścānye yajante tāmasā janāḥ ||4||*

**4.** The *sāttvikas* worship the gods, the *rājasas* worship spirits benign, malign, and innocuous. The others, the *tāmasas*, worship ghosts.

अशास्त्रविहितं घोरं तप्यन्ते ये तपो जनाः ।
दम्भाहङ्कारसंयुक्ताः कामरागबलान्विताः ॥५॥

*aśāstravihitaṁ ghoraṁ tapyante ye tapo janāḥ |*
*dambhāhaṅkārasaṁyuktāḥ kāmarāgabalānvitāḥ ||5||*

**5.** Those that practice severe austerities – not prescribed by the scriptures and full of hypocrisy and egotism – are bound by desire and attachment.

कर्शयन्तः शरीरस्थं भूतग्राममचेतसः ।
मां चैवान्तः शरीरस्थं तान् विद्ध्यासुरनिश्चयान् ॥६॥

*karśayantaḥ śarīrasthaṁ bhūtagrāmamacetasaḥ |*
*māṁ caivāntaḥ śarīrasthaṁ tān viddhyāsuraniścayān ||6||*

**6.** [Such] unscrupulous people weaken the organs and also Me who inhabits the body. Know that such people are of *asura* convictions.

आहारस्त्वपि सर्वस्य त्रिविधो भवति प्रियः ।
यज्ञस्तपस्तथा दानं तेषां भेदमिमं शृणु ॥७॥

*āhārastvapi sarvasya trividho bhavati priyaḥ |*
*yajñastapastathā dānaṁ teṣāṁ bhedamimaṁ śṛṇu ||7||*

**7.** Moreover, the food preferred by all – just as ritual, austerity and offerings – are of three kinds. Hear now the difference among them!

आयुः सत्त्वबलारोग्यसुखप्रीतिविवर्धनाः ।
रस्याः स्निग्धाः स्थिरा हृद्या आहाराः सात्त्विकप्रियाः ॥८॥

*āyuḥ sattvabalārogyasukhaprītivivardhanāḥ |*
*rasyāḥ snigdhāḥ sthirā hṛdyā āhārāḥ sāttvikapriyāḥ ||8||*

**8.** The foods that increase life, clarity of mind, strength, health, well-being, satisfaction, which are savory, oligeaginous, wholesome and pleasant, are foods dear to *sāttvikas*.

कट्वम्ललवणात्युष्णतीक्ष्णरूक्षविदाहिनः ।
आहारा राजसस्येष्टा दुःखशोकामयप्रदाः ॥९॥

*kaṭvamlalavaṇātyuṣṇatīkṣṇarūkṣavidāhinaḥ |*
*āhārā rājasasyeṣṭā duḥkhaśokāmayapradāḥ ||9||*

**9.** Foods very bitter, very sour, very salty, very hot, very spicy, very dry, very burning – causing pain, suffering and sickness – are dear to *rājasas*.

यातयामं गतरसं पूति पर्युषितं च यत् ।
उच्छिष्टमपि चामेध्यं भोजनं तामसप्रियम् ॥१०॥

*yātayāmaṁ gatarasaṁ pūti paryuṣitaṁ ca yat |*
*ucchiṣṭamapi cāmedhyaṁ bhojanaṁ tāmasapriyam ||10||*

**10.** Inadequately cooked food, without nourishment, of strong smell, stale, discarded by another, and also impure, is dear to the *tāmasas*.

अफलाकाङ्क्षिभिर्यज्ञो विधिदृष्टो य इज्यते ।
यष्टव्यमेवेति मनः समाधाय स सात्त्विकः ॥११॥

*aphalākāṅkṣibhiryajño vidhidṛṣṭo ya ijyate |*
*yaṣṭavyameveti manaḥ samādhāya sa sāttvikaḥ ||11||*

**11.** The *sāttvika* ritual is that which is known by scripture, performed by those that do not desire its result [and] that fix the mind [on the following decision]: “the ritual should be done”.

अभिसन्धाय तु फलं दम्भार्थमपि चैव यत् ।
इज्यते भरतश्रेष्ठ तं यज्ञं विद्धि राजसम् ॥१२॥

*abhisandhāya tu phalaṁ dambhārthamapi caiva yat |*
*ijyate bharataśreṣṭha taṁ yajñaṁ viddhi rājasam ||12||*

**12.** But that which is performed with an eye on its result and for ostentation, O *Bharataśreṣṭha* [*Arjuna*], know that such ritual is *rājasa*.

विधिहीनमसृष्टान्नं मन्त्रहीनमदक्षिणम् ।
श्रद्धाविरहितं यज्ञं तामसं परिचक्षते ॥१३॥

*vidhihīnamasṛṣṭānnaṁ mantrahīnamadakṣiṇam |*
*śraddhāvirahitaṁ yajñaṁ tāmasaṁ paricakṣate ||13||*

**13.** It is said that *tāmasa* is a ritual contrary to scriptures, without the offering of food, without reciting the *mantras* properly, without appropriate distribution of wealth [and] without faith.

देवद्विजगुरुप्राज्ञपूजनं शौचमार्जवम् ।
ब्रह्मचर्यमहिंसा च शारीरं तप उच्यते ॥१४॥

*devadvijaguruprājñapūjanaṁ śaucamārjavam |*
*brahmacaryamahiṁsā ca śārīraṁ tapa ucyate ||14||*

**14.** Physical austerities are the reverence to God, to the knower of the *Vedas*, to the gurus, and to the wise; purity; rectitude; discipline; and non-violence.

अनुद्वेगकरं वाक्यं सत्यं प्रियहितं च यत् ।
स्वाध्यायाभ्यसनं चैव वाङ्मयं तप उच्यते ॥१५॥

*anudvegakaraṁ vākyaṁ satyaṁ priyahitaṁ ca yat |*
*svādhyāyābhyasanaṁ caiva vāṅ mayaṁ tapa ucyate ||15||*

**15.** Verbal austerities are words that do not cause distress, which are truthful, agreeable and beneficial, as well as the study of the *Vedas*.

मनःप्रसादः सौम्यत्वं मौनमात्मविनिग्रहः ।
भावसंशुद्धिरित्येतत्तपो मानसमुच्यते ॥१६॥

*manaḥprasādaḥ saumyatvaṁ maunamātmavinigrahaḥ |*
*bhāvasaṁśuddhirityetattapo mānasamucyate ||16||*

**16.** Mental austerity is mental tranquility, contentment, silence, command of the mind, purity in attitude [honesty].

श्रद्धया परया तप्तं तपस्तत्त्रिविधं नरैः ।
अफलाकाङ्क्षिभिर्युक्तैः सात्त्विकं परिचक्षते ॥१७॥

*śraddhayā parayā taptaṁ tapastattrividhaṁ naraiḥ |*
*aphalākāṅkṣibhiryuktaiḥ sāttvikaṁ paricakṣate ||17||*

**17.** They say that these three types of austerites practiced with great faith by those disciplined [and] free from the desire for results [except for mental preparedness] are *sāttvikas*.

सत्कारमानपूजार्थं तपो दम्भेन चैव यत् ।
क्रियते तदिह प्रोक्तं राजसं चलमध्रुवम् ॥१८॥

*satkāramānapūjārthaṁ tapo dambhena caiva yat |*
*kriyate tadiha proktaṁ rājasaṁ calamadhruvam ||18||*

**18.** The austerity practiced with hypocrisy – for the sake of [receiving] reverence, honor or worship – is called *rājasa*, [and its result] is temporary [and] fickle.

मूढग्राहेणात्मनो यत्पीडया क्रियते तपः ।
परस्योत्सादनार्थं वा तत्तामसमुदाहृतम् ॥१९॥

*mūḍhagrāheṇātmano yatpīḍayā kriyate tapaḥ |*
*parasyotsādanārthaṁ vā tattāmasamudāhṛtam ||19||*

**19.** The austerity practiced with deluded determination, with self-torture or for the destruction of others is called *tāmasa*.

दातव्यमिति यद्दानं दीयतेऽनुपकारिणे ।
देशे काले च पात्रे च तद्दानं सात्त्विकं स्मृतम् ॥२०॥

*dātavyamiti yaddānaṁ dīyate'nupakāriṇe |*
*deśe kāle ca pātre ca taddānaṁ sāttvikaṁ smṛtam ||20||*

**20.** The gift from someone who expects nothing in return, offered because "it should be given" – at the proper time and place [and] for a worthy person – is considered *sāttvika*.

यत्तु प्रत्युपकारार्थं फलमुद्दिश्य वा पुनः ।
दीयते च परिक्लिष्टं तद्दानं राजसं स्मृतम् ॥२१॥

*yattu pratyapakārārthaṁ phalamuddiśya vā punaḥ |*
*dīyate ca parikliṣṭaṁ taddānaṁ rājasaṁ smṛtam ||21||*

**21.** But that which is given expecting something in return, or with an eye on its result, and with reluctance, this gift is considered *rājasa*.

अदेशकाले यद्दानमपात्रेभ्यश्च दीयते ।
असत्कृतमवज्ञातं तत्तामसमुदाहृतम् ॥२२॥

*adeśakāle yaddānamapātrebhyaśca dīyate |*
*asatkṛtamavajñātaṁ tattāmasamudāhṛtam ||22||*

**22.** A gift given at an inappropriate time and place and for unworthy people, with disrespect [and] contempt, is called *tāmasa*.

ओं तत्सदिति निर्देशो ब्रह्मणस्त्रिविधः स्मृतः ।
ब्राह्मणास्तेन वेदाश्च यज्ञाश्च विहिताः पुरा ॥२३॥

*oṁ tatsaditi nirdeśo brahmaṇastrividhaḥ smṛtaḥ |*
*brāhmaṇāstena vedāśca yajñāśca vihitāḥ purā ||23||*

**23.** "*Oṁ tat sat*", has been declared as the threefold designation of *Brahman*. By this the *brāhmaṇas*, the *Vedas* and the rituals were created in the past.

तस्मादोमित्युदाहृत्य यज्ञदानतपः क्रियाः ।
प्रवर्तन्ते विधानोक्ताः सततं ब्रह्मवादिनाम् ॥२४॥

*tasmādomityudāhṛtya yajñadānatapaḥ kriyāḥ |*
*pravartante vidhānoktāḥ satataṁ brahmavādinām ||24||*

**24.** Therefore, pronouncing "*oṁ*", acts, such as sacrifice, offerings and austerities, are begun as prescribed by those who know the *Vedas*.

तदित्यनभिसन्धाय फलं यज्ञतपः क्रियाः ।
दानक्रियाश्च विविधाः क्रियन्ते मोक्षकाङ्क्षिभिः ॥२५॥

*tadityanabhisandhāya phalaṁ yajñatapaḥ kriyāḥ |*
*dānakriyāśca vividhāḥ kriyante mokṣakāṅkṣibhiḥ ||25||*

**25.** [Upon pronouncing] "*tat*", various acts are done, such as rituals, austerities and offerings, without expecting any result, by those that desire liberation.

सद्भावे साधुभावे च सदित्येतत्प्रयुज्यते ।
प्रशस्ते कर्मणि तथा सच्छब्दः पार्थ युज्यते ॥२६॥

*sadbhāve sādhubhāve ca sadityetatprayujyate |*
*praśaste karmaṇi tathā sacchabdaḥ pārtha yujyate ||26||*

**26.** "*Sat*" is used in the sense of "existence" and in the sense of "goodness", and also, O *Pārtha* [*Arjuna*], the word "*sat*" is used to refer to an auspicious act.

यज्ञे तपसि दाने च स्थितिः सदिति चोच्यते ।
कर्म चैव तदर्थीयं सदित्येवाभिधीयते ॥२७॥

*yajñe tapasi dāne ca sthitiḥ saditi cocyate |*
*karma caiva tadarthīyaṁ sadityevābhidhīyate ||27||*

**27.** Steadfastness in ritual, austerity and offering is also called "*sat*". And an act for That [*Īśvara*] is also called "*sat*".

अश्रद्धया हुतं दत्तं तपस्तप्तं कृतं च यत् ।
असदित्युच्यते पार्थ न च तत्प्रेत्य नो इह ॥२८॥

*aśraddhayā hutaṁ dattaṁ tapastaptaṁ kṛtaṁ ca yat |*
*asadityucyate pārtha na ca tatpretya no iha ||28||*

**28.** Without faith, anything offered, given, or practiced as an austerity, is called "*asat*", O *Pārtha* [*Arjuna*]. And it is neither [fruitful] here nor in the hereafter.

ओं तत्सदिति श्रीमद्भगवद्गीतासूपनिषत्सु ब्रह्मविद्यायां योगशास्त्रे श्रीकृष्णार्जुनसंवादे श्रद्धात्रयविभागयोगो नाम सप्तदशोऽध्यायः॥

*oṁ tatsaditi śrīmadbhagavadgītāsūpaniṣatsu*
*brahmavidyāyāṁ yogaśāstre śrīkṛṣṇārjunasaṁvāde*
*śraddhātrayavibhāgayogo nāma saptadaśo'dhyāyaḥ ||*

*Oṁ*, this is the Truth. Thus is the seventeenth chapter, the subject [of which] is called "*śraddhātrayavibhāga*" [the distinction among the three faiths], in the glorious *Bhagavadgītā*, [which is equivalent to] the *Upaniṣads*, [the subject of which is] the knowledge of *Brahman* [and] *yoga*, in the dialogue between *śrī Kṛṣṇa* and *Arjuna*.

# Chapter 18

## *Renunciation for liberation*

In this chapter, the purpose of the entire *Gītā* is presented, as well as the goal of the *Vedas* - because the objective of the two are one and the same. Upon saying this, *Śrī Kṛṣṇa* further adds that all that has been said in the other chapters may be comprehended right here in chapter 18.

Just as in chapter 2, this chapter is long and covers the two main themes of the *Vedas* and the *Bhagavadgītā*: *brahmavidyā* and a life of action as *yoga*, self-knowledge and the preparation of the mind for self-knowledge, respectively. The indivisible identity between *jīva* and *Īśvara* is the subject of self-knowledge; a lifestyle for acquiring an emotionally mature mind for liberation, *mokṣa*, as well as command of the mind and the capacity to direct it, is *yoga*. There are two ways of life with the same objective: renunciation of all action (except those related to study) or a life of action according to *dharma* (which includes listening to, reflecting upon and contemplating self-knowledge). However, despite the two different ways of life, both must be a bhakta, a devotee of *Īśvara* - meaning that one comprehends the cosmic order in which one takes part.

An individual who renounces action is free from the obligation of family and society upon doing a specific Vedic ritual from which point this individual assumes the commitment of total dedication to study and contemplation, as well as compassion for all living beings. These two ways of life for liberation are the vision of the *Gītā* and the *Vedas*. The clear and definitive objective in life is to free oneself from suffering and the sense of limitation via the knowledge of *Ātman*;

in this knowledge, *jīva* and *Īśvara* are revealed as essentially being the same.

To begin the chapter, *Arjuna* asks a question. He wants to know the difference between *sannyāsa* and *tyāga*, because both words mean "renunciation".

Throughout the *Gītā*, *Arjuna* has asked many questions to *Kṛṣṇa*. These questions all appear different, but in fact, he is often asking the same thing. His doubt is whether or not he should renounce in order to attain liberation.

*Kṛṣṇa* surely did not want to give him direct advice as to what he should do. As a teacher, he wanted *Arjuna* to comprehend what was best for him to do. However, up to now, *Arjuna* still does not have a grasp on what he should do.

*Kṛṣṇa*'s answer is confusing because he describes two ways of life that lead to the same objective - *mokṣa*. It is impossible to say which way is best: it depends on the individual qualifications either to dedicate oneself solely to study or to a life of action while studying. For liberation, only self-knowledge is necessary. If one does not have the necessary qualifications, then such qualifications must first be acquired through a life of action.

In order to better understand that *karmayoga* and *karmasannyāsa* have equal value as ways of life for self-knowledge, *Kṛṣṇa* mentions the true renunciation that makes the difference is *jñānena sannyāsa*, the renunciation that comes from knowledge.

The choice between taking action and not taking action is secondary. Possessing the knowledge of one's true nature is the highest goal, which is liberation. Renouncing the identification of the body, mind and senses as the Self is attained via the self-knowledge. With this self-knowledge, one is able to witness the body, mind and senses as the agents of action. The highest renunciation is equivalent to knowing the Self, which is, in fact, none other than *Brahman*: the nature of the Self that is *akartṛ*, free and exempt from any action whatsoever.

After chapter 5, *Arjuna* seems to have understood what *Kṛṣṇa* said. However, he wants a better understanding of the kinds of renunciation, since there are two different words used to indicate renunciation: *sannyāsa* and *tyāga*.

Analyzing the *Bhagavadgītā* where the two words are employed, we can see the meanings often differ throughout the verses. We can also note that the word *yoga* is more often associated with *karmayoga*, and the word *sannyāsa* is more often associated to a lifestyle of renunciation in action, *karma-sannyāsa*. *Karmayoga*, therefore, may be called *karma-phala-tyāga*, the renunciation of the result of action. This perspective clarifies what *Kṛṣṇa* says in the beginning of chapter 3 regarding the two ways of life for attaining liberation: *karma-phala-tyāga* and *karma-sannyāsa*.

In order to answer this question, *Kṛṣṇa* first analyzes the various factors related to renunciation and also action, so that *Arjuna* remains without any doubt.

*Kṛṣṇa* speaks once more about the *guṇas* and says that nothing in this universe is free from the *guṇas*, the qualities.

While on this topic, *Kṛṣṇa* says that the *Vedas* divide people into four groups, according to their respective combination of the three *guṇas*. Each one of these divisions, called *varṇa*, have their role to fulfill, and all of them together constitute society.

When each and everyone does what they have the capacity to do, according to each one's qualities, all may enjoy the harmony of society. To do what must be done and contribute to society brings the contentment and maturity that gives one the opportunity to question the point of life. Therefore, it can be seen that the social structure as proposed by the

*Vedas* is clearly intended to be conducive to final liberation.

In verse 46 of this chapter, *Śrī Kṛṣṇa* explains *karmayoga*, and, together with verse 47 of chapter 2, the attitude that is *karmayoga* becomes clear. It is here in chapter 18 that *Arjuna* realizes that he must choose action, but may never choose the result of action, which is solely determined by *Īśvara*, He who creates and sustains all beings. One's action should be performed as an offering to *Īśvara*; this attitude is *karmayoga* and the comprehension of *Īśvara* is *bhakti*, devotion. This attitude comes from this comprehension and is the means to *mokṣa*.

In just a few verses *Kṛṣṇa* sumarizes the entire message of the *Gītā*.

The knowledge of *Ātman*, the Self that is *Brahman*, is acquired by listening to the teaching and reflecting upon it. The steadfastness of the knowledge, *jñānaniṣṭhā*, is reached by contemplation, *nididhyāsana*, on what has been heard and understood.

Finally, *Kṛṣṇa* concluded the instruction of *Arjuna* and says that he may do what he wishes. *Kṛṣṇa* knows that his disciple will do what must be done. He says that *Arjuna* is loved by Him, and by surrendering to *Īśvara*, he will not suffer.

Furthermore, *Kṛṣṇa* mentions the qualifications necessary for both people who teach and who receive this knowledge.

The result of the teaching for both is also mentioned. *Kṛṣṇa* asks if *Arjuna* has understood all that has been taught by Him - asking if his delusion has dissipated. *Arjuna* answers that his delusion has gone and that he shall act according to the teaching of *Kṛṣṇa*.

Following, the *Gītā* returns us to the palace where *Sañjaya* tells king *Dhṛtarāṣṭra* of everything that was happening on the battlefield of *Kurukṣetra*. Blessed by *Vyāsa*, he sees the dialogue between *Kṛṣṇa* and his disciple *Arjuna*, just before the beginning of the war.

*Sañjaya*, mesmerized, remembers the dialogue and the cosmic form of *Kṛṣṇa*, and ends by saying that for as long as there is *Kṛṣṇa* and *Arjuna*, there shall always be wealth, victory, prosperity and justice.

**Summary of the verses**

Verse 1: In order to better understanding about all that *Kṛṣṇa* has said about self-knowledge, *Arjuna* asks about the difference between two words that both mean "renunciation", as used throughout the *Gītā*: *sannyāsa* and *tyāga*.

Verses 2 and 3: *Kṛṣṇa* responds, citing the perspective of different leaned men, and summarizes all that will be taught in the upcoming verses.

Verse 4: According to *Kṛṣṇa*, there is no difference between *sannyāsa* and *tyāga*.

Verses 5 and 6: In these verses, *Kṛṣṇa* explains what must be done and what must be renounced. One must never give up *yajña*, *dāna* and *tapas* (ritual or prayer, offerings and austerities): They must be done; they prepare the mind for self-knowledge.

Actions considered mandatory by the *Vedas* are called *nitya-naimittika-karma*, and they should be done without any expectation as to results of such actions. In other words, not with the attitude of "I shall perform these rites in order to receive these fruits", but rather with the attitude of "I shall do what must be done".

Therefore, the renunciation *Kṛṣṇa* refers to is that of attachment, not the renunciation of action.

Verses 7 to 9: In these verses, *Kṛṣṇa* divides renunciation into three types: *tāmasa*, *rājasa* and *sāttvika*, meaning the renunciation of the *tamas*, *rajas* or *sattva* characteristics.

Verse 10: *Kṛṣṇa* explains what happens to the mind of the person that has *sāttvika-tyāga*; this person is a *karmayogin*: doing what must be done, free from the attachment to the results, which leads to a mind purified from reactions, and thereby reaching some contentment. Thus, the mind is prepared for self-knowledge. Dedicated to knowledge, this person becomes free from doubt and free from action and its results. This liberation comes from the comprehension that "I do no action".

Verse 11: However, one that still identifies oneself with the body as the "doer" will not be able to renounce action completely. Therefore, this individual may renounce the results alone.

Verse 12: The result of action from someone who is not a renunciant may be desireable, undesirable or a mix of the two; there will be no result from action for the renunciant, who is aware that the Self is free from action.

Therefore, the wise have completely renounced; the *karmayogin* has partially renounced.

Verses 13 a 15: *Kṛṣṇa* stipulates the five factors responsible for action, since knowing these causes of action is paramount to understanding that *Ātman* is not one of them: *Ātman* is *akartṛ*, not the agent of action and completely apart from action.

The five factors are: the physical body, *prāṇa*, the mind and senses, the ego, and *daiva* - the deities that preside over the functions of the mind-body. *Īśvara*, seen through each one of these functions and the cosmic laws that govern them, is a *devatā*. In this verse He is called *daiva*.

These five factors are the cause for the three types of *karma*, action: physical, oral and mental: *kāyika*, *vācika* and *mānasa*.

These actions may be either *nyāyya*, legitimate action that is aligned with *dharma*, or *viparīta*, action against this order.

Verse 16: *Kṛṣṇa* concludes that *Ātman* is not part of this action, but due to the errant identification of the Self with these five factors, one identifies the Self as the agent of action.

Verse 17: In the previous verse, *Kṛṣṇa* mentions that the person that does not see the truth of *Ātman* is durmati. In this verse, He defines sumati: one who possesses clear discernment, and who does not hold any misconceptions regarding the Self; one who is free from *karma* even when in action, since this individual is clearly aware that the Self neither acts nor is subject to the fruit of action.

Verse 18: *Śrī Kṛṣṇa* analyzes the three components of action: the knower, the object of knowledge and knowledge; or rather, the agent of action, the object of action and the instrument of action.

Verse 19: *Śrī Kṛṣṇa* takes these three elements - knowledge, the agent of action and action - and elaborates on them considering the three *guṇas*.

Verses 20 to 22: Knowledge is thus presented as having three kinds: *sattva*, *rajas* and *tamas*. However, knowledge is not exactly of three types, since all knowledge is *sattva*. Therefore, this affirmation refers to *antaḥkaraṇa*, meaning the type of mind where knowledge occurs.

*Sattva* is the knowledge in which a person sees many objects but ascertains the sole truth even in duality.

*Rajas* is the knowledge in which a person sees duality and difference.

*Tamas* is the knowledge in which a person sees one thing as if it were everything. For example, this knowledge might conclude that the Self is one's body, and this purported "truth" becomes the basis for conclusions on reality. Such knowledge may even lead a person to worship an idol as a god and adore it as such.

Verses 23 to 25: the three types of *karma* are presented. *Sāttvika-karma,* action predominated by *sattva,* is aligned to *dharma* - that which must be done in certain situations; it is the action performed by a person whose mind is predominately *sattva.* According to *Śrī Kṛṣṇa, sattva* action is *karmayoga;* it is free from the attachment to tastes and aversions and its results.

*Rājasa-karma* is action done with a strong desire for results, done with much arrogance and effort.

*Tāmasa-karma* is action done with no consideration for the consequences, losses, or the fact that such action may affect or damage others. Such action is also done without taking into consideration one's own internal and external resources necessary for the success of an endeavor.

Verses 26 to 28: Three types of *kartṛ,* the agent of action, are presented [the word *kartṛ* becomes *kartā* when declined in the first case, as the subject of the phrase. *Kartṛ* is its root word].

*Sāttvika-kartṛ* is one whose mind is predominately *sattva,* free from attachment, and not affected by the result of action; this individual is resolute and enthusiastic.

Verse 29: *Śrī Kṛṣṇa* also divides the intellect and willpower according to the three *guṇas.*

Verses 30 to 32: The intellect in which *sattva* predominates comprehends what is action and what is renunciation, what must be done and what must be avoided, and what one must and musn't fear; it also understands what is limitation and what is freedom.

The intellect in which *rajas* dominates understands things incorrectly and not the way they are in fact.

*Tamas* intellect is the one that resolutely concludes that a thing is in fact its opposite. Since *tamas* is ignorance, it is capable of concluding that which is inappropriate as correct.

Verses 33 to 35: The three types of willpower are presented.

The willpower that is predominately *sattva* is steadfast and allows an individual to maintain mental and physical activities. Willpower is useful to this person, and it may be used as an instrument for the benefit of the individual.

The willpower that is predominately *rajas* allows an individual to maintain activities for the purpose of security, pleasure and merit (*puṇya*) to be used either in this life or the next.

Lastly, the willpower that is predominately *tamas* is the willpower in which the person cannot give up what should be given up. No matter what happens, this person is attached to lethargy, fear, sadness, and depression, which accompany this individual daily throughout activities.

Verses 36 to 39: Therefore, action and its accessories - knowledge, the agent of action, the intellect and willpower - have been mentioned as being of three types according to the three *guṇas*. Next, the types of happiness are covered. They depend on how happiness is reached, how long it lasts, and it nature.

*Sattva* happiness is reached via the discipline of listening, reflecting and contemplating the truth. This happiness comes from recognizing the plenitude that is the nature of *Ātman*. *Śrī Kṛṣṇa* says that this happiness may be like a poison at the first contact, since it requires an initial effort, but in the end, with a mind transformed by maturity, this happiness is like nectar. This happiness is due to the predominance of *sattva* in the mind, thus it is called *sattva*, in Sanskrit, *sāttvika-sukha*.

Happiness with the predominancy of *rajas* occurs upon the contact of the sense organs and their respective objects. At first, it is nectar, since this pleasure is easily reached, being dependent on neither maturity nor mental preparedness. However, during this process, when there is an exaggeration in sense pleasures, there is a loss of strength, health, the capacity of the senses, and ageing – which makes this happiness seem like poison, because the person is not capable of having the same pleasure as experienced previously.

Finally, happiness that is predominately *tamas* is that which is characterized by delusion at the beginning and in the end. It is the happiness of sleep, lethargy and negligence. There is no positive experience of happiness, yet there is an absence of unhappiness.

Verse 40: With this verse, *Śrī Kṛṣṇa* concludes this subject on the actions and the three *guṇas*, stating that there is nothing in this universe that is free from the power of these three qualities of *Prakṛti*.

Verses 41 to 45: People may be divided into four groups according to their predominant *guṇas*. The *brāhmaṇas* are primarily *sattva* and are occupied with *sattva* activities. *Kṣatriyas* are primarily *rajas*, and have *sattva* in second place. *Vaiśyas* are primarily *rajas*, with *tamas* in second place.

*Śudras* are predominately *tamas*. Each one of these four groups is able to perform the activities that are demanded from them by the respective predominance of the *guṇa*.

The functions of each group are characterized accordingly.

*Kṛṣṇa* says that the commitment to the action required of each one of these groups leads to success. Each individual is capable of determining action according to their specific nature. The satisfactory fulfillment of these duties contributes to the cosmic order, which is *Īśvara* - and that is *karmayoga*. This attitude prepares the mind for self-knowledge.

Verse 46: In this verse, *Śrī Kṛṣṇa* completes verse 47 of chapter 2, where He explains how to transform action, *karma*, into *karmayoga*.

In chapter 2, *Kṛṣṇa* mentions karmaphalahetu, the cause of the result of action, which is *Īśvara*. Here in chapter 18, He elaborates on He who causes the result of action, which is *Īśvara*, which is both the cause of and That which sustains the entire universe. Moreover, *Īśvara* is worshipped by performing the actions that must be done by each and every one, thereby not only creating a harmony throughout society, but also happiness in the appreciation of the connection with *Īśvara*, and also in the satisfaction of doing what must be done.

Verses 47 to 48: It is always best to do what must be done, which is our *dharma*, svadharma, than to do the duty of another - even if well done. What must be done by another suits that individual and is an exercise or a challenge to be met. The duty of each and every one of us is a challenge that must be met. Not complying with what an individual must do generates conflict, and thus, suffering. Therefore, *Kṛṣṇa* says that one's duty should never be abandoned, since abandoning action liberates no one. All actions contain a natural defect; they are limited by the three *guṇas* and they produce a positive and negative result, *puṇya* or *pāpa*, to which a person remains bound. When action is performed as an offering to *Īśvara*, which is the order of *dharma*, one is freed from the bondage of the tastes and aversions and becomes qualified for self-knowledge.

Verse 49: *Kṛṣṇa* now explains what is the goal, siddhi, as mentioned in verse 46, which is what a *karmayogin* is qualified to reach. It is called *naiṣkarmya*: total freedom in action.

Beforehand, *Kṛṣṇa* says that it is impossible not to do action. Therefore, this freedom in action is knowledge. It is in the comprehension that *jīva* is *Brahman*, which is free from action, and thus does nothing. With this knowledge, a person is *niṣkarman*, and one's state of being totally free from action is called *naiṣkarmya*. This concept is not about doing or not doing action: it is the nature of the Self, of *Ātman* that is free from action.

Verses 50 to 55: *Kṛṣṇa* explains that the process of self-knowledge begins with the maturity that comes from *karmayoga* and the relationship with *Īśvara*. With the mind thus capacitated, one listens to the knowledge of, reflects upon, and contemplates *Ātman*. In this process, the qualifications are acquired and an awareness of being *Brahman* is assimilated; this is the knowledge of one's identity with *Īśvara*, which is called complete devotion. *Kṛṣṇa* says that this person becomes one with *Īśvara*, meaning that one leaves behind the notion of being seperate or different - this is called *jñānaniṣṭha*.

Verses 56 to 62: *Kṛṣṇa* once again points out *karmayoga* together with *bhakti*, devotion to *Īśvara* through renouncing the arrogance of the ego.

*Īśvara* is seated in the intellect of everyone. He is responsible for all action that is done, via the three *guṇas* of *Prakṛti*. Thus, through this awareness of *Īśvara*, the ego - despite its wish to control its own life and all that happens around - bows before *Īśvara*, that which governs everything.

Verses 63: With this verse, *Śrī Kṛṣṇa* ends his teaching and says that *Arjuna* may do what he wishes.

Verses 64 to 66: Then *Kṛṣṇa* is overtaken by his affection for *Arjuna* and indicates what is good for him: liberation, *mokṣa*, and knowing exactly what leads a person to liberation, *mokṣa sādhana*, both of which are covered in verses 65 and 66.

Verse 66 is the last verse of the teaching of *Kṛṣṇa*, the first is verse 11 of chapter 2. The first words of the initial verse and the final verse of the *Bhagavadgītā* speak of the elimination of suffering via renunciation and the comprehension of *Īśvara*. Knowledge is the means for liberation.

Verses 67 to 71: These verses contain the rules, vidhi, for a person to teach *Vedas* and particularly for teaching the *Gītā*. The tradition of teaching is called *saṁpradāya*. Therefore, *saṁpradāya* vidhi are the rules on the qualifications necessary for those who teach and who listen.

Furthermore, the result of study is also mentioned.

Verse 72: *Kṛṣṇa* asks *Arjuna* if all that He has taught is clear to him.

Verse 73: *Arjuna* responds that his delusion has gone and demonstrates his gratitude for the teaching he has received from *Kṛṣṇa*. Finally, he says that he will do what must be done, according to the teaching of *Kṛṣṇa*.

Verses 74 to 78: *Sañjaya*, then, speaks to king *Dhṛtarāṣṭra*. He praises the words of Lord *Kṛṣṇa* and feels blessed by having had the opportunity to hear the teaching. He remembers the words of *Kṛṣṇa* and his cosmic form with great emotion. Finally in verse 78, *Sañjaya* declares his regard for *Kṛṣṇa* and *Arjuna*, and the dialogue between them.

With his own last words, finally, *Sañjaya* declares to the king what will be the final result of the war.

# अथ अथाष्टादशोऽध्यायः

## *atha athāṣṭādaśo'dhyāyaḥ*

## Chapter eighteen

अर्जुन उवाच
संन्यासस्य महाबाहो तत्त्वमिच्छामि वेदितुम् ।
त्यागस्य च हृषीकेश पृथक्केशिनिषूदन ॥१॥

*arjuna uvāca*
*saṁnyāsasya mahābāho tattvamicchāmi veditum |*
*tyāgasya ca hṛṣīkeśa pṛthakkeśiniṣūdana ||1||*

**1.** *Arjuna* spoke:
— O *Mahābāhu* [*Kṛṣṇa*], I wish to know, distinctly, the nature of *saṁnyāsa* and of *tyāga*, O *Keśiniṣūdana* [*Kṛṣṇa*], O *Hṛṣīkeśa* [*Kṛṣṇa*]!

श्रीभगवानुवाच
काम्यानां कर्मणां न्यासं संन्यासं कवयो विदुः ।
सर्वकर्मफलत्यागं प्राहुस्त्यागं विचक्षणाः ॥२॥

*śrībhagavānuvāca*
*kāmyānāṁ karmaṇāṁ nyāsaṁ saṁnyāsaṁ kavayo viduḥ |*
*sarvakarmaphalatyāgaṁ prāhustyāgaṁ vicakṣaṇāḥ ||2||*

**2.** The Lord [*Kṛṣṇa*] spoke:
— The wise consider *saṁnyāsa* the renunciation of action compelled by desire. The studious call *tyāga* the renunciation of the result of all action.

त्याज्यं दोषवदित्येके कर्म प्राहुर्मनीषिणः ।
यज्ञदानतपः कर्म न त्याज्यमिति चापरे ॥३॥

*tyājyaṁ doṣavadityeke karma prāhurmanīṣiṇaḥ |*
*yajñadānatapaḥ karma na tyājyamiti cāpare ||3||*

**3.** Some pundits declare that [all] actions have defects [and therefore] should be abandoned; and others declare that actions of ritual, offerings and austerities are not to be abandoned.

निश्चयं शृणु मे तत्र त्यागे भरतसत्तम ।
त्यागो हि पुरुषव्याघ्र त्रिविधः सम्प्रकिर्तितः ॥४॥

*niścayaṁ śṛṇu me tatra tyāge bharatasattama |*
*tyāgo hi puruṣavyāghra trividhaḥ samprakirtitaḥ ||4||*

**4.** Hear my conclusion regarding renunciation, O *Bharatasattama* [*Arjuna*]: renunciation is truly of three types, O *Puruṣavyāghra* [*Arjuna*].

यज्ञदानतपःकर्म न त्याज्यं कार्यमेव तत् ।
यज्ञो दानं तपश्चैव पावनानि मनीषिणाम् ॥५॥

*yajñadānatapaḥkarma na tyājyaṁ kāryameva tat |*
*yajño dānaṁ tapaścaiva pāvanāni manīṣiṇām ||5||*

**5.** Action in the form of ritual, offering and austerity must not be abanodoned. It is what must be done. Ritual, offering and austerity are truly purifying for the discriminating.

एतान्यपि तु कर्माणि सङ्गं त्यक्त्वा फलानि च ।
कर्तव्यानीति मे पार्थ निश्चितं मतमुत्तमम् ॥६॥

*etānyapi tu karmāṇi saṅgaṁ tyaktvā phalāni ca |*
*kartavyānīti me pārtha niścitaṁ matamuttamam ||6||*

**6.** But these actions must be done [while] renunciating attachment and results – this is my clear and definitive point, O *Pārtha* [*Arjuna*].

नियतस्य तु संन्यासः कर्मणो नोपपद्यते ।
मोहात्तस्य परित्यागस्तामसः परिकीर्तितः ॥७॥

*niyatasya tu saṁnyāsaḥ karmaṇo nopapadyate |*
*mohāttasya parityāgastāmasaḥ parikīrtitaḥ ||7||*

**7.** The renunciation of dutiful action is inappropriate; the abandonment of this [duty], due to delusion, is called *tāmasa*.

दुःखमित्येव यत्कर्म कायक्लेशभयात्त्यजेत् ।
स कृत्वा राजसं त्यागं नैव त्यागफलं लभेत् ॥८॥

*duḥkhamityeva yatkarma kāyakleśabhayāttyajet |*
*sa kṛtvā rājasaṁ tyāgaṁ naiva tyāgaphalaṁ labhet ||8||*

**8.** Out of fear of physical suffering, [if one] renounces an action [considered] painful, [then] one's renunciation is *rājasa* [and] shall never reach the result of renunciation.

कार्यमित्येव यत्कर्म नियतं क्रियतेऽर्जुन ।
सङ्गं त्यक्त्वा फलं चैव स त्यागः सात्त्विको मतः ॥९॥

*kāryamityeva yatkarma niyataṁ kriyate'rjuna |*
*saṅgaṁ tyaktvā phalaṁ caiva sa tyāgaḥ sāttviko mataḥ ||9||*

**9.** O *Arjuna*, renouncing attachment and results, [if] the dutiful action is exacted only because it must be done, [then] this renunciation is considered *sāttvika*.

न द्वेष्ट्यकुशलं कर्म कुशले नानुषज्जते ।
त्यागी सत्त्वसमाविष्टो मेधावी छिन्नसंशयः ॥१०॥

*na dveṣṭyakuśalaṁ karma kuśale nānuṣajjate |*
*tyāgī sattvasamāviṣṭo medhāvī chinnasaṁśayaḥ ||10||*

**10.** The renunciant, established in *sattva*, possessing knowledge [of *Ātman*], whose doubts have been eliminated, neither hates inauspicious action nor is attached to auspicious [action].

न हि देहभृता शक्यं त्यक्तुं कर्माण्यशेषतः ।
यस्तु कर्मफलत्यागी स त्यागीत्यभिधीयते ॥११॥

*na hi dehabhṛtā śakyaṁ tyaktuṁ karmāṇyaśeṣataḥ |*
*yastu karmaphalatyāgī sa tyāgītyabhidhīyate ||11||*

**11.** Indeed, for he who identifies himself with the body, it is impossible to renounce action completely, but he who renounces the fruit of action is called a renunciant.

अनिष्टमिष्टं मिश्रं च त्रिविधं कर्मणः फलम् ।
भवत्यत्यागिनां प्रेत्य न तु संन्यासिनां क्वचित् ॥१२॥

*aniṣṭamiṣṭaṁ miśraṁ ca trividhaṁ karmaṇaḥ phalam |*
*bhavatyatyāginām pretya na tu saṁnyāsināṁ kvacit ||12||*

**12.** For the non-renouncer, there are three fruits of action after death: desired, undesired and mixed – but never for the renunciant.

पञ्चैतानि महाबाहो कारणानि निबोध मे ।
साङ्ख्ये कृतान्ते प्रोक्तानि सिद्धये सर्वकर्मणाम् ॥१३॥

*pañcaitāni mahābāho kāraṇāni nibodha me |*
*sāṅkhye kṛtānte proktāni siddhaye sarvakarmaṇām ||13||*

**13.** O *Mahābāhu* [*Arjuna*], know by Me that there are five causes for the accomplishment of all action. They are spoken of in the knowledge that is *Vedānta*.

अधिष्ठानं तथा कर्ता करणं च पृथग्विधम् ।
विविधाश्च पृथक्चेष्टा दैवं चैवात्र पञ्चमम् ॥१४॥

*adhiṣṭhānaṁ tathā kartā karaṇaṁ ca pṛthagvidham |*
*vividhāśca pṛthakceṣṭā daivaṁ caivātra pañcamam ||14||*

**14.** [They are:] the physical body, the agent of action, the various instruments [the organs of perception and action], the many and varied funcitons [of the *prāṇas*] and the deities that preside over all the functions of the Universe, which is the fifth [cause] among them.

शरीरवाङ्मनोभिर्यत्कर्म प्रारभते नरः ।
न्याय्यं वा विपरीतं वा पञ्चैते तस्य हेतवः ॥१५॥

*śarīravāṅ manobhiryatkarma prārabhate naraḥ |*
*nyāyyaṁ vā viparītaṁ vā pañcaite tasya hetavaḥ ||15||*

**15.** These are the five causes of any action a person undertakes with body, speech [or] mind – be it right or wrong.

तत्रैवं सति कर्तारमात्मानं केवलं तु यः ।
पश्यत्यकृतबुद्धित्वान्न स पश्यति दुर्मतिः ॥१६॥

*tatraivaṁ sati kartāramātmānaṁ kevalaṁ tu yaḥ |*
*paśyatyakṛtabuddhitvānna sa paśyati durmatiḥ ||16||*

**16.** Thus, the ignorant – those who see the pure Self as the agent of action due to an unprepared intellect – do not [really] see.

यस्य नाहङ्कृतो भावो बुद्धिर्यस्य न लिप्यते ।
हत्वापि स इमांल्लोकान्न हन्ति न निबध्यते ॥१७॥

*yasya nāhaṅkṛto bhāvo buddhiryasya na lipyate |*
*hatvāpi sa imāṁllokānna hanti na nibadhyate ||17||*

**17.** For whom there is no notion of the agent of action, whose mind is not attached [to the fruit of action], even though he slays these people, he neither slays nor is bound [to the fruit of action].

ज्ञानं ज्ञेयं परिज्ञाता त्रिविधा कर्मचोदना ।
करणं कर्म कर्तेति त्रिविधः कर्मसङ्ग्रहः ॥१८॥

*jñānaṁ jñeyaṁ parijñātā trividhā karmacodanā |*
*karaṇaṁ karma karteti trividhaḥ karmasaṅgrahaḥ ||18||*

**18.** Knowledge, the known [object] [and] the knower are the threefold impulse to action; the instrument, the goal [and] the agent of action are the threefold basis of action.

ज्ञानं कर्म च कर्ता च त्रिधैव गुणभेदतः ।
प्रोच्यते गुणसङ्ख्याने यथावच्छृनु तान्यपि ॥१९॥

*jñānaṁ karma ca kartā ca tridhaiva guṇabhedataḥ |*
*procyate guṇasaṅkhyāne yathāvacchṛnu tānyapi ||19||*

**19.** It has been said of the categorization of the *guṇas* that action and the agent of action are of three types, according to the *guṇas*. Hear about these also:

सर्वभूतेषु येनैकं भावमव्ययमीक्षते ।
अविभक्तं विभक्तेषु तज्ज्ञानं विद्धि सात्त्विकम् ॥२०॥

*sarvabhūteṣu yenaikaṁ bhāvamavyayamīkṣate |*
*avibhaktaṁ vibhakteṣu tajjñānaṁ viddhi sāttvikam ||20||*

**20.** Know that *sāttvika* knowledge is that by which one sees the one, immutable reality [that is] not divided into all the divided beings.

पृथक्त्वेन तु यज्ज्ञानं नानाभावान्पृथग्विधान् ।
वेत्ति सर्वेषु भूतेषु तज्ज्ञानं विद्धि राजसम् ॥२१॥

*pṛthaktvena tu yajjñānaṁ nānābhāvānpṛthagvidhān |*
*vetti sarveṣu bhūteṣu tajjñānaṁ viddhi rājasam ||21||*

**21.** But know that *rājasa* knowledge is that by which one identifies [by mistake] the different and varied natures in all beings as being different

यत्तु कृत्स्नवदेकस्मिन्कार्ये सक्तमहैतुकम् ।
अतत्त्वार्थवदल्पं च तत्तामसमुदाहृतम् ॥२२॥

*yattu kṛtsnavadekasminkārye saktamahaitukam |*
*atattvārthavadalpaṁ ca tattāmasamudāhṛtam ||22||*

**22.** Furthermore, *tāmasa* [knowledge] is said to be that which is focused on the individual body as if it were all that is; [it is the knowledge that is] limited, illogical and unreal.

नियतं सङ्गरहितमरागद्वेषतः कृतम् ।
अफलप्रेप्सुना कर्म यत्तत्सात्त्विकमुच्यते ॥२३॥

*niyataṁ saṅgarahitamarāgadveṣataḥ kṛtam |*
*aphalaprepsunā karma yattatsāttvikamucyate ||23||*

**23.** *Sāttvika* action is said to be that which is obligatory, done without attachment, without tastes and aversions, by a person who is free from the desire for the fruit of action.

यत्तु कामेप्सुना कर्म साहङ्कारेण वा पुनः ।
क्रियते बहुलायासं तद्राजसमुदाहृतम् ॥२४॥

*yattu kāmepsunā karma sāhaṅkāreṇa vā punaḥ |*
*kriyate bahulāyāsaṁ tadrājasamudāhṛtam ||24||*

**24.** But *rājasa* action is said to be that done by a person seeking results, with much arrogance and with great effort.

अनुबन्धं क्षयं हिंसामनपेक्ष्य च पौरुषम् ।
मोहादारभ्यते कर्म यत्तत्तामसमुच्यते ॥२५॥

*anubandhaṁ kṣayaṁ hiṁsāmanapekṣya ca pauruṣam |*
*mohādārabhyate karma yattattāmasamucyate ||25||*

**25.** *Tāmasa* action is said to be that which is undertaken due to delusion, without considering the consequences, loss, injury [to oneself and others] and [one's own] capacity.

मुक्तसङ्गोऽनहंवादी धृत्युत्साहसमन्वितः ।
सिद्ध्यसिद्ध्योर्निर्विकारः कर्ता सात्त्विक उच्यते ॥२६॥

*muktasaṅgo'nahaṁvādī dhṛtyutsāhasamanvitaḥ |*
*siddhyasiddhyornirvikāraḥ kartā sāttvika ucyate ||26||*

**26.** The *sāttvika* agent of action is said to be that which is free from attachment [and] egotism. [It is] endowed with resolution and enthusiasm, unaffected by success or failure.

रागी कर्मफलप्रेप्सुर्लुब्धो हिंसात्मकोऽशुचिः ।
हर्षशोकान्वितः कर्ता राजसः परिकीर्तितः ॥२७॥

*rāgī karmaphalaprepsurlubdho hiṁsātmako'śuciḥ |*
*harṣaśokānvitaḥ kartā rājasaḥ parikīrtitaḥ ||27||*

**27.** The *rājasa* agent of action is said to be that which is impassioned, lustful for the fruit of action, greedy, violent, impure [and] subject to joy and sorrow.

अयुक्तः प्राकृतः स्तब्धः शठो नैष्कृतिकोऽलसः ।
विषादी दीर्घसूत्री च कर्ता तामस उच्यते ॥२८॥

*ayuktaḥ prākṛtaḥ stabdhaḥ śaṭho naiṣkṛtiko'lasaḥ |*
*viṣādī dīrghasūtrī ca kartā tāmasa ucyate ||28||*

**28.** The *tāmasa* agent of action is said to be that which is immature, arrogant, deceitful, cruel, indolent, depressed, procrastinating, and undisciplined.

बुद्धेर्भेदं धृतेश्चैव गुणतस्त्रिविधं शृणु ।
प्रोच्यमानमशेषेण पृथक्त्वेन धनञ्जय ॥२९॥

*buddherbhedaṁ dhṛteścaiva guṇatastrividhaṁ śṛṇu |*
*procyamānamaśeṣeṇa pṛthaktvena dhanañjaya ||29||*

**29.** O *Dhanañjaya* [*Arjuna*], now hear the threefold distinction of intellect and willpower, according to the *guṇas*, taught completely [and] separately [by me].

प्रवृत्तिं च निवृत्तिं च कार्याकार्ये भयाभये ।
बन्धं मोक्षं च या वेत्ति बुद्धिः सा पार्थ सात्त्विकी ॥३०॥

*pravṛttiṁ ca nivṛttiṁ ca kāryākārye bhayābhaye |*
*bandhaṁ mokṣaṁ ca yā vetti buddhiḥ sā pārtha sāttvikī ||30||*

**30.** O *Pārtha* [*Arjuna*], the *sāttvika* intellect is that which is aware of action and renunciation, of what must and must not be done, of what is [the source of] fear and fearlessness, and of bondage and liberation.

यया धर्ममधर्मं च कार्यं चाकार्यमेव च ।
अयथावत्प्रजानाति बुद्धिः सा पार्थ राजसी ॥३१॥

*yayā dharmamadharmaṁ ca kāryaṁ cākāryameva ca |*
*ayathāvatprajānāti buddhiḥ sā pārtha rājasī ||31||*

**31.** O *Pārtha* [*Arjuna*], the *rājasa* intellect is that by which one mistakenly comprehends what is appropriate and inappropriate, as well as what must and must not be done.

अधर्मं धर्ममिति या मन्यते तमसावृता ।
सर्वार्थान्विपरीतांश्च बुद्धिः सा पार्थ तामसी ॥३२॥

*adharmaṁ dharmamiti yā manyate tamasāvṛtā |*
*sarvārthānviparītāṁśca buddhiḥ sā pārtha tāmasī ||32||*

**32.** O *Pārtha* [*Arjuna*], the *tāmasa* intellect is that which is enshrouded by *tamas*; it confuses right for wrong and it mistakes all objects for their opposites.

धृत्या यया धारयते मनः प्राणेन्द्रियक्रियाः ।
योगेनाव्यभिचारिण्या धृतिः सा पार्थ सात्त्विकी ॥३३॥

*dhṛtyā yayā dhārayate manaḥ prāṇendriyakriyāḥ |*
*yogenāvyabhicāriṇyā dhṛtiḥ sā pārtha sāttvikī ||33||*

**33.** O *Pārtha* [*Arjuna*], *sāttvika* willpower becomes steadfast by *yoga*. It is that by which one disciplines the activities of the senses, of *prāṇa* and of the mind.

यया तु धर्मकामार्थान्धृत्या धारयतेऽर्जुन ।
प्रसङ्गेन फलाकाङ्क्षी धृतिः सा पार्थ राजसी ॥३४॥

*yayā tu dharmakāmārthāndhṛtyā dhārayate'rjuna |*
*prasaṅgena phalākāṅkṣī dhṛtiḥ sā pārtha rājasī ||34||*

**34.** However, O *Pārtha* [*Arjuna*], *rājasa* willpower is that by which one lusts for the fruit of action due to attachment – that by which one focuses on *dharma* [merit for a future life], *kāma* [pleasure] and *artha* [security], O *Arjuna*.

यया स्वप्नं भयं शोकं विषादं मदमेव च ।
न विमुञ्चति दुर्मेधा धृतिः सा पार्थ तामसी ॥३५॥

*yayā svapnaṁ bhayaṁ śokaṁ viṣādaṁ madameva ca |*
*na vimuñcati durmedhā dhṛtiḥ sā pārtha tāmasī ||35||*

**35.** O *Pārtha* [*Arjuna*], *tāmasa* willpower is that by which a fool does not give up sleeping, fear, grief and lust.

सुखं त्विदानीं त्रिविधं शृणु मे भरतर्षभ ।
अभ्यासाद्रमते यत्र दुःखान्तं च निगच्छति ॥३६॥

*sukhaṁ tvidānīṁ trividhaṁ śṛṇu me bharatarṣabha |*
*abhyāsādramate yatra duḥkhāntaṁ ca nigacchati ||36||*

**36.** O *Bharatarṣabha* [*Arjuna*], now hear me on the three forms of happiness, enjoyed through practice, and by which one ends suffering.

यत्तदग्रे विषमिव परिणामेऽमृतोपमम् ।
तत्सुखं सात्त्विकं प्रोक्तमात्मबुद्धिप्रसादजम् ॥३७॥

*yattadagre viṣamiva pariṇāme'mṛtopamam |*
*tatsukhaṁ sāttvikaṁ proktamātmabuddhiprasādajam ||37||*

**37.** *Sāttvika* happiness is said to be that which is like poison in the beginning, like nectar in the end, [and] is born from the clarity of self-knowledge.

विषयेन्द्रियसंयोगाद्यत्तदग्रेऽमृतोपमम् ।
परिणामे विषमिव तत्सुखं राजसं स्मृतम् ॥३८॥

*viṣayendriyasaṁyogādyattadagre'mṛtopamam |*
*pariṇāme viṣamiva tatsukhaṁ rājasaṁ smṛtam ||38||*

**38.** *Rājasa* happiness is that which is considered nectar in the beginning, poison in the end, [and] is born from the contact of the sense organs with objects.

यदग्रे चानुबन्धे च सुखं मोहनमात्मनः ।
निद्रालस्यप्रमादोत्थं तत्तामसमुदाहृतम् ॥३९॥

*yadagre cānubandhe ca sukhaṁ mohanamātmanaḥ |*
*nidrālasyapramādotthaṁ tattāmasamudāhṛtam ||39||*

**39.** The happiness called *tāmasa* is that which deludes one in the beginning and the end, and is born from sleep, lethargy and indifference.

न तदस्ति पृथिव्यां वा दिवि देवेषु वा पुनः ।
सत्त्वं प्रकृतिजैर्मुक्तं यदेभिः स्यात्त्रिभिर्गुणैः ॥४०॥

*na tadasti pṛthivyāṁ vā divi deveṣu vā punaḥ |*
*sattvaṁ prakṛtijairmuktaṁ yadebhiḥ syāttribhirguṇaiḥ ||40||*

**40.** Among all the divine beings of Heaven or [beings] on Earth, there is not one who is free from these three *guṇas* born from *Prakṛti.*

ब्राह्मणक्षत्रियविशां शूद्राणां च परन्तप ।
कर्माणि प्रविभक्तानि स्वभावप्रभवैर्गुणैः ॥४१॥

*brāhmaṇakṣatriyaviśāṁ śūdrāṇāṁ ca parantapa |*
*karmāṇi pravibhaktāni svabhāvaprabhavairguṇaiḥ ||41||*

**41.** According to the *guṇas*, which are born from *Prakṛti*, duties have been established for *brāhmaṇas, kṣatriyas, vaiśyas* and *śūdras*, O *Parantapa* [*Arjuna*].

शमो दमस्तपः शौचं क्षान्तिरार्जवमेव च ।
ज्ञानं विज्ञानमास्तिक्यं ब्रह्मकर्म स्वभावजम् ॥४२॥

*śamo damastapaḥ śaucaṁ kṣāntirārjavameva ca |*
*jñānaṁ vijñānamāstikyaṁ brahmakarma svabhāvajam ||42||*

**42.** Control of the mind, control fo the senses, austerity, purity, acceptance, integrity, knowledge, wisdom and faith are the duties of the *brāhmaṇa* [and] these are born from their very nature.

शौर्यं तेजो धृतिर्दाक्ष्यं युद्धे चाप्यपलायनम् ।
दानमीश्वरभावश्च क्षात्रं कर्म स्वभावजम् ॥४३॥

*śauryaṁ tejo dhṛtirdākṣyaṁ yuddhe cāpyapalāyanam |*
*dānamīśvarabhāvaśca kṣātraṁ karma svabhāvajam ||43||*

**43.** Having courage, self-confidence, determination, skill, generosity and the capacity to govern and not flee from the battlefield are the duties of the *kṣatriya*, [and] these are born from their very nature.

कृषिगौरक्ष्यवाणिज्यं वैश्यकर्म स्वभावजम् ।
परिचर्यात्मकं कर्म शूद्रस्यापि स्वभावजम् ॥४४॥

*kṛṣigaurakṣyavāṇijyaṁ vaiśyakarma svabhāvajam |*
*paricaryātmakaṁ karma śūdrasyāpi svabhāvajam ||44||*

**44.** Farming, cow-herding and commerce are the duties of the *vaiśya*, [and] these are born from their very nature. And for the *śudra*, the duty born from his very nature is service.

स्वे स्वे कर्मण्यभिरतः संसिद्धिं लभते नरः ।
स्वकर्मनिरतः सिद्धिं यथा विन्दति तच्छृणु ॥४५॥

*sve sve karmaṇyabhirataḥ saṁsiddhiṁ labhate naraḥ |*
*svakarmanirataḥ siddhiṁ yathā vindati tacchṛṇu ||45||*

**45.** Engaged in one's own duty, one attains success. Hear how a person engaged in his own duty attains success:

यतः प्रवृत्तिर्भूतानां येन सर्वमिदं ततम् ।
स्वकर्मणा तमभ्यर्च्य सिद्धिं विन्दति मानवः ॥४६॥

*yataḥ pravṛttirbhūtānāṁ yena sarvamidaṁ tatam |*
*svakarmaṇā tamabhyarcya siddhiṁ vindati mānavaḥ ||46||*

**46.** Worshipping He who is the creator of all beings [and] who sustains everything, one attains success by performing the actions that are one's own duty.

श्रेयान्स्वधर्मो विगुणः परधर्मात्स्वनुष्ठितात् ।
स्वभावनियतं कर्म कुर्वन्नाप्नोति किल्बिषम् ॥४७॥

*śreyānsvadharmo viguṇaḥ paradharmātsvanuṣṭhitāt |*
*svabhāvaniyataṁ karma kurvannāpnoti kilbiṣam ||47||*

**47.** [Performing] one's own duty – even if imperfect – is better than [performing] the duty of another [even if] well-done. Following the duty as determined by own's own nature, one acquires no negative result.

सहजं कर्म कौन्तेय सदोषमपि न त्यजेत् ।
सर्वारम्भा हि दोषेण धूमेनाग्निरिवावृताः ॥४८॥

*sahajaṁ karma kaunteya sadoṣamapi na tyajet |*
*sarvārambhā hi doṣeṇa dhūmenāgnirivāvṛtāḥ ||48||*

**48.** O *Kaunteya* [*Arjuna*], one must not abandon the duty that comes from one's birth – even if defective – since all endeavors are surrounded by defects, as fire is by smoke.

असक्तबुद्धिः सर्वत्र जितात्मा विगतस्पृहः ।
नैष्कर्म्यसिद्धिं परमां संन्यासेनाधिगच्छति ॥४९॥

*asaktabuddhiḥ sarvatra jitātmā vigataspṛhaḥ |*
*naiṣkarmyasiddhiṁ paramāṁ saṁnyāsenādhigacchati ||49||*

**49.** One whose mind is free from the attachment to all things, who has command of oneself, who is free from lust, reaches the highest fulfillment that is the state of being free from action through renunciation.

सिद्धिं प्राप्तो यथा ब्रह्म तथाप्नोति निबोध मे ।
समासेनैव कौन्तेय निष्ठा ज्ञानस्य या परा ॥५०॥

*siddhiṁ prāpto yathā brahma tathāpnoti nibodha me |*
*samāsenaiva kaunteya niṣṭhā jñānasya yā parā ||50||*

**50.** O *Kaunteya* [*Arjuna*], learn from Me, in just a few words, how one who is successful [in preparing the mind] attains *Brahman*, which is the highest state of knowledge.

बुद्ध्या विशुद्धया युक्तो धृत्यात्मानं नियम्य च ।
शब्दादीन्विषयांस्त्यक्त्वा रागद्वेषौव्युदस्य च ॥५१॥

*buddhyā viśuddhayā yukto dhṛtyātmānaṁ niyamya ca |*
*śabdādīnviṣayāṁstyaktvā rāgadveṣauvyudasya ca ||51||*

**51.** Possessing a purified mind; having disciplined oneself by willpower; renouncing the objects of the senses, such as sound, etc; leaving behind tastes and aversions;

विविक्तसेवी लघ्वाशी यतवाक्कायमानसः ।
ध्यानयोगपरो नित्यं वैराग्यं समुपाश्रितः ॥५२॥

*viviktasevī laghvāśī yatavākkāyamānasaḥ |*
*dhyānayogaparo nityaṁ vairāgyaṁ samupāśritaḥ ||52||*

**52.** seeking isolated places; eating little; disciplining one's word, body and mind; constantly devoted to meditation; [and] endowed with dispassion;

अहङ्कारं बलं दर्पं कामं क्रोधं परिग्रहम् ।
विमुच्य निर्ममः शान्तो ब्रह्मभूयाय कल्पते ॥५३॥

*ahaṅkāraṁ balaṁ darpaṁ kāmaṁ krodhaṁ parigraham |*
*vimucya nirmamaḥ śānto brahmabhūyāya kalpate ||53||*

**53.** relinquishing the false notion of the self [egotism], power, arrogance, desire, anger, possession and free from the notion of "mine" [selfishness]; [and] tranquil; one is ready for the state of being *Brahman*.

ब्रह्मभूतः प्रसन्नात्मा न शोचति न काङ्क्षति ।
समः सर्वेषु भूतेषु मद्भक्तिं लभते पराम् ॥५४॥

*brahmabhūtaḥ prasannātmā na śocati na kāṅkṣati |*
*samaḥ sarveṣu bhūteṣu madbhaktiṁ labhate parām ||54||*

**54.** One who has become *Brahman*, whose mind is satisfied, feels neither sorrow nor desire, who is impartial to all beings, attains the highest devotion to Me.

भक्त्या मामभिजानाति यावान्यश्चास्मि तत्त्वतः ।
ततो मां तत्त्वतो ज्ञात्वा विशते तदनन्तरम् ॥५५॥

*bhaktyā māmabhijānāti yāvānyaścāsmi tattvataḥ |*
*tato māṁ tattvato jñātvā viśate tadanantaram ||55||*

**55.** By devotion, one truly knows Me – both what and how I am; thereby truly knowing Me, afterwards, one enters Me.

सर्वकर्माण्यपि सदा कुर्वाणो मद्व्यपाश्रयः ।
मत्प्रसादादवाप्नोति शाश्वतं पदमव्ययम् ॥५६॥

*sarvakarmāṇyapi sadā kurvāṇo madvyapāśrayaḥ |*
*matprasādādavāpnoti śāśvataṁ padamavyayam ||56||*

**56.** Performing all actions, always taking refuge in Me, one attains the eternal, immutable goal through my blessing.

चेतसा सर्वकर्माणि मयि संन्यस्य मत्परः ।
बुद्धियोगमुपाश्रित्य मच्चित्तः सततं भव ॥५७॥

*cetasā sarvakarmāṇi mayi saṁnyasya matparaḥ |*
*buddhiyogamupāśritya maccittaḥ satataṁ bhava ||57||*

**57.** Be one whose mind is always on Me, mentally surrendering all actions to Me, holding Me as the highest [goal], taking refuge in *karmayoga*.

मच्चित्तः सर्वदुर्गाणि मत्प्रसादात्तरिष्यसि ।
अथ चेत्त्वमहङ्कारान्न श्रोष्यसि विनङ्क्ष्यसि ॥५८॥

*maccittaḥ sarvadurgāṇi matprasādāttariṣyasi |*
*atha cettvamahaṅkārānna śroṣyasi vinaṅkṣyasi ||58||*

**58.** With the mind on Me, you shall surpass all obstacles through my blessing; however, if out of ego you do not listen, you shall be destroyed.

यद्यहङ्कारमाश्रित्य न योत्स्य इति मन्यसे ।
मिथ्यैष व्यवसायस्ते प्रकृतिस्त्वां नियोक्ष्यति ॥५९॥

*yadyahaṅkāramāśritya na yotsya iti manyase |*
*mithyaiṣa vyavasāyaste prakṛtistvāṁ niyokṣyati ||59||*

**59.** [If] seeking refuge in the ego, you think "I shall not fight", this your decision is in vain: [your very] nature shall oblige you [to fight].

स्वभावजेन कौन्तेय निबद्धः स्वेन कर्मणा ।
कर्तुं नेच्छसि यन्मोहात्करिष्यस्यवशोऽपि तत् ॥६०॥

*svabhāvajena kaunteya nibaddhaḥ svena karmaṇā |*
*kartuṁ necchasi yanmohātkariṣyasyavaśo'pi tat ||60||*

**60.** O *Kaunteya* [*Arjuna*], bound by your own duty, which is born from your nature, against your will, you shall do that which you do not want to do out of delusion.

ईश्वरः सर्वभूतानां हृद्देशेऽर्जुन तिष्ठति ।
भ्रामयन्सर्वभूतानि यन्त्रारूढानि मायया ॥६१॥

*īśvaraḥ sarvabhūtānāṁ hṛddeśe'rjuna tiṣṭhati |*
*bhrāmayansarvabhūtāni yantrārūḍhāni māyayā ||61||*

**61.** O *Arjuna, Īśvara* is in the heart of all beings, causing movement in all beings, [as if] mounted on a machine, [moving] by magic.

तमेव शरणं गच्छ सर्वभावेन भारत ।
तत्प्रसादात्परां शान्तिं स्थानं प्राप्स्यसि शाश्वतम् ॥६२॥

*tameva śaraṇaṁ gaccha sarvabhāvena bhārata |*
*tatprasādātparāṁ śāntiṁ sthānaṁ prāpsyasi śāśvatam ||62||*

**62.** O *Bhārata* [*Arjuna*], seek refuge in Him with all your being. You shall reach the highest peace – the eternal abode – by His blessing.

इति ते ज्ञानमाख्यातं गुह्याद्गुह्यतरं मया ।
विमृश्यैतदशेषेण यथेच्छसि तथा कुरु ॥६३॥

*iti te jñānamākhyātaṁ guhyādguhyataraṁ mayā |*
*vimṛśyaitadaśeṣeṇa yathecchasi tathā kuru ||63||*

**63.** Thus [this] knowledge, which is the greatest secret among secrets, has been taught by Me to you. Having fully reflected upon it, do as you wish.

सर्वगुह्यतमं भूयः शृणु मे परमं वचः ।
इष्टोऽसि मे दृढमिति ततो वक्ष्यामि ते हितम् ॥६४॥

*sarvaguhyatamaṁ bhūyaḥ śṛṇu me paramaṁ vacaḥ |*
*iṣṭo'si me dṛḍhamiti tato vakṣyāmi te hitam ||64||*

**64.** Once again, hear my important word, the greatest secret among secrets. You are greatly loved by Me, therefore I shall tell you what is best for you:

मन्मना भव मद्भक्तो मद्याजी मां नमस्कुरु ।
मामेवैष्यसि सत्यं ते प्रतिजाने प्रियोऽसि मे ॥६५॥

*manmanā bhava madbhakto madyājī māṁ namaskuru |*
*māmevaiṣyasi satyaṁ te pratijāne priyo'si me ||65||*

**65.** Be one whose mind is on Me, be devoted to Me, one who makes offerings to Me, one who worships Me. You will certainly reach Me. I tell you the truth for you are dear to Me.

सर्वधर्मान्परित्यज्य मामेकं शरणं व्रज ।
अहं त्वा सर्वपापेभ्यो मोक्षयिष्यामि मा शुचः ॥६६॥

*sarvadharmānparityajya māmekaṁ śaraṇaṁ vraja |*
*ahaṁ tvā sarvapāpebhyo mokṣayiṣyāmi mā śucaḥ ||66||*

**66.** Having renounced all actions, take refuge in Me alone. I shall free you from all negative [and positive] action. Do not grieve.

इदं ते नातपस्काय नाभक्ताय कदाचन ।
न चाशुश्रूषवे वाच्यं न च मां योऽभ्यसूयति ॥६७॥

*idaṁ te nātapaskāya nābhaktāya kadācana |*
*na cāśuśrūṣave vācyaṁ na ca māṁ yo'bhyasūyati ||67||*

**67.** This [knowledge given] to you should not be spoken to someone without discipline, who is not devout, who does not wish to listen, and who slanders Me.

य इमं परमं गुह्यं मद्भक्तेष्वभिधास्यति ।
भक्तिं मयि परां कृत्वा मामेवैष्यत्यसंशयः ॥६८॥

*ya imaṁ paramaṁ guhyaṁ madbhakteṣvabhidhāsyati |*
*bhaktiṁ mayi parāṁ kṛtvā māmevaiṣyatyasaṁśayaḥ ||68||*

**68.** One who teaches this great secret to my devotees, having great devotion to Me, shall only reach Me. [Of this] there is no doubt.

न च तस्मान्मनुष्येषु कश्चिन्मे प्रियकृत्तमः ।
भविता न च मे तस्मादन्यः प्रियतरो भुवि ॥६९॥

*na ca tasmānmanuṣyeṣu kaścinme priyakṛttamaḥ |*
*bhavitā na ca me tasmādanyaḥ priyataro bhuvi ||69||*

**69.** And, among men, there neither is nor shall there be anyone on Earth more loved by Me.

अध्येष्यते च य इमं धर्म्यं संवादमावयोः ।
ज्ञानयज्ञेन तेनाहमिष्टः स्यामिति मे मतिः ॥७०॥

*adhyeṣyate ca ya imaṁ dharmyaṁ saṁvādamāvayoḥ |*
*jñānayajñena tenāhamiṣṭaḥ syāmiti me matiḥ ||70||*

**70.** And I shall be worshipped by *jñānayajña* [the ritual in the form of knowledge] by he who studies this our dialogue on *dharma*. This is my conviction.

श्रद्धावाननसूयश्च शृणुयादपि यो नरः ।
सोऽपि मुक्तः शुभांल्लोकान्प्राप्नुयात्पुण्यकर्मणाम् ॥७१॥

*śraddhāvānanasūyaśca śṛṇuyādapi yo naraḥ |*
*so'pi muktaḥ śubhāṁllokānprāpnuyātpuṇyakarmaṇām ||71||*

**71.** Even one who only listens with faith and without criticizing shall become free [and] shall reach the auspicious worlds of those that exact appropriate action.

कच्चिदेतच्छ्रुतं पार्थ त्वयैकाग्रेण चेतसा ।
कच्चिदज्ञानसंमोहः प्रनष्टस्ते धनञ्जय ॥७२॥

*kaccidetacchrutaṁ pārtha tvayaikāgreṇa cetasā |*
*kaccidajñānasaṁmohaḥ pranaṣṭaste dhanañjaya ||72||*

**72.** O *Pārtha* [*Arjuna*], has this been heard with a focused mind? Has your delusion caused by ignorance been erradicated, *Dhanañjaya* [*Arjuna*]?

अर्जुन उवाच
नष्टो मोहः स्मृतिर्लब्धा त्वत्प्रसादान्मयाच्युत ।
स्थितोऽस्मि गतसन्देहः करिष्ये वचनं तव ॥७३॥

*arjuna uvāca*
*naṣṭo mohaḥ smṛtirlabdhā tvatprasādānmayācyuta |*
*sthito'smi gatasandehaḥ kariṣye vacanaṁ tava ||73||*

**73.** *Arjuna* spoke:
— [My] delusion has gone, I have acquired wisdom through your blessing, O *Acyuta* [*Kṛṣṇa*]! I remain free of doubt. I shall follow your word.

सञ्जय उवाच
इत्यहं वासुदेवस्य पार्थस्य च महात्मनः ।
संवादमिममश्रौषमद्भुतं रोमहर्षणम् ॥७४॥

*sañjaya uvāca*
*ityahaṁ vāsudevasya pārthasya ca mahātmanaḥ |*
*saṁvādamimamaśrauṣamadbhutaṁ romaharṣaṇam ||74||*

**74.** *Sañjaya* spoke:
— Thus I heard this wonderful [and] moving dialogue between *Vāsudeva* [*Kṛṣṇa*] and the great *Pārtha* [*Arjuna*].

व्यासप्रसादाच्छ्रुतवानेतद्गुह्यमहं परम् ।
योगं योगेश्वरात्कृष्णात्साक्षात्कथयतः स्वयम् ॥७५॥

*vyāsaprasādācchrutavānetadguhyamahaṁ param |*
*yogaṁ yogeśvarātkṛṣṇātsākṣātkathayataḥ svayam ||75||*

**75.** By the blessing of *Vyāsa*, I have heard this great secret that is *yoga*, from *Kṛṣṇa*, the Lord of *yoga*, taught directly by Him.

राजन्संस्मृत्य संस्मृत्य संवादमिममद्भुतम् ।
केशवार्जुनयोः पुण्यं हृष्यामि च मुहुर्मुहुः ॥७६॥

*rājansaṁsmṛtya saṁsmṛtya saṁvādamimamadbhutam |*
*keśavārjunayoḥ puṇyaṁ hṛṣyāmi ca muhurmuhuḥ ||76||*

**76.** O king, remembering again and again this wonderful and sacred dialogue between *Keśava* [*Kṛṣṇa*] and *Arjuna*, I rejoice again and again.

तच्च संस्मृत्य संस्मृत्य रूपमत्यद्भुतं हरेः ।
विस्मयो मे महान् राजन् हृष्यामि च पुनः पुनः ॥७७॥

*tacca saṁsmṛtya saṁsmṛtya rūpamatyadbhutaṁ hareḥ |*
*vismayo me mahān rājan hṛṣyāmi ca punaḥ punaḥ ||77||*

**77.** And my amazement is still great! Remembering again and again that marvellous [cosmic] form of *Hari* [*Kṛṣṇa*], I am enchanted again and again, O king.

यत्र योगेश्वरः कृष्णो यत्र पार्थो धनुर्धरः ।
तत्र श्रिर्विजयो भूतिर्ध्रुवा नीतिर्मतिर्मम ॥७८॥

*yatra yogeśvaraḥ kṛṣṇo yatra pārtho dhanurdharaḥ |*
*tatra śrirvijayo bhūtirdhruvā nītirmatirmama ||78||*

**78.** For wherever there is *Kṛṣṇa*, the Lord of *yoga*, for wherever there is *Pārtha* [*Arjuna*], the archer, there shall be wealth, victory, prosperity, and unwavering justice. This is my conviction.

ओं तत्सदिति श्रीमद्भगवद्गीतासूपनिषत्सु ब्रह्मविद्यायां योगशास्त्रे
श्रीकृष्णार्जुनसंवादे मोक्षसंन्यासयोगो नामाष्टादशोऽध्यायः॥

*oṁ tatsaditi śrīmadbhagavadgītāsūpaniṣatsu*
*brahmavidyāyāṁ yogaśāstre śrīkṛṣṇārjunasaṁvāde*
*mokṣasaṁnyāsayogo nāmāṣṭādaśo'dhyāyaḥ ||*

*Oṁ*, this is the Truth. Thus is the eighteenth chapter, the subject [of which] is called "*mokṣasaṁnyāsa*" [renunciation for liberation], in the glorious *Bhagavadgītā*, [which is equivalent to] the *Upaniṣads*, [the subject of which is] the knowledge of *Brahman* [and] *yoga*, in the dialogue between *śrī Kṛṣṇa* and *Arjuna*.

# Epithets of Arjuna

*Anagha* → Sinless One
*Bharatasattama* → Purest among *Bhāratas*
*Bharatarṣabha* → Special among *Bhāratas*
*Bharataśreṣṭha* → Best among *Bhāratas*
*Bhārata* → Decendent of *Bharata*
*Dhanañjaya* → He who has conquered all wealth
*Dehabhṛtām Vara* → Best among the living
*Guḍākeśa* → Lord of the Night
*Kapidhvaja* → He whose banner is a monkey (*Hanumān*)
*Kaunteya* → Son of *Kuntī*
*Kirīṭī* → the Crowned One
*Kurunandana* → Descendent of *Kuru*
*Kurupravīra* → Best among *Kurus*
*Kurusattama* → Best among *Kurus*
*Kuruśreṣṭha* → Best among *Kurus*
*Mahābāhu* → Strong-armed warrior
*Parantapa* → Destoyer of Enemies
*Pāṇḍava* → Son of *Pāṇḍu*
*Pārtha* → Son of *Pṛthā* (*Kuntī*)
*Puruṣarṣabha* → Best among men
*Puruṣavyāghra* → Tiger among men
*Savyasācin*→ Ambidextrous archer

# Epithets of Śrī Kṛṣṇa

*Acyuta* → He who is never destroyed
*Ananta* → Eternal one
*Anantarūpa* → Inifinite Form
*Arisūdana* → Destroyer of the Enemy
*Deva* → Lord
*Deveśa* → Lord of Gods
*Devavara* → Lord of Lords
*Govinda* → Protector of the Herds and the *Vedas*
*Hari* → Destroyer bondage
*Hṛṣīkeśa* → Master of his own senses
*Jagannivāsa* → Abode of the Universe
*Janārdana* → Protector of the Tormented
*Kamalapatrākṣa* → He with eyes of lotus petals
*Keśava* → Handsome-haired one; he who killed the demon *Keśin*
*Mādhava* → Descendent of a *Yadhava*, called *Madhu*
*Madhusūdana* → He who killed the demon *Madhu*
*Mahābāhu* → Great Warrior
*Mahātman* → He whose self is limitless
*Mahāyogeśvara* → Great Lord of *yoga*
*Parameśvara* → Great Lord
*Prabhu* → Lord
*Puruṣottama* → Highest of Beings
*Sahasrabāhu* → Lord of 1000 arms
*śrībhagavān* → Great Lord
*Vārṣṇeya* → Descendent of *Vṛṣṇi*
*Vāsudeva* → Son of *Vasudeva*
*Viśvamūrti* → He of Cosmic Form
*Viṣṇu* → He who everything pervades
*Yogeśvara* → Lord of *yoga*

# References

**Swami Dayananda Saraswati:**
Bhagavad Gita
*Arsha Vidya Research and Publication*
*Chennai, India*

The Teachings of the Bhagavad Gita
*Vision Books Pvt. Ltd*
*New Delhi, India*

Bhagavad Gita Home Study Course - 4 volumes
*Arsha Vidya Research and Publication Trust*
*Chennai, India*

**Swami Paramarthananda Saraswati:**
Srimad Bhagavadgita - 18 booklets
*www.sastraprakasika.org*